THEORIES OF MYTH

From Ancient Israel and Greece to Freud, Jung, Campbell, and Lévi-Strauss

Series Editor

ROBERT A. SEGAL

University of Lancaster

A GARLAND SERIES

SERIES CONTENTS

VOLUME

5

RITUAL AND MYTH

ROBERTSON SMITH,
FRAZER, HOOKE, AND
HARRISON

Edited with introductions by

ROBERT A. SEGAL
University of Lancaster

GARLAND PUBLISHING, INC.
New York & London
1996

Library of Congress Cataloging-in-Publication Data

Ritual and myth : Robertson Smith, Frazer, Hooke, and Harrison /
edited with introductions by Robert A. Segal.
    p.   cm. — (Theories of myth ; 5)
    Includes bibliographical references.
    ISBN 0-8153-2259-3 (alk. paper)
    1. Myth. 2. Ritual. 3. Myth—Study and teaching—History—
Sources. I. Segal, Robert Alan. II. Series.
BL304.R577 1996
291.1'3—dc20   95-36270
                                                    CIP

Printed on acid-free, 250-year-life paper
Manufactured in the United States of America

CONTENTS

SERIES INTRODUCTION

The modern study of myth is already more than a hundred years old and is the work of many disciplines. This six-volume collection of 113 essays brings together both classic and contemporary analyses of myth from the disciplines that have contributed most to its study: psychology, anthropology, folklore, philosophy, religious studies, and literature. Because myth has been analyzed for so long by specialists in so many fields, knowledge of the range of sources and access to them are difficult to secure. The present collection provides a comprehensive and systematic selection of the most important writings on myth.

All of the essays in this collection are theoretical. All are concerned with myth per se, not with a single myth or set of myths. Many of the essays make explicit claims about myth generally. Others use individual myths to make or to test those claims. Most of the essayists are proponents of the theories they employ. Some are critics.

By no means has each of the disciplines considered here developed a single, unified theory of myth. Multiple, competing theories have arisen within disciplines as well as across them. The leading theories from each discipline are represented in the collection.

Theories of myth are never theories of myth alone. Myth always falls under a larger rubric such as the mind, culture, knowledge, religion, ritual, symbolism, and narrative. The rubric reflects the discipline from which the theory is derived. For example, psychological theories see myth as an expression of the mind. Anthropological theories view myth as an instance of culture. Literary theories regard myth as a variety of narrative. Within a discipline, theories differ about the nature of myth because they differ about the nature of the rubric involved. At the same time, theorists qualify as theorists of myth only when they single out myth for the application of the larger rubric. Writings that completely subsume myth under its larger rubric—discussing only religion or symbolism, for example—fail to qualify as writings on myth.

Theories of myth purport to answer one or more of the fundamental questions about myth: what is its origin, what is its function, what is its subject matter? Theories differ, first, in the answers they give to these questions. For most theorists, myth originates and functions to satisfy a need, but that need can be for anything—for example, for food, information, hope, or God. The need can be on the part of individuals or on the part of the community. Similarly, the subject matter, or referent, of myth can be anything. It can be the literal, apparent subject matter—for example, gods or the physical world—or a symbolic one—for example, human beings or society.

Theories differ even more basically in the questions they seek to answer. Few theories claim to answer all three of the major questions about myth. Some theories focus on the origin of myth, others on the function, still others on the subject matter. The answer a theory gives to one question doubtless shapes the answer it gives to another, but most theories concentrate on only one or two of the questions. Writings that merely describe or categorize myths fail to qualify as theories, as do writings that are skeptical of any universal claims about myths.

Still more basically, theories differ in the definition of myth. By some definitions myth can be a sheer belief or conviction—for example, the American "myth" of the frontier or of the self-made man. By other definitions myth must be a story. By some definitions the agents in a story can be humans or even animals. By others the agents must be either gods or extraordinary humans such as heroes. Theories employ definitions that reflect the disciplines from which they come. For example, theories from literature assume myth to be a story. Theories from religious studies assume the agents in myth to be gods or other superhuman figures.

Theorizing about myth is as old as the Presocratics. But only since the development of the social sciences in the last half of the nineteenth century has the theorizing become scientific. Some social scientific theories may find counterparts in earlier ones (see Burton Feldman and Robert D. Richardson's introduction to *The Rise of Modern Mythology* [Bloomington: Indiana University Press, 1972]), but social scientific theorizing still differs in kind from earlier theorizing. Where earlier theorizing was largely speculative and philosophical in nature, social scientific theorizing is far more empirical. The anthropologist John Beattie best sums up the differences, which apply to all of the social sciences and to the study of more than myth:

> Thus it was the reports of eighteenth- and nineteenth-century missionaries and travellers in Africa, North America,

the Pacific and elsewhere that provided the raw material upon which the first anthropological works, written in the second half of the last century, were based. Before then, of course, there had been plenty of conjecturing about human institutions and their origins; to say nothing of earlier times, in the eighteenth century Hume, Adam Smith and Ferguson in Britain, and Montesquieu, Condorcet and others on the Continent, had written about primitive institutions. But although their speculations were often brilliant, these thinkers were not empirical scientists; their conclusions were not based on any kind of evidence which could be tested; rather, they were for the most part implicit in their own cultures. They were really philosophers and historians of Europe, not anthropologists. (*Other Cultures* [New York: Free Press, 1964], 5–6)

By no means do all of the theories represented in this collection come from the social sciences. But even theories from philosophy, religious studies, and literature reflect strongly the impact of these fields.

The first four volumes in this collection are organized by disciplines. The selections in each volume typify the nature of the theorizing in the discipline. By far the most influential psychological theories of myth have been Freudian and Jungian. Anthropological theories have proved both more numerous and more disparate, with no one theory dominating the field. Folklorists have been particularly concerned with distinguishing myth from other verbal genres. Many theories of myth from philosophy and especially from religious studies grow out of attempts to decipher the classics and the Bible. Literary critics have understandably been preoccupied with both the similarities and the differences between myth and literature.

The final two volumes of the collection are grouped by theories rather than by disciplines. While the number of essays written on any major theory would readily fill a volume, the number written on the myth-ritualist theory and more recently on structuralism has been so large as to necessitate individual volumes about them. The burgeoning of writing on these theories stems in part from the array of disciplines that have adopted the theories. The myth-ritualist theory originated in the fields of classics and biblical studies but soon spread to the study of myth everywhere and, even more, to the study of secular literature. As a theory of myth, structuralism began in anthropology but has since been incorporated by many other fields.

Space does not permit inclusion in this collection of any essays that survey the field of theories of myth. Some useful surveys in

English are the following:

Campbell, Joseph. "The Historical Development of Mythology," *Daedalus* 88 (Spring 1959): 234–54.

Cohen, Percy S. "Theories of Myth," *Man*, n.s., 4 (September 1969): 337–53.

Dorson, Richard M. "Theories of Myth and the Folklorist," *Daedalus* 88 (Spring 1959): 280–90.

———. "Current Folklore Theories," *Current Anthropology* 4 (February 1963): 93–112.

Eliade, Mircea. "Myth," *Encyclopaedia Britannica*, 14th ed. (1970), vol. 15, 1132–40.

———. "Myth in the Nineteenth and Twentieth Centuries," in *Dictionary of the History of Ideas*, ed. Philip P. Wiener (New York: Scribner, 1973–74), vol. 3, 307–18.

Farnell, L. R. "The Value and the Methods of Mythologic Study," *Proceedings of the British Academy* (1919–20): 37–51.

Fischer, J. L. "The Sociopsychological Analysis of Folktales," *Current Anthropology* 4 (June 1963): 235–73, 292–95.

Georges, Robert A. "Prologue" to *Studies on Mythology*, ed. Georges (Homewood, IL: Dorsey, 1968), 1–14.

Halpern, Ben. "'Myth' and 'Ideology' in Modern Usage," *History and Theory* 1 (1961): 129–49.

Herskovits, Melville J. and Frances S. *Dahomean Narrative* (Evanston, IL: Northwestern University Press, 1958), 80–122.

Kaines, J. "The Interpretation of Mythology," *Anthropologia* 1 (1873–75): 465–75.

Kluckhohn, Clyde. "Recurrent Themes in Myths and Mythmaking," *Daedalus* 88 (Spring 1959): 268–79.

Larson, Gerald James. "Introduction: The Study of Mythology and Comparative Mythology," in *Myth in Indo-European Antiquity*, ed. Larson (Berkeley: University of California Press, 1974), 1–16.

MacIntyre, Alasdair. "Myth," *Encyclopedia of Philosophy* (1968), vol. 5, 434–37.

Maranda, Elli Köngäs. "Five Interpretations of a Melanesian Myth," *Journal of American Folklore* 86 (January-March 1973): 3–13.

Patterson, John L. "Mythology and Its Interpretation," *Poet Lore* 37 (Winter 1926): 607–15.

Puhvel, Jaan. *Comparative Mythology* (Baltimore: Johns Hopkins University Press, 1987), 7–20.

Reinach, Solomon. "The Growth of Mythological Study," *Quarterly Review* 215 (October 1911): 423–41.

Rogerson, J. W. "Slippery Words: V. Myth," *Expository Times* 90 (October 1978): 10–14.

Segal, Robert A. "In Defense of Mythology: The History of Modern Theories of Myth," *Annals of Scholarship* 1 (Winter 1980): 3–49.

Simon, Ulrich. "A Key to All Mythologies?" *Church Quarterly Review* 117 (1956): 251–61.

INTRODUCTION

The myth and ritual, or myth-ritualist, theory of myth maintains that myths and rituals operate together. This theory claims not that myths and rituals happen to go hand in hand but that they must. In its most uncompromising form, the myth-ritualist theory contends that myths and rituals cannot exist without each other. In a tamer form, it asserts that myths and rituals originally exist together but may eventually go their separate ways. In a still tamer form of the theory, myths and rituals can arise separately but subsequently coalesce.

First proposed by William Robertson Smith, the myth-ritualist theory was developed much further by James Frazer and carried to its fullest form by Jane Harrison and S.H. Hooke. Harrison led the group that applied the theory to the classics; Hooke, the group that applied the theory to the Bible. Disciples of Frazer, Harrison, and Hooke have applied the theory to dead and living religions worldwide. At least as important has been the application of the theory to secular literature, which has been interpreted as the outgrowth of myth.

Because the myth-ritualist theory maintains that myths and rituals operate in tandem, it has repeatedly been castigated by those who argue that the two phenomena operate independently of each other and come together only episodically. This volume therefore includes selections from not only the leading myth-ritualists but also critics and revisionists.

THE MYTH-RITUAL THEORY

By William Bascom

T HE theory that various forms of folklore and literature are ultimately derived from ritual has been expounded at considerable length by an active group of scholars,[1] but has received very little attention from American folklorists. Some of our colleagues in related fields have assumed that the ritual theory has been accepted, apparently without demurrer, and it comes as something of a surprise to learn that this is not the case. If not, why have American folklorists not criticized or queried it, or challenged the vigorous campaign of such men as Lord Raglan and Stanley Edgar Hyman? It is only in the recent Myth issue of the *JAF*, to which both Raglan and Hyman contributed, that Stith Thompson has injected a few carefully chosen reservations. I propose to undertake an analysis of the ritual theory as presented in Raglan's *The Hero*, the broadest in scope and of most interest to folklorists of the many relevant publications.

HISTORICITY

Raglan's argument is in large part that myths and tales must have their origin in ritual because they do not have them either in actual history or in folk imagination. Almost half of *The Hero* is devoted to an attack on scholars who assume myths and legends to be based on history and use them to supplement or interpret the available written documents. He disposes of the historicity of traditional family pedigrees, local traditions, Robin Hood, the Norse Sagas, King Arthur, Hengist and Horsa, Cuchulainn, the tale of Troy, and traditions of other lands. Much of this argument is based on demonstrating historical inaccuracies in verbal traditions. With this there can be no quarrel except as to the question of degree, which Raglan carries to the ultimate extreme. "Tradition never preserves historical facts." "There are no valid grounds for believing in the historicity of tradition." "As we must continue to point out, there is no good reason to believe that a myth or any other traditional narrative has ever embodied an historic fact."[2]

A major weakness in this argument is that the mass of evidence of historical inaccuracies in folklore, which could easily be extended, does not disprove the possibility of historical origins. If some myths and tales can have their origins in human social situations or other historical events, however inaccurately they may be reported, it is not necessary to look for their origins in ritual any more than in natural phenomena. The fact that verbal tradition is not an accurate historical account does not mean that it cannot have its basis in historical event. Raglan, however, says "If one traditional tale, told as a tale of fact, is completely devoid of fact, then the belief that such stories must have a historical basis is clearly ill-founded" (p. 44). Even the fact that one tale is completely contradicted by historical records does not prove that it, or any other tale, has no basis in historical events. Having been called a "neo-euhemerist" by Hyman on an earlier occasion,[3] I should state clearly that I do not maintain either

1

that all tales have a historical basis or that any of them are completely accurate. But I do believe that some tales can have their origins in human social situations or other historical events, and that some historical facts are transmitted in verbal tradition.

Raglan maintains that peasants and non-literate peoples have no concept of history as such, and no interest in it. "History . . . is the recital in chronological sequence of events which are known to have occurred. Without precise chronology there can be no history, since the essence of history is the relation of events in their correct sequence" (p. 2). And without writing there can be no chronology (p. 4). "Since history depends upon written chronology, and the savage has no written chronology, the savage can have no history. And since interest in the past is induced solely by books, the savage can take no interest in the past; the events of the past are, in fact, completely lost" (p. 6).

Polynesian genealogies and traditions of exploration at once come to mind, as well as American Indian traditions of migration, African accounts of wars and succession of kings, and other legends. "Most illiterate communities have, of course, traditional stories, and these stories may seem to be memories of historical events. They tell of the journeys and victories of heroes, and with some rationalization and rearrangement these journeys and victories can be made to represent historical migrations and conquests. These stories, however, are really myths" (p. 8). Raglan quotes Alfred Nutt, who asked in 1891 and again in 1901, "Is there such a thing as historic myth at all? Do men commemorate tribal wanderings, settlements, conquests, subjugations, acquisitions of new forms of culture, or any other incidents in the collective life of a people in the form of stories about individual men and women? I do not deny the possibility of their so doing; all I ask for is evidence of the fact."[4] Raglan comments, "I cannot learn that anyone ever gave Mr. Nutt the evidence for which he asked, no doubt for the very good reason that there is no such evidence" (p. 121).

Van Gennep stated that the French peasantry had completely forgotten the facts of Napoleon's career within fifty years of his death (p. 8), and believed than an incident which is not recorded in writing cannot be remembered more than 200 years. Raglan believes this is too long. "After much consideration I have fixed on the term of one hundred and fifty years as the maximum. I have arrived at this figure, which is of course approximate, in various ways. A careful study of what is known of my grandparents and great-grandparents has convinced me that any fact about a person which is not placed on record within a hundred years of his death is lost. Giving a person about fifty years of active life, we get a hundred and fifty years as the limit. Among ourselves the names of the dead are recorded in various ways, but I believe that among the illiterate, anyone who has been dead a hundred years is completely forgotten. Again I have known cases in which old men have succeeded in impressing incidents of their own lives upon children in such a way that the children remember them; but they cannot impress in this way incidents which have not made an impression upon themselves. Matter that is not part of the group tradition thus dies out in the second generation" (p. 12).

This of course does not prove that children upon whom the incidents of their fathers' lives have been impressed may not in turn impress these incidents on their own children. One may therefore ask what about matter which thus becomes a part of the verbal tradition and does not die out in the second, or third, or fourth generation? Raglan's position is clear: it does not exist. "The fact is that all history, except in so far as it has been recorded, or as it can be recovered by archaeologists, is completely lost" (p. 36). "Such evidence as I have been able to collect, then, shows firstly that the alleged historical facts embodied in local tradition are not facts at all, and secondly, that the real facts of history are never preserved by local tradition" (p. 37).

Most anthropologists who have attempted an ethnohistorical reconstruction of the past would probably agree that while an informant's accounts of events which happened during his lifetime can be accepted with the usual cautions, those going back farther than this are questionable but can often be verified by historical documents, and those beyond a century or two are highly suspect and often impossible to verify because of the absence of written documents. The question, however, is whether actual events beyond this point in time can be preserved in verbal traditions.

This is the crux of Raglan's anti-historical argument. He maintains that historical events cannot be remembered longer than 150 years, and that unless they are preserved longer than this they are not truly traditional. It is to the lore that is traditional in this sense that Raglan imputes a ritual origin. It is no problem to find legendary accounts of wars, migrations, and other historically verifiable events, but most of these are relatively recent. By implication Raglan admits that these forms, to which I refer as legends, and which constitute a sizeable portion of the folklore of many societies, have a historical basis. But the real answer to the question he raises must be sought in any historical event, whether perpetuated in verbal tradition or elaborated into myth, legend, or folktale, which has survived more than 150 years.

An answer is to be found in a recent dissertation by Charles Edward Fuller, "An Ethnohistoric Study of Continuity and Change in Gwambe Culture" (Northwestern University, 1955), based on a comparison of the early historical records with the contemporary culture of the Gwambe of Mozambique. The Gwambe, who call their present home Wutonga, claim "that their ancestors came to Wutonga from the Karanga country prior to or during the reign of Gamba, their early chief" (Fuller, p. 12). Recording the experience of the survivors of the shipwreck of the *Sao Thome* in 1589, Diago do Couto wrote "They went to the city of this King Gamba, who would be a league and a half from the river. He, knowing of their coming already, gave orders to receive them well, and to entertain them. The king and his children were Christians baptized by the Padre Goncalo da Silveira, of the Company of Jesuits, who in the year 1560-1561, travelled in these parts among the Barbarians, preaching the law of the Holy Gospel" (Fuller, p. 19). King Gamba's son was baptized in the port of Mozambique in 1559, and arranged for Fr. Goncalo da Silveira and his companion, Fr. Andre Fernandes, to visit Gwambe country, where they spent almost two years as guests of chief Gamba. In their letters they reported that the people of Gwambe were Makaranga from the highlands of the interior (Fuller, p. 16). "The wording of the account suggests that the chief Gamba, their host, had been the actual leader of the group which left Karanga, his father having been defeated by a stronger Karanga chief" (Fuller, p. 17). Because of a classificatory system of kinship terms, a person other than Gamba's biological father may be referred to, but written records document the fact that Gamba was actually the chief of the Gwambe 400 years ago, and that the tradition of Karanga origin has persisted for four centuries.

The Gwambe also occasionally tell legends about early European contacts, probably derived from the Tembe, Maputo, Inyaka, or other coastal neighbors. One reports a disagreement among the chiefs of the Delagoa Bay area as to whether Euro-

3

peans should be refused permission to pass through their territories, since they were so dirty, disease ridden, and destructive. Another legend—according to a personal communication from Fuller—tells of the killing and prompt burial of white cannibals in the region south of Delagoa Bay. Both of these legends find confirmation in Portuguese records referring to historical events 400 years ago. "When the galleon, *S. Joao* was wrecked on May 25, 1553, off the Natal coast, over 500 persons, half slaves and half Europeans were saved. Their mistreatment of African benefactors on the coastal route north caused trouble which brought death to many. . . . Elsewhere, news of cannibalism, which occurred when Portuguese sailors sought relief from starvation, shocked natives, who killed the offenders who had eaten their fellow tribesmen. Word of this travelled over long distances, and persisted over many years, as other shipwrecked travellers learned later. . . . When, in 1554, the survivors of the *Sao Bento* travelled the same coast they found Africans remembering the ill treatment meted out to them earlier . . ." (Fuller, p. 17). Legendary accounts of mistreatments or hard bargains driven by Europeans might have originated in later periods. But it is most unlikely that the coastal chiefs would have continued for 250 years to debate whether or not to allow Europeans passage through their territories, after having established a precedent in the 1550's, or that they could have been able to persist in killing Europeans on the grounds of intra-tribal cannibalism, even if later European survivors had practiced it. These two historical events, which have been elaborated into legends, have clearly, according to the available evidence, persisted in the verbal traditions of the peoples near Delagoa Bay for far more than two centuries.

IMAGINATION

The second part of Raglan's argument denies that folklore arises from imagination or creative fantasy. Raglan begins by disposing of the nature allegorical school, and then rejects the idea that myths are an attempt to explain nature and the world about him, citing Malinowski's criticism of the latter position (pp. 126-128). He then attacks the idea that the folktale or Märchen is a type of fiction and the product of creative imagination, offering four arguments (p. 133) against it.

First, "No popular story-teller has ever been known to invent anything." In support of this he cites several examples, such as the Eskimo, which show that the narrator is expected to recite a tale "as nearly as possible in the words of the original version" (p. 134). There are, however, societies such as Zuni, where this is clearly not the case. Originality and improvisation operate within certain limits, to be sure, but it cannot be maintained that creativity is lacking in all societies. Raglan continues "in illiterate communities the people as a whole not merely do not invent stories, but they do not even tell stories. The telling of stories may only be done by recognized story tellers, and . . . among many tribes they may tell only the particular stories which they have a recognized right to tell" (pp. 134-135). Granted that invention is an individual, not a group act, does this show that it cannot occur? Even if this statement were true for all societies, which it is not, it has no bearing on the proposition it is purported to support.

Second, "Not only are the incidents in folk-tales the same all over the world, but in areas of the same language they are commonly narrated in the same actual words." Raglan shows that "the fairy-tales of England and France contain not merely the same incidents, but the same or equivalent names" (p. 135) as in Bluebeard and

Barbe-bleu, and Little Red Riding Hood and Le Petit Chaperon Rouge. "We must conclude," he says "that one set of tales is a translation" (p. 135), implying that all of the tales of either France or England were borrowed from the other country. "The above seems enough to show that the fairy-tales of one country are not of popular origin, and this being so, we have no reason to assume that the fairy-tales of another country are of popular origin" (p. 135). Here, I confess, I am again unable to follow his reasoning. If some, or even all, English tales are borrowed from France, this is no demonstration that some, or even all of them, were not originated in France. Yet he continues, "If we find reason to believe that a folk-story has been borrowed, even from the next village, its popular origin becomes suspect, since if one community borrows instead of inventing, another may well do the same, and if one item of what passes as folk-lore is borrowed, it is at least possible that all is borrowed" (p. 136).

Diffusion is of course a most important process, but every element in culture, and every plot and incident in folklore, must have been invented at least once, by some individual somewhere. To show that a plot or motif has spread by diffusion even as widely as the Magic Flight does not by any means establish that it could not have had a secular origin or have been the product of some individual's imagination.

Third, "Folk-tales deal as a rule with subjects of which the folk can have no knowledge." They deal, he says, with supernatural beings, kings and queens, princes and princesses; their scenes are laid in palaces and castles, not in the farmyard or the harvest field. If folktales were really composed by the folk, he maintains, they would deal with everyday subjects such as courtship and marriage, seed-time and harvest, or hunting and fishing, with which the folk are familiar, rather than heroic feats of arms and succession to kingdoms. "Even when the characters are supposed to be peasants, the situations and incidents are quite unreal" (p. 138), as in the story of Red Riding Hood. Two possible explanations of this can be put forward, neither of which involve ritual origins. One is that these European folktales originated in the palaces and castles, and eventually seeped down to the peasants. The other is that the peasants found the same gratification in tales of royalty that Americans find in movies about romance and success. Gossip about the affairs of the castle was probably as interesting as the latest romances and scandals of Hollywood or royalty are to Americans today. There is nothing surprising in the fact that people find enjoyment in talking about things that they will never have or about events that will never happen to them.

Raglan continues, "It seems to be supposed, though I have nowhere seen this clearly stated, that the peasant and the savage, although they are great hands at making up stories, are nevertheless incapable of making up the simplest story of the doings of ordinary human beings, and are therefore obliged to have recourse to ogres, fairies, talking animals, and people endowed with supernatural powers, to which conceptions they are led by some mysterious but universal force. It has been suggested that this force operates by means of dreams and hallucinations, but those who make this suggestion fail to realize that dreams and hallucinations cannot put new ideas into the mind" (p. 139). What Raglan seems clearly to be stating is that although they are great hands at making up ritual, the peasant and the savage are nevertheless incapable of making up even the simplest folktale. As Stith Thompson has said, "None of these writers tells us how the ritual itself evolved and how the inventive process which moved from ritual into a story about the gods and heroes is any easier than any other form of invention."[5] Nor does Raglan tell us why it requires

5

greater genius to invent myths or folktales than the complex rituals from which they are claimed to be derived.

It is worth noting, also, that this argument is based on European folklore exclusively. The fact that kings and castles are not found in North American Indian folklore is not surprising, but is most pertinent here. Moreover, although they involve a variety of wondrous events, one also finds descriptions of hunting, grinding meal, courtship and desertion, and other ordinary human activities. In fact, in most bodies of living folklore one can find enough descriptions of technology, economics, social and political organization, as well as religion and ritual, to extract a description of the daily life, as Boas did using Tsimshian myths.

Fourth, "The exercise of the imagination consists not in creating something out of nothing, but in the transmutation of matter already present in the mind." The argument presented here is that the teller of a folktale, like the architect who designs a house and the literary poet or author, largely reworks familiar materials. I agree with this, but not with Raglan's conclusions that genius and true originality are restricted to the literates, and that it is absurd to suppose the unlettered rustic capable of composing the story of Cinderella. "Every literary community has certain types of story outside which none but exceptional geniuses can venture. As for the folk, they may make minor alterations, mostly for the worse, in existing poems, stories, or plays, but they never compose them for themselves" (p. 143). If the aborigines of the Americas could invent the igloo, snowshoe, toboggan, smoking, *cire perdue* casting, the zero concept, and so forth, could they not also have composed a folktale?

Summarizing the argument thus far, Raglan states "The position which we have now reached is that the folk-tale is never of popular origin, but is merely one form of the traditional narrative; that the traditional narrative has no basis either in history or in philosophical speculation, but is derived from the myth; and that the myth is a narrative connected with a rite" (p. 144). Nothing is traditional unless it is more than 150 years old, and a myth by definition is "a narrative connected with a rite." Raglan cites Hooke's definition of a myth as "the spoken part of a ritual; the story which the ritual enacts," and Jane Harrison, who says "A *mythos* to the Greek was primarily just a thing spoken, uttered by the *mouth*. Its antithesis or rather correlative is the thing done, enacted. . . . The primary meaning of myth in religion is just the same as in early literature; it is the spoken correlative of the acted rite."[6] Like Stith Thompson, I do not believe that Raglan's argument is intended to be as circular as it seems, when he begins his recent article by saying that a myth is simply a narrative associated with a rite, and "then proceeds to show that a myth (that is, a narrative associated with a rite) is indeed associated with a rite."[7]

In support of the theory that all traditional narratives are connected with ritual, Raglan (p. 144) recapitulates five arguments: "(1) That there is no other satisfactory way in which they can be explained. . . . (2) That these narratives are concerned primarily and chiefly with supernatural beings, kings, and heroes. (3) That miracles play a large part in them. (4) That the same scenes and incidents appear in many parts of the world. (5) That many of these scenes and incidents are explicable in terms of known rituals." In my opinion Raglan has failed to demonstrate either that myths and tales cannot have their origin in actual events and situations, or that it is impossible to ascribe them to creative imagination. It is not necessary, therefore, to look to ritual as their only satisfactory explanation. But his evidence for this explanation remains to be examined.

JOCASTA AND OEDIPUS

The ritual with which Raglan and many of the others of this school are primarily concerned is that of the early inhabitants of the Nile, Euphrates, and the Indus valleys. It is described as a complex ritual, in which they pretended to destroy the old world and create a new one, and as the means by which the divine king insured the regular flooding of the rivers and general fertility and prosperity. It consisted of a "dramatic ritual representing the death and resurrection of the king, who was also the god, performed by priests and members of the royal family. It comprised a sacred combat in which was enacted the victory of the god over his enemies, a triumphal procession in which the neighbouring gods took part, an enthronement, a ceremony by which the destinies of the state for the coming year were determined, and a sacred marriage." "Whereas the existing accounts of the ritual of Egypt and Mesopotamia provide only for a pretence of killing the king, the traditions of Greece and less civilized countries point to a ritual in which the king was actually killed, either annually, at the end of some longer term, or when his strength fails."[8] An essential and equally potent part of this ritual was the recitation of the myth which outlined the ritual itself.

This ritual is viewed by Raglan not only as the probable origin of the flood myths, but also as the basis for the Oedipus myth. Oedipus, who kills his father Laius, marries his mother Jocasta, and himself becomes king, is the new king who must defeat his predecessor either in battle or mock contest, be enthroned, and enter into a sacred marriage. Raglan's theory substitutes regicide, based on ancient ritual, for Freudian patricide, based on innate sexual desires.

Yet there is no criticism of the Freudian interpretation of this myth. In *The Hero* the Oedipus complex is not even mentioned, all of the ammunition being spent on the theory of ancient Euhemerus. Earlier, in *Jocasta's Crime* (London, 1933), Raglan devoted some pages (70-75) to a criticism of the "two different and indeed contradictory theories of the incest taboo" in Freud's *Totem and Taboo,* including a page-long discussion of the Oedipus complex. Raglan writes: "There seems to be no doubt that this complex occurs among European neurotics, and it may occur to some extent among normal Europeans; but even Freud's own followers have been unable to find it among savages, and have been reduced to the necessity of postulating a repressed repression in order to account for its apparent absence. . . . Among the classes from which Freud drew his data, women often retain their sexual attractiveness until after their sons have reached puberty. . . . Among savages, on the other hand, women age rapidly, and the result of this, combined with low birth-rate and high infant death-rate, is that by the time a boy reaches puberty his mother is normally a withered hag." Aside from the single sentence quoted previously from *The Hero* about dreams and hallucinations, I have found only one other reference to the Freudian interpretation of myths; in *Jocasta's Crime* (p. 136) Raglan mentions "the psychoanalysts, who produce myths from the subconscious much as conjurors produce rabbits from hats."

This is worth nothing, not only because Jocasta's crime and the Oedipus complex stem from the same myth, but also because the rest of Raglan's analysis of myths is closely paralleled by Rank's prior analysis in "The Myth of the Birth of the Hero."[9] As early as 1908 Rank had arrived at the following pattern, which he interprets in Freudian terms: "The hero is the child of most distinguished parents; usually the son of a king. His origin is preceded by difficulties, such as continence, or prolonged barrenness, or secret intercourse of the parents, due to external prohibition or ob-

7

stacles. During the pregnancy, or antedating the same, there is a prophecy in form of a dream or oracle, cautioning against his birth, and usually threatening danger to the father, or his representative. As a rule, he is surrendered to the water, in a box. He is then saved by animals, or lowly people (shepards) and is suckled by a female animal, or by a humble woman. After he has grown up, he finds his distinguished parents, in a highly versatile fashion; takes his revenge on his father, on the one hand, and is acknowledged on the other, and finally achieves rank and honors" (Rank, p. 61).

In 1936, Raglan (pp. 178-179) compared the Oedipus myth with twenty others, abstracting a pattern of twenty-two points, of which the first thirteen are strikingly similar to Rank's analysis. "(1) The hero's mother is a royal virgin; (2) his father is a king, and (3) often a near relative of his mother, but (4) the circumstances of his conception are unusual, and (5) he is also reputed to be the son of a god. (6) At birth an attempt is made, usually by his father or maternal grandfather, to kill him, but (7) he is spirited away, and (8) reared by foster-parents in a far country. (9) We are told nothing of his childhood, but (10) on reaching manhood he returns or goes to his future kingdom. (11) After a victory over the king and/or a giant, dragon or wild beast, (12) he marries a princess, often the daughter of his predecessor, and (13) becomes king.

"(14) For a time he reigns uneventfully, and (15) prescribes laws, but (16) later he loses favour with the gods and/or his subjects, and (17) is driven from the throne and city, after which (18) he meets with a mysterious death, (19) often at the top of a hill. (20) His children, if any, do not succeed him. (21) His body is not buried, but nevertheless (22) he has one or more holy sepulchres."

Raglan applies this pattern to Oedipus and finds he scores the full twenty-two points. Theseus, Romulus, Heracles, Perseus, Jason, Bellerophon, Pelops, Asclepios, Dionysos, Apollo, and Zeus, also in classical mythology, are given scores ranging from eleven to twenty points. Elijah, Joseph, and Moses from the Old Testament score from nine to twenty points. Siegfried, Llew Llawgyffes, Robin Hood, and King Arthur from European folklore score from eleven to nineteen points. Nyikang, the cult hero of the Shilluk of Africa, scores fourteen and Wata Gunung, a Javanese hero, scores eighteen.

Rank's analysis, to which Raglan makes no reference, had included six of these myths. Rank had considered Oedipus, Romulus, Heracles, Perseus, Paris, Telephos, Kyros, Karna, Sargon, Gilgamos, Moses, Jesus, Siegfried, Tristan, and Lohengrin, with subsidiary analyses of Ion, Amphion and Zethos, Darab, Kaikhosrav, Zal, Feridun, Zoroaster, Abraham, Isaac, Judas, St. Gregory, Arthur, Tristram, Wolfdietrich, Horn, Wieland, Helias, and Sceaf. Rank interprets these heroes, all of whom come from Europe, the Middle East, and India, in terms of the Oedipus complex and the exposure of the child in a box, basket, or cave, which symbolizes not a return to the womb, but the process of birth (Rank, p. 70).

These two analyses confirm the pattern, but obviously neither of the two very different interpretations. As far as the Freudian interpretation is concerned, the hero marries his mother in only four of these forty-eight myths: Oedipus himself, Judas, St. Gregory, and Wata Gunung, who marries his mother and his sister. Zeus marries his sister, Theseus marries several princesses, St. Gregory is "the child of the incestuous union of royal lovers," Darab is the child of father-daughter incest, and Heracles' parents are parallel first cousins, suggesting the violation of taboos, but not the Oedipus complex. Rank himself (p. 88) notes that the myths emphasize the hostility toward the father or father surrogate, but not the sexual desire for the mother: "The mother, and her relation to the hero, appear relegated to the background in the myth of the birth of the hero."

Yet again, in only four of the forty-eight myths, Oedipus, Judas, Theseus, and Romulus, does the hero kill his father or cause his death. This supports neither the theory of patricide nor that of regicide. Perseus and Kaikhoarav kill their mother's father, Jason his father's brother, Heracles his foster father, Romulus his twin brother, but Amphion and Zethos kill their mother's father's brother's wife, Helias causes his father's mother to be burned, and Karna is himself killed by his brother. It is difficult to interpret all of these as father surrogates. In other cases the hero kills or overcomes monsters, performs feats, overcomes death, wins actual or magical victories or, in the case of Joseph, wins "a contest in dream-interpretation and weather-forecasting" (Raglan, p. 184). The pattern as abstracted by Raglan and Rank seems less compatible with Oedipal interpretations and ritual origins than with Hollywood's formulae. The hero overcomes insurmountable obstacles, marries a princess, and becomes a king. But many of the details and incidents would be censored by Hollywood.

In another very important point the theory of ritual regicide fails to account for the hero pattern outlined by Raglan, namely the fact that the hero himself is not slain by his successor, but is driven away after losing favor and meets a mysterious death on top of a hill. Raglan himself remarks, "We may conclude that deposition and a mysterious death is a part of the pattern, but a puzzling feature is that there is nothing to suggest that the hero suffers a defeat. As he has gained the throne by a victory, one would expect him to lose it by a defeat, but this he never does" (pp. 197-198). Raglan's only explanation is that the divine king may have been burned on a pyre erected on a hill-top, but he admits that there is nothing to suggest that before being burned he is compelled to fight with and be defeated by his successor. Yet if the death of the old king is to be found in ritual regicide, so must the death of the new king. Point 18 should equal point 11. Raglan himself says earlier, "History is what happens once, but things that happen once only are nothing to the ritualist, who is concerned only with things that are done again and again" (p. 150). The same criticism, of course, applies with equal force to the Freudian interpretation, since the Oedipus complex is held to be inherent in every man.

NYIKANG AND WATA GUNUNG

I do not propose an alternative theory of origin of Raglan or Rank's hero pattern. Perhaps its origin is in ritual regicide or sexual patricide, and perhaps it is in imaginative fantasy or actual human situations. I do not regard any of these as either proven or impossible. It is important to note, however, that all of Rank's heroes and all but two of Raglan's are derived from the societies of India, the Middle East and Europe, whose cultures are historically related. The similarities in these tales could be explained by diffusion from a common source, as Raglan suggests, and this might also account for Nyikang and Wata Gunung. The Shilluk are not too remote from Mohammedan peoples, and perhaps this tale spread to Java along with either Islam or Buddhism. But, if similarities are due to diffusion from a single source, is there any reason to look for ritual origins to explain them? Documenting the similarities at

9

least proves nothing about their origin in ritual, history, or fantasy, Freudian or other-wise.

In a recent paper, Lessa has discussed Oedipus-type tales in Sumatra, Java, and Lombok, and beyond the area of Buddhistic and Islamic influence, on Ulithi, Truk, Ponape, Kusaie, the Marshalls, Kapingamarangi, New Guinea, and the Marquesas.[10] In the Maori creation myth in which Tanemahuta severs his father and mother, Lang had found a close parallel to the Cronus myth,[11] and as other analogues had cited the Indian myth in which Indra severs Dyaus and Prthivi and the Chinese myth of Puang-ku to which Tylor had previously referred.[12] Lessa concludes that the Oedipus-type story spread by diffusion from the patriarchal Euro-Asiatic societies to Oceanic societies in which the Oedipal situation is lacking. Although I have as yet found no references to it in Burma, Siam, Indo-China, or Malaya, this is at least a reasonable hypothesis. Lessa says that "we find such stories limited to a continuous belt extend-ing from Europe to the Near and Middle East and south-eastern Asia, and from there into the islands of the Pacific. It seems to be absent from such vast areas as Africa, China, central Asia, northeastern Asia, North America, South America, and Aus-tralia."[13]

Rank and other classical Freudians would explain these analogues in terms of innate Oedipal drives. Yet if these drives are innate and universal, why are not such myths found in all societies? And why are the Oedipus myths of closely related cultures more similar than those separated by greater time, space, and cultural differences?

Raglan apparently does not claim that all myths have a common source in a single ritual. "It may be urged," he writes, "that if all myths are derived from the royal ritual of the Nile-Indus region, then all myths should be alike. In fact, many myths are extremely widespread; this fact has been generally realized, except by exponents of the 'Aryan' theory, but has been attributed to the alleged similar working of the human mind. This theory breaks down, however, when it is realized that however widespread certain features of myth and ritual may be, other myths and rites have a distribution comparable, let us say, to that of the Moslem religion. Nobody asserts that, because we find in Java and in Nigeria men who marry four wives and pray five times a day, the human mind works naturally in the direction of four wives and five daily prayers. No belief or practice can be claimed as natural unless it is universal, and even the most widespread myths and rites are not that" (p. 150).

Yet he goes on to say, "The myth varies with the ritual, and both, especially among the illiterate, tend to reflect political and economic conditions. A ritual de-veloped among a people who both kept cattle and cultivated the soil might spread on the one hand to pastoral nomads, and on the other to cultivators who kept no cattle. One part of the ritual would then die out, and as it would, of course, not be the same part, it might come to be supposed that the two rituals were quite inde-pendent. . . . The original, so far as can be judged from the general pattern, was based on the existence of a king who was killed and replaced annually. A hundred myths describe his death and the installation of his successor" (p. 151). I can only conclude that Raglan does not mean to imply that all myths have a single source, and that if he did, he has certainly not demonstrated this to be the case.

In his recent article, Raglan cites Parson's statement that the Hopi Emergence myth is too explanatory of the ceremonial life to be told to rank outsiders.[14] Although in the same passage Parsons refers to it as less esoteric than Pueblo chants, this quotation suggests that it is a narrative of the events enacted in rituals. It is not clear from this passage whether the Emergence story, which among the Zuni differs markedly from one version to another in the details which are introduced,[15] is similar in this respect to what Parsons (I, 215) calls "the archeological or topographic legends." "Into this legendary frame a considerable number of narratives are embroidered and a few songs, for ritual recitation or for edification. Versions vary, for there will be stressed or introduced myth bearing upon the ceremony or organization the particular narrator is connected with." In similar accounts, which Benedict (I, xxxii, xxxix) refers to as "myths," the Zuni narrator is free to incorporate details of rituals of which he has special knowledge, drawing on his own personal experience. It is clear that the relation between these Zuni myths and ritual is secondary. Although these details are derived from rituals and are enacted in rituals, the myths are not. The passage cited by Raglan does not show that this is not also the case with regard to the Hopi Emergence myth.

In support of ritual associations, Raglan might better have quoted from Parson's previous paragraph (I, 215): "As yet only a few ritual recitals or chants have been recorded, mostly Zuni. These ritual versions are known only to those in charge of them; even when recited semipublicly, like the Shalako and Sayatasha myths, they are not attended to by outsiders; they are merely part of the ceremony. In this respect these unique Zuni recitals suggest the all-night song myths of the Mohave which constitute Mohave ceremony or the Athapascan song myths which are also a part of the ceremony. In general, however, Pueblo mythology and ceremonial are far more separate than are Navaho-Apache song myths and ceremonial."

It is not difficult to recognize other myths, even in Raglan's special sense of narratives associated with rituals, in societies outside the stream of Western culture. The totemic myths of the Murngin of Australia, as described by Warner, also fulfill in detail the definitions of Harrison and Hooke. "A fundamental conceptual scheme runs through all the ceremonies; the various dramatic sections portray the myth by dance and song. For the Western European, this whole totemic ceremonial behavior might be compared to a Wagnerian opera, with the myth as libretto; the motifs, like that of the snake swallowing the women, first expressed in a phrase or two, are later elaborated; and certain motifs, highly elaborate in some of the ceremonies are only hinted at in others. For the reason that here we have ceremonies treated separately by the natives which they yet realize fit into a larger whole, the totality may, without too much stretching, be compared with the Nibelungen Ring. The fundamental difference is that the story is not a myth to them, but a dogma and has the same ceremonial significance to the Murngin as the Mass to a believing Catholic."[16]

These instances, and others which might be cited, are reason enough for anthropologists to pay more attention to the relation of myth to ritual, and to test cross-culturally what the ritual school often puts forth as its own dogma or at least as unsupported hypotheses.[17] Are what the ritualists define as myths universal in all societies? Or to restate the question, are all myths as more commonly defined connected with ritual? I would doubt that this is the case, but before these questions can be answered there must be some further agreement among the ritualists and a clearer statement of whether a myth is (1) a narrative which is recited as a part of a ritual, (2) a narrative, the events of which are enacted in a ritual, (3) a narrative which is both recited and enacted in a ritual, or (4) a narrative which is only indirectly and secondarily associated with ritual.

There is an equal need for anthropologists and folklorists, as a whole, to arrive at some agreement as to what they mean by myth, and at least some tentative distinctions between myth, legend, and folktale. In the American Indian field as a whole it is particularly difficult to distinguish between them, as Parsons' reference to legends and Benedict's reference to myths, for which she also uses the term folktales, indicate. Warner, in saying that what he has called myth is "not a myth, but a dogma," and Bidney, in defining myth as something which is untrue, have simply added to the confusion. This is no place to present my own system of classification, but in it myths are by definition regarded as true in the society in which they are told. They are regarded as fact, rather than fiction, while legends are also, folktales are not.

NOTES

[1] The extensive literature of these scholars has been summarized by Stanley Edgar Hyman in "The Ritual View of Myth and the Mythic," *JAF*, LXVIII (1955), 462-472; and in an earlier review, *JAF*, LXVII (1954), 86-89.

[2] Quotations from Lord Raglan, *The Hero* (London, 1949; first published 1936), pp. 36, 120, 121, respectively. Subsequent page references, to the 1949 edition, are given parenthetically in the text.

[3] Stanley Edgar Hyman, "Dissent on a Dictionary," *Kenyon Review*, XII (1950), 726.

[4] Raglan, *The Hero*, p. 121; Alfred Nutt, "History, Tradition, and Historic Myths," *Folk-Lore*, XII (1901), 339.

[5] Stith Thompson, "Myths and Folktales," *JAF*, LXVIII (1955), 483.

[6] Raglan, *The Hero*, p. 128; S. H. Hooke, *Myth and Ritual* (Oxford, 1933), p. 3; J. E. Harrison, *Themis* (Cambridge, Eng., 1912), p. 328.

[7] Thompson, "Myths and Folktales," p. 484.

[8] Raglan, *The Hero*, p. 153; S. H. Hooke, *The Labyrinth* (London, 1935), v.

[9] Otto Rank, *The Myth of the Birth of the Hero*, Nervous and Mental Disease Mono. Ser., No. 18 (New York, 1914). Page references are to this edition. This study had been published as *Der Mythus von der Geburt des Helden*, Schriften zur Angewandten Seelenkunde, V, ed. S. Freud (1908), with a second and enlarged edition in 1922. The English edition has been republished by R. Brunner (New York, 1952).

[10] William A. Lessa, "Oedipus-Type Tales in Oceania," *JAF*, LXIX (1956), 63.

[11] Andrew Lang, *Custom and Myth* (New York, 1885), pp. 45-51.

[12] Edward B. Tylor, *Primitive Culture* (London, 1871), I, 294.

[13] Lessa, p. 68. Li Hwei has traced fifty-one flood myths in Formosa, South China, the Indo-China Peninsula, the Malay Archipelago, and westward to central India, in which a brother and sister survive by floating in "a wooden box, or the like." Being the only living beings, they mate with each other and give birth to the ancestors of mankind; see Li Hwei, "The Deluge Legend of the Sibling-Mating Type in Aboriginal Formosa and Southeast Asia," *Bull. of the Ethno. Soc.* (Taiwan, 1955), I, 205-206. Although not Oedipus-type myths, these would have to be considered in any comprehensive study, since they overlap in distribution and in at least one motif.

[14] Lord Raglan, "Myth and Ritual," *JAF*, LXVIII (1955), 461; Elsie Clews Parsons, *Pueblo Indian Religion* (Chicago, 1939), I, 216.

[15] Ruth Benedict, *Zuni Mythology*, Columbia Univ. Contr. to Anthro., No. 21 (New York, 1935), I, xxx.

[16] W. Lloyd Warner, *A Black Civilization* (New York and London, 1937), p. 260.

[17] For example, Raglan's interpretation of William Tell and the tale of the Faithful Hound, "Myth and Ritual," p. 459.

Northwestern University
Evanston, Illinois

THE MYTH AND RITUAL POSITION CRITICALLY CONSIDERED

by S. G. F. BRANDON

SINCE the year 1795, when Charles-François Dupuis set forth the view[1] that behind the figures of Christ and Osiris, of Bacchus and Mithra, there lay a common tendency to personify the sun in its annual course, the comparative study of religions has been generally characterized by attempts to find some common interpretative principle which will account either for the origin of religion or for its essential structure. The motive behind such attempts is intelligible, and it may well be compared to the tendency manifest in many other disciplines to seek one simple formula which will explain an immense corpus of otherwise amorphous data. But these attempts, which have generally occurred successively and often in consequence of each other, have resulted in the history of the comparative study of religions assuming the appearance of a chronological record of the rise and fall of various so-called 'schools', which are severally distinguished by the peculiar theories concerning the origin or nature of religion which their members advanced or defended. Thus, to name but a few representative examples: the so-called 'Philological School' of Max Müller and his followers sought to account for religious origins in terms of a solar mythology by means of comparative philology;[2] the reactions which this line of interpretation provoked found a common expression in the efforts of those scholars who turned for a solution to anthropological research and of whom one of the earliest and most distinguished representatives, Sir Edward B. Tylor, set forth animism, i.e. 'belief in Spiritual Beings' as what he termed 'the minimum definition of Religion'.[3] An even greater name in this

---

[1] *L'Origine de tous les cultes ou la religion universelle* (nouv. éd., Paris, 1822). On Dupuis see *La Grande Encyclopédie*, t. 15, p. 97. Cf. G. Berguer in *Histoire générale des religions*, ed. M. Gorce et R. Mortier, t. i (Paris, 1948), p. 8.

[2] e.g. Max Müller, 'Comparative Mythology' (1856), in *Chips from a German Workshop* ii (London, 1867). Cf. L. Spence, *Introduction to Mythology* (London, 1921), pp. 47–51.

[3] *Primitive Culture* i (London, 1929, 1st ed. 1871), 424.

'Anthropological School' is that of Sir James G. Frazer—indeed by reason of his prodigious labours in assembling material and in advancing certain hypotheses in the interpretation of it his name still remains, despite criticism and changing modes of thought, the most significant in this field of study. The work of Frazer, based as that of the 'Anthropological School' generally on the assumption of the soundness of the evolutionary principle in the interpretation of culture,[1] was largely devoted to showing how profoundly the needs of the agriculturalist's life had affected religious concept and practice. The spectacle of the annual cycle of Nature's year, with its recurrent drama of the death and revival of vegetation, inspired, so he maintained, the pregnant idea of the dying-god, of which Adonis, Attis, and Osiris are the classic examples, and from which derived the institution of divine kingship, whereby communities at a certain level of cultural development believed that their well-being was essentially bound up with the well-being of their king, who impersonated or was the incarnation of the spirit of vegetation.[2]

Frazer in his interpretation of religious origins had also advanced the thesis that an 'Age of Magic' had preceded the 'Age of Religion',[3] and in support of this view he had cited a great abundance of evidence concerning the magical rites practised by primitive peoples whereby mainly by the action of miming they sought to cause the recurrence of phenomena advantageous to themselves. This evaluation of the importance of ritual was in due course so developed by the late Professor Gilbert Murray[4] and the late Dr. Jane Harrison[5] in interpreting ancient Greek religion that the claims of ritual magic to be one of the

---

[1] But Frazer fully realized the complexity of the issue and the vital part played by cultural diffusion, cf. *Balder the Beautiful* (*Golden Bough, VIII*), i, Preface, pp. vi–vii; *Folklore in the Old Testament*, i. 106–7; 'Sur l'étude des origines humaines' in *The Gorgon's Head and other Literary Pieces* (London, 1927), pp. 348–55.

[2] The theme in its various aspects finds expression throughout the constitutive parts of *The Golden Bough*.   [3] *The Dying God* (*Golden Bough*, iii. 1936), p. 2.

[4] 'Excursus on Ritual Forms preserved in Greek Tragedy', in J. E. Harrison, *Themis* (Cambridge, 1912); *Five Stages of Greek Religion*, chap. i (the substance of the book was originally delivered as lectures in 1912).

[5] *Prolegomena to the Study of Greek Religion* (Cambridge, 1907); *Ancient Art and Ritual* (London, 1913).

primary factors in the origin of religious concept became generally recognized. Closely associated with this new appreciation of ritual came a re-evaluation of myth. In early times myth had been generally regarded either as the poetic imaginings of primitive peoples or it was interpreted aetiologically, i.e. as being the naïve explanations of natural phenomena concocted by the primitive mind. But now attention was given to the close connexion holding between ritual and myth, and since the former was generally believed to be prior in order of appearance, myth in its original form was held to be an explanation of the ritual, a kind of libretto designed to make intelligible sacro-magical acts when the original emotions which prompted them were no longer remembered or understood.[1]

It was in this setting, constituted by the trend of thought in the field of *Religionsgeschichte,* that the so-called 'Myth and Ritual School' emerged in the third decade of the present century. As seen in that context, it appears as an intelligible derivation from the work of Frazer[2] and the new estimate of the function of ritual and myth, and it may also be fairly regarded as another instance of that same tendency to seek a formula which will neatly explain the origin or nature of a complex of religious faith and practice.

Intelligible though it be when seen in such a context, the 'Myth and Ritual' thesis is not thereby adequately explained in the matter of original inspiration, and it would seem that there is yet another factor of considerable significance concerning which a reckoning must be made. A clue to the nature of this factor is surely to be found in the fact that the majority of those scholars who co-operated with Professor S. H. Hooke in the original publication of the thesis in 1933 were men who were

---

[1] Cf. W. R. Smith, *Religion of the Semites* (3rd ed., London, 1927), pp. 17–20, see also S. A. Cook's notes, op. cit., pp. 500–3; A. N. Whitehead, *Religion in the Making* (Cambridge, 1927), pp. 8–17; E. O. James, *Comparative Religion* (London, 1938), pp. 97–100; G. van der Leeuw, *La Religion dans son essence et ses manifestations* (Paris, 1948), pp. 404–5; M. Éliade, *Traité d'histoire des religions* (Paris, 1949), pp. 350–73; Chantepie de la Saussaye, *Lehrbuch der Religionsgeschichte* (ed. A. Bertholet u. E. Lehman, Tübingen, 1925), i. 93–94; E. Cassirer, *An Essay on Man* (New Haven, 1944), pp. 79–83; T. H. Gaster, 'Myth and Story', *Numen,* i (1954), pp. 184–212.
[2] The work of A. M. Hocart should also be noted in this connexion: his *Kingship* was published in 1927 and he contributed to the symposium *The Labyrinth.*

profoundly concerned with the interests of the Christian religion;
most of them, moreover, were Old Testament scholars.[1] It is,
therefore, not altogether surprising that five out of the original
eight lectures, which formed the symposium *Myth and Ritual*,
were concerned with the various aspects of the so-called 'Myth
and Ritual pattern' as manifest in the cultures of Palestine, and
as constituting issues which ¦ultimately had significance for
Christian theology.[2] And to what may be described as this
general professional interest there may have been an even
deeper-lying motive, which can be reasonably defined, although
its existence cannot be demonstrated. It is that the 'Myth and
Ritual' thesis represents a reaction on the part of certain scholars
to the great emphasis which had hitherto been laid upon the
essential significance of the prophetic movement and tradition
in the religion of Israel. The prophet had been exalted to the
detriment of the priest, the inspirational element in religion at
the expense of the cultic. Whether such considerations were
consciously felt or subconsciously operative,[3] the 'Myth and
Ritual' thesis did in fact help to redress the balance by showing
that in the cultus of Israel there was a factor which proved as
influential as that of prophecy in shaping the thought and
aspirations, not only of Israel, but also of Christianity, and it is
surely significant that this tacit *apologia* for the cultus coincided
with a renewed interest in this country and on the Continent in
the liturgical heritage of the Christian Church.[4]

   To complete the account of those factors which appear to
have been influential in the genesis of the 'Myth and Ritual'
thesis consideration must also be given to the theory concerning

---

   [1] The Preface to *Myth and Ritual* (Oxford, 1933) by Canon D. C. Simpson is
significant in this connexion.

   [2] In the succeeding symposium edited by S. H. Hooke entitled *The Labyrinth*
(London, 1935) the same interest manifests itself in the majority of the essays.

   [3] In his Preface to *Myth and Ritual*, pp. xiii–xiv, Dr. Simpson was evidently
conscious of the issue.

   [4] The controversy aroused by the measures to revise the *Book of Common Prayer*
in 1927 and 1928 and the publication by the S.P.C.K. of the symposium *Liturgy and
Worship* in 1932 may be mentioned in this connexion.

   [*Editor's note*: The statements on this page must be corrected by what is said
in the first essay.]

the diffusion of culture propounded by Sir Grafton Elliot Smith and W. J. Perry, according to which certain fundamental inventions and institutions of human society, having been first achieved in Egypt, had gradually been diffused among the other peoples of the ancient world: among such institutions was notably that of divine kingship.[1] As will be noticed at greater length presently, the exponents of the 'Myth and Ritual' thesis have variously based themselves upon the diffusionist and the evolutionary theories of culture; nevertheless it is evident in the earliest statements of the thesis that the view that the pharaonic kingship of Egypt had powerfully influenced the ideas and institutions of neighbouring peoples was accepted as virtually axiomatic.[2]

As seen now across more than twenty subsequent years of discussion, discovery, and research, the original exposition of the 'Myth and Ritual' thesis may also be reckoned as the first notable effort to reap the harvest which the archaeology of the Near East had been steadily producing. From the discovery of the celebrated Amarna tablets in 1887 to the uncovering of the ancient city of Ugarit, at the modern Ras Shamra, in 1929, evidence had been accumulating to show that among the peoples occupying what the late Professor J. H. Breasted had aptly called the 'Fertile Crescent' there had been a lively commerce, with its consequent intermingling of cultural elements and influences, so that justification was given for thinking of the ancient Near East as an integral culture-area.[3] Viewed in this light, similarities which were found to exist between the ideas

---

[1] The chief works in which the diffusionist theory was expounded prior to 1933 were G. Elliot Smith, *The Ancient Egyptian and the Origins of Civilization* (London, 1911, 2nd ed. 1923), *Human History* (London, 1930); W. J. Perry, *The Children of the Sun: a Study in the Early History of Civilization* (London, 1923); *The Growth of Civilization* (1924). Cf. A. J. Toynbee, *A Study of History* i (London, 1935), 424–40.

[2] *Myth and Ritual*, pp. 6, 8–9, 11–12, 71–73, 86 (S. H. Hooke), 87–88 (F. J. Hollis), 117, 118, 121, 123–4, 129 (W. O. E. Oesterley), 149 (E. O. James). It is significant that the Egyptologist, Prof. A. M. Blackman, who contributed to the volume, ends his essay by noting 'an indication that the original "pattern" was not a product of Egypt but was imported thither, possibly from Syria' (op. cit., p. 39).

[3] Cf. Ed. Meyer, *Geschichte des Altertums* (Stuttgart u. Berlin, 1913), i. 680–3; A. Moret, *Des clans aux empires* (Paris, 1923), pp. 185–6, 246, 341–8, 401–3; W. F. Albright, *From the Stone Age to Christianity* (Baltimore, 1946), pp. 1–33, 35–36.

and institutions of the various peoples dwelling in that area were naturally suggestive of a common attitude and response to certain situations. Moreover, this predisposition in particular was conducive to an appreciation of that which in the culture of Israel, traditionally regarded as the 'peculiar people', attested the basic integration of Israelite culture with that which seemed common to the area. But, as will be shown in greater detail presently, by making of the undoubted similarities occurring in the cultures of the ancient Near East the basic assumption of the existence throughout the area of a common cultural tradition in the matter of the institution of kingship, the exponents of the 'Myth and Ritual' thesis tended to disregard the equally or even more significant differences which existed in the *Weltanschauungen* of the cultures concerned.

With this basic assumption there was closely linked in the 'Myth and Ritual' thesis another, namely, the validity of the concept of 'culture-pattern' and the possibility of its effective diffusion outside the sphere in which it was created. In the two volumes in which the 'Myth and Ritual' thesis was first published no formal definition of a 'culture-pattern' was given,[1] but from the use of the term in many passages it is evident that the authors believed that in certain cultures there can be perceived a number of interrelated ideas and practices which may be considered as constituting a unified whole which has its own logic and is expressive of a specific communal endeavour to deal with some situation which threatens the common good and/or which might be made to serve the common welfare. This complex of idea and practice, or in the 'Myth and Ritual' terminology the 'culture-pattern',[2] it is further maintained, can be, in fact has

---

[1] In *Myth and Ritual*, p. 8, S. H. Hooke does give this partial definition: 'The ritual pattern represents the things which were done to and by the king in order to secure the prosperity of the community in every sense for the coming year.' In *The Labyrinth*, p. 260, E. O. James makes what may be deemed a definition of certain aspects of the 'pattern': 'Around the divine kingship a series of religious activities was set in motion in the great agricultural civilizations of the ancient East which had for their purpose the maintenance of the food supply and the prosperity of society in general, as well as the satisfaction of individual needs.' Cf. E. O. James, *Comparative Religion*, pp. 94–95.

[2] It is to be noted that often the term 'ritual pattern' is used when its connotation

been, diffused from the culture in which it originated and established effectively within alien cultures or at least among alien peoples. Now the mode of such a diffusion is never explicitly described, and the most that may be inferred from various allusions and references is that such 'culture-patterns' were diffused in consequence of war or trade or colonization. But the issue involved here is too important to permit the assumption to be passed without a closer scrutiny of its practical aspects. Accordingly it may be noted that in a pertinent passage Professor Hooke maintains that, just as the symbol of the winged sun-disk was diffused from Egypt to Assyria, Cappadocia and Persia, so 'it is also possible to conceive of the carrying of the larger ritual pattern with its associated myth from one country to another by one of the various ways of "culture spread", such as commerce, conquest, or colonization'.[1] However, the very example which is here chosen in support of the theory does itself raise doubt about the soundness of that theory, because it is evident that, while Hittite, Assyrian, and Iranian artists did copy this famous Egyptian symbol, its original significance was not understood by them—quite obviously it was the general form of the symbol which impressed the foreigner and he reproduced it without insight into its intrinsic meaning, changing its pregnant details according to his own fancy or needs.[2] If this then happened in the transmission of the concrete symbol of the winged sun-disk of Egypt, the question may well be asked how far is the assumption justified that a complex of religious ideas and practice, such as that presupposed in the 'Myth and Ritual' thesis, which had been created by a particular people in response to its experience of life in a given geographical environment, could be effectively

is clearly meant to include other elements than the 'ritual'. Cf. R. F. Benedict, *Patterns of Culture* (New York, 1934), pp. 23–24, 46, 254. See also J. de Fraine, *L'Aspect religieux de la royauté israélite* (Roma, 1954), pp. 27–32; A. Bentzen, *Messias-Moses redivivus Menschensohn* (Zürich, 1948), p. 16; *King and Messiah* (London, 1955), p. 83 n. 8, p. 84 n. 11. [1] *Myth and Ritual*, p. 4.

[2] An example of this can be noted in op. cit., fig. i, in the reproduction of the *uraeus* serpents by the foreign artists: quite clearly they did not appreciate this part of the symbol and treated it as a pair of decorative streamers. On the significance of the Egyptian winged sun-disk see H. Bonnet, *Reallexikon der ägyptischen Religionsgeschichte* (Berlin, 1952), *sub nominibus* 'Behdeti' and 'Uräus'.

transmitted to alien peoples? It will be well here to consider again the instance of the winged sun-disk, since it has further significance in this connexion. Because such a symbol was a visible object and could be seen by a traveller on many Egyptian buildings or on objects circulated outside Egypt through trade or diplomatic policy, it was easy for a foreign artist to reproduce it, or something like it, in his own land; but, if the foreigner had not been content merely with an approximate reproduction of such a symbol and had sought to understand its spiritual meaning, he would have been obliged to make special inquiry of the competent Egyptian authorities, an undertaking which would have required considerable knowledge of a foreign language and insight into alien modes of thought.[1] It may accordingly be asked who in the countries of the ancient Near East would have been sufficiently interested in, or capable of, surmounting such immense difficulties in order to transmit to their own people the esoteric 'culture-pattern' of some alien folk? Merchants, soldiers, or colonists are certainly not cast for this role, and it is instructive to note what happened when educated men in the ancient world did specially seek to understand and interpret a culture alien to their own—the strange accounts which Herodotus gave of Egyptian customs and Plutarch's version of the Osirian myth have provided several generations of Egyptologists with a fascinating task of trying to identify their queer statements with what is known of ancient Egyptian faith and practice from the native records; and the general verdict is that these Greek savants utterly failed to apprehend the true nature of Egyptian religion.[2]

[1] The Egyptians' fear of dying and being buried in a foreign land, which is graphically described in the Middle Kingdom story of Sinuhe (Erman–Blackman, *Literature of the Ancient Egyptians*, pp. 14–29), is evidence of their conviction that foreigners could not really understand the essentials of Egyptian religion. The Phoenician attempts at embalming the bodies of certain magnates and their burial in anthropoid sarcophagi were obviously inspired by knowledge of Egyptian funerary practice, but it is equally obvious that such imitation did not imply an intelligent adoption of the Egyptian mortuary faith; cf. G. Contenau, *La Civilisation phénicienne* (Paris, 1949), pp. 155–6, 197–202, plates xi, xii; E. A. W. Budge, *The Mummy* (Cambridge, 1925), p. 431. See also H. Frankfort *The Art and Architecture of the Ancient Orient* (London, 1954), pp. 66, 117, 157–61, 197–201.

[2] Cf. Sourdille, *Hérodote et la religion de l'Égypte* (Paris, 1910), pp. 363, 365–6, 401; W. Spiegelberg, *Die Glaubwürdigkeit der Herodots Berichte über Ägypten im*

The assumption that 'culture-patterns' existed and could be effectively disseminated from their original centre among the peoples of the ancient Near East prepares the way for the next assumption, namely, that there existed a definitive 'culture-pattern' centred on the institution of divine kingship which was thus disseminated and which came to constitute a common tradition of faith and practice throughout that area. It is a crucial part of the 'Myth and Ritual' thesis that this 'culture-pattern' found dramatic expression at an annual festival in which the king played an essential part. The constitutive elements of the ritual enacted at this festival are defined as 'the dramatic representation of the death and resurrection of the god'; 'the recitation or symbolic representation of the myth of creation'; 'the ritual combat, in which the triumph of the god over his enemies was depicted'; 'the sacred marriage'; 'the triumphal procession, in which the king played the part of the god followed by a train of lesser gods or visiting deities'.[1] The clarity with which these liturgical moments are defined and their articulation in the assumed ἱερὸς λόγος demonstrated is certainly impressive, but when a search is made in the relevant expositions of the 'Myth and Ritual' thesis for an account of the actual origin of this 'ritual-pattern' and for evidence of its occurrence as such in the records of the various cultures concerned, the result is curiously vague and unsatisfactory. If the influence of the pharaonic kingship had been such as is assumed, it is reasonable to expect that in the Egyptian records there should be ample evidence of the existence of this 'ritual pattern' as a regular feature of the state-religion of Egypt and, further, of its great antiquity. However, the essay which was contributed to the original symposium by the Egyptologist, Professor A. M. Blackman, despite its considerable value to Egyptological studies, is notable for its generally negative character in this respect. Although, by ranging throughout the

Lichte der ägyptischen Denkmäler (Heidelberg, 1926), pp. 16–18, 34–40; A. Erman, *Die Religion der Ägypter* (Berlin u. Leipzig, 1934), pp. 86–87, 333, 425–6; E. A. W. Budge, *Osiris and the Egyptian Resurrection* i (London, 1911), 18. Megasthenes's identification of two Indian gods with Dionysos and Herakles is also significant in this connexion; cf. C. Eliot, *Hinduism and Buddhism* ii (London, 1954), 137–8, 139 n. 1.

[1] *Myth and Ritual*, p. 8 (S. H. Hooke).

whole course of Egyptian history, a number of instances were found which had a certain degree of correspondence to certain moments of the hypothetical 'ritual-pattern', nowhere was it shown that there was a regular annual festival in Egypt which reproduced this 'pattern' in its essential entirety and thus presumably provided the prototype of such a festival, which was diffused from the valley of the Nile throughout the lands of the Fertile Crescent.[1]

The most convincing evidence of the occurrence of such a 'ritual-pattern' at an annual festival is actually provided by the records of the New Year festival at Babylon.[2] But the significance of this evidence may well be questioned; the actual documents concerned are relatively late in date and Babylon cannot, without qualification, be regarded as representative of Mesopotamia generally back to the era of Sumerian hegemony,[3] and still less may it be taken as typical in the matter of the religious faith and practice of various states, not all of them of Semitic origin, lying far to the west and north, unless it can be shown that the culture of Babylon or of some older Mesopotamian state was effectively diffused throughout the area of the Near East.

[1] See the statement of Blackman quoted on p. 265 n. 2, above. Cf. H. Frankfort, *Kingship and the Gods* (Chicago, 1948), pp. 34–35, 183–5, 204, 207–9. See also the account of Egyptian kingship given by Bonnet, op. cit., *sub nomin.* 'Dreißigjahrfest', 'Feste', 'König', 'Krönung', 'Kult', 'Theokratie'; see also under 'Ernte'. Reference might also be made to the account of H. W. Fairman ('Worship and Festivals in an Egyptian Temple', in *B.J.R.L.*, xxxvii. 1954) of the annual festivals, in which the king participated, at the Ptolemaic temple of Edfu: the sacred marriage there had nothing of the character of that assumed in the 'Myth and Ritual' thesis (cf. op. cit., pp. 196–7, 200).

[2] Cf. C. J. Gadd, *Myth and Ritual*, pp. 47 ff.; S. H. Hooke, *The Origins of Early Semitic Ritual* (Schweich Lectures, 1935), pp. 8–19, *Babylonian and Assyrian Religion* (London, 1953), pp. 58–60, 103–11; I. Engnell, *Studies in Divine Kingship in the Ancient Near East* (Uppsala, 1943), pp. 18 ff.

[3] The Babylonian evidence for the sacred marriage is actually wanting and the 'pattern' has to be completed in this respect from other sources, see Gadd, op. cit., p. 56. 'La spéculation théologique doit adapter les anciens mythes au nouvel état politique et puisque rien n'existe en ce monde, si ce n'est par l'ordre des dieux et le destin qu'ils ont fixé, à l'élévation de Babylone au-dessus des autres cités doit répondre nécessairement l'exaltation de son dieu au-dessus de tous les autres dieux', L. Delaporte, *La Mésopotamie* (Paris, 1923), p. 154. Some allowance must also be made for the religious 'reformation' effected about the time of Ḥammurabi, cf. Delaporte, *Le Proche-Orient Asiatique* (Paris, 1948), p. 139–40.

This consideration leads back to an issue which has already been briefly noticed. It is that in the exposition of the 'Myth and Ritual' thesis there appears to be some uncertainty as to whether an original 'myth and ritual pattern' was diffused throughout the Near East from some single centre or whether in various places throughout that area similar 'patterns' were independently evolved in response to the challenge of similar environments. Each of these alternatives has its own particular set of problems. Generally it would seem that the diffusionist view has prevailed, but with uncertainty as to the original source of the movement. The continuous reference which is made to the pharaonic monarchy as the supreme example of divine kingship suggests that often Egypt is regarded as the original source of the 'myth and ritual pattern'.[1] But no attempt is made to demonstrate this, which perhaps is not surprising in view of the fact just previously noticed that the Egyptian records provide no evidence of the hypothetical 'cult-pattern' having existed as such in the state-religion of the land. That Mesopotamia is assumed to be the original point of diffusion seems to be indicated in certain other statements of the thesis,[2] but here again no definitive attempt has been made to prove that this was so; moreover, as has already been noted, there is a vagueness about the presumed place of origin of the 'pattern' in Mesopotamia itself, which in view of the nature of the relevant data is understandable. It is, accordingly, found on examination that not only have the exponents of the 'Myth and Ritual' thesis neglected to deal with the practical problems which the idea of a diffusion of an esoteric complex of religious concept and practice inevitably entails, but they themselves do not appear to be clear in their minds on the fundamental point of the location of the original centre from which the 'pattern' was diffused.[3]

[1] See above, p. 265 n. 2; to which may be added the later references of E. O. James, *The Labyrinth*, pp. 244, 249–50, 253–4, *Christian Myth and Ritual* (London, 1937), pp. 1–6, 40–41, 58–62.

[2] Cf. *Myth and Ritual*, pp. 66 (Gadd), 70, 81, 86 (Hooke—in this essay a compromise sometimes seems to appear in the use of the term 'Egyptian-Babylonian pattern'), 112–13, 120, 124, 129, 135 (Oesterley): Hooke, *Origins of Early Semitic Ritual*, p. 1.

[3] That the 'pattern' might have been diffused from two separate centres, namely,

In the final paragraph of his contribution to the symposium *Myth and Ritual* Professor W. O. E. Oesterley suggested that, while the diffusionist theory accounted for the recurrence of the 'pattern' among various peoples in what might be termed its classic form, the true cause of its being lay deeper. The passage deserves quotation:[1]

> Behind the central 'pattern' with all its varying modifications in different centres among diverse peoples, there were certain underlying conceptions common to the entire world of the Near East, and beyond. Whether expressed in the developed and elaborate ritual of the city-god of Babylon, or in the somewhat similar rites in Erech and Asshur, or in those of the Egyptians on the morning of their New Year, or in those of the Zoroastrian *Naurūz* (New Year Festival), or in the celebrations in Jerusalem in honour of Jahweh, the underlying *motif*, expressed in various ways by different peoples, was the attempt to explain the mysteries of the dying vegetation at the approach of winter, and of the revival of Nature in the spring. While it is clear that in the case both of ideas and ritual the influence of more powerful and cultured peoples exerted itself on the less advanced, yet behind and beneath all was the insistent urge to answer the questions: Why does the vegetation die; how can it be revivified?

In this passage Dr. Oesterley touches upon an issue which must be much in the mind of one who seeks to study religion with comparative reference when he finds himself confronted with the 'Myth and Ritual' thesis. If the alleged recurrence of the

Egypt and Mesopotamia, as some statements seem to imply, must encounter the objection either that it is very improbable that such a 'pattern' would have been spontaneously and contemporaneously generated in two different places, or, that, if one of these centres had originally borrowed from the other, there is still the same 'diffusionist' problem to be solved.

[1] *Myth and Ritual*, p. 146. In this connexion the curiously obscure statement of Engnell (op. cit., p. 72) should be noted: 'However, as a possible contrary conception one may consider the west-Semitic type as an autochthonous development of an otherwise homogeneous schedule that has actually never been brought together and worked out or, in a word, urbanized, but has remained standing half-way.... It offers greater possibilities of doing justice to the original features found in the western area. Yet I am fully aware of the fact that we have at the same time to reckon with an extraordinarily strong influence from abroad, from the Egyptian and the 'Hittite', but far more still from the eastern Sumero-Accadian culture. We come, I think, nearest to the truth if we merely say that this western pattern is only an offshoot of the general Near East pattern.'

so-called 'pattern' is not to be explained by some theory of cultural diffusion but is regarded as constituting specific expressions of a common endeavour to answer some problem basic to the life of man (in this case that of the death and revival of vegetation), ought not similar manifestations of the 'pattern' to be found among other peoples than those of the Near East, when they were at a similar state of cultural development and living under similar environmental conditions? A test case at once suggests itself, namely, ancient China, where civilized life was based on agriculture and where climatic conditions produced those tensions arising from the need of certain kinds of weather at different times of the year, which were such potent factors in the religious conception of the Near Eastern peoples. Here indeed the ruler had an essential part in securing the prosperity of the land and this role involved him in the performance of an elaborate ritual, which was regulated by the calendar; he was, moreover, the 'Son of Heaven', who alone could perform those sacrifices which, it was believed, were vital to the well-being of the state.[1] However, despite all this apparent similarity between Chinese kingship and that which existed in the Near East, in Chinese faith and practice there is no trace of those elements which are fundamental to the Near Eastern 'ritual-pattern', namely, the concept of the 'dying-rising god', the ritual combat, or the sacred marriage.[2] And it may further be noted that in ancient India at a comparable stage of cultural development the

[1] Cf. M. Granet, *Chinese Civilization* (London, 1930), pp. 379–89, 400–2; L. Wieger, *History of Religious Beliefs and Philosophical Opinions in China* (Hsien-hsien Press, 1927), pp. 57–60, 63–64; W. E. Soothill, *The Hall of Light* (London, 1950), *passim*. See also 'The Mythico-Ritual Pattern in Chinese Civilization', by J. J. L. Duyvendak, and 'Zur konfuzianischen Staatsmoral' by E. Haenisch in *Proceedings of the 7th Congress for the History of Religions* (Amsterdam, 1951). The issue here is discussed at length by D. H. Smith in an article entitled 'Divine Kingship in Ancient China', which is due to appear in a future number of *Numen*.

[2] The thesis recently advanced by H. G. Quaritch Wales (*The Mountain of God*, London, 1953, pp. 38 ff) that 'a new religion, as part of a cultural pattern originating in Mesopotamia, was introduced to the Yellow River basin in the middle of the second millenium B.C.', must be considered improbable on two basic points (i) its interpretation of the role of Enlil in Mesopotamian religion is not demonstrated, (ii) the diffusion of the 'cultural pattern' from Mesopotamia to China is rather assumed than proved: indeed on the evidence available for that period it could not be otherwise.

5789   T

power of the Brahman caste effectively prevented the political rulers from acquiring and exercising sacerdotal status and function, and, so far as a claim was made to divinity, it was made pre-eminently by the Brahmans themselves.[1] Accordingly, it seems necessary to conclude that the so-called 'ritual-pattern' cannot be regarded as the natural expression in cultic imagery and practice of human societies when living at a specific cultural level and faced with the common challenges of the agriculturist's life. The 'pattern', as it has been defined, is clearly an artificial composition and as such it must have had its origin in some specific community of peculiar genius, which inference naturally points to the necessity of adopting some theory of diffusion to account for the alleged recurrence of the 'pattern' in a number of different localities; but of the soundness of such a theory it has been found that serious doubt exists.

From this critical estimate of what might be called the assumptive basis of the 'Myth and Ritual' thesis attention must now be turned to the interpretation of the data relevant to the establishment of that thesis. Here invaluable work has been done by Professor H. Frankfort in his great study entitled *Kingship and the Gods*[2] and in his Frazer Memorial Lecture;[3] and his demonstration of the fundamental difference between the insti-

---

[1] 'Verily, there are two kinds of gods; for, indeed, the gods are the gods, and the Brahmans who have studied and teach sacred lore are the human gods', *Satapatha Brahmana*, ii. ii. 2–6, trans. J. N. Farquhar, *A Primer of Hinduism* (Madras, 1911), p. 19. 'An examination of all passages in which the masculine *brahmán* is found shows that it denotes in general a distinct class, if not a caste, with their dependents, and is frequently used in direct contrast with the king', A. Hillebrandt in *Encyclopaedia of Religion and Ethics* (ed. J. Hastings), ii. 798a. Divinity was ascribed to kings in honorific titles, but the fact is without significance in the present context, cf. J. Filliozat in *Anthropologie religieuse* (ed. C. J. Bleeker, Leiden, 1955), pp. 115–17. Cf. L. H. Gray in *Encyclopaedia of Religion and Ethics*, vii. 720–1; A. L. Basham, *The Wonder that was India* (London, 1954), pp. 34, 81–93, who shows that ancient Indian kingship was essentially a political institution; see also pp. 120, 138, 141. It is also significant that the only instance of a 'dying-god' in Hindu mythology, namely, the death of Krishna, appears in that part of his legend which contains other non-Indian *motifs*.

[2] Chicago, 1948.

[3] *The Problem of Similarity in Ancient Near Eastern Religions* (Oxford, 1951). Cf. S. G. F. Brandon, 'Divine Kings and Dying Gods', in *The Hibbert Journal*, liii (1955). For a criticism along somewhat different lines see de Fraine, op. cit., pp. 27–54.

tution of kingship in Egypt and in Mesopotamia is so satisfactory that the case may be deemed established,[1] so that consideration may now be given to some other issues.[2]

The exponents of the 'Myth and Ritual' thesis have rightly emphasized the essentiality of the connexion of the god Osiris with the pharaonic kingship. Osiris was indeed the vegetation god *par excellence* of Egypt, and his cultus, as it found expression in the royal ritual and in certain annual festivals, made manifest the Egyptian belief that the prosperity of the land was vitally integrated with the king's being and function. But to concentrate interest on this aspect of Osiris is to run the risk of misunderstanding or misrepresenting what appears to have been the greater significance of this deity for the inhabitants of the valley of the Nile. Osiris, the 'dying-rising god' of Egypt, was pre-eminently the centre of one of the most remarkable mortuary cults ever practised by mankind.[3] Whatever may have been the origins of this deity and whatever part he had in the state cult as a vegetation god,[4] from the earliest documents of Egyptian thought Osiris is the god to whom the individual turned in fervent hope when confronted by the dread prospect of death. It is of the pharaoh's faith in this respect that we are first informed, but a process of democratization can be traced until by the New Kingdom period the ordinary man and woman sought salvation through Osiris.[5] The means by which it was believed

---

[1] But cf. above, p. 69, n. 1. Ed.

[2] The evidence assembled by T. Fish in his article 'Some Aspects of Kingship in the Sumerian City and Kingdom of Ur' (*B.J.R.L.*, xxxii. 1951) should also be noted in this connexion. The account of kingship which C. J. Gadd gives in his Schweich Lectures entitled *Ideas of Divine Rule in the Ancient East* (London, 1948), pp. 33 ff., is significant in view of the fact of his being one of the original contributors to *Myth and Ritual*.

[3] H. Kees, *Totenglauben und Jenseitsvorstellungen der alten Ägypter* (Leipzig, 1926), p. 190; Erman, *Die Religion der Ägypter*, pp. 40, 68–69, 217–21; G. Roeder, *Volksglaube im Pharaonenreich* (Stuttgart, 1952), pp. 156–60; Bonnet, op. cit., *sub nomin.* 'Osiris', 'Jenseitsglaube' (pp. 344b ff.); J. Vandier, *La Religion égyptienne* (Paris, 1949), pp. 81–107; J. Černý, *Ancient Egyptian Religion* (London, 1952), pp. 84–90.

[4] Cf. A. Moret, *Le Nil et la civilisation égyptienne* (Paris, 1926), pp. 92–112; Vandier, op. cit., pp. 67–69; Frankfort, *Kingship and the Gods*, pp. 200–3, 207–9.

[5] This was first done in a masterly way by the late J. H. Breasted in his *Development of Religion and Thought in Ancient Egypt* (London, 1912), lecture viii. Cf.

that this salvation might be achieved was that of the magical assimilation of the deceased with the god, so that, as the devotee was identified with the god in death, he would be one with him in his resurrection.[1] And this death and resurrection was no piece of mystical symbolism, but was conceived of in the most realistic terms. Thus, the myth of Osiris is set forth essentially as a human drama, and the horrors of death are depicted with a brutal realism—for example in the *Pyramid Texts*, in a passage in which the ritual of embalmment is represented in terms of the Osirian drama, a spell against physical decomposition is provided for the deceased pharaoh Pepi:

> Isis comes and Nephthys: the one from the right and the other from the left. . . . They find Osiris, as his brother Set laid him low in *Nḏi.t*. Then speaks Osiris Pepi: 'Hasten thou to me !' and thus he exists in his name Sokaris. They prevent thee from perishing in thy name *inpw* (Anubis); they prevent thy putrefaction from flowing on the earth according to thy name *sꜣb imꜥ*; they prevent the odour of thy corpse from being evil for thee in thy name of *Ḥrw ḫꜣti.* . . .[2]

Then:

> Isis brings a libation to thee, Nephthys cleanses thee; thy two great sisters restore thy flesh, they reunite thy members, they cause thy two eyes to appear in thy face.[3]

It is seen then that primarily for the Egyptians Osiris was not a vegetation deity, with whose being the king was intimately associated and whose life-cycle constituted critical points in the course of the year; rather Osiris was the saviour to whom men

Frankfort, *Ancient Egyptian Religion* (New York, 1948), pp. 103–5. There is evidence in the Pyramid Texts that Osiris was an ancient mortuary deity whose prestige the Heliopolitan priesthood sought to controvert in favour of their god Atum. Cf. H. Kees, 'Das Eindringen des Osiris in die Pyramidtexte', Excursus XXVII in S. A. B. Mercer, *The Pyramid Texts* (London, 1952), iv. 123–39.

[1] The pattern is set in the Pyramid Texts: see P.T., 167 (K. Sethe, *Die altägyptischen Pyramidtexten*, i. 93–94). Cf. G. Thausing, *Der Auferstehungsgedanke in ägyptischen religiösen Texten* (Leipzig, 1943), pp. 21–22.

[2] P.T., 1255–7 (text in Sethe, op. cit. ii. 210–11; trans. L. Speleers, *Les Textes des pyramides égyptiennes* (Bruxelles, 1923), i. 83; S. A. B. Mercer, *The Pyramid Texts*, i. 207). Cf. Thausing, op. cit., pp. 115–16. See also P.T. 722, 725.

[3] P.T. 1981 (text in Sethe, op. cit. i. 478; trans. Speleers, op. cit. i. 115; Mercer, op. cit. i. 295). Cf. Thausing, op. cit., p. 133; Mercer, op. cit. iii. 892.

and women turned for the assurance of immortality and before whom they believed that they would be judged in the next world.[1] Hence, although he may have been solicited for a good harvest, the real significance of Osiris lay in his mortuary role, a fact which is graphically attested by his iconography, for he is ever represented as one who is embalmed for burial and yet holds the emblems of sovereignty and power.[2] And it is only by appreciating this aspect of Osiris that the peculiarity of the Egyptian *Weltanschauung* may be understood. Although the Egyptian was intensely concerned with the prosperity of his land and enthusiastically participated in those festivals which were designed to promote it, he was obsessed by the thought of his own personal fate when death should strike him down.[3] Consequently it is not strange that the vast bulk of the evidence which has survived of Egyptian life and thought is of a mortuary character, while little remains to illustrate concern with those issues which, according to the 'Myth and Ritual' thesis, should have been primary.

This conclusion in respect of Egypt inevitably raises the question whether the impression created by the 'Myth and Ritual' thesis in its interpretation of the Mesopotamian data may not similarly place too great an emphasis on certain aspects of religious faith and practice in that land and so obstruct the forming of a balanced estimate. If the New Year festival at Babylon, thus interpreted, were representative of a long-established tradition of faith and practice throughout that cultural area, it must next be asked to what degree was that tradition influential in the formation of the Mesopotamian *Weltanschauung*. At first sight it would appear that, in comparison with the Egyptian faith, religion in Mesopotamia was singularly

---

[1] Eloquent witness of the reality of this judgement before Osiris is afforded by the vignettes to Chapters 30 and 125 of the *Book of the Dead*. Cf. *The Book of the Dead: Facsimile of the Papyrus of Ani* (British Museum, 1894), sheet 3.

[2] Cf. Budge, *Osiris and the Egyptian Resurrection*, i. 30–54.

[3] Cf. S. G. F. Brandon, *Time and Mankind* (London, 1951), pp. 32–39; to the references there given add C. E. Sander-Hansen, *Der Begriff des Todes bei den Ägyptern* (Copenhagen, 1942); C. J. Bleeker, 'Die Idee des Schicksals in der altägyptischen Religion', in *Numen*, ii (1955), pp. 28–46.

deficient in encouraging those who professed it to look beyond the scope of this life—indeed, far to the contrary, its grim eschatology was calculated to invest death with the utmost terror.[1] However, despite the consequent concentration of interest on life in this world, it does not appear that state rituals, such as those in which the 'Myth and Ritual pattern' presumably found expression, satisfied the spiritual needs of the people, however necessary they were felt to be to the well-being of the community as a whole. Instead the great mass of divinatory and exorcismal texts, which have been recovered by archaeological research, attests the preoccupation of the people with warding off all manner of ills which were believed to be due to the action of evil spirits.[2] And of particular significance is it that in those texts in which Dumu-zi or Tammuz, the dying-rising god of vegetation, is invoked, the deliverance which is sought through his instrumentality is never from the common fate after death but from some evil which spoilt the enjoyment of this life. Indeed, if the *Epic of Gilgamesh* may be taken, as it surely must be in view of its great popularity, as a faithful reflection of the Meso-potamian view of life, then the advice which Siduri gives to the hero in his quest constitutes the best comment on the matter at issue here:

> Gilgamesh, whither runnest thou?
> The life thou seekest thou wilt not find;
> (For) when the gods created mankind,
> They allotted death to mankind,
> But life they retained in their keeping.
> Thou, O Gilgamesh, let thy belly be full;

[1] See the *Epic of Gilgamesh*, Tab. VII, vol. iv. 31–41, Tab. XII, 84–153; *Ishtar's Descent to the Underworld* (trans. A. Heidel in *The Epic of Gilgamesh and Old Testament Parallels*, Chicago, 1949, pp. 60, 99–101, 119–28; A. Ungnad, *Die Religion der Babylonier und Assyrer*, Jena, 1921, pp. 86–87, 117–18, 142–50). Cf. A. Jeremias, *Die babylonisch-assyrischen Vorstellungen vom Leben nach dem Tode* (Leipzig, 1887); F. Jeremias in Chantepie de la Saussaye, *Lehrbuch der Religionsgeschichte* (Tübingen, ed. 1925), i. 585–8; M. David, *Les Dieux et le destin en Babylonie* (Paris, 1949), pp. 39–40; T. Jacobsen, in *The Intellectual Adventure of Ancient Man* (Chicago, 1946), pp. 202–18, in *Before Philosophy* (Penguin Books), pp. 217–34.

[2] Cf. E. Ebeling, *Tod und Leben nach Vorstellungen der Babylonier* (Leipzig, 1931), pp. 122–62; Hooke, *Babylonian and Assyrian Religion*, pp. 77 ff.; Ed. Dhorme, *Les Religions de Babylonie et d'Assyrie* (Paris, 1945), pp. 260 ff.

Day and night be thou merry;
Make every day (a day of) rejoicing.
Let thy raiment be clean,
Thy head be washed, (and) thyself bathed in water.
Cherish the little one holding thy hand,
(And) let thy wife rejoice in thy bosom.
This is the lot of [mankind. . . .][1]

It has already been noted that many of the original exponents of the 'Myth and Ritual' thesis were evidently profoundly concerned with the interests of Christian theology; indeed on consideration it may fairly be asked how far the idea of the 'pattern' was itself suggested by the Christian *mythos*, because the form which that *mythos* had attained by the end of the first century reproduced in a remarkable way all the constitutive elements of the 'pattern'. The Christ was a god incarnate and of royal status by virtue of His Davidic descent; He had struggled with the power of evil and descended into Death but had revived again to a new and more glorious life; in triumph He had ascended into the heavens, where He reigned in majesty and dispensed new life to those who served Him. The *motif* of the sacred marriage was there too: the Bride of Christ was the Church and from that union was born the company of the faithful.[2] Indeed so complete did the parallels appear that Professor E. O. James was led to write:

Thus at the beginning of the Christian era the stage was set for a new act in the ancient drama of the divine kingship and its ritual pattern. . . . With the break-up of the Roman Empire the scattered fragments were again brought together, like the dismembered body of Osiris, this time round the figure of a spiritual Divine king 'incarnated once and for all in order ever after to rule the souls of men'; invested in a scarlet robe, a crown of thorns, and a reed for a sceptre, and dying to live on a cross which has become symbolized as the tree of life.[3]

[1] Tab. X, col. iii. 1–14; translated by A. Heidel, *The Epic of Gilgamesh and Old Testament Parallels* (University of Chicago Press, 1949), p. 70. For another recent translation see that of E. A. Speiser in *Ancient Near Eastern Texts* (ed. J. B. Pritchard, Princeton, 1955), p. 90a.

[2] Rev. xxi. 2, xxii. 17; cf. Eph. v. 23–32; 2 Cor. xi. 2. Cf. the vision of the Church as a woman in the *Shepherd of Hermes*.

[3] *Christian Myth and Ritual*, pp. 40–41. See also his essay in *The Labyrinth*

The apparent fulfilment in the Christian *mythos* of the ancient 'pattern' is truly impressive, and Professor James ably interpreted it as a notable instance of the *Praeparatio Evangelii*, but it must be recognized that it could with equal aptness be interpreted adversely to the orthodox Christian claim, in that it might be contended that the ancient 'Myth and Ritual' pattern provided a set of inherited categories in terms of which Christian soteriology was inevitably formed. However, it appears on closer examination of the issues involved here that the definitive form which the Christian *mythos* achieved by the end of the first century is not to be explained primarily as due either to divine predestination or to the influence of inherited modes of thought, but as the outcome of a peculiar combination of events which can only be properly understood by a detailed investigation of the relevant data. Although such an investigation cannot be attempted here, a summary of a study published elsewhere[1] may be conveniently utilized to demonstrate the need of substantiating each alleged instance of the occurrence of the 'Myth and Ritual' pattern by an adequate examination of its historical context.

In the history of Christian doctrine there is perhaps no more significant fact, although it has been consistently disregarded by Christian scholars, than St. Paul's attestation that within some twenty years of the Crucifixion there were current two different and rival interpretations of the faith. This attestation is contained in two distinct passages in his Epistles, namely, Gal. i. 6–8 and 2 Cor. xi. 3–4. In view of the fundamental importance of the witness of these passages they must be quoted *in extenso*. In the Galatian passage Paul writes to his converts:

I marvel that ye are so quickly removing from him that called you in the grace of Christ unto a different gospel (εἰς ἕτερον εὐαγγέλιον); which is not another gospel (ὃ οὐκ ἔστιν ἄλλο);[2] only there be some

entitled 'The Sources of Christian Ritual'. It should be noted that A. Ehrhardt has attempted to show that Christian myth and ritual originated in reaction to Roman emperor-worship (see 'Myth and Ritual from Alexander to Constantine', in *Studi in onore di Pietro de Francisci* (Milano, 1955), iv, pp. 423–44.

[1] S. G. F. Brandon, *The Fall of Jerusalem and the Christian Church* (London, 1951, 2nd. ed. 1957).

[2] 'This is not an admission in favour of the false teachers, as though they taught the

that trouble you, and would pervert the gospel of Christ. But though we, or an angel from heaven, should preach (unto you) any gospel other (or contrary to: παρ' ὅ) than that we preached unto you, let him be anathema.

In the other passage the Apostle writes in admonition to his Corinthian converts:

But I fear, lest by any means, as the serpent beguiled Eve in his craftiness, your minds should be corrupted from the simplicity and the purity that is toward Christ. For if he that cometh preacheth another Jesus (ἄλλον Ἰησοῦν), whom we did not preach, or if ye receive a different spirit (πνεῦμα ἕτερον), which ye did not receive, or a different gospel (εὐαγγέλιον ἕτερον), which ye did not accept, ye welcome it (καλῶς ἀνέχεσθε).[1]

Quite clearly in these two places Paul acknowledges that the interpretation of the person and mission of Jesus, of which he was the protagonist, was being challenged in its authority for his converts by another interpretation, which seriously differed from it. Now the significance of the situation obviously depends upon the identity of the exponents of this rival version of the faith. Unfortunately Paul nowhere explicitly states who they were, but it is patent from the profound concern which he shows about their activities that they were no mere group of irresponsible heretics but men who were capable of challenging his authority among his own converts. On further investigation there can be little doubt that these exponents of the rival gospel were none other than the emissaries of the Church of Jerusalem, which means that their teaching represented the interpretation of the status and role of Jesus held by those original apostles and 'eye-witnesses' who constituted the *Urgemeinde* of Christianity.[2]

one Gospel, however perverted (comp. Phil. i. 15, 18)', J. B. Lightfoot, *Saint Paul's Epistle to the Galatians* (London, 1881), p. 76. After a survey of the comparative meanings of ἄλλος and ἕτερος, Lightfoot concluded (ibid.); 'Thus while ἄλλος is generally confined to a negative of identity, ἕτερος sometimes implies the negation of resemblance.' Cf. K. Lake, *The Earlier Epistles of St. Paul* (London, 1930), p. 267 n. 1. ἄλλος ein anderer v. Art'., W. Bauer, *Wörterbuch zum Neuen Testament* (Giessen 1928), p. 61a, cf. p. 491a *sub* ἕτερος.

[1] Cf. A. Menzies, *The Second Epistle to the Corinthians* (London, 1912), p. 78.

[2] Cf. *Fall of Jerusalem*, chap. 4 and pp. 136–153; to the references given therein add M. Simon, *Les Premiers Chrétiens* (Paris, 1952), pp. 70–82.

That the teaching of the Mother Church of the faith differed so seriously from that of Paul is clearly a matter of supreme moment, but one also that is most unfortunately complicated by the fact that no documents of that church survived its obliteration when Jerusalem was destroyed by the Romans in A.D. 70. However, the situation is not completely hopeless, and it is possible by patient research to reconstruct the main tenets of its gospel from scattered allusions and references found in the writings of Paul, in the Acts of the Apostles, the Gospels, in the surviving fragments of Hegesippus, and in the Pseudo-Clementine literature. Accordingly it is found that Jesus was primarily proclaimed as the Messiah of Israel, who would shortly return with supernatural power and glory to 'restore again the kingdom to Israel'. This proclamation had apparently encountered the serious objection that Jesus had died the accursed death of the Law, and, to meet it, it had been necessary to elaborate an apologetic whereby it could be shown that this death had been foretold by the prophets, pre-eminently by Isaiah in the figure of the Suffering Servant of Yahweh. But such an apologetic, it must be noted, contained no elements of soteriology; the invocation of the Isaianic Servant as a prototype of the crucified Jesus was strictly a defensive move, for it could not have been otherwise in a Judaic milieu, where such an idea as that of the Messiah of Israel dying to save the Gentiles would have been an inconceivable, let alone an outrageous, thing. Consequently, in the definition of their gospel the Jerusalem Christians represented the Crucifixion as an unfortunate accident done in ignorance, but which had been anticipated by divine revelation; no emphasis was placed upon its significance and attention was directed instead to the imminent return of Jesus to redeem Israel. There seems to be evidence also for thinking that the prominence given to the Davidic descent of Jesus meant that his Messiahship was interpreted in a political sense.[1]

To this presentation of Jesus and His mission we know that Paul was vehemently opposed, but unfortunately no formal

---

[1] Cf. *Fall of Jerusalem*, chap. 5; H. J. Schoeps, *Theologie und Geschichte des Judenchristentums* (Tübingen, 1949), pp. 71–73, 78–98, 157.

statement of his own gospel appears in his writings which have survived; however, it is possible to piece together from various parts of the Epistles a coherent outline of the contents of that gospel.

Of key importance is the fact that for Paul the Crucifixion was of supreme significance and its proclamation stood in the forefront of his message. To him it was a supernatural event preordained by God before the aeons. Its explanation was comprised in an esoteric doctrine of mankind's state and destiny which is briefly sketched in 1 Cor. ii. 6–8 and Gal. iv. 1–7. Herein man is represented as held in bondage by the daemonic powers which ruled in the present world-order and which were closely associated with the celestial phenomena; to rescue men from this dire condition God had sent a supernatural pre-existent being, a veritable *deuteros theos*, to earth in an incarnated human form, and the daemonic powers, not recognizing his true nature, had crucified him and so, presumably by exceeding their rights, they had forfeited their hold over man. Paul, of course, identified this divine saviour with the historical Jesus, whom he accordingly calls 'the Son of God', *Kyrios* and *Soter*. Thus Paul's gospel was a soteriology of universal significance. The *mythos* also had its ritual expression, for in his references to baptism in Rom. vi. 2–5 it is evident that the Apostle taught that salvation was effected by the ritual assimilation, through the baptismal rite, of the neophyte to the saviour in both his death and resurrection.[1]

What would have been the outcome, if these two rival interpretations of the faith had been left to struggle together for the allegiance of the Church, is unknown. Judging by the resources of the rival exponents of them it would seem that victory must ultimately have gone to the Jerusalem leaders, because their authority and prestige as the first disciples far outweighed the claims of Paul. However, it was fated that the issue should be decided by extraneous forces. In the year 66 the Jewish nationalists revolted against the Roman suzerainty and four years later, after a disastrous struggle, the cause of Israel was

[1] Cf. op. cit., chap. 4.

lost with the utter destruction of Jerusalem and its Temple. In this catastrophe the Christian community of Jerusalem was in some way involved, because after A.D. 70 it disappears completely from the life of the Church. It was in the reconstruction of Christian life and thought which followed these shattering events that there was born that synthesis of the rival gospels of Paul and the Jerusalem *Urgemeinde* which constitutes the classic *mythos* of Christian soteriology and which first found expression in the Markan Gospel. Herein were fused into a single figure the picture of the historical Jesus, of royal descent, the Messiah of Israel, and the concept of the incarnated divine saviour of Paul, who by his vicarious death had redeemed mankind and whose mystic bride was the Church.[1] And thus in the Christ of Catholic theology was sublimely manifest the apparent fulfilment of those ancient adumbrations of a divine king who dies to give his people new life. But the fulfilment was apparent only, because it was not the achievement of forces of which the operation may be consistently traced; it was the fortuitous result of a combination of disparate and generically unconnected factors— yet to the eye of faith, it must be admitted, the fortuitous element here may be deemed providential and the events of A.D. 66–70 be seen as evidence of that divine intervention in history which is the basic concept of the Christian interpretation of the past.

The 'Myth and Ritual' thesis by implication raises an important question in another field, but one which is also of vital concern for the comparative study of religion.

By postulating the 'Myth and Ritual' complex as the basic religious pattern common to the cultures of the ancient Near East and by attempting to show that this pattern found expression in a series of annual festivals which were related to the course of Nature's year, a situation is implied from which it may reasonably be inferred on *a priori* grounds that a cyclic view of existence must have been held by those who practised such rituals.[2] That

[1] Cf. op. cit., chaps. 7, 9, 10.

[2] Cf. M. Éliade, *Traité d'histoire des religions* (Paris, 1949), pp. 332–49; *Le Mythe de l'éternel retour* (Paris, 1949), pp. 83–99.

such a view was actually held there is a certain amount of confirmatory evidence in Egyptian[1] and Mesopotamian[2] documents, although the fact leaves unanswered the question whether such a view had been inspired by some 'myth and ritual' pattern or whether that pattern, if it existed, would have been a specific expression of a *Weltanschauung* which had been formed by the operation of other causes. However that may be, the vital issue here lies in the fact that among the cultures of the ancient Near East there were two of which the *Weltanschauungen* were notably teleological and not cyclic in outlook. The cultures concerned were the Iranian, as conditioned by Zarathustra's reform, and the Hebrew. Since in the present context the significance of the Iranian estimate is more peripheral, attention may be devoted to that of the Hebrews.

If the 'Myth and Ritual' thesis be sound in its suggestion that the 'pattern' had once an effective currency in Israel through the institution of kingship, it would appear that, not only did a cyclic view of the temporal process never establish itself there, but, on the contrary, the teleological interpretation emerged at a very early period.

The origin of what might justly be called the 'Hebrew philosophy of History' is admittedly obscure, but there is reason for thinking that its roots are to be found in the propaganda of the Yahwist party which sought to maintain allegiance to Yahweh among the Israelite tribes after the settlement in Canaan.[3] If Professor Martin Noth's interpretation of the original confederacy of the Twelve Tribes on the analogy of the Greek and

---

[1] 'Re showeth himself in the morning, and Atum goeth down in Manu. Men beget, women conceive, and every nose breatheth air—day dawneth, and their children go one and all to their place.' (Quoted from the so-called 'Song of the Harper' of the New Kingdom period; Eng. trans. by A. M. Blackman in A. Erman's *Literature of the Ancient Egyptians* (Methuen, London, 1927), p. 252.)

[2] Cf. A. Jeremias, *Handbuch der altorientalischen Geisteskultur* (Leipzig, 1913), pp. 193–204, in Hastings, *Encycl. Rel. and Ethics*, i. 185 : A. Rey, *La Science orientale avant les Grecs* (Paris, 1930), pp. 155 ff. The decreeing of destinies for the ensuing year was an important factor in the Babylonian New Year festival as C. J. Gadd shows in *Myth and Ritual*, pp. 55–56. Cf. Éliade, *Le Mythe de l'éternel retour*, pp. 89–94; F. Jeremias in Chantepie de la Saussaye, *Lehrbuch der Religionsgeschichte* (Tübingen, 1925), i. 505–12.

[3] Cf. S. G. F. Brandon, *Time and Mankind* (London, 1951), pp. 63–72.

Italian amphictyonies be accepted,[1] and there is much reason for so doing, then a situation can reasonably be envisaged after the invasion of Canaan, in which the constituent tribes tended to revert to their former independence, which meant devotion to their own tribal deities and a corresponding forgetfulness of Yahweh, under whose patronage they had achieved their first successful lodgement in the Promised Land. This centrifugal movement had the effect of weakening the invaders militarily, the consequences of which were soon felt in terms of conquest by the reviving power of the Canaanites and perhaps by the newly-arrived Philistines. The situation provided the devotees of Yahweh with a unique opportunity to press the claims of their deity with considerable assurance of success. Their message to their compatriots naturally took the form of an appeal to the memory of the past—that, when they had been faithful, Yahweh had done mighty deeds for their fathers: if now they would return to their allegiance to him, he would forgive them and redeem them. The appeal rested on a sound military logic, for return to Yahweh meant the unification of their forces, and, hence, increased military strength and a better chance of victory against their oppressors.

Thus Yahwism acquired its characteristic preoccupation with history, or at least an accepted tradition about the past. In its earliest form this attitude probably found expression in cultic formulae[2] and the exhortations of prophets. Whether it would have survived long in such form is a matter for speculation, but its survival was guaranteed from about the ninth or tenth century by a creation which is quite unparalleled in any other ancient religion. A writer (or a school of writers), usually designated the Yahwist, composed out of various fragments of tradition, legend, and folk-lore, a unique conspectus of the past from the very act of Creation. The composition was a work of

[1] M. Noth, *Das System der Zwölf Stämme Israels* (*Beiträge z. Wiss. v. Alt. u. N. Test.*, Vierte Folge, Heft 1, Stuttgart, 1930). Cf. W. F. Albright, *From the Stone Age to Christianity* (Baltimore, 1946), p. 215; H. H. Rowley, *From Joseph to Joshua* (Schweich Lectures, 1948, London, 1950), pp. 102 ff., 126; Brandon, op. cit., pp. 71–72.

[2] Cf. Brandon, op. cit., pp. 69, 72.

genius, because out of such disparate material a coherent narrative was fashioned in which Yahweh was shown as guiding the course of history in order to fulfil his promise to the nation's ancestor, Abraham, that of his descendants he would make a great people and settle them in the land of Canaan. Yahweh's character as the 'Lord of History' was thus exhibited in a dramatic narrative and the Israelite tribes acquired thereby the sense of a common ancestry and a divinely guided past.[1]

The influence of this Yahwist achievement was profound, and it set the pattern for all subsequent Hebrew thought. Even the great vicissitudes of fortune which the nation subsequently suffered failed to shake its conviction in the providence of its god, and the darker Israel's political situation became the more fervent grew Israel's hopes that Yahweh would eventually intervene to save them and destroy their enemies. Accordingly, the distinctive Hebrew *Weltanschauung* was formed, whereby the passage of time was regarded teleologically as the gradual unfolding of the divine purpose and its irresistible achievement. Hence, whatever encouragement the periodic festivals of kingship may have given to a cyclic view of existence, that encouragement was too weak a thing to challenge the teleologically conceived *Weltanschauung* of Yahwism.

And the Yahwist teleological interpretation of the past was destined to exercise an even greater influence, outside the bounds of Judaism, through Christianity. The scheme of Jewish apocalyptic clearly shows itself in the earliest Christian documents, and from their testimony it is evident that primitive Christian thought was essentially teleological in outlook. Even the problem caused by the continued delay of the expected *Parousia* of Christ did not disturb this mode of thought, nor did the subsequent process of Hellenization, which might have introduced the cyclic view of time which was native to Greek thought. Indeed, far to the contrary, by utilizing Paul's apologetic theory of 'Godly Remnant', which was the true Israel, the Church was able to lay claim to the traditional Jewish philosophy of History and so

[1] Cf. Brandon, op. cit., pp. 63–84, and the references there given. See also G. Hölscher, *Geschichtsschreibung in Israel* (Lund, 1952), pp. 119, 134–5.

to formulate the theory of the two divine covenants, the Old and the New, which eventually found abiding expression in the chronology which divides the stream of time by the Incarnation into two parts, designated respectively the era 'Before Christ' and that of the *anni domini*.[1]

Accordingly, it must be deemed remarkable, if the 'myth and ritual pattern' had succeeded in establishing itself in both Hebrew religion and Christianity, that the influence of the concomitant cyclic view of existence never seriously challenged the dominance of that peculiar teleology of Yahwism which by its very genius was inimical to the premises of the 'myth and ritual' complex.

In the phenomenology of religion the ritual pattern envisaged in the 'myth and ritual' thesis belongs to the class of seasonal rites which expresses a consciousness that human life is faced with recurrent crisis through the cyclic process of nature's year.[2] In this sense it is to be distinguished from another class of ritual practice which is concerned with the perpetuation or re-creation of the efficacy of a unique event of the past.[3] The principle involved here may be described as the magical or ritual perpetuation of the past, and it represents a mode of primitive thought and action which has had a very long and remarkable history. It appears in Palaeolithic times in the famous painting of the so-called 'Dancing Sorcerer' in the cavern of the Trois Frères in the *département* of Ariège. The motive behind the production of this picture would seem to be that of perpetuating the potency of a magical dance after the action of that dance had finished in time.[4] The idea which was thus adumbrated at this remote period finds some notable forms of expression in subsequent ages. One of the most remarkable is that enshrined in the

---

[1] Cf. Brandon, op. cit., chap. viii and the references given therein.

[2] See p. 284 n. 2 above.

[3] Cf. Brandon, op. cit., p. 23. 'Le temps qui a vu l'événement commémoré ou répété par le rituel en question est *rendu* présent, 're-présenté' si l'on peut dire, si reculé qu'on l'imagine dans le temps', Éliade, *Traité d'histoire des religions*, p. 336.

[4] Cf. Brandon, op. cit., pp. 17–18. For a photograph and drawing of this figure, which is partly painted and partly engraved, see the Abbé Breuil, *Quatre cents siècles d'art pariétal* (Montignac, 1952), p. 166, see also pp. 176–7.

40

Osirian mortuary ritual, which we have already noticed. Herein it was sought by the use of imitative magic to make available to the devotee, on whose behalf the rites were being celebrated, the efficacy of a past event, namely, the resurrection of Osiris.[1] The same principle found expression in the ritual of the Christian Eucharist; indeed it may truly be said that therein it achieved its classic form. The quintessence of the rite lies in a ritual re-presentation of the historical death of Christ on Calvary for the purpose of pleading that Sacrifice again before God and for making its efficacy available to the faithful, then assembled, or on behalf of certain specified objects. Although in the course of the liturgical calendar this rite assumes the guise of a cyclically recurring festival, its reference to a unique historical event remains essential.[2]

In view of these considerations, doubt must again surely be felt about the presumed ubiquity of the so-called 'Myth and Ritual' pattern in the ancient Near East and also about its supposed influence. Indeed it would be ironical, if the 'Myth and Ritual' hypothesis be sound, that it was just in that cultural area in which the 'pattern' was supposed to have originated and flourished that the tradition of a teleological *Weltanschauung* developed, while in India, where it had no such currency, a cyclic view of existence was generated to become the basic premiss of both Hinduism and Buddhism.

According to its terms of reference this essay has been consistently critical of the 'Myth and Ritual' thesis. Moreover, since it is designed to be a contribution to a symposium on this subject, care has been taken not to enter too deeply into those fields which were being specifically covered by other contributors. Observance of these limitations has inevitably meant that little or no account has been given here of those aspects of the thesis which have met with general approval in the academic circles concerned and which have been very adequately and ably described by Professor Hooke and Professor Widengren in their papers. But the present

---

[1] Cf. Brandon, op. cit., pp. 29–30, 31.
[2] Ibid., pp. 169, 177–8, 180–1.

contributor would not like the impression to be given by his own critical consideration of the thesis that he is not appreciative of the significance of those aspects and that he does not recognize the achievement of those scholars who originally expounded the thesis. He sees the 'Myth and Ritual' thesis as one of the major developments in the comparative study of religion, and he believes that, despite all the opposition which it has encountered, when the final adjustments are made it will be found that its contribution has been of the highest importance and that its value is abiding.[1] To particularize, it would seem that the exponents of the thesis have established beyond all doubt the fundamental importance of kingship as a religious institution throughout the various cultures of the ancient Near East. Secondly, that they have succeeded in showing that kingship in Israel must be evaluated in this light, and that, if this is done, many hitherto obscure passages in Hebrew literature gain a new and convincing meaning, and truer appreciation of the peculiar genius of Israelite religion is thereby made possible. Another aspect of this contribution, which is of the highest import for the study of religion, is constituted by the demonstration which has thereby been given of the fundamental importance of the evidence of ritual and myth for understanding both the ethos and the *Weltanschauung* of ancient cultures.

But what is perhaps the most significant indication of the achievement of the 'Myth and Ritual' thesis is to be found by way of a comparison. Between the years 1903 and 1921 the twelve volumes comprising Hastings's *Encyclopaedia of Religion and Ethics* were published. In this great corpus of information under 'Ritual' only a cross-reference was given to 'Prayer' and 'Worship', while the article on 'Mythology' treated the question

---

[1] A measure of the influence of the 'Myth and Ritual' thesis is to be seen in the fact that the theme of the 7th International Congress for the History of Religions, held at Amsterdam in 1950, was 'the mythical-ritual pattern in civilization', and that of the 8th Congress, held in Rome in 1955, was 'the king-god and the sacral character of kingship'. Cf. *Proceedings of the 7th Congress for the History of Religions* (Amsterdam, 1951); *Atti dell'VIII Congresso internazionale di Storia delle Religioni* (Florence, 1956). The full text of the relevant papers is to be published under the title of *La royauté sacrée.*

of the ritual origin of myth solely from the aetiological point of view.[1] When one contemplates the great output of works which has been inspired by the 'Myth and Ritual' thesis and the interest and reorientation of view which those works represent, it would seem that a veritable renaissance (or reformation) was inaugurated in this field of study in 1933, when Professor Hooke and his colleagues published their symposium.

[1] In vol. x, p. 666a of this work, some notice is given of the 'myth versus ritual' controversy, reference being made to such books as W. R. Smith, *Religion of the Semites*. Reference to other standard works in the field of *Religionsgeschichte* is of significance in this connexion. The *Histoire générale des religions* (ed. M. Gorce et R. Mortier), 5 tomes, Paris, 1948–52, pays no attention to the 'Myth and Ritual' thesis. In the 1950 edition of the *Encyclopaedia Britannica* an article is given under 'Myth and Ritual', but it contains no reference to the thesis of Professor Hooke or the work of the so-called Uppsala school in this respect. The last (French) edition of G. van der Leeuw's great work on the phenomenology of religion (*La Religion dans son essence et ses manifestations*, Paris, 1948) takes no cognizance of the thesis. M. Éliade, in his *Traité d'histoire des religions* (Paris, 1949), accepts A. R. Johnson's interpretation of Yahweh's victory over Rahab (p. 343), but has nothing to say of the thesis as a whole beyond making a bibliographical reference to it (p. 371). The *Eranos-Jahrbuch*, Bd. XVII, 1949 (Zürich, 1950), contains a paper by E. O. James entitled 'Myth and Ritual'; A. Bertholet in his *Wörterbuch der Religionen* (Stuttgart, 1952), pp. 327–8, says briefly that 'die Begründung des Kultus durch den Mythus das Sekundäre ist'. He does not apparently discuss 'Myth and Ritual' as such. G. Mensching, in his *Vergleichende Religionswissenschaft* (Heidelberg, 1949), merely mentions *Myth and Ritual* in a bibliographical note (p. 100). It may also be noted that the 'Myth and Ritual' thesis appears to have played no part in the 'Entmythologisierung' controversy associated with Rudolf Bultmann. H.-C. Puech in the *Bibliographie générale* to the *Mana* collection on the History of Religion (printed in J. Vandier, *La Religion égyptienne*, Paris, 1948), after noticing the two fundamental studies, contents himself with a reference to C. Kluckhohn's estimate 'Myth and Ritual' in the *Harvard Theological Review*, xxx (1942) (p. xxx). N. Turchi in his *Storia delle religioni*, 2 vols. (Florence, 1954), merely gives a bibliographical reference under 'Myth and Ritual' (vol. i, p. 73) to Kluckhohn's article in the *Harvard Theological Review* and to the *Eranos-Jahrbuch*, xvii (1949). No notice is taken of the 'Myth and Ritual' thesis in the following general works: *De Godsdiensten der Wereld* (ed. G. van der Leeuw, Amsterdam, 1948, 2 vols.); *Christus und die Religionen der Erde* (ed. F. König, 3 Bände, Vienna, 1951); *Christus (Manuel d'histoire des religions* (ed. J. Huby, 8th ed., Paris, 1947); *Histoire des religions* (ed. M. Brillant et R. Aigrain, t. i, Paris, 1953); *Storia delle religioni* (ed. P. T. Venturi, 2 vols., Turin, 4th ed., 1954).

A RITUAL BASIS FOR HESIOD'S
THEOGONY

PROFESSOR Mazon has recently described Hesiod's *Theogony* as 'a genealogy interrupted by episodes'. These episodes are myths, and Professor Mazon rightly remarks that their authenticity ought not to be suspected merely because they interrupt the genealogy, or because they are not consistent with one another. The texts produced by higher critics, who have given rein to such suspicions, leave the impression that the poem consists mainly of interpolations, like a bad sponge consisting mostly of holes. They are approaching the point at which the critics of the Pauline Epistles, having condemned them all, one after another, were left with no means of knowing what a genuine Pauline Epistle would be like. If the game was to go on, it was necessary to restore at least one to serve as a criterion for rejecting the remainder; and when that had been done, most of the others crept back again one by one into the canon.

This paper is inspired by the hope of rescuing some of the so-called episodes now jettisoned from the *Theogony*. I shall call in question what seems to be the current view, that the narrative parts of the poem are a mere patchwork of unconnected stories drawn from a variety of sources: Homer's account of the Olympian society; local cult-legends; other myths universally current in Greece; and a few stories too crudely indecent to be acknowledged as Hellenic.[1] I shall argue that the bulk of the episodes fit into the pattern of a very old myth of Creation, known to us from eastern sources and ultimately based on ritual.

Hesiod's own programme, laid down in the prelude, mentions three elements that are to figure in the poem: (1) theogony proper, i.e. the generations of the gods; (2) cosmogony, or the formation of the physical world-order and the creation of mankind; and (3) the story of how the gods took possession of

[1] So Ziegler in Roscher, *Lex. Myth.* s.v. 'Theogonien'.

95

Olympus under the supreme kingship of Zeus, who apportioned to the other gods their several provinces and honours.

(1) We can quickly pass over the first element—the genealogies of the gods. Hesiod gives three main lines of descent: (*a*) The children of Night prove to be a list of allegorical abstractions: Death, Sleep, the Fates, and all the afflictions which plague mankind. (*b*) The children of the Sea (Pontos), including a Dragon of the Waters with a brood of monsters, of whom we shall hear more later on. (*c*) Finally there are the offspring of Ouranos and Gaia: the earlier generation of Titans, Cyclopes, and the Hundred-Armed, and the second generation of the sons of Cronos, Zeus and the other Olympians and their descendants. These genealogies, though bewilderingly complicated, can be understood as an effort to combine in one pantheon a very miscellaneous collection of supernatural beings, ranging from the most concrete and anthropomorphic to the barest allegorical abstractions.

(2) Setting aside the genealogies, we come next to the second factor, cosmogony: 'how at the first the gods and earth came into being, and the rivers, and the swelling rage of the boundless sea, an the shining stars, and the broad heaven above' (108–10). The cosmogony, so announced in the prelude, follows immediately. It is quite short, occupying seventeen lines of which three or four are possibly spurious (116–32).

We are here told how the main divisions of the existing cosmos came into being: the earth with its dry land and seas, and the sky above with its stars. The veil of mythological language is so thin as to be quite transparent. Ouranos and Gaia, for instance, are simply the sky and the earth that we see every day. They are not here supernatural persons with mythical biographies and adventures. Even when Earth is said to 'give birth' to the mountains and the sea, Hesiod himself tells us that this is conscious metaphor: a 'birth' can only follow upon a marriage, but here it occurs 'without love or marriage', ἄτερ φιλότητος ἐφιμέρου (132). The metaphor means no more than that this cosmogony is of the evolutionary type. There are no personal gods to make the world

96

out of pre-existing materials according to the alternative pattern, the creational. The personal gods come later, when the world-order is already complete.

At that moment (132) Gaia and Ouranos suddenly become mythical persons, who marry and have children—Gaia is now a goddess, who can plot with her son Cronos to mutilate her husband Ouranos. We have passed into the world of myth, where the characters acquire the solidity and opaqueness of anthropomorphic individuals, with the whole apparatus of human motive and action.

(3) The remainder of the poem—the third of our three elements— moves in this genuine mythical atmosphere. It is a story of the adventures which led from the birth of the earliest gods to the final establishment of Zeus, triumphant over his enemies, as king of the gods and of the universe.

My object is to show that we have here not 'a genealogy interrupted by episodes', but a sequence of episodes, most of which once formed parts of a connected pattern, interrupted by genealogies, which serve to explain how the characters in the mythical action came into existence. The sequence of episodes itself constitutes what is, in essence, a hymn to Zeus and also a hymn of Creation—a mythical account of the beginning of things, immeasurably more primitive in character than the evolutionary cosmogony that precedes it. These two elements—the cosmogony and the hymn of Creation—are not in origin what Hesiod has made them, two chapters in a single story. The hymn is based on a genuine myth of enormous antiquity, itself founded on ritual. The cosmogony, on the other hand, has almost completely emerged from the atmosphere of myth. It is only just on the wrong side of the line we draw between mythical thinking and the earliest rational philosophy—the system of the Milesians.

CONTENTS OF THE COSMOGONY

Let us look first at the cosmogony.

I can only deal very shortly with its contents. I think it can be shown to conform to a pattern which also appears in the Orphic cosmogonies and underlies the Ionian systems of philosophy from Anaximander onwards.

(1) '*First of all Chaos came into being.*' There should be no doubt about the meaning of Chaos.[1] Etymologically, the word means a yawning gap; and in the Greek poets, including Hesiod himself (*Theog.* 700), it denotes the gap or void space between sky and earth. Bacchylides (v, 27) and Aristophanes (*Birds*, 192) speak of birds as flying in or through this space (διὰ τοῦ χάους, ἐν χάει).

A gap or yawn *comes into being* (Hesiod says γένετο, not ἦν) by the separation of two things that were formerly together. What these things were we learn from a fifth-century Ionian system, preserved by Diodorus (1, 7).[2] It opens with the words: 'Originally, heaven and earth had one form (μίαν ἰδέαν), their natures being mingled; then, when these bodies had taken up their stations apart from one another, the world embraced the whole order now seen in it.' Diodorus cites as parallel the famous lines of Euripides' Melanippe: 'The tale is not mine—I had it from my mother: how heaven and earth were once one form, and when they were separated apart, they gave birth to all things.'

Orpheus (Apollonius Rhodius, *Argon.* 1, 496) sang 'how earth and heaven and sea were once joined together in one form, and by deadly strife were separated from each other', then the heavenly bodies, mountains and rivers (dry land and water) were formed; and finally all living things.

Thus all these cosmogonies begin with a primal unity, which is separated apart, when the sky is lifted up from the earth, leaving the yawning gap of void or air between.

(2) By the opening of the gap, the broad bosom of Earth is revealed (γαῖα εὐρύστερνος), and Eros. Eros is an allegorical figure.

---

[1] Most modern discussions of this term are vitiated by the introduction of the later idea of infinite empty space, and by modern associations with disorder. I do not think Chaos is ever described as ἄπειρον, and if it were, that would mean no more than 'immeasurable', as when the word is used of the earth or the sea.

[2] This system is now ascribed (Diels–Kranz *Vors.*[5], II, 135) to Democritus; but there is no mention of atoms.

98

His function is to reunite the sundered parents, Heaven and Earth, in the marriage from which all life, mortal and immortal, is born. So we are told in the parabasis of the *Birds*: 'Before that there was no race of immortals, until Eros mixed all things together', συνέμειξεν: the use of μιγῆναι for marriage needs no illustration. Eros is the allegorical image of that intercourse of the separated opposites which will generate life.

His physical equivalent is the rain, the seed of the Heaven-father which fertilises the womb of mother Earth.

(3) Another physical consequence of the opening of the gap is that light is let in between the sundered parts. Accordingly we hear next of the appearance of light out of darkness. In genealogical terms, Darkness, as the male Erebos and the female Nyx, generates Light as the male Aither and the female Hemera. Day dawns from Night.

In one form of the Orphic cosmogony Eros is replaced by the spirit of light, Phanes, who appears when the world-egg is separated apart, the upper half forming the dome of heaven, the lower containing the moist slime from which the dry earth and the sea will emerge.

(4) The next event is startling. In spite of the fact that the gap separating heaven and earth has already come into being, we now hear that 'Earth first generated the starry heaven, equal to herself, to envelop her all round, that there might be for the blessed gods a seat secure for ever'.

Here is another separation of heaven from earth duplicating the opening of the gap. We shall soon encounter this duplication again, and when we get back to the original myth we shall be able to explain it.

Meanwhile let us note the epithet of heaven—'starry' (ἀστερόεις). This is expanded in Hesiod's proem: 'the shining stars of the broad heaven above' (110). Strange as it seems to us, the Ionian philosophers likewise regard the heavenly bodies as derived from the earth. They were explained mechanically as huge rocks, flung off to a distance, which became incandescent because of the speed of their motion.

(5) Then comes the distinction of the dry land from the sea: 'Earth gave birth to the high hills and to the sea (Pontos) with swelling waves.' This was *not* the result of a marriage, but ἄτερ φιλότητος ἐφιμέρου, another act of separation.

So again, in the Ionian systems, the last stage is the separation of dry from moist, when part of the earth is dried by the sun's heat, and the seas shrink into their beds.

The world-order is now complete as we see it, with its four great divisions: earth, sea, the gap of air, and starry sky above. From first to last the process is the separation or division, out of a primal indistinct unity, of parts which successively became distinct regions of the cosmos.

This cosmogony, as I have remarked, is not a myth, or rather it is *no longer* a myth. It has advanced so far along the road of rationalisation that only a very thin partition divides it from those early Greek systems which historians still innocently treat as purely rational constructions. Comparison with those systems shows that, when once the cosmic order has been formed, the next chapter should be an account of the origin of life. In the philosophies, life arises from the interaction or intercourse of the separated elements: animal life is born of the action of the heavenly heat on the moist slime of earth. This is the rationalised equivalent of the marriage of Heaven and Earth. And sure enough this marriage follows immediately in Hesiod: Gaia lay with Ouranos and brought forth the Titans. And so the genealogies begin—the theogony proper.

But here comes the sudden change I mentioned.

These gods are supernatural persons, with human forms and characters and well-known biographies. So at this point we turn back into that world of mythical representation which the rationalised cosmogony had left so far behind. Sky and Earth are re-transformed into a god and goddess, whose love and hate are depicted in all too human terms.

Here, where the mythical hymn to Zeus begins with the birth of the eldest gods, we must leave Hesiod for the moment to note a curiously close parallel to this sudden shift from rationalised cosmogony back to pure myth.

100

The first three chapters of Genesis contain two alternative accounts of Creation. The first account, in its present form, was composed not earlier than the Exile; it is considerably later than Hesiod, it may even be later than Anaximander. In this Hebrew cosmogony, moreover, we find nearly the same sequence of events. Let us recall what happened on the six days of Creation.

(1) There is the original confusion, the unformed watery mass wrapped in darkness. Light appears, divided from darkness, as day from night.

(So Hesiod's gap opened and Day was born from Night.)

(2) The sky as a solid firmament (στερέωμα) is lifted up to form a roof separating the heavenly waters, whence the rain comes, from the waters on the earth.

(This corresponds to Hesiod's Earth generating the sky as a secure seat for the gods. There is the same duplication that we noted.)

(3) The dry land is separated from the sea, and clothed with plants and trees.

(4) The heavenly bodies, sun, moon, and stars are made.

(As in the Greek myths and philosophies, their formation follows that of the earth.)

(5) & (6) Then came the moving creatures with life—birds, fishes, and creeping things—and finally man.

(Thus life appears when the cosmic frame is complete.)

The most striking difference from the Greek cosmogonies is that Hebrew monotheism has retained the Divine Creator as the sole first cause. Otherwise there are no mythical personifications, no allegorical figures like Eros or Phanes. And the action of the Elohim is confined to the utterance of the creative word. He has become extremely abstract and remote. If you eliminate the divine command: 'Let there be' so-and-so, and leave only the event commanded: 'There was' so-and-so, and then link these events in a chain of natural causation, the whole account is transformed into a quasi-scientific evolution of the world-order. The process is the same as in the Greek cosmogonies—separation or differentiation out of a primitive confusion. And as measured

101

by the absence of allegorical personifications, Genesis is less mythical than Hesiod's *Theogony*, and even closer to the rationalised system of the Milesians.

When we turn to the second account of Creation in Genesis ii–iii, we find ourselves back once more in the world of myth. The utterly remote Elohim of the first chapter is replaced by an anthropomorphic Jahweh, who moulds man out of dust, breathes life into his nostrils, plants a garden with trees, takes the man's rib and makes out of it a woman, walks in the garden in the cool of the day, and speaks to Adam with a human voice. The substance of the story also is composed of genuine myths: the woman Eve and the trouble she brings recall Hesiod's Pandora; there is the myth explaining man's mortality by failure to eat the fruit of the tree of life; and so on.

These myths may represent the concluding episodes in a primitive Creation myth. The earlier part, dealing with the formation of the world-order before man was made, has been suppressed by the priestly compilers of Genesis. They substituted for it their own expurgated and semi-philosophical cosmogony in the first chapter.

There is thus a curious parallel between Hesiod and Genesis. In both we find a prosaic cosmogony followed by a shift back into the world of poetry, peopled by the concrete human figures of mythical gods. This is no mere accident. In each case the cosmogony is the final product of a long process of rationalisation, in which the expurgation of mythical imagery has been carried so far that the result might almost be mistaken for a construction of the intellect reasoning from observation of the existing world. Only when we reflect on certain features do we realise that it can be nothing of the kind. There is nothing whatever in the obvious appearance of the world to suggest that the sky ever had to be lifted up from the earth, or that the heavenly bodies were formed after the earth, and so on. The same remark applies to the slightly more rationalised cosmogonies of the Ionian philosophers. They follow the same pattern, which pattern could never have been designed by inference from the observation of nature.

Now the value of the parallel I have drawn with Hebrew cosmogony lies in the fact that the Old Testament has preserved elsewhere other traces of the original myth of Creation which the priestly authors of Genesis have largely obliterated. This myth has been restored by scholars, and, what is more, traced to its origin in ritual. And behind this Palestinian myth and ritual lie the Babylonian Hymn of Creation and the corresponding New Year rites. If we follow this track, we shall, I believe, discover the framework of those episodes which make up the third element in Hesiod's *Theogony*—the mythical hymn to Zeus.

THE OPENING OF CHAOS

We may start from that curious feature I have emphasised: the fact that, both in Hesiod and Genesis, the separation of sky from earth occurs twice over. We will take the two versions of this event separately.

First there is the opening of the gap and the appearance of light in the primaeval darkness. Turning from Hesiod's cosmogony to the hymn which follows, we find that this event has its counterpart in the first episode of the myth. Fifty years ago Andrew Lang pointed out that the mutilation of the sky-god by his son Cronos could be 'explained as a myth of the violent separation of the earth and sky, which some races, for example the Polynesians, supposed to have originally clasped each other in a close embrace'. I quote these words from Frazer's *Adonis* (I, 283); and this explanation is adopted by Nilsson in his *History of Greek Religion* (p. 73).

After mentioning the Orphic world–egg, Nilsson writes: 'Still more crude is the cosmogonic myth in Hesiod. Ouranos (the sky) settled down upon Gaia (the earth), completely covering her, and hid their children in her entrails. Gaia persuaded her son Kronos to part them by cutting off the genitalia of Ouranos. There are curious parallels in the Egyptian myth of Keb and Nut, the earth-god and the goddess of heaven, and in the Maori myth of Rangi and Papa.'

In this myth we read:[1] 'From Rangi, the Heaven, and Papa, the Earth, sprang all men and things; but sky and earth clave together,

---

[1] Tylor, *Primitive Culture* I, 322.

103

and darkness rested upon them and the beings they had begotten, till at last their children took counsel whether they should rend apart their parents or slay them.'

Tane Mahute separated them and raised up the sky. The gods then departed each to his separate place in air, earth, and sea, and thus the world was established. We may note further that as, in Hesiod's Cosmogony, the opening of the gap is followed by the appearance of Eros, so in his myth the sundering of Ouranos and Gaia is followed by the birth of Aphrodite, who has Eros and Himeros in her train and whose prerogative (τιμή and μοῖρα) is to preside over marriage (201–6).

The Polynesian myth brings out more clearly than Hesiod does the purpose for which heaven and earth were forced apart: it was to give the gods room in which to be born and distinct regions they could occupy in a world-order. In the language of myth, it enables Gaia to give birth to her children, Pontos and the other gods. In the language of rationalised cosmogony, it is followed by the separation of the sea from the dry land and the appearance of living things. Once you have granted the fundamental axiom that 'heaven and earth were once one form' (or, as the philosophers put it, 'all things were together', ἦν ὁμοῦ πάντα), theogony and cosmogony alike must begin with the separation of the two parents of the gods or the two primary regions of the cosmos.

The agent in the mythical version is Cronos, instigated by Gaia herself. To that extent Cronos fills the role of creator. Also he was the king, who originally distributed among the Titans their privileges and provinces in the order of the world (*Theog.* 392 ff.). But his reign has receded into the dim past. In the hymn the foreground is occupied by his son, the young king, Zeus. Zeus is the hero whose exploits established the world as it now is.

THE DRAGON

So much, then, for the original opening of the gap. We will now go on to the second version of this act of separation. In Hesiod, Earth gives birth to the heaven and the shining stars. In Genesis, Elohim lifts up the firmament to support the heavenly ocean and creates the sun, moon, and stars. What is the mythical counterpart of this episode in cosmogony?

Once more the answer is to be found in the pages of the *Golden Bough*. Frazer writes:

> The Babylonian myth relates how in the beginning the mighty god Marduk fought and killed the great dragon Tiamat, an embodiment of the primaeval watery chaos, and how after his victory he created the present heaven and earth by splitting the huge carcase of the monster into halves and setting one of them up to form the sky, while the other half apparently he used to fashion the earth. Thus the story is a myth of creation.... The account of creation given in the first chapter of Genesis, which has been so much praised for its simple grandeur and sublimity, is merely a rationalised version of the old myth of the fight with the dragon, a myth which for crudity of thought deserves to rank with the quaint fancies of the lowest savages.[1]

Frazer is referring to the Babylonian so-called 'Epic of Creation'. We there read how Tiamat the dragon of the waters, seeking vengeance on the younger gods for killing her husband Apsu, organised a host of monsters. She defeats the first champion of the gods, who then appeal to Marduk. He undertakes to save them, if he is promised kingship over the whole world. Exalted as a great god, he kills the dragon and imprisons her monsters in the lower world. He then splits her body in half to make sky and earth; fixes the regions of the world-order, and assigns the three provinces of heaven, earth, and sea to Anu, Enlil, and Ea. He orders the year and the signs of the Zodiac and other heavenly bodies. There is a long description of the constellations.

Here we have, in its oldest known form, the lifting-up of the starry heaven from the earth followed by the ordering of the stars and of the provinces in the cosmos. We have seen how all this is rationalised in Genesis i and reduced to the formation of the firmament, the creation of the heavenly bodies, the separation of land and sea.

Now the link connecting the Babylonian myth with Genesis i is provided by references in the Psalms and Prophets to the myth

[1] *The Dying God*, p. 105.

105

of Jahweh slaying the dragon Rahab or Leviathan. Here is one of many:

> God is my king of old, working salvation in the midst of the earth.
> Thou didst divide the sea by thy strength; thou brakest the heads of the dragons in the waters.
> Thou breakest the heads of leviathan in pieces....
> The day is thine, the night also is thine; thou hast prepared the light and the sun.
> Thou hast set all the borders of the earth: thou hast made summer and winter.[1]

Here the dividing of the waters by the firmament is equated with the breaking of the dragon in pieces. It is followed by the creation of light and the sun, the ordering of the seasons, and fixing of the borders of the earth.

Now in Hesiod, one of the most exciting episodes is the slaying of the dragon by Zeus. This is one of the passages which the editors condemn on account of some inconsistency and dislocation. Among the descendants of Pontos we find the half-human dragon Echidna, who in marriage with Typhaon produces a brood of monsters (*Theog.* 295 ff.). Later (820), after the expulsion of the Titans from heaven, comes the battle of Zeus with the dragon Typhoeus, here the child of Earth and Tartarus. The whole of nature is involved in the turmoil of this terrific struggle. After his victory, Zeus, like Marduk, is established as king over the gods, and apportions to them their stations in the world-order.

On the strength of the Hebrew and Babylonian parallels (not to mention others), I claim that the battle of Zeus and the dragon Typhoeus is an original feature of the Greek Creation myth, which should be followed by the lifting up of the sky and the formation of the heavenly bodies. Of this sequel just a trace remains in the cosmogony, where the earth gives birth to the heaven and the shining stars—the second of those two separations of heaven and earth which we have noted.

It is now possible to explain why this separation occurs twice.

[1] Ps. lxxiv. 12-17.

106

In the rationalised cosmogonies it is inexplicable; but the reason appears in the myth. There the work of creation is the exploit of a personal god—Marduk, Jahweh, Zeus—who can bring light out of darkness, order out of formlessness, only by first triumphing over the powers of evil and disorder embodied in the dragon of the waters and her brood of monsters.[1] But this exploit must happen *somewhere*: the drama requires a stage. Also the hero must have a birth and history; and if he is to be the son of Heaven and Earth, his parents must have become distinct before they could marry and have a child.

Hence the necessity that the whole story should begin with the gap coming into being. In Hesiod's cosmogony, this simply happens: the first event has no cause behind it. But in myth all events are apt to have personal causes. So we find that Ouranos and Gaia are forced apart by Cronos, before the gods can be born, including Zeus himself. The result is this curious duplication. Heaven and earth are first separated in order to give birth to the god, who will create the world by separating heaven from earth as the two parts of the dragon.

But it is high time for me to fulfil the promise of my title which suggests that Hesiod's *Theogony* is, in the last resort, based on ritual. So far I have only argued that his all-but philosophical cosmogony is a rational reflection of his mythical hymn of Zeus, just as Genesis i is a reflection of the myths of Jahweh and Marduk. But I have only dealt with two episodes in the myth. In the light of the oriental material we can now go further and ask whether other episodes in the hymn of Zeus will not fit into a connected pattern, and whether this pattern may not be referred ultimately to a sequence of ritual acts.

It is now certainly established that the killing of Leviathan by Jahweh or of Tiamat by Marduk was not what Frazer called a 'quaint fancy' of primitive and problematical savages, sitting round the fire and speculating on the origin of the world. Nor was this conflict an isolated event without a context. Biblical

---

[1] Roscher, *Lex.* s.v. 'Ophion'. Jensen suggested that the battle of Χρόνος-Κρόνος with Ophioneus in Pherecydes' cosmogony is equivalent to the battle of Marduk and Tiamat.

107

students[1] have made out that the Psalm celebrating it belong to a group of liturgical songs, which were recited, as part of the Temple worship, at the Feast of Tabernacles. This feast inaugurated the New Year; and in its dramatic ritual the events these Psalms describe were annually re-enacted.

It is inferred from the Psalms that the fight with the dragon was one episode in the drama, in which, as throughout the festival, the part of Jahweh was taken by the king. There was also a triumphal procession, conducting the divine king in his chariot up the hill of Zion to be enthroned in the temple. Emblems of new vegetation, fertility, and moisture were carried and waved as a charm to secure a sufficiency of rain for the coming year. There are also signs that, at some point in the king's progress, there was another ritual combat. The procession was assailed by the powers of darkness and death, who are also the enemies of Israel, the kings of the earth who took counsel together against the Lord's anointed. The god who wields the thunder intervened to save his royal son and to dash his enemies in pieces. This episode has a parallel in the annual ritual at Abydos in Egypt. The procession conducting Osiris to his shrine was attacked by a band representing Set and his followers, who were repelled by a company led by Horus. At Jerusalem there was probably also a sacred marriage in a grove, commemorated by the booths made of branches from which the festival took its name, Tabernacles.

It appears, then, that the slaying of the dragon by the king-god, which was the initial act of creation, was one feature in the dramatic ritual of the New Year festival. What is the connection between a New Year festival and the myth of Creation?

This question has been convincingly answered by oriental scholars. The festival was much more than the civic inauguration of another year. It was in the first place a ceremony whose magical efficacy was to secure, during the coming year, the due supply of rain and the consequent fertility of plants and animals, on which man's life depends. This purpose was never forgotten. It is stated in the simplest terms by the prophet Zechariah (xiv. 16), who

[1] Prof. W. O. E. Oesterley in *Myth and Ritual*, chap. vi; A. R. Johnson in *The Labyrinth*.

108

foretells that, when the Lord is King over the whole earth, every one that is left of all the nations which came against Jerusalem shall go up from year to year to worship the King, the Lord of Hosts, and to keep the feast of Tabernacles—'And it shall be, that whoso will not come up...*upon them shall be no rain*.'

So the central figure in the New Year rites was the rain-maker, the divine king. But at the advanced stage of civilisation we are now considering in Babylon, Egypt, and Palestine, the king has become much more than a rain-making magician. To control the rain is to control the procession of the seasons and their powers of drought and moisture, heat and cold; and these again are linked with the orderly revolutions of sun, moon, and stars. The king is thus regarded as the living embodiment of the god who instituted this natural order and must perpetually renew and maintain its functioning for the benefit of man. The king embodies that power and also the life-force of his people, concentrated in his official person. He is the maintainer of the social order; and the prosperity of the nation depends upon his righteousness, the Hebrew *Sedek*, the Greek δίκη. He protects his people from the evil powers of death and disorder, as well as leading them in war to victory over their enemies.

The purpose of the New Year festival is to renovate—to recreate—the ordered life of the social group and of the world of nature, after the darkness and defeat of winter. The power which gives one more turn to the wheel of the revolving year is vested in the king, but derived from the god whom he embodies, the god who first set the wheel in motion. So the rites are regarded as an annual re-enactment of Creation.

Commenting on the features common to the New Year festivals of Babylon and Egypt, Professor Oesterley remarks[1] that, while there are many gods,

there is one who assumes supremacy in the role of productive creator; and the earthly king is identified with him. Osiris among the Egyptians, and Marduk among the Babylonians, are the supreme gods, and in each case the earthly king is identified with his god. During the annual New Year Festival held in honour of the deity he is proclaimed king;

[1] *Myth and Ritual*, p. 123.

109

and this is graphically set forth in the drama of his ascent upon his throne; he is thereby acknowledged as lord of creation. The mystery-rite not only symbolised, but was believed actually to bring about, the revivification of Nature.

Now, what Osiris was to the Egyptians, and what Marduk was to the Babylonians, that Jahweh was to the Israelites. The New Year Festival of the Israelites was held on the first day of the Feast of Taber-nacles (Sukkoth), when the Kingship of their God Jahweh was cele-brated, and he was worshipped and honoured as Lord of Creation. By his will...the produce of the soil during the coming year would be abundant; thus, annually there was the renewed manifestation of His creative power, so that every New Year Festival was a memorial of the Creation, since at each New Year the land was recreated.... It may be said that the New Year Festival was, as it were, a repetition of the Creation.

To the same effect Professor Hooke has written of the Babylo-nian ceremony:

It was, in a literal sense, the making of a New Year, the removal of the guilt and defilement of the old year, and the ensuring of security and prosperity for the coming year. By this ceremony was secured the due functioning of all things, sun, moon, stars, and seasons, in their appointed order. Here lies the ritual meaning of Creation: there is a new creation year by year, as a result of these ceremonies. The conception of creation in this stage of the evolution of religion is not cosmological but ritual. It has not come into existence in answer to speculations about the origin of things, but as a ritual means of maintaining the necessary order of things essential for the well-being of the community.[1]

We can now define the relation between the Creation myth and the New Year rites. It is the relation called 'aetiological'. Here the Babylonian evidence is conclusive. We possess a large part of the myth in the tablets now misleadingly entitled 'The Epic of Creation'. This is not an epic, but a hymn. Epics do not reflect ritual action; nor were they recited as incantations to reinforce the efficacy of a rite every time it was performed. This document is a hymn to Marduk, recounting his exploits in creating and ordering the world of gods and men.

[1] *Origins of Early Semitic Ritual*, p. 19.

We know, moreover, that, on the fourth day of the New Year festival of the spring equinox, this hymn was recited, from beginning to end, by the high priest, shut up alone in the sanctuary. This was done before the king arrived to take the leading part in the principal ceremonies.

Further, fragments of a priestly commentary on the ritual explain that a whole series of actions performed by the king symbolised the exploits of Marduk in the story of Creation. That story is, in fact, the aetiological myth of the New Year festival.

Now we know that an aetiological myth is not really the historical record of a supernatural series of events instituting the rite which professes to re-enact these events on a miniature scale. The rite itself is the only historical event, repeated annually. Every spring the king-god actually recreates the natural and social order. The myth is a transcription of that performance on a higher plane, where the corresponding actions are imagined as performed once for all by the god whom the king is conceived to embody and represent. But that god is simply a projection, made up of the official character and functions of the king, abstracted from the accidental human personality who is invested with those functions so long as his vitality lasts in full vigour. When he grows old or dies, the divine character is transmitted to a successor. The god is related to the individual king as the Platonic Idea to a series of particulars which for a time manifest its character. The myth is similarly the universalised transcript of the recurrent ritual action, projected on to the superhuman plane.

It follows that the contents of the Creation myth are not 'quaint fancies', or baseless speculations; nor are they derived from the observation of natural phenomena. Starting from the given appearance of the starry sky above our heads and the broad earth at our feet, no one but a lunatic under the influence of hashish could ever arrive at the theory that they were originally formed by splitting the body of a dragon in half. But suppose you start with a ritual drama, in which the powers of evil and disorder, represented by a priestly actor with a dragon's mask, are overcome by the divine king, as part of a magical regeneration of the natural and social order. Then you may compose a hymn, in which this

III

61

act is magnified, with every circumstance of splendour and horror, as a terrific battle between the king of the gods and the dragon of the deep. And you will recite this hymn, every time the ritual drama is performed, to reinforce its efficacy with all the majesty of the superhuman precedent.

Now so long as the myth remains part of a living ritual, its symbolic meaning is clear. But when the ritual has fallen into disuse, the myth may survive for many centuries. The action will now appear crude, grotesque, monstrous; and yet a poet may instinctively feel that the story is still charged with significance, however obscure, owing to the intense emotions that went to its making when it was part of vitally important religious action. Symbols like the dragon still haunt the dreams of our most civilised contemporaries.

The suggestion, then, to which all this intricate argument has led, is that the mythical element in the *Theogony* consists mainly in the debris of a Creation myth which is also a hymn to Zeus. By Hesiod's time it had long been detached from the ritual it once reflected, and the episodes have naturally suffered some dislocation. Also, since Hesiod was unaware of the ritual origin which alone makes them intelligible, the outlines are sometimes blurred. But if we pass them briefly in review, the ancient pattern can still be traced.

(1) Hesiod's myth is linked with the preceding cosmogony by the marriage of Ouranos and Gaia, parents of the elder gods; the Cyclopes, who will furnish Zeus with his thunder; the Hundred-Armed, who will fight for him against the Titans; and the Titans themselves.

Ouranos hates his children, who cannot get born until Cronos castrates his father and forces the pair apart.

In the Babylonian myth the first parents are the male and female powers of the primaeval deep, Apsu and Tiamat, whose waters at first were mingled together. Apsu wishes to destroy his children, the elder gods. Ea plots against Apsu, kills him, and castrates his messenger, Mummu.

(2) Here follow in Hesiod three genealogies. The children of Night include Death and all the evils that plague mankind.

112

Among the descendants of Pontos is the dragon Echidna with her consort Typhaon and their brood of monsters.

In the Babylonian hymn, Tiamat plans to avenge Apsu, with the help of monsters born of the sea. She exalts Kingu among her first-born to be king over her other children, much as Gaia chose Cronos to take the lead among the Titans.

(3) Both poems then tell of the birth of the young God— Marduk, Zeus—who is to become king and order the world of men and gods.

This part of the story of Zeus is of Cretan origin. Once more the old king tries to destroy his sons who will rob him of his kingship, and is defeated by a stratagem.

It will be remembered how in the Palaikastro hymn the fertility aspect of the young Zeus appears when he leads the dancing Kouretes, and is invoked to bring fruitfulness for the coming year.

In Hesiod Zeus releases the Hundred-Armed and the Cyclopes, who give him the thunder that will assure his kingship.

As Nilsson remarks, a fertility god who is annually reborn must also die annually. The death of Zeus was a part of the Cretan myth which the Greeks suppressed.

It is noteworthy that the death of Marduk does not figure in the Creation myth; but we possess tablets recording the ritual of his death and resurrection, which somehow accompanied the New Year festival. The ritual resembled that of Tammuz; and, while Bel-Marduk was in the underworld, the hymn of Creation was sung as an incantation to secure his return to life.

(4) Hesiod's story is here interrupted by the genealogy of Iapetus, which leads to the cheating of Zeus by Prometheus, the theft of fire, and the creation of woman to plague mankind. These events, which imply that man has already been created, are obviously out of place. At line 617 Hesiod goes back to the release of the Hundred-Armed. Zeus gives them the food of immortality, and they undertake to fight the Titans, who are attacking Olympus. The battle is indecisive until Zeus, now armed with the thunder, intervenes. The Titans are blasted and imprisoned in Tartarus.

These Titans who assail Olympus can hardly be the same as the children of Ouranos called Titans in the earlier genealogy. We cannot believe that the lovely Tethys, the gold-crowned Phebe, and two brides of Zeus, Themis and Mnemosyne, can have been battered with rocks, blasted by the lightning, and permanently chained in Tartarus.

This story has grown out of the ritual combat in which the forces of death and disorder, the followers of Set, the kings of the earth, attack the company of the young king, and are defeated by the god whom he represents. If this is so, the Titanomachy perpetuates a feature of New Year ritual.

(5) In the Babylonian myth the enemies of the younger gods are Tiamat and her host of monsters. She defeats their first champion, Anu. The gods then appeal to Marduk, who undertakes to save them if he is promised kingship over the whole world. The gods do homage to him and invest him with the insignia of royalty. There is a terrific battle, told at great length. Tiamat is slain and her monsters imprisoned.

Marduk then splits her body to make heaven and earth, fixes the regions of the world-order, and assigns heaven, earth, and sea to Anu, Enlil, and Ea as their provinces. (Compare the δασμός of these same regions to the three sons of Cronos.)

Marduk orders the year, the signs of the Zodiac, and the other heavenly bodies.

Man is created by Ea from the blood of Tiamat's consort, Kingu.

Marduk then gives laws to the gods and fixes their prerogatives. In gratitude, they build the temple of E-Sagila, where they assemble every year for the New Year festival—that very festival of which this hymn reflects the ritual.

In Hesiod the battle with the dragon Typhoeus comes after the expulsion of the Titans, as the last exploit of Zeus. It cannot be followed by the work of Creation, since the formation of the world-order has already been described in the cosmogony prefixed to the whole myth and Hesiod is too logical to repeat it here. But it is followed by the final recognition of Zeus as king over the gods, to whom he apportions their prerogatives.

Thus Zeus institutes the natural and social order. This royal function is allegorically expressed by the marriage of Zeus with

114

Themis (social order) and the birth of their children, the Seasons (whose names are Good Government, Justice, and Peace) and the Moirai, who give men their portions of good and evil.

So the last event in the hymn of Marduk is that the seven gods of fate fix the destinies for all mankind.

The parallel I have drawn might be illustrated in much greater detail. But perhaps there is now a *prima facie* case for the thesis that Hesiod's hymn of Zeus is not a genealogy interrupted by unconnected episodes, but reflects the features of an ancient New Year ritual of recreation, in which the king impersonated Zeus. The myth may have been for a long time detached from the ritual. Hesiod cannot have been aware of its origin; but he must have been dimly conscious that just these episodes were relevant to the story of Creation. Further research in Crete and Asia Minor may show whether there is any ground for the guess that the New Year festival in question was once performed in the palace of King Minos.

NOTE

The following is added at the end of the MS. of this essay, with a note saying that it was occasioned by a criticism of Prof. A. B. Cook to the effect that it ought to be possible to point to a ritual *on Greek soil*, of which the myth discussed might be the aetiology.   W. K. C. G.

I am wondering whether this New Year festival is not the original parent of a lot of festivals, including the Dionysia (New Year festivals need not be in spring), which have diverged by emphasising different features of the original until they may seem to have as little in common as a horse's leg, the human forearm and hand, and a bird's wing. Thus the death and resurrection element may be almost entirely suppressed in one form (as at Babylon, where it survived only as an extraneous rite and in the humiliation of the divine king by the high priest, of which there is a trace still in the coronation rite). Elsewhere this feature might become central and all-important: then you have the ritual which yields tragedy and comedy. Hocart's *Kingship* suggests that you might derive from the one source also the coronation ritual and the initiation ceremonies of Eleusinian type (which were agricultural-fertility rites, *not* tribal initiations). In Osiris's case the death and resurrection *motif* is central, but other features survive.

There is only one fundamental theme behind all these: renewal of life; rebirth; the young king superseding the old.

What excited me was the idea (which I got from Hooke's books) that early philosophic cosmogony is not only a transcription of mythical cosmogony, but finally has its root in *ritual*, something tangibly existing, not baseless 'fancies' and speculation.

116

CHAPTER I

OEDIPUS REX: THE TRAGIC RHYTHM
OF ACTION

. . . quel secondo regno
dove l'umano spirito si purga.
—*Purgatorio,* CANTO I

I SUPPOSE there can be little doubt that *Oedipus Rex* is a crucial instance of drama, if not *the* play which best exemplifies this art in its essential nature and its completeness. It owes its position partly to the fact that Aristotle founded his definitions upon it. But since the time of Aristotle it has been imitated, rewritten, and discussed by many different generations, not only of dramatists, but also of moralists, psychologists, historians, and other students of human nature and destiny.

Though the play is thus generally recognized as an archetype, there has been little agreement about its meaning or its form. It seems to beget, in every period, a different interpretation and a different dramaturgy. From the seventeenth century until the end of the eighteenth, a Neoclassic and rationalistic interpretation of *Oedipus,* of Greek tragedy, and of Aristotle, was generally accepted; and upon this interpretation was based the dramaturgy of Corneille and Racine. Nietzsche, under the inspiration of Wagner's *Tristan und Isolde,* developed a totally different view of it, and thence a different theory of drama. These two views of Greek tragedy, Racine's and Nietzsche's, still provide indispensable perspectives upon *Oedipus.* They show a great deal about modern principles of dramatic composition; and they show, when compared, how central and how essential Sophocles' drama is. In the two essays following, the attempt is made to develop the analogies, the similarities and differences, between these three conceptions of drama.

13

In our day a conception of *Oedipus* seems to be developing which is neither that of Racine nor that of Nietzsche. This view is based upon the studies which the Cambridge School, Fraser, Cornford, Harrison, Murray, made of the ritual origins of Greek tragedy. It also owes a great deal to the current interest in myth as a way of ordering human experience. *Oedipus*, we now see, is both myth and ritual. It assumes and employs these two ancient ways of understanding and representing human experience, which are prior to the arts and sciences and philosophies of modern times. To understand it (it now appears) we must endeavor to recapture the habit of significant make-believe, of the direct perception of action, which underlies Sophocles' theater.

If *Oedipus* is to be understood in this way, then we shall have to revise our ideas of Sophocles' dramaturgy. The notion of Aristotle's theory of drama, and hence of Greek dramaturgy, which still prevails (in spite of such studies as Butcher's of the *Poetics*) is largely colored by Neoclassic taste and rationalistic habits of mind. If we are to take it that Sophocles was imitating action before theory, instead of after it, like Racine, then both the elements and the form of his composition appear in a new light.

In the present essay the attempt is made to draw the deductions, for Sophocles' theater and dramaturgy, which the present view of *Oedipus* implies. We shall find that the various traditional views of this play are not so much wrong as partial.

Oedipus, Myth and Play

When Sophocles came to write his play he had the myth of Oedipus to start with. Laius and Jocasta, King and Queen of Thebes, are told by the oracle that their son will grow up to kill his father and marry his mother. The infant, his feet pierced, is left on Mount Kitharon to die. But a shepherd finds him and takes care of him; at last gives him to another shepherd, who takes him to Corinth, and there the King and Queen bring him up as their own son. But Oedipus—"Clubfoot"— is plagued in his turn by the oracle; he hears that he is fated to kill his father and marry his mother; and to escape that fate he leaves Corinth

14

never to return. On his journey he meets an old man with his servants; gets into a dispute with him, and kills him and all his followers. He comes to Thebes at the time when the Sphinx is preying upon that City; solves the riddle which the Sphinx propounds, and saves the City. He marries the widowed Queen, Jocasta; has several children by her; rules prosperously for many years. But, when Thebes is suffering under a plague and a drought, the oracle reports that the gods are angry because Laius' slayer is unpunished. Oedipus, as King, undertakes to find him; discovers that he is himself the culprit and that Jocasta is his own mother. He blinds himself and goes into exile. From this time forth he becomes a sort of sacred relic, like the bones of a saint; perilous, but "good medicine" for the community that possesses him. He dies, at last, at Athens, in a grove sacred to the Eumenides, female spirits of fertility and night.

It is obvious, even from this sketch, that the myth, which covers several generations, has as much narrative material as *Gone with the Wind*. We do not know what versions of the story Sophocles used. It is the way of myths that they generate whole progenies of elaborations and varying versions. They are so suggestive, seem to say so much, yet so mysteriously, that the mind cannot rest content with any single form, but must add, or interpret, or simplify—reduce to terms which the reason can accept. Mr. William Troy suggests that "what is possibly most in order at the moment is a thoroughgoing refurbishment of the medieval four-fold method of interpretation, which was first developed, it will be recalled, for just such a purpose—to make at least partially available to the reason that complex of human problems which are embedded, deep and imponderable, in the Myth."* It appears that Sophocles, in his play, succeeded in preserving the suggestive mystery of the Oedipus myth, while presenting it in a wonderfully unified dramatic form; and this drama has all the dimensions which the fourfold method was intended to explore.

Everyone knows that when Sophocles planned the plot of the play itself, he started almost at the end of the story, when the plague descends upon the City of Thebes which Oedipus and

*"Myth, Method and the Future," by William Troy. *Chimera*, spring, 1946.

15

Jocasta had been ruling with great success for a number of years. The action of the play takes less than a day, and consists of Oedipus' quest for Laius' slayer—his consulting the Oracle of Apollo, his examination of the Prophet, Tiresias, and of a series of witnesses, ending with the old Shepherd who gave him to the King and Queen of Corinth. The play ends when Oedipus is unmistakably revealed as himself the culprit.

At this literal level, the play is intelligible as a murder mystery. Oedipus takes the role of District Attorney; and when he at last convicts himself, we have a twist, a *coup de théâtre*, of unparalleled excitement. But no one who sees or reads the play can rest content with its literal coherence. Questions as to its meaning arise at once: Is Oedipus really guilty, or simply a victim of the gods, of his famous complex, of fate, of original sin? How much did he know, all along? How much did Jocasta know? The first, and most deeply instinctive effort of the mind, when confronted with this play, is to endeavor to reduce its meanings to some set of rational categories.

The critics of the Age of Reason tried to understand it as a fable of the enlightened moral will, in accordance with the philosophy of that time. Voltaire's version of the play, following Corneille, and his comments upon it, may be taken as typical. He sees it as essentially a struggle between a strong and righteous Oedipus, and the malicious and very human gods, aided and abetted by the corrupt priest Tiresias; he makes it an antireligious tract, with an unmistakable moral to satisfy the needs of the discursive intellect. In order to make Oedipus "sympathetic" to his audience, he elides, as much as possible, the incest motif; and he adds an irrelevant love story. He was aware that his version and interpretation were not those of Sophocles but, with the complacent provinciality of his period, he attributes the difference to the darkness of the age in which *Sophocles* lived.

Other attempts to rationalize *Oedipus Rex* are subtler than Voltaire's, and take us further toward an understanding of the play. Freud's reduction of the play to the concepts of his psychology reveals a great deal, opens up perspectives which we are still exploring. If one reads *Oedipus* in the light of Fustel de Coulanges' *The Ancient City*, one may see it as the expression

16

of the ancient patriarchal religion of the Greeks. And other interpretations of the play, theological, philosophical, historical, are available, none of them wrong, but all partial, all reductions of Sophocles' masterpiece to an alien set of categories. For the peculiar virtue of Sophocles' presentation of the myth is that it preserves the ultimate mystery by focusing upon the tragic human at a level beneath, or prior to any rationalization whatever. The plot is so arranged that we see the action, as it were, illumined from many sides at once.

By starting the play at the end of the story, and showing on-stage only the last crucial episode in Oedipus' life, the past and present action of the protagonist are revealed together; and, in each other's light, are at last felt as one. Oedipus' quest for the slayer of Laius becomes a quest for the hidden reality of his own past; and as that slowly comes into focus, like repressed material under psychoanalysis—with sensory and emotional immediacy, yet in the light of acceptance and understanding—his immediate quest also reaches its end: he comes to see himself (the Savior of the City) and the guilty one, the plague of Thebes, at once and at one.

This presentation of the myth of Oedipus constitutes, in one sense, an "interpretation" of it. What Sophocles saw as the essence of Oedipus' nature and destiny, is not what Seneca or Dryden or Cocteau saw; and one may grant that even Sophocles did not exhaust the possibilities in the materials of the myth. But Sophocles' version of the myth does not constitute a "reduction" in the same sense as the rest.

I have said that the action which Sophocles shows is a quest, the quest for Laius' slayer; and that as Oedipus' past is unrolled before us his whole life is seen as a kind of quest for his true nature and destiny. But since the object of this quest is not clear until the end, the seeking action takes many forms, as its object appears in different lights. The object, indeed, the final perception, the "truth," looks so different at the end from what it did at the beginning that Oedipus' action itself may seem not a quest, but its opposite, a flight. Thus it would be hard to say, simply, that Oedipus either succeeds or fails. He succeeds; but his success is his undoing. He fails to find what, in one way, he

17

sought; yet from another point of view his search is brilliantly successful. The same ambiguities surround his effort to discover who and what he is. He seems to find that he is nothing; yet thereby finds himself. And what of his relation to the gods? His quest may be regarded as a heroic attempt to escape their decrees, or as an attempt, based upon some deep natural faith, to discover what their wishes are, and what true obedience would be. In one sense Oedipus suffers forces he can neither control nor understand, the puppet of fate; yet at the same time he wills and intelligently intends his every move.

The meaning, or spiritual content of the play, is not to be sought by trying to resolve such ambiguities as these. The spiritual content of the play is the tragic action which Sophocles directly presents; and this action is in its essence *zweideutig:* triumph and destruction, darkness and enlightenment, mourning and rejoicing, at any moment we care to consider it. But this action has also a shape: a beginning, middle, and end, in time. It starts with the reasoned purpose of finding Laius' slayer. But this aim meets unforeseen difficulties, evidences which do not fit, and therefore shake the purpose as it was first understood; and so the characters suffer the piteous and terrible sense of the mystery of the human situation. From this suffering or passion, with its shifting visions, a new perception of the situation emerges; and on that basis the purpose of the action is redefined, and a new movement starts. This movement, or *tragic rhythm of action*, constitutes the shape of the play as a whole; it is also the shape of each episode, each discussion between principals with the chorus following. Mr. Kenneth Burke has studied the tragic rhythm in his *Philosophy of Literary Form,* and also in *A Grammar of Motives,* where he gives the three moments traditional designations which are very suggestive: *Poiema, Pathema, Mathema.* They may also be called, for convenience, Purpose, Passion (or Suffering) and Perception. It is this tragic rhythm of action which is the substance or spiritual content of the play, and the clue to its extraordinarily comprehensive form.

In order to illustrate these points in more detail, it is convenient to examine the scene between Oedipus and Tiresias with the chorus following it. This episode, being early in the play (the

18

first big agon), presents, as it were, a preview of the whole action and constitutes a clear and complete example of action in the tragic rhythm.

Hero and Scapegoat: The Agon between Oedipus and Tiresias

The scene between Oedipus and Tiresias comes after the opening sections of the play. We have seen the citizens of Thebes beseeching their King to find some way to lift the plague which is on the City. We have had Oedipus' entrance (majestic, but for his tell-tale limp) to reassure them, and we have heard the report which Creon brings from the Delphic Oracle: that the cause of the plague is the unpunished murder of Laius, the former king. Oedipus offers rewards to anyone who will reveal the culprit, and he threatens with dire punishment anyone who conceals or protects him. In the meantime, he decides, with the enthusiastic assent of the chorus, to summon Tiresias as the first witness.

Tiresias is that suffering seer whom Sophocles uses in *Antigone* also to reveal a truth which other mortals find it hard and uncomfortable to see. He is physically blind, but Oedipus and chorus alike assume that if anyone can see who the culprit is, it is Tiresias, with his uncanny inner vision of the future. As Tiresias enters, led by a boy, the chorus greets him in these words:[*]

> CHORUS. But the man to convict him is here. Look: they are bringing the one human being in whom the truth is native, the godlike seer.

Oedipus is, at this point in the play, at the opposite pole of experience from Tiresias: he is hero, monarch, helmsman of the state; the solver of the Sphinx's riddle, the triumphant being. He explains his purpose in the following proud clear terms:

> OEDIPUS. O Tiresias, you know all things: what may be told, and the unspeakable: things of earth and things of heaven.

[*]I am responsible for the English of this scene. The reader is referred to *Oedipus Rex*, translated by Dudley Fitts and Robert Fitzgerald (New York: Harcourt, Brace and Co., 1949), a very handsome version of the whole play.

19

You understand the City (though you do not see it) in its present mortal illness—from which to save us and protect us, we find, Lord, none but you. For you must know, in case you haven't heard it from the messengers, that Apollo, when we asked him, told us there was one way only with this plague: to discover Laius' slayers, and put them to death or send them into exile. Therefore you must not jealously withhold your omens, whether of birds or other visionary ·way, but save yourself and the City—save me, save all of us—from the defilement of the dead. In your hand we are. There is no handsomer work for a man, than to bring, with what he has, what help he can.

This speech is the prologue of the scene, and the basis of the agon or struggle which follows. This struggle in effect analyzes Oedipus' purpose; places it in a wider context, reveals it as faulty and dubious. At the end of the scene Oedipus loses his original purpose altogether, and suffers a wave of rage and fear, which will have to be rationalized in its turn before he can "pull himself together" and act again with a clear purpose.

In the first part of the struggle, Oedipus takes the initiative, while Tiresias, on the defensive, tries to avoid replying:

TIRESIAS. Oh, oh. How terrible to know, when nothing can come of knowing! Indeed, I had lost the vision of these things, or I should never have come.

OEDIPUS. What things? . . . In what discouragement have you come to us here!

TIR. Let me go home. I shall endure this most easily, and so will you, if you do as I say.

OED. But what you ask is not right. To refuse your word is disloyalty to the City that has fed you.

TIR. But I see that your demands are exorbitant, and lest I too suffer such a—

OED. For the sake of the gods, if you know, don't turn away! Speak to us, we are your suppliants here.

TIR. None of you understands. But I—I never will tell my misery. Or yours.

OED. What are you saying? You know, but tell us nothing?

20

74

You intend treachery to us, and death to the City?

T<small>IR</small>. I intend to grieve neither myself nor you. Why then do you try to know? You will never learn from me.

O<small>ED</small>. Ah, evil old man! You would anger a stone! You will say *nothing?* Stand futile, speechless before us?

T<small>IR</small>. You curse my temper, but you don't see the one that dwells in you; no, you must blame me.

O<small>ED</small>. And who would *not* lose his temper, if he heard you utter your scorn of the City?

T<small>IR</small>. It will come. Silent though I be.

O<small>ED</small>. Since it will come, it is your duty to inform me.

T<small>IR</small>. I shall say no more. Now, if you like, rage to your bitter heart's content.

O<small>ED</small>. Very well: in my "rage" I shall hold back nothing which I now begin to see. I think you planned that deed, even performed it, though not with your own hands. If you could see, I should say that the work was yours alone.

In the last speech quoted, Oedipus changes his tack, specifying his purpose differently; he accuses Tiresias, and that makes Tiresias attack. In the next part of the fight the opponents trade blow for blow:

T<small>IR</small>. You would? I charge you, abide by the decree you uttered: from this day forth, speak neither to these present, nor to me, unclean as you are, polluter of the earth!

O<small>ED</small>. You have the impudence to speak out words like these! And now how do you expect to escape?

T<small>IR</small>. I have escaped. The truth strengthens and sustains me.

O<small>ED</small>. Who taught you the truth? Not your prophet's art.

T<small>IR</small>. You did; you force me against my will to speak.

O<small>ED</small>. Speak what? Speak again, that I may understand better.

T<small>IR</small>. *Didn't* you understand? Or are you goading me?

O<small>ED</small>. I can't say I really grasp it: speak again.

T<small>IR</small>. I say you are the murderer of the man whose murderer you seek.

O<small>ED</small>. You won't be glad to have uttered that curse twice.

T<small>IR</small>. Must I say more, so you may rage the more?

O<small>ED</small>. As much as you like—all is senseless.

21

TIR. I say you do not know your own wretchedness, nor see in what shame you live with those you love.

OED. Do you think you can say that forever with impunity?

TIR. If the truth has power.

OED. It has, with all but you: helpless is truth with you: for you are blind, in eye, in ear, in mind.

TIR. You are the impotent one: you utter slanders which every man here will apply to you.

OED. You have your being only in the night; you couldn't hurt me or any man who sees the sun.

TIR. No. Your doom is not to fall by me. Apollo suffices for that, he will bring it about.

OED. Are these inventions yours, or Creon's?

TIR. Your wretchedness is not Creon's, it is yours.

OED. O wealth, and power, and skill—which skill, in emulous life, brings low—what envy eyes you! if for this kingly power which the City gave into my hands, unsought—if for *this* the faithful Creon, my friend from the first, has stalked me in secret, yearning to supplant me! if he has bribed this juggling wizard, this deceitful beggar, who discerns his profit only, blind in his own art!

Tell me now, tell me where you have proved a true diviner? Why, when the song-singing sphinx was near, did you not speak deliverance to the people? Her riddles were not for any comer to solve, but for the mantic art, and you were apparently instructed neither by birds nor by any sign from the gods. Yet when I came, I, Oedipus, all innocent, I stopped her song. No birds taught me, by my own wit I found the answer. And it is I whom you wish to banish, thinking that you will then stand close to Creon's throne.

You and your ally will weep, I think, for this attempt; and in fact, if you didn't seem to be an old man, you would already have learned, in pain, of your presumption.

In this part the beliefs, the visions, and hence the purposes of the antagonists are directly contrasted. Because both identify themselves so completely with their visions and purposes, the

22

76

fight descends from the level of dialectic to a level below the rational altogether: it becomes cruelly *ad hominem*. We are made to see the absurd incommensurability of the very beings of Oedipus and Tiresias; they shrink from one another as from the uncanny. At the end of the round, it is Oedipus who has received the deeper wound; and his great speech, "O wealth and power," is a far more lyric utterance than the ordered exposition with which he began.

The end of this part of the fight is marked by the intervention of the chorus, which endeavors to recall the antagonists to the most general version of purpose which they supposedly share: the discovery of the truth and the service of the gods:

> CHORUS. To us it appears that this man's words were uttered in anger, and yours too, Oedipus. No need for that: consider how best to discharge the mandate of the god.

The last part of the struggle shows Tiresias presenting his whole vision, and Oedipus, on the defensive, shaken to the depths:

> TIR. Although you rule, we have equally the right to reply; in that I too have power. Indeed, I live to serve, not you, but Apollo; and I shall not be enrolled under Creon, either. Therefore I say, since you have insulted even my blindness, that though you have eyesight, you do not see what misery you are in, nor where you are living, nor with whom. Do you know whence you came? No, nor that you are the enemy of your own family, the living and the dead. The double prayer of mother and father shall from this land hound you in horror—who now see clearly, but then in darkness.
>
> Where then will your cry be bounded? What part of Kitharon not echo it quickly back, when you shall come to understand that marriage, to which you sailed on so fair a wind, homelessly home? And many other evils which you do not see will bring you to yourself at last, your children's equal.
>
> Scorn Creon, therefore, and my words: you will be struck down more terribly than any mortal.

23

OED. Can I really hear such things from him? Are you not gone? To death? To punishment? Not fled from this house?

TIR. I should never have come if you hadn't called me.

OED. I didn't know how mad you would sound, or it would have been a long time before I asked you here to my house.

TIR. This is what I am; foolish, as it seems to you; but wise, to the parents who gave you birth.

OED. To whom? Wait: *who* gave me birth?

TIR. This day shall give you birth, and death.

OED. In what dark riddles you always speak.

TIR. Aren't you the best diviner of riddles?

OED. Very well: mock that gift, which, you will find, is mine.

TIR. That very gift was your undoing.

OED. But if I saved the City, what does it matter?

TIR. So be it. I am going. Come, boy, lead me.

OED. Take him away. Your presence impedes and trips me; once you are gone, you can do no harm.

TIR. I shall go when I have done my errand without fear of your frowns, for they can't hurt me. I tell you, then, that the man whom you have long been seeking, with threats and proclamations, Laius' slayer, is here. He is thought to be an alien, but will appear a native Theban, and this circumstance will not please him. Blind, who once could see; destitute, who once was rich, leaning on a staff, he will make his way through a strange land. He will be revealed as brother and father of his own children; of the woman who bore him, both son and husband; sharer of his father's bed; his father's killer.

Go in and ponder this. If you find it wrong, say then I do not understand the prophetic vision.

Oedipus rushes off-stage, his clear purpose gone, his being shaken with fear and anger. Tiresias departs, led by his boy. The chorus is left to move and chant, suffering the mixed and ambivalent feelings, the suggestive but mysterious images, which the passion in which the agon eventuated produces in them:

24

CHORUS

Strophe I. Who is it that the god's voice from the Rock of
   Delphi says
   Accomplished the unspeakable with murderous hands?
   Time now that windswift
   Stronger than horses
   His feet take flight.
   In panoply of fire and lightning
   Now springs upon him the son of Zeus
   Whom the dread follow,
   The Fates unappeasable.

Antistrophe I. New word, like light, from snowy Parnassus:
   Over all the earth trail the unseen one.
   For in rough wood,
   In cave or rocks,
   Like bull bereft—stampeded, futile
   He goes, seeking with futile foot to
   Flee the ultimate
   Doom, which ever
   Lives and flies over him.

Strophe II. In awe now, and soul's disorder, I neither accept
   The augur's wisdom, nor deny: I know not what to say.
   I hover in hope, see neither present nor future.
   Between the House of Laius
   And Oedipus, I do not hear, have never heard, of any feud:
   I cannot confirm the public charge against him, to help
   Avenge the dark murder.

Antistrophe II. Zeus and Apollo are wise, and all that is mortal
   They know: but whether that human seer knows more
      than I
   There is no way of telling surely, though in wisdom
   A man may excel.
   Ah, never could I, till I see that word confirmed, consent
      to blame him!
   Before all eyes the winged songstress, once, assailed him;
   Wise showed he in that test, and to the City, tender; in my
      heart
   I will call him evil never.

25

The chorus is considered in more detail below. At this point I merely wish to point out that Oedipus and Tiresias show, in their agon, the "purpose" part of the tragic rhythm; that this turns to "passion," and that the chorus presents the passion and also the new perception which follows. This new perception is that of Oedipus as the possible culprit. But his outlines are vague; perhaps the vision itself is illusory, a bad dream. The chorus has not yet reached the end of its quest; that will come only when Oedipus, in the flesh before them, is unmistakably seen as the guilty one. We have reached merely a provisional resting-place, the end of the first figure in which the tragic rhythm is presented. But this figure is a reduced version of the shape of the play as a whole, and the fleeting and unwelcome image of Oedipus as guilty corresponds to the final perception or epiphany, the full-stop, with which the play ends.

Oedipus: Ritual and Play

The Cambridge School of Classical Anthropologists has shown in great detail that the form of Greek tragedy follows the form of a very ancient ritual, that of the *Enniautos-Daimon*, or seasonal god.* This was one of the most influential discoveries of the last few generations, and it gives us new insights into *Oedipus* which I think are not yet completely explored. The clue to Sophocles' dramatizing of the myth of Oedipus is to be found in this ancient ritual, which had a similar form and meaning—that is, it also moved in the "tragic rhythm."

Experts in classical anthropology, like experts in other fields, dispute innumerable questions of fact and of interpretation which the layman can only pass over in respectful silence. One of the thornier questions seems to be whether myth or ritual came first. Is the ancient ceremony merely an enactment of the Ur-Myth of the year-god—Attis, or Adonis, or Osiris, or the "Fisher-King"—in any case that Hero-King-Father-High-Priest who fights with his rival, is slain and dismembered, then rises anew with the spring season? Or did the innumerable myths of

*See especially Jane Ellen Harrison's *Ancient Art and Ritual,* and her *Themis* which contains an "Excursus on the ritual forms preserved in Greek Tragedy" by Professor Gilbert Murray.

26

this kind arise to "explain" a ritual which was perhaps mimed or danced or sung to celebrate the annual change of season?

For the purpose of understanding the form and meaning of *Oedipus*, it is not necessary to worry about the answer to this question of historic fact. The figure of Oedipus himself fulfills all the requirements of the scapegoat, the dismembered king or god-figure. The situation in which Thebes is presented at the beginning of the play—in peril of its life; its crops, its herds, its women mysteriously infertile, signs of a mortal disease of the City, and the disfavor of the gods—is like the withering which winter brings, and calls, in the same way, for struggle, dismemberment, death, and renewal. And this tragic sequence is the substance of the play. It is enough to know that myth and ritual are close together in their genesis, two direct imitations of the perennial experience of the race.

But when one considers *Oedipus* as a ritual one understands it in ways which one cannot by thinking of it merely as a dramatization of a story, even that story. Harrison has shown that the Festival of Dionysos, based ultimately upon the yearly vegetation ceremonies, included *rites de passage*, like that celebrating the assumption of adulthood—celebrations of the mystery of individual growth and development. At the same time, it was a prayer for the welfare of the whole City; and this welfare was understood not only as material prosperity, but also as the natural order of the family, the ancestors, the present members, and the generations still to come, and, by the same token, obedience to the gods who were jealous, each in his own province, of this natural and divinely sanctioned order and proportion.

We must suppose that Sophocles' audience (the whole population of the City) came early, prepared to spend the day in the bleachers. At their feet was the semicircular dancing-ground for the chorus, and the thrones for the priests, and the altar. Behind that was the raised platform for the principal actors, backed by the all-purpose, emblematic façade, which would presently be taken to represent Oedipus' palace in Thebes. The actors were not professionals in our sense, but citizens selected for a religious office, and Sophocles himself had trained them and the chorus.

27

This crowd must have had as much appetite for thrills and diversion as the crowds who assemble in our day for football games and musical comedies, and Sophocles certainly holds the attention with an exciting show. At the same time his audience must have been alert for the fine points of poetry and dramaturgy, for *Oedipus* is being offered in competition with other plays on the same bill. But the element which distinguishes this theater, giving it its unique directness and depth, is the *ritual expectancy* which Sophocles assumed in his audience. The nearest thing we have to this ritual sense of theater is, I suppose, to be found at an Easter performance of the *Mattias Passion*. We also can observe something similar in the dances and ritual mummery of the Pueblo Indians. Sophocles' audience must have been prepared, like the Indians standing around their plaza, to consider the playing, the make-believe it was about to see—the choral invocations, with dancing and chanting; the reasoned discourses and the terrible combats of the protagonists; the mourning, the rejoicing, and the contemplation of the final stage-picture or epiphany—as imitating and celebrating the mystery of human nature and destiny. And this mystery was at once that of individual growth and development, and that of the precarious life of the human City.

I have indicated how Sophocles presents the life of the mythic Oedipus in the tragic rhythm, the mysterious quest of life. Oedipus is shown seeking his own true being; but at the same time and by the same token, the welfare of the City. When one considers the ritual form of the whole play, it becomes evident that it presents the tragic but perennial, even normal, quest of the whole City for its well-being. In this larger action, Oedipus is only the protagonist, the first and most important champion. This tragic quest is realized by all the characters in their various ways; but in the development of the action as a whole it is the chorus alone that plays a part as important as that of Oedipus; its counterpart, in fact. The chorus holds the balance between Oedipus and his antagonists, marks the progress of their struggles, and restates the main theme, and its new variation, after each dialogue or agon. The ancient ritual was probably performed by a chorus alone without individual developments and

28

82

variations, and the chorus, in *Oedipus*, is still the element that throws most light on the ritual form of the play as a whole.

The chorus consists of twelve or fifteen "Elders of Thebes." This group is not intended to represent literally all of the citizens either of Thebes or of Athens. The play opens with a large delegation of Theban citizens before Oedipus' palace, and the chorus proper does not enter until after the prologue. Nor does the chorus speak directly for the Athenian audience; we are asked throughout to make-believe that the theater is the agora at Thebes; and at the same time Sophocles' audience is witnessing a ritual. It would, I think, be more accurate to say that the chorus represents the point of view and the faith of Thebes as a whole, and, by analogy, of the Athenian audience. Their errand before Oedipus' palace is like that of Sophocles' audience in the theater: they are watching a sacred combat, in the issue of which they have an all-important and official stake. Thus they represent the audience and the citizens in a particular way—not as a mob formed in response to some momentary feeling, but rather as an organ of a highly self-conscious community: something closer to the "conscience of the race" than to the overheated affectivity of a mob.

According to Aristotle, a Sophoclean chorus is a character that takes an important role in the action of the play, instead of merely making incidental music between the scenes, as in the plays of Euripides. The chorus may be described as a group personality, like an old Parliament. It has its own traditions, habits of thought and feeling, and mode of being. It exists, in a sense, as a living entity, but not with the sharp actuality of an individual. It perceives; but its perception is at once wider and vaguer than that of a single man. It shares, in its way, the seeking action of the play as a whole; but it cannot act in all the modes; it depends upon the chief agonists to invent and try out the detail of policy, just as a rather helpless but critical Parliament depends upon the Prime Minister to act but, in its less specific form of life, survives his destruction.

When the chorus enters after the prologue, with its questions, its invocation of the various gods, and its focus upon the hidden and jeopardized welfare of the City—Athens or Thebes—the list

29

of essential *dramatis personae*, as well as the elements needed to celebrate the ritual, is complete, and the main action can begin. It is the function of the chorus to mark the stages of this action, and to perform the suffering and perceiving part of the tragic rhythm. The protagonist and his antagonists develop the "purpose" with which the tragic sequence begins; the chorus, with its less than individual being, broods over the agons, marks their stages with a word (like that of the chorus leader in the middle of the Tiresias scene), and (expressing its emotions and visions in song and dance) suffers the results, and the new perception at the end of the fight.

The choral odes are lyrics but they are not to be understood as poetry, the art of words, only, for they are intended also to be danced and sung. And though each chorus has its own shape, like that of a discrete lyric—its beginning, middle, and end—it represents also one passion or pathos in the changing action of the whole. This passion, like the other moments in the tragic rhythm, is felt at so general or, rather, so deep a level that it seems to contain both the mob ferocity that Nietzsche felt in it and, at the other extreme, the patience of prayer. It is informed by faith in the unseen order of nature and the gods, and moves through a sequence of modes of suffering. This may be illustrated from the chorus I have quoted at the end of the Tiresias scene.

It begins (close to the savage emotion of the end of the fight) with images suggesting that cruel "Bacchic frenzy" which is supposed to be the common root of tragedy and of the "old" comedy: "In panoply of fire and lightning / The son of Zeus now springs upon him." In the first antistrophe these images come together more clearly as we relish the chase; and the fleeing culprit, as we imagine him, begins to resemble Oedipus, who is lame, and always associated with the rough wilderness of Kitharon. But in the second strophe, as though appalled by its ambivalent feelings and the imagined possibilities, the chorus sinks back into a more dark and patient posture of suffering, "in awe," "hovering in hope." In the second antistrophe this is developed into something like the orthodox Christian attitude of prayer, based on faith, and assuming the possibility of a hitherto

30

unimaginable truth and answer: "Zeus and Apollo are wise," etc. The whole chorus then ends with a new vision of Oedipus, of the culprit, and of the direction in which the welfare of the City is to be sought. This vision is still colored by the chorus's human love of Oedipus as Hero, for the chorus has still its own purgation to complete, cannot as yet accept completely either the suffering in store for it, or Oedipus as scapegoat. But it marks the end of the first complete "purpose-passion-perception" unit, and lays the basis for the new purpose which will begin the next unit.

It is also to be noted that the chorus changes the scene which we, as audience, are to imagine. During the agon between Oedipus and Tiresias, our attention is fixed upon their clash, and the scene is literal, close, and immediate: before Oedipus' palace. When the fighters depart and the choral music starts, the focus suddenly widens, as though we had been removed to a distance. We become aware of the interested City around the bright arena; and beyond that, still more dimly, of Nature, sacred to the hidden gods. Mr. Burke has expounded the fertile notion that human action may be understood in terms of the scene in which it occurs, and vice versa: the scene is defined by the mode of action. The chorus's action is not limited by the sharp, rationalized purposes of the protagonist; its mode of action, more patient, less sharply realized, is cognate with a wider, if less accurate, awareness of the scene of human life. But the chorus's action, as I have remarked, is not that of passion itself (Nietzsche's cosmic void of night) but suffering informed by the faith of the tribe in a human and a divinely sanctioned natural order: "If such deeds as these are honored," the chorus asks after Jocasta's impiety, "why should I dance and sing?" (lines 894, 895). Thus it is one of the most important functions of the chorus to reveal, in its widest and most mysterious extent, the theater of human life which the play, and indeed the whole Festival of Dionysos, assumed. Even when the chorus does not speak, but only watches, it maintains this theme and this perspective—ready to take the whole stage when the fighters depart.

If one thinks of the movement of the play, it appears that the tragic rhythm analyzes human action temporally into successive

31

modes, as a crystal analyzes a white beam of light spatially into the colored bands of the spectrum. The chorus, always present, represents one of these modes, and at the recurrent moments when reasoned purpose is gone, it takes the stage with its faith-informed passion, moving through an ordered succession of modes of suffering, to a new perception of the immediate situation.

Sophocles and Euripides, the Rationalist

Oedipus Rex is a changing image of human life and action which could have been formed only in the mirror of the tragic theater of the Festival of Dionysos. The perspectives of the myth, of the rituals, and of the traditional *hodos*, the way of life of the City—"habits of thought and feeling" which constitute the traditional wisdom of the race—were all required to make this play possible. That is why we have to try to regain these perspectives if we are to understand the written play which has come down to us: the analysis of the play leads to an analysis of the theater in which it was formed.

But though the theater was there, everyone could not use it to the full: Sophocles was required. This becomes clear if one considers the very different use which Euripides, Sophocles' contemporary, makes of the tragic theater and its ritual forms.

Professor Gilbert Murray has explained in detail how the tragic form is derived from the ritual form; and he has demonstrated the ritual forms which are preserved in each of the extant Greek tragedies. In general, the ritual had its agon, or sacred combat, between the old King, or god or hero, and the new, corresponding to the agons in the tragedies, and the clear "purpose" moment of the tragic rhythm. It had its *Sparagmos*, in which the royal victim was literally or symbolically torn asunder, followed by the lamentation and/or rejoicing of the chorus: elements which correspond to the moments of "passion." The ritual had its messenger, its recognition scene, and its epiphany; various plot devices for representing the moment of "perception" which follows the "pathos." Professor Murray, in a word, studies the art of tragedy in the light of ritual forms, and thus, throws a really new light upon Aristotle's *Poetics*. The

32

86

parts of the ritual would appear to correspond to parts of the plot, like recognitions and scenes of suffering, which Aristotle mentions, but, in the text which has come down to us, fails to expound completely. In this view, both the ritual and the more highly elaborated and individualized art of tragedy would be "imitating" action in the tragic rhythm; the parts of the ritual, and the parts of the plot, would both be devices for showing forth the three moments of this rhythm.

Professor Murray, however, does not make precisely these deductions. Unlike Aristotle, he takes the plays of Euripides, rather than Sophocles' *Oedipus*, as the patterns of the tragic form. That is because his attitude to the ritual forms is like Euripides' own: he responds to their purely theatrical effectiveness, but has no interest or belief in the prerational image of human nature and destiny which the ritual conveyed; which Sophocles felt as still alive and significant for his generation, and presented once more in *Oedipus*. Professor Murray shows that Euripides restored the literal ritual much more accurately than Sophocles— his epiphanies, for example, are usually the bodily showing-forth of a very human god, who cynically expounds his cruel part in the proceedings; while the "epiphany" in *Oedipus*, the final tableau of the blind old man with his incestuous brood, merely conveys the moral truth which underlay the action, and implies the anagoge: human dependence upon a mysterious and divine order of nature. Perhaps these distinctions may be summarized as follows: Professor Murray is interested in the ritual forms in abstraction from all content; Sophocles saw also the spiritual content of the old forms: understood them at a level deeper than the literal, as imitations of an action still "true" to life in his sophisticated age.

Though Euripides and Sophocles wrote at the same time and for the same theater, one cannot understand either the form or the meaning of Euripides' plays on the basis of Sophocles' dramaturgy. The beautiful lyrics sung by Euripides' choruses are, as I have said, incidental music rather than organic parts of the action; they are not based upon the feeling that all have a stake in the common way of life and therefore in the issue of the present action. Euripides' individualistic heroes find no light

33

in their suffering, and bring no renewal to the moral life of the community: they are at war with the very clear, human, and malicious gods, and what they suffer, they suffer unjustly and to no good end. Where Sophocles' celebrated irony seems to envisage the *condition humaine* itself—the plight of the psyche in a world which is ultimately mysterious to it—Euripides' ironies are all aimed at the incredible "gods" and at the superstitions of those who believe in them. In short, if these two writers both used the tragic theater, they did so in very different ways.

Verral's *Euripides the Rationalist* shows very clearly what the basis of Euripides' dramaturgy is. His use of myth and ritual is like that which Cocteau or, still more exactly, Sartre makes of them—for parody or satirical exposition, but without any belief in their meaning. If Euripides presents the plight of Electra in realistic detail, it is because he wants us to feel the suffering of the individual without benefit of any objective moral or cosmic order—with an almost sensational immediacy: he does not see the myth, as a whole, as significant as such. If he brings Apollo, in the flesh, before us, it is not because he "believes" in Apollo, but because he disbelieves in him, and wishes to reveal this figment of the Greek imagination as, literally, incredible. He depends as much as Sophocles upon the common heritage of ritual and myth: but he "reduces" its form and images to the uses of parody and metaphorical illustration, in the manner of Ovid and of the French Neoclassic tradition. And the human action he reveals is the extremely modern one of the psyche caught in the categories its reason invents, responding with unmitigated sharpness to the feeling of the moment, but cut off from the deepest level of experience, where the mysterious world is yet felt as real and prior to our inventions, demands, and criticisms.

Though Sophocles was not using the myths and ritual forms of the tragic theater for parody and to satirize their tradition, it does not appear that he had any more naïve belief in their literal validity than Euripides did. He would not, for his purpose, have had to ask himself whether the myth of Oedipus conveyed any historic facts. He would not have had to believe that the performance of *Oedipus,* or even the Festival of Dionysos itself, would assure the Athenians a good crop of children and olives.

34

On the contrary he must have felt that the tragic rhythm of action which he discerned in the myth, which he felt as underlying the forms of the ritual, and which he realized in so many ways in his play, was a deeper version of human life than any particular manifestation of it, or any conceptual understanding of it, whether scientific and rationalistic, or theological; yet potentially including them all. If one takes Mr. Troy's suggestion, one might say, using the Medieval notion of fourfold symbolism, that Sophocles might well have taken myth and ritual as literally "fictions," yet still have accepted their deeper meanings—trope, allegory, and anagoge—as valid.

Oedipus: The Imitation of an Action

The general notion we used to compare the forms and spiritual content of tragedy and of ancient ritual was the "imitation of action." Ritual imitates action in one way, tragedy in another; and Sophocles' use of ritual forms indicates that he sensed the tragic rhythm common to both.

But the language, plot, characters of the play may also be understood in more detail and in relation to each other as imitations, in their various media, of the one action. I have already quoted Coleridge on the unity of action: "not properly a rule," he calls it, "but in itself the great end, not only of the drama, but of the epic, lyric, even to the candle-flame cone of an epigram —not only of poetry, but of poesy in general, as the proper generic term inclusive of all the fine arts, as its species."* Probably the influence of Coleridge partly accounts for the revival of this notion of action which underlies the recent studies of poetry which I have mentioned. Mr. Burke's phrase, "language as symbolic action," expresses the idea, and so does his dictum: "The poet spontaneously knows that 'beauty *is* as beauty *does*' (that the 'state' must be embodied in an 'actualization')." (*Four Tropes.*)

This idea of action, and of the play as the imitation of an action, is ultimately derived from the *Poetics*. This derivation is explained in the Appendix. At this point I wish to show how the complex form of *Oedipus*—its plot, characters, and discourse

*The essay on *Othello*.

35

—may be understood as the imitation of a certain action.

The action of the play is the quest for Laius' slayer. That is the over-all aim which informs it—"to find the culprit in order to purify human life," as it may be put. Sophocles must have seen this seeking action as the real life of the Oedipus myth, discerning it through the personages and events as one discerns "life in a plant through the green leaves." Moreover, he must have seen this particular action as a type, or crucial instance, of human life in general; and hence he was able to present it in the form of the ancient ritual which also presents and celebrates the perennial mystery of human life and action. Thus by "action" I do not mean the events of the story but the focus or aim of psychic life from which the events, in that situation, result.

If Sophocles was imitating action in this sense, one may schematically imagine his work of composition in three stages, three mimetic acts: 1. He makes the plot: i.e., arranges the events of the story in such a way as to reveal the seeking action from which they come. 2. He develops the characters of the story as individualized forms of "quest." 3. He expresses or realizes their actions by means of the words they utter in the various situations of the plot. This scheme, of course, has nothing to do with the temporal order which the poet may really have followed in elaborating his composition, nor to the order we follow in becoming acquainted with it; we start with the words, the "green leaves." The scheme refers to the "hierarchy of actualizations" which we may eventually learn to see in the completed work.

1. The first act of imitation consists in making the plot or arrangement of incidents. Aristotle says that the tragic poet is primarily a maker of plots, for the plot is the "soul of a tragedy," its formal cause. The arrangement which Sophocles made of the events of the story—starting near the end, and rehearsing the past in relation to what is happening now—already to some degree actualizes the tragic quest he wishes to show, even before we sense the characters as individuals or hear them speak and sing.

(The reader must be warned that this conception of the plot is rather unfamiliar to us. Usually we do not distinguish between the plot as the form of the play and the plot as producing a cer-

36

tain effect upon the audience—excitement, "interest," suspense, and the like. Aristotle also uses "plot" in this second sense. The mimicry of art has a further purpose, or final—as distinguished from its formal—cause, i.e., to reach the audience. Thinking of the Athenian theater, he describes the plot as intended to show the "universal," or to rouse and purge the emotions of pity and terror. These two meanings of the word—the form of the action, and the device for reaching the audience—are also further explained in the Appendix. At this point I am using the word *plot* in the first sense: as the form, the first actualization, of the tragic action.)

2. The characters, or agents, are the second actualization of the action. According to Aristotle, "the agents are imitated mainly with a view to the action"—i.e., the soul of the tragedy is there already in the order of events, the tragic rhythm of the life of Oedipus and Thebes; but this action may be more sharply realized and more elaborately shown forth by developing individual variations upon it. It was with this principle in mind that Ibsen wrote to his publisher, after two years' of work on *The Wild Duck,* that the play was nearly complete, and he could now proceed to "the more energetic individuation of the characters."

If one considers the Oedipus-Tiresias scene which I have quoted, one can see how the characters serve to realize the action of the whole. They reveal, at any moment, a "spectrum of action" like that which the tragic rhythm spread before us in temporal succession, at the same time offering concrete instances of almost photographic sharpness. Thus Tiresias "suffers" in the darkness of his blindness while Oedipus pursues his reasoned "purpose"; and then Tiresias effectuates his "purpose" of serving his mantic vision of the truth, while Oedipus "suffers" a blinding passion of fear and anger. The agents also serve to move the action ahead, develop it in time, through their conflicts. The chorus meanwhile, in some respects between, in others deeper, than the antagonists, represents the interests of that resolution, that final chord of feeling, in which the end of the action, seen ironically and sympathetically as one, will be realized.

3. The third actualization is in the words of the play. The

37

seeking action which is the substance of the play is imitated first in the plot, second in the characters, and third in the words, concepts, and forms of discourse wherein the characters "actualize" their psychic life in its shifting forms, in response to the everchanging situations of the play. If one thinks of plotting, characterization, and poetry as successive "acts of imitation" by the author, one may also say that they constitute, in the completed work, a hierarchy of forms; and that the words of the play are its "highest individuation." They are the "green leaves" which we actually perceive; the product and the sign of the one "life of the plant" which, by an imaginative effort, one may divine behind them all.

At this point one encounters again Mr. Burke's theory of "language as symbolic action," and the many contemporary studies of the arts of poetry which have been made from this point of view. It would be appropriate to offer a detailed study of Sophocles' language, using the modern tools of analysis, to substantiate my main point. But this would require the kind of knowledge of Greek which a Jebb spent his life to acquire; and I must be content to try to show, in very general terms, that the varied forms of the poetry of *Oedipus* can only be understood on a histrionic basis: i.e., as coming out of a direct sense of the tragic rhythm of *action*.

In the Oedipus-Tiresias scene, there is a "spectrum of the forms of discourse" corresponding to the "spectrum of action" which I have described. It extends from Oedipus' opening speech—a reasoned exposition not, of course, without feeling but based essentially upon clear ideas and a logical order—to the choral chant, based upon sensuous imagery and the "logic of feeling." Thus it employs, in the beginning, the principle of composition which Mr. Burke calls "syllogistic progression," and, at the other end of the spectrum, Mr. Burke's "progression by association and contrast." When the Neoclassic and rationalistic critics of the seventeenth century read *Oedipus*, they saw only the order of reason; they did not know what to make of the chorus. Hence Racine's drama of "Action as Rational": a drama of static situations, of clear concepts and merely illustrative images. Nietzsche, on the other hand, saw only the passion of

38

92

the chorus; for his insight was based on *Tristan*, which is composed essentially in sensuous images, and moves by association and contrast according to the logic of feeling: the drama which takes "action as passion." Neither point of view enables one to see how the scene, as a whole, hangs together.

If the speeches of the characters and the songs of the chorus are only the foliage of the plant, this is as much as to say that the life and meaning of the whole is never literally and completely present in any one formulation. It takes *all* of the elements—the shifting situation, the changing and developing characters, and their reasoned or lyric utterances, to indicate, in the round, the action Sophocles wishes to convey. Because this action takes the form of reason as well as passion, and of contemplation by way of symbols; because it is essentially moving (in the tragic rhythm); and because it is shared in different ways by all the characters, the play has neither literal unity nor the rational unity of the truly abstract idea, or "univocal concept." Its parts and its moments are one only "by analogy"; and just as the Saints warn us that we must believe in order to understand, so we must "make believe," by a sympathetic and imitative act of the histrionic sensibility, in order to get what Sophocles intended by his play.

It is the histrionic basis of Sophocles' art which makes it mysterious to us, with our demands for conceptual clarity, or for the luxury of yielding to a stream of feeling and subjective imagery. But it is this also which makes it so crucial an instance of the art of the theater in its completeness, as though the author understood "song, spectacle, thought, and diction" in their primitive and subtle roots. And it is the histrionic basis of drama which "undercuts theology and science."

Analogues of the "Tragic Rhythm"

In the present study I propose to use *Oedipus* as a landmark, and to relate subsequent forms of drama to it. For it presents a moving image at the nascent moment of highest valency, of a way of life and action which is still at the root of our culture.

Professor Buchanan remarks, in *Poetry and Mathematics*, that the deepest and most elaborate development of the tragic

39

93

rhythm is to be found in the *Divine Comedy*. The *Purgatorio* especially, though an epic and not a drama, evidently moves in the tragic rhythm, both as a whole and in detail. The daylight climb up the mountain, by moral effort, and in the light of natural reason, corresponds to the first moment, that of "purpose." The night, under the sign of Faith, Hope and Charity, when the Pilgrim can do nothing by his own unaided efforts, corresponds to the moments of passion and perception. The Pilgrim, as he pauses, mulls over the thoughts and experiences of the day; he sleeps and dreams, seeing ambivalent images from the mythic dreaming of the race, which refer, also, both to his own "suppressed desires" and to his own deepest aspirations. These images gradually solidify and clarify, giving place to a new perception of his situation. This rhythm, repeated in varied forms, carries the Pilgrim from the superficial but whole-hearted motivations of childhood, in the Antipurgatorio, through the divided counsels of the growing soul, to the new innocence, freedom, and integrity of the Terrestrial Paradise—the realm of *The Tempest* or of *Oedipus at Colonos*. The same rhythmic conception governs also the detail of the work, down to the *terza rima* itself—that verse-form which is clear at any moment in its literal fiction yet essentially moving ahead and pointing to deeper meanings.

Because Dante keeps his eye always upon the tragic moving of the psyche itself, his vision, like that of Sophocles, is not limited by any of the forms of thought whereby we seek to fix our experience—in which we are idolatrously expiring, like the coral animal in its shell. But Professor Buchanan shows that the abstract shape, at least, of the tragic rhythm is to be recognized in other and more limited or specialized cultural forms as well. "This pattern," he writes, "is the Greek view of life. It is the method of their and our science, history and philosophy. . . . The Greek employment of it had been humanistic in the main. . . . The late Middle Ages and the Renaissance substituted natural objects for the heroes of vicarious tragedies, the experiments in the laboratory. They put such objects under controlled conditions, introduced artificial complications, and waited for the answering pronouncement of fate. The crucial experiment is the

40

crisis of an attempt to rationalize experience, that is, to force it into our analogies. Purgation and recognition are now called elimination of false hypotheses and verification. The shift is significant, but the essential tragic pattern of tragedy is still there."

The tragic rhythm is, in a sense, the shape of Racinian tragedy, even though Racine was imitating action as essentially rational, and would have called the moments of the rhythm exposition, complication, crisis, and denouement, to satisfy the reason. It is in a way the shape of *Tristan*, though action in that play is reduced to passion, the principles of composition to the logic of feeling. Even the over-all shape of *Hamlet* is similar, though the sense of pathos predominates, and the whole is elaborated in such subtle profusion as can only be explained with reference to Dante and the Middle Ages.

The next two chapters are devoted respectively to *Bérénice* and *Tristan*. It is true that neither Racine nor Wagner understood the dramatic art in the exact spirit of Aristotle's definition, "the *imitation* of action." Wagner was rather expressing an emotion, and Racine was *demonstrating* an essence. But expression of emotion and rational demonstration may themselves be regarded as modes of action, each analogous to one moment in Sophocles' tragic rhythm.

CHAPTER I

THE MYTH OF ADONIS

THE spectacle of the great changes which annually pass over the face of the earth has powerfully impressed the minds of men in all ages, and stirred them to meditate on the causes of transformations so vast and wonderful. Their curiosity has not been purely disinterested ; for even the savage cannot fail to perceive how intimately his own life is bound up with the life of nature, and how the same processes which freeze the stream and strip the earth of vegetation menace him with extinction. At a certain stage of development men seem to have imagined that the means of averting the threatened calamity were in their own hands, and that they could hasten or retard the flight of the seasons by magic art. Accordingly they performed ceremonies and recited spells to make the rain to fall, the sun to shine, animals to multiply, and the fruits of the earth to grow. In course of time the slow advance of knowledge, which has dispelled so many cherished illusions, convinced at least the more thoughtful portion of mankind that the alternations of summer and winter, of spring and autumn, were not merely the result of their own magical rites, but that some deeper cause, some mightier power, was at work behind the shifting scenes of nature. They now pictured to themselves the growth and decay of vegetation, the birth and death of living creatures, as effects of the waxing or waning strength of divine beings, of gods and goddesses, who were born and died, who married and begot children, on the pattern of human life.

3

97

Magical
ceremonies
to revive
the failing
energies of
the gods.

Thus the old magical theory of the seasons was displaced, or rather supplemented, by a religious theory. For although men now attributed the annual cycle of change primarily to corresponding changes in their deities, they still thought that by performing certain magical rites they could aid the god, who was the principle of life, in his struggle with the opposing principle of death. They imagined that they could recruit his failing energies and even raise him from the dead. The ceremonies which they observed for this purpose were in substance a dramatic representation of the natural processes which they wished to facilitate ; for it is a familiar tenet of magic that you can produce any desired effect by merely imitating it. And as they now explained the fluctuations of growth and decay, of reproduction and dissolution, by the marriage, the death, and the rebirth or revival of the gods, their religious or rather magical dramas turned in great measure on these themes. They set forth the fruitful union of the powers of fertility, the sad death of one at least of the divine partners, and his joyful resurrection. Thus a religious theory was blended with a magical practice. The combination is familiar in history. Indeed, few religions have ever succeeded in wholly extricating themselves from the old trammels of magic. The inconsistency of acting on two opposite principles, however it may vex the soul of the philosopher, rarely troubles the common man ; indeed he is seldom even aware of it. His affair is to act, not to analyse the motives of his action. If mankind had always been logical and wise, history would not be a long chronicle of folly and crime.[1]

---

[1] As in the present volume I am concerned with the beliefs and practices of Orientals I may quote the following passage from one who has lived long in the East and knows it well : " The Oriental mind is free from the trammels of logic. It is a literal fact that the Oriental mind can accept and believe two opposite things at the same time. We find fully qualified and even learned Indian doctors practising Greek medicine, as well as English medicine, and enforcing sanitary restrictions to which their own houses and families are entirely strangers. We find astronomers who can predict eclipses, and yet who believe that eclipses are caused by a dragon swallowing the sun. We find holy men who are credited with miraculous powers and with close communion with the Deity, who live in drunkenness and immorality, and who are capable of elaborate frauds on others. To the Oriental mind, a thing must be incredible to command a ready belief " (" Riots and Unrest in the Punjab, from a corre-

Of the changes which the seasons bring with them, the most striking within the temperate zone are those which affect vegetation. The influence of the seasons on animals, though great, is not nearly so manifest. Hence it is natural that in the magical dramas designed to dispel winter and bring back spring the emphasis should be laid on vegetation, and that trees and plants should figure in them more prominently than beasts and birds. Yet the two sides of life, the vegetable and the animal, were not dissociated in the minds of those who observed the ceremonies. Indeed they commonly believed that the tie between the animal and the vegetable world was even closer than it really is ; hence they often combined the dramatic representation of reviving plants with a real or a dramatic union of the sexes for the purpose of furthering at the same time and by the same act the multiplication of fruits, of animals, and of men. To them the principle of life and fertility, whether animal or vegetable, was one and indivisible. To live and to cause to live, to eat food and to beget children, these were the primary wants of men in the past, and they will be the primary wants of men in the future so long as the world lasts. Other things may be added to enrich and beautify human life, but unless these wants are first satisfied, humanity itself must cease to exist. These two things, therefore, food and children, were what men chiefly sought to procure by the performance of magical rites for the regulation of the seasons.

Nowhere, apparently, have these rites been more widely

The principles of animal and of vegetable life confused in these ceremonies.

---

spondent," *The Times Weekly Edition*, May 24, 1907, p. 326). Again, speaking of the people of the Lower Congo, an experienced missionary describes their religious ideas as "chaotic in the extreme and impossible to reduce to any systematic order. The same person will tell you at different times that the departed spirit goes to the nether regions, or to a dark forest, or to the moon, or to the sun. There is no coherence in their beliefs, and their ideas about cosmogony and the future are very nebulous. Although they believe in punishment after death their faith is so hazy that it has lost all its deterrent force. If in the following pages a lack of logical unity is observed, it must be put to the debit of the native mind, as that lack of logical unity really represents the mistiness of their views." See Rev. John H. Weeks, "Notes on some Customs of the Lower Congo People," *Folk-lore*, xx. (1909) pp. 54 *sq.* Unless we allow for this innate capacity of the human mind to entertain contradictory beliefs at the same time, we shall in vain attempt to understand the history of thought in general and of religion in particular.

Prevalence
of these
rites in
Western
Asia and
Egypt.
and solemnly celebrated than in the lands which border the
Eastern Mediterranean. Under the names of Osiris, Tammuz, Adonis, and Attis, the peoples of Egypt and Western
Asia represented the yearly decay and revival of life,
especially of vegetable life, which they personified as a god
who annually died and rose again from the dead. In name
and detail the rites varied from place to place : in substance
they were the same. The supposed death and resurrection of this oriental deity, a god of many names but of
essentially one nature, is the subject of the present inquiry.
We begin with Tammuz or Adonis.[1]

Tammuz
or Adonis
in Babylonia.
The worship of Adonis was practised by the Semitic
peoples of Babylonia and Syria, and the Greeks borrowed it
from them as early as the seventh century before Christ.[2]
The true name of the deity was Tammuz : the appellation
of Adonis is merely the Semitic *Adon*, "lord," a title of
honour by which his worshippers addressed him.[3] In the
Hebrew text of the Old Testament the same name Adonai,

---

[1] The equivalence of Tammuz and
Adonis has been doubted or denied by
some scholars, as by Renan (*Mission de
Phénicie*, Paris, 1864, pp. 216, 235)
and by Chwolsohn (*Die Ssabier und
der Ssabismus*, St. Petersburg, 1856,
ii. 510). But the two gods are identified by Origen (*Selecta in Ezechielem*,
Migne's *Patrologia Graeca*, xiii. 797),
Jerome (*Epist.* lviii. 3 and *Commentar.
in Ezechielem*, *viii. 13, 14*, Migne's
Patrologia Latina, xxii. 581, xxv. 82),
Cyril of Alexandria (*In Isaiam*, lib. ii.
tomus. iii., and *Comment. on Hosea*,
iv. 15, Migne's *Patrologia Graeca*, lxx.
441, lxxi. 136), Theodoretus (*In
Ezechielis cap. viii.*, Migne's *Patrologia
Graeca*, lxxxi. 885), the author of the
Paschal Chronicle (Migne's *Patrologia
Graeca*, xcii. 329) and Melito (in W.
Cureton's *Spicilegium Syriacum*, London, 1855, p. 44) : and accordingly
we may fairly conclude that, whatever their remote origin may have
been, Tammuz and Adonis were in the
later period of antiquity practically
equivalent to each other. Compare
W. W. Graf Baudissin, *Studien zur
semitischen Religionsgeschichte* (Leipsic,
1876 1878), i. 299 ; *id.*, in *Realency-*

*clopädie für protestantische Theologie
und Kirchengeschichte*,[3] *s.v.* "Tammuz" ; *id., Adonis und Esmun* (Leipsic,
1911), pp. 94 *sqq.* ; W. Mannhardt,
Antike Wald- und Feldkulte (Berlin,
1877), pp. 273 *sqq.* ; Ch. Vellay, "Le
dieu Thammuz," *Revue de l'Histoire
des Religions*, xlix. (1904) pp. 154-162.
Baudissin holds that Tammuz and
Adonis were two different gods sprung
from a common root (*Adonis und
Esmun*, p. 368). An Assyrian origin
of the cult of Adonis was long ago
affirmed by Macrobius (*Sat.* i. 21. 1).
On Adonis and his worship in general
see also F. C. Movers, *Die Phoenizier*,
i. (Bonn, 1841) pp. 191 *sqq.*; W. H.
Engel, *Kypros* (Berlin, 1841), ii. 536
sqq.; Ch. Vellay, *Le culte et les fêtes
d'Adonis-Thammouz dans l'Orient
antique* (Paris, 1904).

[2] The mourning for Adonis is mentioned by Sappho, who flourished about
600 B.C. See Th. Bergk's *Poetae Lyrici
Graeci*,[3] iii. (Leipsic, 1867) p. 897 ;
Pausanias, ix. 29. 8.

[3] Ed. Meyer, *Geschichte des Alter-
tums*,[2] i. 2 (Berlin, 1909), pp. 394 *sq.*;
W. W. Graf Baudissin, *Adonis und
Esmun*, pp. 65 *sqq.*

originally perhaps Adoni, " my lord," is often applied to Jehovah.[1] But the Greeks through a misunderstanding converted the title of honour into a proper name. While Tammuz or his equivalent Adonis enjoyed a wide and lasting popularity among peoples of the Semitic stock, there are grounds for thinking that his worship originated with a race of other blood and other speech, the Sumerians, who in the dawn of history inhabited the flat alluvial plain at the head of the Persian Gulf and created the civilization which was afterwards called Babylonian. The origin and affinities of this people are unknown ; in physical type and language they differed from all their neighbours, and their isolated position, wedged in between alien races, presents to the student of mankind problems of the same sort as the isolation of the Basques and Etruscans among the Aryan peoples of Europe. An ingenious, but unproved, hypothesis would represent them as immigrants driven from central Asia by that gradual desiccation which for ages seems to have been converting once fruitful lands into a waste and burying the seats of ancient civilization under a sea of shifting sand. Whatever their place of origin may have been, it is certain that in Southern Babylonia the Sumerians attained at a very early period to a considerable pitch of civilization ; for they tilled the soil, reared cattle, built cities, dug canals, and even invented a system of writing, which their Semitic neighbours in time borrowed from them.[2] In the pantheon

His worship seems to have originated with the Sumerians.

---

[1] *Encyclopaedia Biblica*, ed. T. K. Cheyne and J. S. Black, iii. 3327. In the Old Testament the title *Adoni*, " my lord," is frequently given to men. See, for example, Genesis xxxiii. 8, 13, 14, 15, xlii. 10, xliii. 20, xliv. 5, 7, 9, 16, 18, 19, 20, 22, 24.

[2] C. P. Tiele, *Geschichte der Religion im Altertum* (Gotha, 1896-1903), i. 134 *sqq.* ; G. Maspero, *Histoire Ancienne des Peuples de l'Orient Classique, les Origines* (Paris, 1895), pp. 550 *sq.* ; L. W. King, *Babylonian Religion and Mythology* (London, 1899), pp. 1 *sqq.*; id., *A History of Sumer and Akkad* (London, 1910), pp. 1 *sqq.*, 40 *sqq.*: H. Winckler, in E. Schrader's *Die Keilinschriften und das alte Testament*[3] (Berlin, 1902),

pp. 10 *sq.*, 349 ; Fr. Hommel, *Grundriss der Geographie und Geschichte des alten Orients* (Munich, 1904), pp. 18 *sqq.*; Ed. Meyer, *Geschichte des Altertums*,[2] i. 2 (Berlin, 1909), pp. 401 *sqq.* As to the hypothesis that the Sumerians were immigrants from Central Asia, see L. W. King, *History of Sumer and Akkad*, pp. 351 *sqq.* The gradual desiccation of Central Asia, which is conjectured to have caused the Sumerian migration, has been similarly invoked to explain the downfall of the Roman empire ; for by rendering great regions uninhabitable it is supposed to have driven hordes of fierce barbarians to find new homes in Europe. See Professor J. W. Gregory's lecture " Is the earth drying up ? "

of this ancient people Tammuz appears to have been one of the oldest, though certainly not one of the most important figures.[1] His name consists of a Sumerian phrase meaning "true son" or, in a fuller form, "true son of the deep water,"[2] and among the inscribed Sumerian texts which have survived the wreck of empires are a number of hymns in his honour, which were written down not later than about two thousand years before our era but were almost certainly composed at a much earlier time.[3]

Tammuz the lover of Ishtar.

In the religious literature of Babylonia Tammuz appears as the youthful spouse or lover of Ishtar, the great mother goddess, the embodiment of the reproductive energies of nature. The references to their connexion with each other in myth and ritual are both fragmentary and obscure, but we gather from them that every year Tammuz was believed to die, passing away from the cheerful earth to the gloomy subterranean world, and that every year his divine mistress journeyed in quest of him "to the land from which there is no returning, to the house of darkness, where dust lies on door and bolt." During her absence the passion of love ceased to operate : men and beasts alike forgot to reproduce their kinds : all life was threatened with extinction. So

Descent of Ishtar to the nether world to recover Tammuz.

---

delivered before the Royal Geographical Society and reported in *The Times*, December 9th, 1913. It is held by Prof. Hommel (*op. cit.* pp. 19 *sqq.*) that the Sumerian language belongs to the Ural-altaic family, but the better opinion seems to be that its linguistic affinities are unknown. The view, once ardently advocated, that Sumerian was not a language but merely a cabalistic mode of writing Semitic, is now generally exploded.

[1] H. Zimmern, "Der babylonische Gott Tamuz," *Abhandlungen der philologisch-historischen Klasse der Königl. Sächsischen Gesellschaft der Wissenschaften*, xxvii. No. xx. (Leipsic, 1909) pp. 701, 722.

[2] *Dumu-zi*, or in fuller form *Dumu-zi-absu*. See P. Jensen, *Assyrisch-Babylonische Mythen und Epen* (Berlin, 1900), p. 560 ; H. Zimmern, *op. cit.* pp. 703 *sqq.* ; *id.*, in E. Schrader's

Die Keilinschriften und das Alte Testament[3] (Berlin, 1902), p. 397 ; P. Dhorme, *La Religion Assyro-Babylonienne* (Paris, 1910), p. 105 ; W. W. Graf Baudissin, *Adonis und Esmun* (Leipsic, 1911), p. 104.

[3] H. Zimmern, "Der babylonische Gott Tamuz," *Abhandl. d. Kön. Sächs. Gesellschaft der Wissenschaften*, xxvii. No. xx. (Leipsic, 1909) p. 723. For the text and translation of the hymns, see H. Zimmern, "Sumerisch-babylonische Tamūzlieder," *Berichte über die Verhandlungen der Königlich Sächsischen Gesellschaft der Wissenschaften zu Leipzig, Philologisch-historische Klasse*, lix. (1907) pp. 201-252. Compare H. Gressmann, *Altorientalische Texte und Bilder* (Tübingen, 1909), i. 93 *sqq.*; W. W. Graf Baudissin, *Adonis und Esmun* (Leipsic, 1911), pp. 99 *sq.*; R. W. Rogers, *Cuneiform Parallels to the Old Testament* (Oxford, N.D.), pp. 179-185.

intimately bound up with the goddess were the sexual functions of the whole animal kingdom that without her presence they could not be discharged. A messenger of the great god Ea was accordingly despatched to rescue the goddess on whom so much depended. The stern queen of the infernal regions, Allatu or Eresh-Kigal by name, reluctantly allowed Ishtar to be sprinkled with the Water of Life and to depart, in company probably with her lover Tammuz, that the two might return together to the upper world, and that with their return all nature might revive.

Laments for the departed Tammuz are contained in several Babylonian hymns, which liken him to plants that quickly fade. He is

Laments for Tammuz

> " *A tamarisk that in the garden has drunk no water,*
> *Whose crown in the field has brought forth no blossom.*
> *A willow that rejoiced not by the watercourse,*
> *A willow whose roots were torn up.*
> *A herb that in the garden had drunk no water.*"

His death appears to have been annually mourned, to the shrill music of flutes, by men and women about midsummer in the month named after him, the month of Tammuz. The dirges were seemingly chanted over an effigy of the dead god, which was washed with pure water, anointed with oil, and clad in a red robe, while the fumes of incense rose into the air, as if to stir his dormant senses by their pungent fragrance and wake him from the sleep of death. In one of these dirges, inscribed *Lament of the Flutes for Tammuz,* we seem still to hear the voices of the singers chanting the sad refrain and to catch, like far-away music, the wailing notes of the flutes :—

> " *At his vanishing away she lifts up a lament,*
>   '*Oh my child!* ' *at his vanishing away she lifts up a lament;*
> '*My Damu!* ' *at his vanishing away she lifts up a lament.*
>   '*My enchanter and priest!* ' *at his vanishing away she lifts up a lament,*
> *At the shining cedar, rooted in a spacious place,*
>   *In Eanna, above and below, she lifts up a lament.*
> *Like the lament that a house lifts up for its master, lifts she up a lament,*
>   *Like the lament that a city lifts up for its lord, lifts she up a lament.*

Her lament is the lament for a herb that grows not in the bed,
Her lament is the lament for the corn that grows not in the ear.
Her chamber is a possession that brings not forth a possession,
A weary woman, a weary child, forspent.
Her lament is for a great river, where no willows grow,
Her lament is for a field, where corn and herbs grow not.
Her lament is for a pool, where fishes grow not.
Her lament is for a thicket of reeds, where no reeds grow.
Her lament is for woods, where tamarisks grow not.
Her lament is for a wilderness where no cypresses (?) grow.
Her lament is for the depth of a garden of trees, where honey and wine
    grow not.
Her lament is for meadows, where no plants grow.
Her lament is for a palace, where length of life grows not." [1]

Adonis
a Greek
mythology
merely a

The tragical story and the melancholy rites of Adonis are better known to us from the descriptions of Greek writers than from the fragments of Babylonian literature or

---

[1] A. Jeremias, *Die babylonisch-as-syrischen Vorstellungen vom Leben nach dem Tode* (Leipsic, 1887), pp. 4 *sqq.*; *id.*, in W. H. Roscher's *Lexikon der griech. und röm. Mythologie*, ii. 808, iii. 258 *sqq.*; M. Jastrow, *The Religion of Babylonia and Assyria* (Boston, 1898), pp. 565-576, 584, 682 *sq.*; W. L. King, *Babylonian Religion and Mythology*, pp. 178-183; P. Jensen, *Assyrisch-babylonische Mythen und Epen*, pp. 81 *sqq.*, 95 *sqq.*, 169; R. F. Harper, *Assyrian and Babylonian Literature* (New York, 1901), pp. 316 *sq.*, 338, 408 *sqq.*; H. Zimmern, in E. Schrader's *Die Keilinschriften und das Alte Testament*,[3] pp. 397 *sqq.*, 561 *sqq.*; *id.*, "Sumerisch-babylonische Tamûzlieder," *Berichte über die Verhandlungen der Königlich Sächsischen Gesellschaft der Wissenschaften zu Leipzig, Philologisch-historische Klasse*, lix. (1907) pp. 220, 232, 230 *sq.*; *id.*, "Der babylonische Gott Tamûz," *Abhandlungen der philologisch-historischen Klasse der Königl. Sächsischen Gesellschaft der Wissenschaften*, xxvii. No. xx. (Leipsic, 1909) pp. 725 *sq.*, 729-735; H. Gressmann, *Altorientalische Texte und Bilder zum Alten Testamente* (Tübingen, 1909), i. 65 *sq.*; R. W. Rogers, *Cuneiform Parallels to the Old Testament* (Oxford, N.D.), pp. 121-131; W. W. Graf Baudissin, *Adonis und*

Esmun (Leipsic, 1911), pp. 99 *sqq.*, 353 *sqq.* According to Jerome (on Ezekiel viii. 14) the month of Tammuz was June; but according to modern scholars it corresponded rather to July, or to part of June and part of July. See F. C. Movers, *Die Phoenizier*, i. 210; F. Lenormant, "Il mito di Adone-Tammuz nei documenti cuneiformi," *Atti del IV. Congresso Internazionale degli Orientalisti* (Florence, 1880), i. 144 *sq.*; W. Mannhardt, *Antike Wald- und Feldkulte*, p. 275; *Encyclopaedia Biblica*, s.v. "Months," iii. 3194. My friend W. Robertson Smith informed me that owing to the variations of the local Syrian calendars the month of Tammuz fell in different places at different times, from midsummer to autumn, or from June to September. According to Prof. M. Jastrow, the festival of Tammuz was celebrated just before the summer solstice (*The Religion of Babylonia and Assyria*, pp. 547, 682). He observes that "the calendar of the Jewish Church still marks the 17th day of Tammuz as a fast, and Houtsma has shown that the association of the day with the capture of Jerusalem by the Romans represents merely the attempt to give an ancient festival a worthier interpretation."

the brief reference of the prophet Ezekiel, who saw the reflection of the Oriental Tammuz.
women of Jerusalem weeping for Tammuz at the north gate
of the temple.[1] Mirrored in the glass of Greek mythology,
the oriental deity appears as a comely youth beloved by
Aphrodite. In his infancy the goddess hid him in a chest,
which she gave in charge to Persephone, queen of the nether
world. But when Persephone opened the chest and beheld
the beauty of the babe, she refused to give him back to
Aphrodite, though the goddess of love went down herself to
hell to ransom her dear one from the power of the grave.
The dispute between the two goddesses of love and death
was settled by Zeus, who decreed that Adonis should abide
with Persephone in the under world for one part of the year,
and with Aphrodite in the upper world for another part.
At last the fair youth was killed in hunting by a wild boar,
or by the jealous Ares, who turned himself into the likeness
of a boar in order to compass the death of his rival.
Bitterly did Aphrodite lament her loved and lost Adonis.[2]
The strife between the divine rivals for the possession of
Adonis appears to be depicted on an Etruscan mirror. The
two goddesses, identified by inscriptions, are stationed on
either side of Jupiter, who occupies the seat of judgment
and lifts an admonitory finger as he looks sternly towards
Persephone. Overcome with grief the goddess of love buries
her face in her mantle, while her pertinacious rival, grasping
a branch in one hand, points with the other at a closed
coffer, which probably contains the youthful Adonis.[3] In

[1] Ezekiel viii. 14.

[2] Apollodorus, *Bibliotheca*, iii. 14.
4 ; Bion, *Idyl*, i. ; J. Tzetzes, *Schol.
on Lycophron*, 831 ; Ovid. *Metam*. x.
503 *sqq.* ; Aristides, *Apology*, edited
by J. Rendel Harris (Cambridge,
1891), pp. 44, 106 *sq.* In Babylonian
texts relating to Tammuz no reference
has yet been found to death by a boar.
See H. Zimmern, "Sumerisch-babylonische Tammuzlieder," p. 451 ; *id.*,
"Der babylonische Gott Tammuz," p.
731. Baudissin inclines to think that
the incident of the boar is a late impor-
tation into the myth of Adonis. See
his *Adonis und Esmun*, pp. 142 *sqq.*
As to the relation of the boar to the

kindred gods Adonis, Attis, and Osiris
see *Spirits of the Corn and of the Wild*,
ii. 22 *sqq.*, where I have suggested
that the idea of the boar as the foe of
the god may be based on the terrible
ravages which wild pigs notoriously
commit in fields of corn.

[3] W. W. Graf Baudissin, *Adonis
und Esmun* (Leipsic, 1911), pp. 152
sq., with plate iv. As to the representation of the myth of Adonis on
Etruscan mirrors and late works of
Roman art, especially sarcophaguses
and wall-paintings, see Otto Jahn,
Archäologische Beiträge (Berlin, 1847),
pp. 45-51.

this form of the myth, the contest between Aphrodite and Persephone for the possession of Adonis clearly reflects the struggle between Ishtar and Allatu in the land of the dead, while the decision of Zeus that Adonis is to spend one part of the year under ground and another part above ground is merely a Greek version of the annual disappearance and reappearance of Tammuz.

CHAPTER IX

THE RITUAL OF ADONIS

THUS far we have dealt with the myth of Adonis and the legends which associated him with Byblus and Paphos. A discussion of these legends led us to the conclusion that among Semitic peoples in early times, Adonis, the divine lord of the city, was often personated by priestly kings or other members of the royal family, and that these his human representatives were of old put to death, whether periodically or occasionally, in their divine character. Further, we found that certain traditions and monuments of Asia Minor seem to preserve traces of a similar practice. As time went on, the cruel custom was apparently mitigated in various ways; for example, by substituting an effigy or an animal for the man, or by allowing the destined victim to escape with a merely make-believe sacrifice. The evidence of all this is drawn from a variety of scattered and often ambiguous indications: it is fragmentary, it is uncertain, and the conclusions built upon it inevitably partake of the weakness of the foundation. Where the records are so imperfect, as they happen to be in this branch of our subject, the element of hypothesis must enter largely into any attempt to piece together and interpret the disjointed facts. How far the interpretations here proposed are sound, I leave to future inquiries to determine.

From dim regions of the past, where we have had to grope our way with small help from the lamp of history, it is a relief to pass to those later periods of classical antiquity on which contemporary Greek writers have shed the light of their clear intelligence. To them we owe almost all that we know for certain about the rites of Adonis. The Semites who practised the worship have said little about it; at all events little that they said has come down to us. Accordingly, the following account of the ritual is derived mainly from Greek authors who saw what they describe; and it applies to ages in which the growth of humane feeling had softened some of the harsher features of the worship.

At the festivals of Adonis, which were held in Western Asia and in Greek lands, the death of the god was annually mourned, with a bitter wailing, chiefly by women; images of him, dressed to resemble corpses, were carried out as to burial and then thrown into the sea or into springs;[1] and in some places his revival was celebrated on the following day.[2] But at different places the ceremonies varied somewhat in the manner and apparently also in the season of their celebration. At Alexandria images of Aphrodite and Adonis were displayed on two couches; beside them were set ripe fruits of all kinds, cakes, plants growing in flower-pots, and green bowers twined with anise. The marriage of the lovers was celebrated one day, and on the morrow women attired as mourners, with streaming hair and bared

---

[1] Plutarch, *Alcibiades*, 18; id., *Nicias*, 13; Zenobius, *Centur.* i. 49; Theocritus, xv. 132 *sqq.*; Eustathius on Homer, *Od.* xi. 590.

[2] Besides Lucian (cited below) see Origen, *Selecta in Ezechielem* (Migne's *Patrologia Graeca*, xiii. 800), δοκοῦσι γὰρ κατ' ἐνιαυτὸν τελετάς τινας ποιεῖν πρῶτον μὲν ὅτι θρηνοῦσιν αὐτὸν [scil. Ἄδωνιν] ὡς τεθνηκότα, δεύτερον δὲ ὅτι χαίρουσιν ἐπ' αὐτῷ ὡς ἀπὸ νεκρῶν ἀναστάντι. Jerome, *Commentar. in Ezechielem*, viii. 13, 14 (Migne's *Patrologia Latina*, xxv. 82, 83): "Quem nos Adonidem interpretati sumus, et Hebraeus et Syrus sermo THAMUZ (תמוז) vocat: unde quia juxta gentilem fabulam, in mense Junis amasius Veneris et pulcherrimus juvenis occisus, et deinceps revixisse narratur, eundem Junium mensem eodem appellant nomine, et anniversariam ei celebrant solemni-tatem, in qua plangitur a mulieribus quasi mortuus, et postea reviviscens canitur atque laudatur . . . interfectionem et resurrectionem Adonidis planctu et gaudio prosequens." Cyril of Alexandria, *In Isaiam*, lib. ii. tomus iii. (Migne's *Patrologia Graeca*, lxx. 441), ἐπλάττοντο τοίνυν Ἕλληνες ἑορτὴν ἐπὶ τούτῳ τοιαύτην. Προσεποιοῦντο μὲν γὰρ λυπουμένῃ τῇ Ἀφροδίτῃ, διὰ τὸ τεθνάναι τὸν Ἄδωνιν, συνολοφύρεσθαι καὶ θρηνεῖν· ἀνελθούσης δὲ ἐξ ᾅδου, καὶ μὴν καὶ ηὑρῆσθαι λεγούσης τὸν ζητούμενον, συνήδεσθαι καὶ ἀνασκιρτᾶν· καὶ μέχρι τῶν καθ' ἡμᾶς καιρῶν ἐν τοῖς κατ' Ἀλεξάνδρειαν ἱεροῖς ἐτελεῖτο τὸ παίγνιον τοῦτο. From this testimony of Cyril we learn that the festival of the death and resurrection of Adonis was celebrated at Alexandria down to his time, that is, down to the fourth or even the fifth century, long after the official establishment of Christianity.

breasts, bore the image of the dead Adonis to the sea-shore and committed it to the waves. Yet they sorrowed not without hope, for they sang that the lost one would come back again.[1] The date at which this Alexandrian ceremony was observed is not expressly stated; but from the mention of the ripe fruits it has been inferred that it took place in late summer.[2] In the great Phoenician sanctuary of Astarte at Byblus the death of Adonis was annually mourned, to the shrill wailing notes of the flute, with weeping, lamentation, and beating of the breast; but next day he was believed to come to life again and ascend up to heaven in the presence of his worshippers. The disconsolate believers, left behind on earth, shaved their heads as the Egyptians did on the death of the divine bull Apis; women who could not bring themselves to sacrifice their beautiful tresses had to give themselves up to strangers on a certain day of the festival, and to dedicate to Astarte the wages of their shame.[3]

The festival at Byblus.

This Phoenician festival appears to have been a vernal one, for its date was determined by the discoloration of the river Adonis, and this has been observed by modern travellers to occur in spring. At that season the red earth washed down from the mountains by the rain tinges the water of the river, and even the sea, for a great way with a blood-red hue, and the crimson stain was believed to be the blood of Adonis, annually wounded to death by the boar on Mount Lebanon.[4] Again, the

Date of the festival at Byblus.

---

[1] Theocritus, xv.

[2] W. Mannhardt, *Antike Wald- und Feldkulte* (Berlin, 1877), p. 277.

[3] Lucian, *De dea Syria*, 6. See above, p. 38. The flutes used by the Phoenicians in the lament for Adonis are mentioned by Athenaeus (iv. 76, p. 174 F), and by Pollux (iv. 76), who say that the same name *gingras* was applied by the Phoenicians both to the flute and to Adonis himself. Compare F. C. Movers, *Die Phoenizier*, i. 243 *sq.* We have seen that flutes were also played in the Babylonian rites of Tammuz (above, p. 9). Lucian's words, ἐς τὸν ἠέρα πέμπουσι, imply that the ascension of the god was supposed to take place in the

presence, if not before the eyes, of the worshipping crowds. The devotion of Byblus to Adonis is noticed also by Strabo (xvi. 2. 18, p. 755).

[4] Lucian, *De dea Syria*, 8. The discoloration of the river and the sea was observed by H. Maundrell on $\frac{17}{27}$ March $\frac{1696}{1697}$. See his *Journey from Aleppo to Jerusalem, at Easter, A.D. 1697*, Fourth Edition (Perth, 1800), pp. 59 *sq.*; *id.*, in Bohn's *Early Travels in Palestine*, edited by Thomas Wright (London, 1848), pp. 411 *sq.* Renan remarked the discoloration at the beginning of February (*Mission de Phénicie*, p. 283). In his well-known lines on the subject

The anemone and the red rose the flowers of Adonis.

scarlet anemone is said to have sprung from the blood of Adonis, or to have been stained by it;[1] and as the anemone blooms in Syria about Easter, this may be thought to show that the festival of Adonis, or at least one of his festivals, was held in spring. The name of the flower is probably derived from Naaman ("darling"), which seems to have been an epithet of Adonis. The Arabs still call the anemone "wounds of the Naaman."[2] The red rose also was said to owe its hue to the same sad occasion; for Aphrodite, hastening to her wounded lover, trod on a bush of white roses; the cruel thorns tore her tender flesh, and her sacred blood dyed the white roses for ever red.[3] It would be idle, perhaps, to lay much weight on evidence drawn from the calendar of flowers, and in particular to press an argument so fragile as the bloom of the rose. Yet so far as it counts at all, the tale which links the damask rose with the death of Adonis points to a summer rather than to a spring celebration of his passion. In Attica, certainly, the festival fell at the height of summer. For the fleet which Athens fitted out against Syracuse, and by the destruction of which her power was permanently crippled, sailed at midsummer, and by an ominous coincidence the sombre rites of Adonis were being celebrated at the very time. As the troops marched down to the harbour to embark, the streets through which they passed were lined with coffins and corpse-like effigies, and the air was rent with the noise of women wailing for the dead Adonis. The circumstance cast a gloom over the sailing of the most splendid armament that Athens ever sent to sea.[4] Many

Festivals of Adonis at Athens and Antioch.

Milton has laid the mourning in summer :—

> " *Thammuz came next behind,*
> *Whose annual wound in Lebanon*
> *   allur'd*
> *The Syrian damsels to lament his fate*
> *In amorous ditties all a summer's day.*"

[1] Ovid, *Metam.* x. 735 ; Servius on Virgil, *Aen.* v. 72 ; J. Tzetzes, *Schol. on Lycophron*, 831. Bion, on the other hand, represents the anemone as sprung from the tears of Aphrodite (*Idyl.* i. 66).

[2] W. Robertson Smith, "Ctesias and the Semiramis Legend," *English*

Historical Review, ii. (1887) p. 307, following Lagarde. Compare W. W. Graf Baudissin, *Adonis und Esmun*, pp. 88 *sq.*

[3] J. Tzetzes, *Schol. on Lycophron*, 831 : *Geoponica*, xi. 17 ; *Mythographi Graeci*, ed. A. Westermann, p. 359. Compare Bion, *Idyl.* i. 66 ; Pausanias vi. 24. 7 ; Philostratus, *Epist.* i. and iii.

[4] Plutarch, *Alcibiades*, 18 ; *id.*, *Nicias*, 13. The date of the sailing of the fleet is given by Thucydides (vi. 30, θέρους μεσοῦντος ἤδη), who, with his habitual contempt for the supersti-

ages afterwards, when the Emperor Julian made his first entry into Antioch, he found in like manner the gay, the luxurious capital of the East plunged in mimic grief for the annual death of Adonis : and if he had any presentiment of coming evil, the voices of lamentation which struck upon his ear must have seemed to sound his knell.[1]

The resemblance of these ceremonies to the Indian and European ceremonies which I have described elsewhere is obvious. In particular, apart from the somewhat doubtful date of its celebration, the Alexandrian ceremony is almost identical with the Indian.[2] In both of them the marriage of two divine beings, whose affinity with vegetation seems indicated by the fresh plants with which they are surrounded, is celebrated in effigy, and the effigies are afterwards mourned over and thrown into the water.[3] From the similarity of these customs to each other and to the spring and midsummer customs of modern Europe we should naturally expect that they all admit of a common explanation. Hence, if the explanation which I have adopted of the latter is correct, the ceremony of the death and resurrection of Adonis must also have been a dramatic representation of the decay and revival of plant life. The inference thus based on the resemblance of the customs is confirmed by the following features in the legend and ritual of Adonis. His affinity with vegetation comes out at once in the common story of his birth. He was said to have been born from a myrrh-tree, the bark of which bursting, after a ten months' gestation, allowed the lovely infant to come forth. According to some, a boar rent the bark with his tusk and so opened a passage for the babe. A faint rationalistic colour was given to the legend by saying that his mother was a woman named Myrrh, who had been

Side notes: Resemblance of these rites to Indian and European ceremonies.

The death and resurrection of Adonis a mythical expression for the annual decay and revival of plant life.

---

tion of his countrymen, disdains to notice the coincidence. Adonis was also bewailed by the Argive women (Pausanias, ii. 20. 6), but we do not know at what season of the year the lamentation took place. Inscriptions prove that processions in honour of Adonis were held in the Piraeus, and that a society of his worshippers existed at Loryma in Caria. See G.

Dittenberger, *Sylloge Inscriptionum Graecarum*,[2] Nos. 726, 741 (vol. ii. pp. 564, 604).
[1] Ammianus Marcellinus, xxii. 9. 15.
[2] *The Dying God*, pp. 261-266.
[3] In the Alexandrian ceremony, however, it appears to have been the image of Adonis only which was thrown into the sea.

turned into a myrrh-tree soon after she had conceived the child.[1] The use of myrrh as incense at the festival of Adonis may have given rise to the fable.[2] We have seen that incense was burnt at the corresponding Babylonian rites,[3] just as it was burnt by the idolatrous Hebrews in honour of the Queen of Heaven,[4] who was no other than Astarte. Again, the story that Adonis spent half, or according to others a third, of the year in the lower world and the rest of it in the upper world,[5] is explained most simply and naturally by supposing that he represented vegetation, especially the corn, which lies buried in the earth half the year and reappears above ground the other half. Certainly of the annual phenomena of nature there is none which suggests so obviously the idea of death and resurrection as the disappearance and reappearance of vegetation in autumn and spring. Adonis has been taken for the sun; but there is nothing in the sun's annual course within the temperate and tropical zones to suggest that he is dead for half or a third of the year and alive for the other half or two-thirds. He might, indeed, be conceived as weakened in winter, but dead he could not be thought to be; his daily reappearance contradicts the supposition.[6] Within the Arctic Circle, where the sun annually disappears for a continuous period which varies from twenty-four hours to six months according to the latitude, his yearly death and resurrection would certainly be an obvious idea; but no one except the unfortunate

[1] Apollodorus, *Bibliotheca*, iii. 14.4; Scholiast on Theocritus, i. 109; Antoninus Liberalis, *Transform.* 34: J. Tzetzes, *Scholia on Lycophron*, 829; Ovid, *Metamorph.* x. 480 *sqq.*; Servius on Virgil, *Aen.* v. 72, and on *Bucol.* x. 18; Hyginus, *Fab.* 58, 164; Fulgentius, iii. 8. The word Myrrha or Smyrna is borrowed from the Phoenician (Liddell and Scott, *Greek Lexicon, s.v.* σμύρνα). Hence the mother's name, as well as the son's, was taken directly from the Semites.

[2] W. Mannhardt, *Antike Wald- und Feldkulte*, p. 383, note 2.

[3] Above, p. 9.

[4] Jeremiah xliv. 17-19.

[5] Scholiast on Theocritus, iii. 48; Hyginus, *Astronom.* ii. 7; Lucian, *Dialog. deor.* xi. 1; Cornutus, *Theologiae Graecae Compendium*, 28, p. 54, ed. C. Lang (Leipsic, 1881); Apollodorus, *Bibliotheca*, iii. 14. 4.

[6] The arguments which tell against the solar interpretation of Adonis are stated more fully by the learned and candid scholar Graf Baudissin (*Adonis und Esmun*, pp. 169 *sqq.*), who himself formerly accepted the solar theory but afterwards rightly rejected it in favour of the view "*dass Adonis die Frühlingsvegetation darstellt, die im Sommer abstirbt*" (*op. cit.* p. 169).

astronomer Bailly[1] has maintained that the Adonis worship came from the Arctic regions. On the other hand, the annual death and revival of vegetation is a conception which readily presents itself to men in every stage of savagery and civilization ; and the vastness of the scale on which this ever-recurring decay and regeneration takes place, together with man's intimate dependence on it for subsistence, combine to render it the most impressive annual occurrence in nature, at least within the temperate zones. It is no wonder that a phenomenon so important, so striking, and so universal should, by suggesting similar ideas, have given rise to similar rites in many lands. We may, therefore, accept as probable an explanation of the Adonis worship which accords so well with the facts of nature and with the analogy of similar rites in other lands. Moreover, the explanation is countenanced by a considerable body of opinion amongst the ancients themselves, who again and again interpreted the dying and reviving god as the reaped and sprouting grain.[2]

[1] Bailly, *Lettres sur l'Origine des Sciences* (London and Paris, 1777), pp. 255 *sq.* ; *id.*, *Lettres sur l'Atlantide de Platon* (London and Paris, 1779), pp. 114-125. Carlyle has described how through the sleety drizzle of a dreary November day poor innocent Bailly was dragged to the scaffold amid the howls and curses of the Parisian mob (*French Revolution*, bk. v. ch. 2). My friend the late Professor C. Bendall showed me a book by a Hindoo gentleman in which it is seriously maintained that the primitive home of the Aryans was within the Arctic regions. See Bâl Gangâdhâr Tilak, *The Arctic Home in the Vedas* (Poona and Bombay, 1903).

[2] Cornutus, *Theologiae Graecae Compendium*, 28, pp. 54 *sq.*, ed. C. Lang (Leipsic, 1881), τοιοῦτον γάρ τι καὶ παρ' Αἰγυπτίοις ὁ ζητούμενος καὶ ἀνευρισκόμενος ὑπὸ τῆς Ἴσιδος Ὄσιρις ἐμφαίνει καὶ παρὰ Φοίνιξιν ὁ ἀνὰ μέρος παρ' ἓξ μῆνας ὑπὲρ γῆν τε καὶ ὑπὸ γῆν γινόμενος Ἄδωνις, ἀπὸ τοῦ ἀδεῖν τοῖς ἀνθρώποις οὕτως ὠνομασμένου τοῦ Δημητριακοῦ καρποῦ. τοῦτον δὲ πλήξας

κάπρος ἀνελεῖν λέγεται διὰ τὸ τὰς ὗς δοκεῖν ληιβοτείρας εἶναι ἢ τὸν τῆς ὕνεως ὀδόντα αἰνιττομένων αὐτῶν, ὑφ' οὗ κατὰ γῆς κρύπτεται τὸ σπέρμα. Scholiast on Theocritus, iii. 48, ὁ Ἄδωνις, ἤγουν ὁ σῖτος ὁ σπειρόμενος, ἓξ μῆνας ἐν τῇ γῇ ποιεῖ ἀπὸ τῆς σπορᾶς καὶ ἓξ μῆνας ἔχει αὐτὸν ἡ Ἀφροδίτη, τουτέστιν ἡ εὐκρασία τοῦ ἀέρος. καὶ ἐκτότε λαμβάνουσιν αὐτὸν οἱ ἄνθρωποι. Origen, *Selecta in Ezechielem* (Migne's *Patrologia Graeca*, xiii. 800), οἱ δὲ περὶ τὴν ἀναγωγὴν τῶν Ἑλληνικῶν μύθων δεινοὶ καὶ μυθικῆς νομιζομένης θεολογίας, φασὶ τὸν Ἄδωνιν σύμβολον εἶναι τῶν τῆς γῆς καρπῶν, ὑπηρουμένων μὲν ὅτε σπείρονται, ἀνισταμένων δέ, καὶ διὰ τοῦτο χαίρειν ποιούντων τοὺς γεωργοὺς ὅτε φύονται. Jerome, *Commentar. in Ezechielem*, viii. 13, 14 (Migne's *Patrologia Latina*, xxv. 83), "*Eadem gentilitas hujuscemodi fabulas poetarum, quae habent turpitudinem, interpretatur subtiliter, interfectionem et resurrectionem Adonidis planctu et gaudio prosequens : quorum alterum in seminibus, quae moriuntur in terra, alterum in*

Tammuz
or Adonis
as a
corn-spirit
bruised and
ground in
a mill.

The character of Tammuz or Adonis as a corn-spirit comes out plainly in an account of his festival given by an Arabic writer of the tenth century. In describing the rites and sacrifices observed at the different seasons of the year by the heathen Syrians of Harran, he says : "Tammuz (July). In the middle of this month is the festival of el-Bûgât, that is, of the weeping women, and this is the Tâ-uz festival, which is celebrated in honour of the god Tá-uz. The women bewail him, because his lord slew him so cruelly, ground his bones in a mill, and then scattered them to the wind. The women (during this festival) eat nothing which has been ground in a mill, but limit their diet to steeped wheat, sweet vetches, dates, raisins, and the like." [1] Tâ-uz, who is no other than Tammuz, is here like Burns's John Barleycorn—

---

segetibus, quibus mortua semina rena-
scuntur, ostendi putat." Amnianus
Marcellinus, xix. 1..11, "in sollemnibus
Adonidis sacris, quod simulacrum ali-
quod esse frugum adultarum religiones
mysticae docent." Id. xxii. 9. 15,
"amato Veneris, ut fabulae fingunt,
apri dente ferali deleto, quod in
adulto flore sectarum est indicium
frugum." Clement of Alexandria,
Hom. 6. 11 (quoted by W. Mannhardt,
Antique Wald- und Feldkulte, p. 281),
λαμβάνουσι δὲ καὶ Ἄδωνιν εἰς ὡραίους
καρπούς. Etymologicum Magnum s.v.
Ἄδωνις κύριον· δύναται καὶ ὁ καρπὸς
εἶναι Ἄδωνις· οἷον ἀδώνειος καρπός,
ἀρέσκων. Eusebius, Praepar. Evang.
iii. 11. 9, Ἄδωνις τῆς τῶν τελείων
καρπῶν ἐκτομῆς σύμβολον. Sallustius
philosophus, "De diis et mundo,"
iv. Fragmenta Philosophorum Graecorum, ed. F. G. A. Mullach, iii. 32,
οἱ Αἰγύπτιοι . . . αὐτὰ τὰ σώματα θεοὺς
νομίσαντες . . . Ἴσιν μὲν τὴν γῆν . . .
Ἄδωνιν δὲ καρπούς. Joannes Lydus,
De mensibus, iv. 4, τῷ Ἀδώνιδι, τουτ-
έστι τῷ Μαΐῳ . . . ἢ ὡς ἄλλοις, δοκεῖ,
Ἄδωνις μέν ἐστιν ὁ καρπός, κτλ. The
view that Tammuz or Adonis is a
personification of the dying and re-
viving vegetation is now accepted by many scholars. See P. Jensen, Kosmo-
logie der Babylonier (Strasburg, 1890),
p. 480 ; id., Assyrisch-babylonische
Mythen und Epen, pp. 411, 560 ; H.
Zimmern, in E. Schrader's Keilinschriften und das Alte Testament,[3] p.
397; A. Jeremias, s.v. "Nergal," in W.
H. Roscher's Lexikon der griech. und
röm. Mythologie, iii. 265 ; R. Wünsch,
Das Frühlingsfest der Insel Malta
(Leipsic, 1902), p. 21; M. J. Lagrange,
Études sur les Religions Sémitiques,[2]
pp. 306 sqq. ; W. W. Graf Baudissin,
"Tammuz," Realencyclopädie für protestantische Theologie und Kirchengeschichte ; id., Esmun und Adonis,
pp. 81, 141, 169, etc. ; and Ed.
Meyer, Geschichte des Altertums,[2] i. 2.
pp. 394, 427. Prof. Jastrow regards
Tammuz as a god both of the sun and
of vegetation (Religion of Babylonia
and Assyria, pp. 547, 564, 574, 588).
But such a combination of disparate
qualities seems artificial and unlikely.

[1] D. Chwolsohn, Die Ssabier und
der Ssabismus (St. Petersburg, 1856),
ii. 27 ; id., Ueber Tammûz und die
Menschenverehrung bei den alten Baby-
loniern (St. Petersburg, 1860), p. 38.
Compare W. W. Graf Baudissin,
Adonis und Esmun, pp. 111 sqq.

"They wasted o'er a scorching flame
The marrow of his bones;
But a miller us'd him worst of all—
For he crush'd him between two stones."

This concentration, so to say, of the nature of Adonis upon the cereal crops is characteristic of the stage of culture reached by his worshippers in historical times. They had left the nomadic life of the wandering hunter and herdsman far behind them; for ages they had been settled on the land, and had depended for their subsistence mainly on the products of tillage. The berries and roots of the wilderness, the grass of the pastures, which had been matters of vital importance to their ruder forefathers, were now of little moment to them: more and more their thoughts and energies were engrossed by the staple of their life, the corn; more and more accordingly the propitiation of the deities of fertility in general and of the corn-spirit in particular tended to become the central feature of their religion. The aim they set before themselves in celebrating the rites was thoroughly practical. It was no vague poetical sentiment which prompted them to hail with joy the rebirth of vegetation and to mourn its decline. Hunger, felt or feared, was the mainspring of the worship of Adonis.

It has been suggested by Father Lagrange that the mourning for Adonis was essentially a harvest rite designed to propitiate the corn-god, who was then either perishing under the sickles of the reapers, or being trodden to death under the hoofs of the oxen on the threshing-floor. While the men slew him, the women wept crocodile tears at home to appease his natural indignation by a show of grief for his death.[2] The theory fits in well with the dates of the festivals, which fell in spring or summer; for spring and summer, not autumn, are the seasons of the barley and wheat harvests in the lands which worshipped Adonis.[3]

The mourning for Adonis interpreted as a harvest rite.

---

[1] The comparison is due to Felix Liebrecht (*Zur Volkskunde*, Heilbronn, 1879, p. 259).

[2] M. J. Lagrange, *Études sur les Religions Sémitiques*[2] (Paris, 1905), pp. 307 *sq.*

[3] Hence Philo of Alexandria dates the corn-reaping in the middle of spring (Μεσοῦντος δὲ ἔαρος ἄμητος ἐνίσταται, *De special. legibus*, i. 183, vol. v. p. 44, ed. L. Cohn). On this subject Professor W. M. Flinders Petrie writes to me: "The Coptic calendar puts on April 2 beginning of wheat harvest in Upper Egypt, May 2 wheat harvest, Lower Egypt.

Further, the hypothesis is confirmed by the practice of th[e] Egyptian reapers, who lamented, calling upon Isis, whe[n] they cut the first corn;[1] and. it is recommended by th[e] analogous customs of many hunting tribes, who testify grea[t] respect for the animals which they kill and eat.[2]

Thus interpreted the death of Adonis is not the natura[l] decay of vegetation in general under the summer heat o[r] the winter cold; it is the violent destruction of the corn by man, who cuts it down on the field, stamps it to pieces on the threshing-floor, and grinds it to powder in the mill. That this was indeed the principal aspect in which Adonis presented himself in later times to the agricultural peoples of the Levant, may be admitted; but whether from the beginning he had been the corn and nothing but the corn,

But probably Adonis was a spirit of fruits, edible roots and grass before he became a spirit of the cultivated corn.

Barley is two or three weeks earlier than wheat in Palestine, but probably less in Egypt. The Palestine harvest is about the time of that in North Egypt." With regard to Palestine we are told that "the harvest begins with the barley in April; in the valley of the Jordan it begins at the end of March. Between the end of the barley harvest and the beginning of the wheat harvest an interval of two or three weeks elapses. Thus as a rule the business of harvest lasts about seven weeks" (J. Benzinger, *Hebräische Archäologie*, Freiburg i. B. and Leipsic, 1894, p. 209). "The principal grain crops of Palestine are barley, wheat, lentils, maize, and millet. Of the latter there is very little, and it is all gathered in by the end of May. The maize is then only just beginning to shoot. In the hotter parts of the Jordan valley the barley harvest is over by the end of March, and throughout the country the wheat harvest is at its height at the end of May, excepting in the highlands of Galilee, where it is about a fortnight later" (H. B. Tristram, *The Land of Israel*, Fourth Edition, London, 1882, pp. 583 *sq.*). As to Greece, Professor E. A. Gardner tells me that harvest is from April to May in the plains and about a month later in the mountains. He adds that "barley may, then, be assigned to the latter part of April, wheat to May in the lower ground, but you know the great difference of climate between different parts; there is the same difference of a month in the vintage." Mrs. Hawes (Miss Boyd), who excavated at Gournia, tells me that in Crete the barley is cut in April and the beginning of May, and that the wheat is cut and threshed from about the twentieth of June, though the dates naturally vary somewhat with the height of the place above the sea. June is also the season when the wheat is threshed in Euboea (R. A. Arnold, *From the Levant*, London, 1868, i. 250). Thus it seems possible that the spring festival of Adonis coincided with the cutting of the first barley in March, and his summer festival with the threshing of the last wheat in June. Father Lagrange (*op. cit.* pp. 305 *sq.*) argues that the rites of Adonis were always celebrated in summer at the solstice of June or soon afterwards. Baudissin also holds that the summer celebration is the only one which is clearly attested, and that if there was a celebration in spring it must have had a different signification than the death of the god. See his *Adonis und Esmun*, pp. 132 *sq.*

[1] Diodorus Siculus, i. 14. 2. See below, vol. ii. pp. 45 *sq.*

[2] *Spirits of the Corn and of the Wild*, ii. 180 *sqq.*, 204 *sqq.*

may be doubted. At an earlier period he may have been to the herdsman, above all, the tender herbage which sprouts after rain, offering rich pasture to the lean and hungry cattle. Earlier still he may have embodied the spirit of the nuts and berries which the autumn woods yield to the savage hunter and his squaw. And just as the husbandman must propitiate the spirit of the corn which he consumes, so the herdsman must appease the spirit of the grass and leaves which his cattle munch, and the hunter must soothe the spirit of the roots which he digs, and of the fruits which he gathers from the bough. In all cases the propitiation of the injured and angry sprite would naturally comprise elaborate excuses and apologies, accompanied by loud lamentations at his decease whenever, through some deplorable accident or necessity, he happened to be murdered as well as robbed. Only we must bear in mind that the savage hunter and herdsman of those early days had probably not yet attained to the abstract idea of vegetation in general ; and that accordingly, so far as Adonis existed for them at all, he must have been the *Adon* or lord of each individual tree and plant rather than a personification of vegetable life as a whole. Thus there would be as many Adonises as there were trees and shrubs, and each of them might expect to receive satisfaction for any damage done to his person or property. And year by year, when the trees were deciduous, every Adonis would seem to bleed to death with the red leaves of autumn and to come to life again with the fresh green of spring.

We have seen reason to think that in early times Adonis was sometimes personated by a living man who died a violent death in the character of the god. Further, there is evidence which goes to show that among the agricultural peoples of the Eastern Mediterranean, the corn-spirit, by whatever name he was known, was often represented, year by year, by human victims slain on the harvest-field.[1] If that was so, it seems likely that the propitiation of the corn-spirit would tend to fuse to some extent with the worship of the dead. For the spirits of these victims

The propitiation of the corn-spirit may have fused with the worship of the dead.

---

[1] W. Mannhardt, *Mythologische Forschungen* (Strasburg, 1884), pp. 1 *sqq.*; *Spirits of the Corn and of the Wild*, i. 216 *sqq.*

might be thought to return to life in the ears which they had fattened with their blood, and to die a second death at the reaping of the corn. Now the ghosts of those who have perished by violence are surly and apt to wreak their vengeance on their slayers whenever an opportunity offers. Hence the attempt to appease the souls of the slaughtered victims would naturally blend, at least in the popular conception, with the attempt to pacify the slain corn-spirit. And as the dead came back in the sprouting corn, so they might be thought to return in the spring flowers, waked from their long sleep by the soft vernal airs. They had been laid to their rest under the sod. What more natural than to imagine that the violets and the hyacinths, the roses and the anemones, sprang from their dust, were empurpled or incarnadined by their blood, and contained some portion of their spirit?

> "*I sometimes think that never blows so red*
> *The Rose as where some buried Caesar bled;*
> *That every Hyacinth the Garden wears*
> *Dropt in her Lap from some once lovely Head.*
>
> "*And this reviving Herb whose tender Green*
> *Fledges the River-Lip on which we lean—*
> *Ah, lean upon it lightly, for who knows*
> *From what once lovely Lip it springs unseen?*"

In the summer after the battle of Landen, the most sanguinary battle of the seventeenth century in Europe, the earth, saturated with the blood of twenty thousand slain, broke forth into millions of poppies, and the traveller who passed that vast sheet of scarlet might well fancy that the earth had indeed given up her dead.[1] At Athens the great Commemoration of the Dead fell in spring about the middle of March, when the early flowers are in bloom. Then the dead were believed to rise from their graves and go about the streets, vainly endeavouring to enter the temples and the dwellings, which were barred against these perturbed spirits with ropes, buckthorn, and pitch. The name of the festival, according to the most obvious and natural interpretation, means the Festival of Flowers, and the title would

The festival of the dead a festival of flowers.

[1] T. B. Macaulay, *History of England*, chapter xx. vol. iv. (London, 1855) p. 410.

fit well with the substance of the ceremonies if at that season the poor ghosts were indeed thought to creep from the narrow house with the opening flowers.[1]   There may therefore be a measure of truth in the theory of Renan, who saw in the Adonis worship a dreamy voluptuous cult of death, conceived not as the King of Terrors, but as an insidious enchanter who lures his victims to himself and lulls them into an eternal sleep.   The infinite charm of nature in the Lebanon, he thought, lends itself to religious emotions of this sensuous, visionary sort, hovering vaguely between pain and pleasure, between slumber and tears.[2]   It would doubtless be a mistake to attribute to Syrian peasants the worship of a conception so purely abstract as that of death in general.   Yet it may be true that in their simple minds the thought of the reviving spirit of vegetation was blent with the very concrete notion of the ghosts of the dead, who come to life again in spring days with the early flowers, with the tender green of the corn and the many-tinted blossoms of the trees.   Thus their views of the death and resurrection of nature would be coloured by their views of the death and resurrection of man, by their personal sorrows and hopes and fears.   In like manner we cannot doubt that Renan's theory of Adonis was itself deeply tinged by passionate memories, memories of the slumber akin to death which sealed his own eyes on the slopes of the Lebanon, memories of the sister who sleeps in the land of Adonis never again to wake with the anemones and the roses.

---

[1] This explanation of the name *Anthesteria,* as applied to a festival of the dead, is due to Mr. R. Wünsch (*Das Frühlingsfest der Insel Malta,* Leipsic, 1902, pp. 43 *sqq.*).   I cannot accept the late Dr. A. W. Verrall's ingenious derivation of the word from a verb ἀναθέσσασθαι in the sense of "to conjure up" ("The Name Anthesteria," *Journal of Hellenic Studies,* xx. (1900) pp. 115-117).   As to the festival see E. Rohde, *Psyche*[3] (Tübingen and Leipsic, 1903), i. 236 *sqq.* ; Miss J. E. Harrison, *Prolegomena to the Study of Greek Religion*[2] (Cambridge, 1908), pp. 32 *sqq.*   In Annam people offer food to their dead on the graves when the earth begins to grow green in spring.   The ceremony takes place on the third day of the third month, the sun then entering the sign of Taurus.   See Paul Giran, *Magie et Religion Annamites* (Paris, 1912), pp. 423 *sq.*

[2] E. Renan, *Mission de Phénicie* (Paris, 1864), p. 216.

CHAPTER X

THE GARDENS OF ADONIS

Pots of corn, herbs, and flowers, called the gardens of Adonis.

PERHAPS the best proof that Adonis was a deity of vegetation, and especially of the corn, is furnished by the gardens of Adonis, as they were called. These were baskets or pots filled with earth, in which wheat, barley, lettuces, fennel, and various kinds of flowers were sown and tended for eight days, chiefly or exclusively by women. Fostered by the sun's heat, the plants shot up rapidly, but having no root they withered as rapidly away, and at the end of eight days were carried out with the images of the dead Adonis, and flung with them into the sea or into springs.[1]

These gardens of Adonis were charms to promote the growth of vegetation.

These gardens of Adonis are most naturally interpreted as representatives of Adonis or manifestations of his power ; they represented him, true to his original nature, in vegetable form, while the images of him, with which they were carried out and cast into the water, portrayed him in his later human shape. All these Adonis ceremonies, if I am right, were originally intended as charms to promote the growth

---

[1] For the authorities see Raoul Rochette, "Mémoire sur les jardins d'Adonis," Revue Archéologique, viii. (1851) pp. 97-123 ; W. Mannhardt, Antike Wald- und Feldkulte, p. 279, note 2, and p. 280, note 2. To the authorities cited by Mannhardt add Theophrastus, Hist. Plant. vi. 7. 3 ; id., De Causis Plant. i. 12. 2 ; Gregorius Cyprius, i. 7 ; Macarius, i. 63 ; Apostolius, i. 34 ; Diogenianus, i. 14 ; Plutarch, De sera num. vind. 17. Women only are mentioned as planting the gardens of Adonis by Plutarch, l.c.; Julian, Convivium, p. 329 ed. Span-heim (p. 423 ed. Hertlein) ; Eustathius on Homer, Od. xi. 590. On the other hand, Apostolius and Diogenianus (ll.cc.) say φυτεύοντες ἢ φυτεύουσαι. The earliest extant Greek writer who mentions the gardens of Adonis is Plato (Phaedrus, p. 276 B). The procession at the festival of Adonis is mentioned in an Attic inscription of 302 or 301 B.C. (G. Dittenberger, Sylloge Inscriptionum Graecarum,2 vol. ii. p. 564, No. 726). Gardens of Adonis are perhaps alluded to by Isaiah (xvii. 10, with the commentators).

236

or revival of vegetation; and the principle by which they were supposed to produce this effect was homoeopathic or imitative magic. For ignorant people suppose that by mimicking the effect which they desire to produce they actually help to produce it; thus by sprinkling water they make rain, by lighting a fire they make sunshine, and so on. Similarly, by mimicking the growth of crops they hope to ensure a good harvest. The rapid growth of the wheat and barley in the gardens of Adonis was intended to make the corn shoot up; and the throwing of the gardens and of the images into the water was a charm to secure a due supply of fertilizing rain.[1] The same, I take it, was the object of throwing the effigies of Death and the Carnival into water in the corresponding ceremonies of modern Europe.[2] Certainly the custom of drenching with water a leaf-clad person, who undoubtedly personifies vegetation, is still resorted to in Europe for the express purpose of producing rain.[3] Similarly the custom of throwing water on the last corn cut at harvest, or on the person who brings it home (a custom observed in Germany and France, and till quite lately in England and Scotland), is in some places practised with the avowed intent to procure rain for the next year's crops. Thus in Wallachia and amongst the Roumanians in Transylvania, when a girl is bringing home a crown made of the last ears of corn cut at harvest, all who meet her hasten to throw water on her, and two farm-servants are placed at the door for the purpose; for they believe that if this were not done, the crops next year would perish from drought.[4] So

The throwing of the "gardens" into water was a rain-charm.

Parallel European customs of drenching the corn with water at harvest or sowing

---

[1] In hot southern countries like Egypt and the Semitic regions of Western Asia, where vegetation depends chiefly or entirely upon irrigation, the purpose of the charm is doubtless to secure a plentiful flow of water in the streams. But as the ultimate object and the charms for securing it are the same in both cases, I have not thought it necessary always to point out the distinction.

[2] *The Dying God*, pp. 232, 233 *sqq.*

[3] *The Magic Art and the Evolution of Kings*, i. 272 *sqq.*

[4] W. Mannhardt, *Der Baumkultus der Germanen und ihrer Nachbar-* *stämme* (Berlin, 1875), p. 214; W. Schmidt, *Das Jahr und seine Tage in Meinung und Brauch der Romänen Siebenbürgens* (Hermannstadt, 1866), pp. 18 *sq.* The custom of throwing water on the last wagon-load of corn returning from the harvest-field has been practised within living memory in Wigtownshire, and at Orwell in Cambridgeshire. See J. G. Frazer, "Notes on Harvest Customs," *Folk-lore Journal*, vii. (1889) pp. 50, 51. (In the first of these passages the Orwell at which the custom used to be observed is said to be in Kent; this was a mistake of mine, which my informant, the Rev.

Use of
water as a
rain-charm
at harvest
and
sowing.

amongst the Saxons of Transylvania, the person who wears
the wreath made of the last corn cut is drenched with water
to the skin; for the wetter he is, the better will be next
year's harvest, and the more grain there will be threshed out.
Sometimes the wearer of the wreath is the reaper who cut
the last corn.[1] In Northern Euboea, when the corn-sheaves
have been piled in a stack, the farmer's wife brings a pitcher
of water and offers it to each of the labourers that he may
wash his hands. Every man, after he has washed his hands,
sprinkles water on the corn and on the threshing-floor,
expressing at the same time a wish that the corn may last
long. Lastly, the farmer's wife holds the pitcher slantingly
and runs at full speed round the stack without spilling a
drop, while she utters a wish that the stack may endure as
long as the circle she has just described.[2] At the spring
ploughing in Prussia, when the ploughmen and sowers
returned in the evening from their work in the fields, the
farmer's wife and the servants used to splash water over
them. The ploughmen and sowers retorted by seizing every
one, throwing them into the pond, and ducking them under
the water. The farmer's wife might claim exemption on
payment of a forfeit, but every one else had to be ducked.
By observing this custom they hoped to ensure a due
supply of rain for the seed.[3] Also after harvest in Prussia,
the person who wore a wreath made of the last corn cut
was drenched with water, while a prayer was uttered that
"as the corn had sprung up and multiplied through the
water, so it might spring up and multiply in the barn and
granary."[4] At Schlanow, in Brandenburg, when the sowers

E. B. Birks, formerly Fellow of Trinity
College, Cambridge, afterwards corrected.) Mr. R. F. Davis writes to
me (March 4, 1906) from Campbell
College, Belfast : "Between 30 and
40 years ago I was staying, as a very
small boy, at a Nottinghamshire farm-
house at harvest-time, and was allowed
—as a great privilege—to ride home
on the top of the last load. All the
harvesters followed the waggon, and
on reaching the farmyard we found the
maids of the farm gathered near the
gate, with bowls and buckets of water,
which they proceeded to throw on the

men, who got thoroughly drenched."

[1] G. A. Heinrich, *Agrarische Sitten
und Gebräuche unter den Sachsen
Siebenbürgens* (Hermanstadt, 1880), p.
24 ; H. von Wlislocki, *Sitten und
Brauch der Siebenbürger Sachsen* (Ham-
burg, 1888), p. 32.

[2] G. Drosinis, *Land und Leute in
Nord-Euböa* (Leipsic, 1884), p. 53.

[3] Matthäus Praetorius, *Deliciae Prus-
sicae* (Berlin, 1871), p. 55 ; W. Mannhardt, *Baumkultus*, pp. 214 *sq.*, note.

[4] M. Praetorius, *op. cit.* p. 60 ; W.
Mannhardt, *Baumkultus*, p. 215,
note.

return home from the first sowing they are drenched with water "in order that the corn may grow."[1] In Anhalt on the same occasion the farmer is still often sprinkled with water by his family ; and his men and horses, and even the plough, receive the same treatment. The object of the custom, as people at Arensdorf explained it, is "to wish fertility to the fields for the whole year."[2] So in Hesse, when the ploughmen return with the plough from the field for the first time, the women and girls lie in wait for them and slyly drench them with water.[3] Near Naaburg, in Bavaria, the man who first comes back from sowing or ploughing has a vessel of water thrown over him by some one in hiding.[4] At Hettingen in Baden the farmer who is about to begin the sowing of oats is sprinkled with water, in order that the oats may not shrivel up.[5] Before the Tusayan Indians of North America go out to plant their fields, the women sometimes pour water on them ; the reason for doing so is that "as the water is poured on the men, so may water fall on the planted fields."[6] The Indians of Santiago Tepehuacan steep the seed of the maize in water before they sow it, in order that the god of the waters may bestow on the fields the needed moisture.[7]

The opinion that the gardens of Adonis are essentially charms to promote the growth of vegetation, especially of the crops, and that they belong to the same class of customs as those spring and midsummer folk-customs of modern Europe which I have described elsewhere,[8] does not rest for its evidence merely on the intrinsic probability of the case. Fortunately we are able to show that gardens of Adonis (if we may use the expression in a general sense) are still planted, first, by a primitive race at their sowing season,

Gardens of Adonis among the Oraons and Mundas of Bengal.

---

[1] H. Prahn, "Glaube und Brauch in der Mark Brandenburg," *Zeitschrift des Vereins für Volkskunde*, i. (1891) p. 186.

[2] O. Hartung, "Zur Volkskunde aus Anhalt," *Zeitschrift des Vereins für Volkskunde*, vii. (1897) p. 150.

[3] W. Kolbe, *Hessische Volks-Sitten und Gebräuche* (Marburg, 1888), p. 51.

[4] *Bavaria, Landes- und Volkskunde des Königreichs Bayern*, ii. (Munich, 1863) p. 297.

[5] E. H. Meyer, *Badisches Volksleben* (Strasburg, 1900), p. 420.

[6] J. Walter Fewkes, "The Tusayan New Fire Ceremony," *Proceedings of the Boston Society of Natural History*, xxvi. (1895) p. 446.

[7] "Lettre du curé de Santiago Tepehuacan à son évèque," *Bulletin de la Société de Géographie* (Paris), Deuxième Série, ii. (1834) pp. 181 *sq.*

[8] *The Magic Art and the Evolution of Kings*, ii. 59 *sqq.*

and, second, by European peasants at midsummer. Amongst the Oraons and Mundas of Bengal, when the time comes for planting out the rice which has been grown in seed-beds, a party of young people of both sexes go to the forest and cut a young Karma-tree, or the branch of one. Bearing it in triumph they return dancing, singing, and beating drums, and plant it in the middle of the village dancing-ground. A sacrifice is offered to the tree; and next morning the youth of both sexes, linked arm-in-arm, dance in a great circle round the Karma-tree, which is decked with strips of coloured cloth and sham bracelets and necklets of plaited straw. As a preparation for the festival, the daughters of the headman of the village cultivate blades of barley in a peculiar way. The seed is sown in moist, sandy soil, mixed with turmeric, and the blades sprout and unfold of a pale-yellow or primrose colour. On the day of the festival the girls take up these blades and carry them in baskets to the dancing-ground, where, prostrating themselves reverentially, they place some of the plants before the Karma-tree. Finally, the Karma-tree is taken away and thrown into a stream or tank.[1] The meaning of planting these barley blades and then presenting them to the Karma-tree is hardly open to question. Trees are supposed to exercise a quickening influence upon the growth of crops, and amongst the very people in question — the Mundas or Mundaris — "the grove deities are held responsible for the crops."[2] Therefore, when at the season for planting out the rice the Mundas bring in a tree and treat it with so much respect, their object can only be to foster thereby the growth of the rice which is about to be planted out; and the custom of causing barley blades to sprout rapidly and then present-ing them to the tree must be intended to subserve the same purpose, perhaps by reminding the tree-spirit of his duty towards the crops, and stimulating his activity by this visible example of rapid vegetable growth. The throwing of the Karma-tree into the water is to be interpreted as a rain-

---

[1] E. T. Dalton, *Descriptive Ethnology of Bengal* (Calcutta, 1872), p. 259.

[2] E. T. Dalton, *op. cit.* p. 188.

As to the influence which trees are supposed to exercise on the crops, see *The Magic Art and the Evolution of Kings*, ii. 47 *sqq.*

charm. Whether the barley blades are also thrown into the water is not said ; but if my interpretation of the custom is right, probably they are so. A distinction between this Bengal custom and the Greek rites of Adonis is that in the former the tree-spirit appears in his original form as a tree ; whereas in the Adonis worship he appears in human form, represented as a dead man, though his vegetable nature is indicated by the gardens of Adonis, which are, so to say, a secondary manifestation of his original power as a tree-spirit.

Gardens of Adonis are cultivated also by the Hindoos, with the intention apparently of ensuring the fertility both of the earth and of mankind. Thus at Oodeypoor in Rajputana a festival is held "in honour of Gouri, or Isani, the goddess of abundance, the Isis of Egypt, the Ceres of Greece. Like the Rajpoot Saturnalia, which it follows, it belongs to the vernal equinox, when nature in these regions proximate to the tropic is in the full expanse of her charms, and the matronly Gouri casts her golden mantle over the verdant Vassanti, personification of spring. Then the fruits exhibit their promise to the eye ; the kohil fills the ear with melody ; the air is impregnated with aroma, and the crimson poppy contrasts with the spikes of golden grain to form a wreath for the beneficent Gouri. Gouri is one of the names of Isa or Parvati, wife of the greatest of the gods, Mahadeva or Iswara, who is conjoined with her in these rites, which almost exclusively appertain to the women. The meaning of *gouri* is 'yellow,' emblematic of the ripened harvest, when the votaries of the goddess adore her effigies, which are those of a matron painted the colour of ripe corn." The rites begin when the sun enters the sign of the Ram, the opening of the Hindoo year. An image of the goddess Gouri is made of earth, and a smaller one of her husband Iswara, and the two are placed together. A small trench is next dug, barley is sown in it, and the ground watered and heated artificially till the grain sprouts, when the women dance round it hand in hand, invoking the blessing of Gouri on their husbands. After that the young corn is taken up and distributed by the women to the men, who wear it in their turbans. Every wealthy family, or at least every sub-division of the city, has its own image. These and other

Gardens of Adonis in Rajputana.

rites, known only to the initiated, occupy several days, and
are performed within doors.   Then the images of the
goddess and her husband are decorated and borne in procession to a beautiful lake, whose deep blue waters mirror
the cloudless Indian sky, marble palaces, and orange groves.
Here the women, their hair decked with roses and jessamine,
carry the image of Gouri down a marble staircase to the
water's edge, and dance round it singing hymns and love-
songs.   Meantime the goddess is supposed to bathe in the
water.   No men take part in the ceremony ; even the
image of Iswara, the husband-god, attracts little attention.[1]
In these rites the distribution of the barley shoots to the
men, and the invocation of a blessing on their husbands by
the wives, point clearly to the desire of offspring as one
motive for observing the custom.   The same motive probably explains the use of gardens of Adonis at the marriage
of Brahmans in the Madras Presidency.   Seeds of five or
nine sorts are mixed and sown in earthen pots, which are
made specially for the purpose and are filled with earth.
Bride and bridegroom water the seeds both morning and
evening for four days ; and on the fifth day the seedlings are
thrown, like the real gardens of Adonis, into a tank or river.[2]

Gardens of Adonis in North-Western and Central India.

In the Himalayan districts of North-Western India the
cultivators sow barley, maize, pulse, or mustard in a basket
of earth on the twenty-fourth day of the fourth month
(*Asárh*), which falls about the middle of July.   Then on the
last day of the month they place amidst the new sprouts
small clay images of Mahadeo and Parvati and worship
them in remembrance of the marriage of those deities.
Next day they cut down the green stalks and wear them in
their head-dress.[3]   Similar is the barley feast known as
Jáyi or Jawára in Upper India and as Bhujariya in the
Central Provinces.   On the seventh day of the light half of
the month Sâwan grains of barley are sown in a pot of
manure, and spring up so quickly that by the end of the

---

[1] Lieut.-Col. James Tod, *Annals and Antiquities of Rajast'han*, i. (Lon-don, 1829) pp. 570-572.

[2] G. F. D'Penha, " A Collection of Notes on Marriage Customs in the Madras Presidency," *Indian Anti-*

quary, xxv. (1896) p. 144 ; E. Thur-ston, *Ethnographic Notes in Southern India* (Madras, 1906), p. 2.

[3] E. T. Atkinson, *The Himalayan Districts of the North-Western Provinces of India*, ii. (Allahabad, 1884) p. 870.

month the vessel is full of long, yellowish-green stalks.   On
the first day of the next month, Bhádon, the women and
girls take the stalks out, throw the earth and manure into
water, and distribute the plants among their male friends,
who bind them in their turbans and about their dress.[1]   At
Sargal in the Central Provinces of India this ceremony is
observed about the middle of September.   None but women
may take part in it, though crowds of men come to look on.
Some little time before the festival wheat or other grain has
been sown in pots ingeniously constructed of large leaves,
which are held together by the thorns of a species of acacia.
Having grown up in the dark, the stalks are of a pale
colour.   On the day appointed these gardens of Adonis, as
we may call them, are carried towards a lake which abuts
on the native city.   The women of every family or circle of
friends bring their own pots, and having laid them on the
ground they dance round them.   Then taking the pots of
sprouting corn they descend to the edge of the water, wash
the soil away from the pots, and distribute the young plants
among their friends.[2]   At the temple of the goddess Padma-
rati, near Pandharpur in the Bombay Presidency, a Nine
Nights' festival is held in the bright half of the month
Ashvin (September–October).   At this time a bamboo frame
is hung in front of the image, and from it depend garlands
of flowers and strings of wheaten cakes.   Under the frame
the floor in front of the pedestal is strewn with a layer of
earth in which wheat is sown and allowed to sprout.[3]   A
similar rite is observed in the same month before the images
of two other goddesses, Ambabai and Lakhubai, who also
have temples at Pandharpur.[4]

[1] W. Crooke, *Popular Religion and
Folk-lore of Northern India* (West-
minster, 1896), ii. 203 *sq.*   Compare
Baboo Ishuree Dass, *Domestic Manners
and Customs of the Hindoos of Northern
India* (Benares, 1860), pp. 111 *sq.*
According to the latter writer, the
festival of Salono [not Salonan] takes
place in August, and the barley is
planted by women and girls in baskets
a few days before the festival, to be
thrown by them into a river or tank
when the grain has sprouted to the

height of a few inches.
[2] Mrs. J. C. Murray - Aynsley,
"Secular and Religious Dances," *Folklore Journal*, v. (1887) pp. 253 *sq.*
The writer thinks that the ceremony
"probably fixes the season for sowing
some particular crop."
[3] *Gazetteer of the Bombay Presidency*,
xx. (Bombay, 1884) p. 454.   This
passage was pointed out to me by my
friend Mr. W. Crooke.
[4] *Gazetteer of the Bombay Presidency*,
xx. 443, 460.

In some parts of Bavaria it is customary to sow flax in a pot on the last three days of the Carnival; from the seed which grows best an omen is drawn as to whether the early, the middle, or the late sowing will produce the best crop.[1] In Sardinia the gardens of Adonis are still planted in connexion with the great Midsummer festival which bears the name of St. John. At the end of March or on the first of April a young man of the village presents himself to a girl, and asks her to be his *comare* (gossip or sweetheart), offering to be her *compare*. The invitation is considered as an honour by the girl's family, and is gladly accepted. At the end of May the girl makes a pot of the bark of the cork-tree, fills it with earth, and sows a handful of wheat and barley in it. The pot being placed in the sun and often watered, the corn sprouts rapidly and has a good head by Midsummer Eve (St. John's Eve, the twenty-third of June). The pot is then called *Erme* or *Nenneri*. On St. John's Day the young man and the girl, dressed in their best, accompanied by a long retinue and preceded by children gambolling and frolicking, move in procession to a church outside the village. Here they break the pot by throwing it against the door of the church. Then they sit down in a ring on the grass and eat eggs and herbs to the music of flutes. Wine is mixed in a cup and passed round, each one drinking as it passes. Then they join hands and sing "Sweethearts of St. John" (*Compare e comare di San Giovanni*) over and over again, the flutes playing the while. When they tire of singing they stand up and dance gaily in a ring till evening. This is the general Sardinian custom. As practised at Ozieri it has some special features. In May the pots are made of cork-bark and planted with corn, as already described. Then on the Eve of St. John the window-sills are draped with rich cloths, on which the pots are placed, adorned with crimson and blue silk and ribbons of various colours. On each of the pots they used formerly to place a statuette or cloth doll dressed as a woman, or a Priapus-like figure made of paste; but this custom, rigorously forbidden by the Church, has fallen into disuse. The village swains go about

---

[1] *Bavaria, Landes- und Volkskunde des Königreichs Bayern* (Munich, 1860-1867), ii. 298.

in a troop to look at the pots and their decorations and to wait for the girls, who assemble on the public square to celebrate the festival.   Here a great bonfire is kindled, round which they dance and make merry.   Those who wish to be " Sweethearts of St. John " act as follows.   The young man stands on one side of the bonfire and the girl on the other, and they, in a manner, join hands by each grasping one end of a long stick, which they pass three times backwards and forwards across the fire, thus thrusting their hands thrice rapidly into the flames.   This seals their relationship to each other.   Dancing and music go on till late at night.[1] The correspondence of these Sardinian pots of grain to the gardens of Adonis seems complete, and the images formerly placed in them answer to the images of Adonis which accompanied his gardens.

Customs of the same sort are observed at the same season in Sicily.   Pairs of boys and girls become gossips of St. John on St. John's Day by drawing each a hair from his or her head and performing various ceremonies over them. Thus they tie the hairs together and throw them up in the air, or exchange them over a potsherd, which they afterwards break in two, preserving each a fragment with pious care.   The tie formed in the latter way is supposed to last for life.   In some parts of Sicily the gossips of St. John present each other with plates of sprouting corn, lentils, and canary seed, which have been planted forty days before the festival.   The one who receives the plate pulls a stalk of the young plants, binds it with a ribbon, and preserves it among his or her greatest treasures, restoring the platter to the giver.   At Catania the gossips exchange pots of basil and great cucumbers ; the girls tend the basil, and the thicker it grows the more it is prized.[2]

[1] Antonio Bresciani, *Dei costumi dell' isola di Sardegna comparati cogli antichissimi popoli orientali* (Rome and Turin, 1866), pp. 427 *sq.* ; R. Tennant, *Sardinia and its Resources* (Rome and London, 1885), p. 187 ; S. Gabriele, " Usi dei contadini della Sardegna," *Archivio per lo Studio delle Tradizioni Popolari*, vii. (1888) pp. 469 *sq.*   Tennant says that the pots are kept in a dark warm place, and that the children leap across the fire.

[2] G. Pitrè, *Usi e Costumi, Credenze e Pregiudizi del Popolo Siciliano* (Palermo, 1889), ii. 271-278.   Compare *id.*, *Spettacoli e Feste Popolari Siciliane* (Palermo, 1881), pp. 297 *sq.* In the Abruzzi also young men and young women become gossips by exchanging nosegays on St. John's Day,

In these
Sardinian
and Sicilian
ceremonies
St. John
may have
taken the
place of
Adonis.

In these midsummer customs of Sardinia and Sicily it is possible that, as Mr. R. Wünsch supposes,[1] St. John has replaced Adonis. We have seen that the rites of Tammuz or Adonis were commonly celebrated about midsummer; according to Jerome, their date was June.[2] And besides their date and their similarity in respect of the pots of herbs and corn, there is another point of affinity between the two festivals, the heathen and the Christian. In both of them water plays a prominent part. At his midsummer festival in Babylon the image of Tammuz, whose name is said to mean " true son of the deep water," was bathed with pure water : at his summer festival in Alexandria the image of Adonis, with that of his divine mistress Aphrodite, was committed to the waves ; and at the midsummer celebration in Greece the gardens of Adonis were thrown into the sea

Custom of
bathing in
water or
washing in
dew on
the Eve or
Day of St.
John (Mid-
summer
Eve or Mid-
summer
Day).

or into springs. Now a great feature of the midsummer festival associated with the name of St. John is, or used to be, the custom of bathing in the sea, springs, rivers, or the dew on Midsummer Eve or the morning of Midsummer Day. Thus, for example, at Naples there is a church dedicated to St. John the Baptist under the name of St. John of the Sea (S. Giovan a mare) ; and it was an old practice for men and women to bathe in the sea on St. John's Eve, that is, on Midsummer Eve, believing that thus all their sins were washed away.[3] In the Abruzzi water is still supposed to acquire certain marvellous and beneficent properties on St. John's Night. They say that on that night the sun and moon bathe in the water. Hence many people take a bath in the sea or in a river at that season, especially at the moment of sunrise. At Castiglione a Casauria they go before sunrise to the Pescara River or to springs, wash their faces and hands, then gird themselves with twigs of bryony (vitalba) and twine the plant round their brows, in order that they may be free from pains. At Pescina boys and girls wash each other's faces in a river or a spring, then exchange kisses, and become gossips. The dew, also, that

and the tie thus formed is regarded as sacred. See G. Finamore, Credenze, Usi e Costumi Abruzzesi (Palermo, 1890), pp. 165 sq.

[1] R. Wünsch, Das Frühlingsfest

der Insel Malta, pp. 47-57.
[2] See above, pp. 10, note [1], 224 sq., 226.
[3] J. Grimm, Deutsche Mythologie,[4] i. 490.

falls on St. John's Night is supposed in the Abruzzi to benefit whatever it touches, whether it be water, flowers, or the human body.   For that reason people put out vessels of water on the window-sills or the terraces, and wash themselves with the water in the morning in order to purify themselves and escape headaches and colds.   A still more efficacious mode of accomplishing the same end is to rise at the peep of dawn, to wet the hands in the dewy grass, and then to rub the moisture on the eyelids, the brow, and the temples, because the dew is believed to cure maladies of the head and eyes.   It is also a remedy for diseases of the skin. Persons who are thus afflicted should roll on the dewy grass.   When patients are prevented by their infirmity or any other cause from quitting the house, their friends will gather the dew in sheets or tablecloths and so apply it to the suffering part.[1]   At Marsala in Sicily there is a spring of water in a subterranean grotto called the Grotto of the Sibyl.   Beside it stands a church of St. John, which has been supposed to occupy the site of a temple of Apollo. On St. John's Eve, the twenty-third of June, women and girls visit the grotto, and by drinking of the prophetic water learn whether their husbands have been faithful to them in the year that is past, or whether they themselves will wed in the year that is to come.   Sick people, too, imagine that by bathing in the water, drinking of it, or ducking thrice in it in the name of the Trinity, they will be made whole.[2]   At Chiaramonte in Sicily the following custom is observed on St. John's Eve.   The men repair to one fountain and the women to another, and dip their heads thrice in the water, repeating at each ablution certain verses in honour of St. John.   They believe that this is a cure or preventive of the scald.[3]   When Petrarch visited Cologne, he chanced to

---

[1] G. Finamore, *Credenze, Usi e Costumi Abruzzesi*, pp. 156-160. A passage in Isaiah (xxvi. 19) seems to imply that dew possessed the magical virtue of restoring the dead to life. In this passage of Isaiah the customs which I have cited in the text perhaps favour the ordinary interpretation of אורת על as "dew of herbs" (compare 2 Kings iv. 39) against the interpretation "dew of lights," which some modern commentators (Dillmann, Skinner, Whitehouse), following Jerome, have adopted.

[2] G. Pitrè, *Feste patronali in Sicilia* (Turin and Palermo, 1900), pp. 488, 491-493.

[3] G. Pitrè, *Spettacoli e Feste Popolari Siciliane*, p. 307.

arrive in the town on St. John's Eve. The sun was nearly setting, and his host at once led him to the Rhine. A strange sight there met his eyes, for the banks of the river were covered with pretty women. The crowd was great but good-humoured. From a rising ground on which he stood the poet saw many of the women, girt with fragrant herbs, kneel down on the water's edge, roll their sleeves up above their elbows, and wash their white arms and hands in the river, murmuring softly some words which the Italian did not understand. He was told that the custom was a very old one, much honoured in the observance; for the common folk, especially the women, believed that to wash in the river on St. John's Eve would avert every misfortune in the coming year.[1] On St. John's Eve the people of Copenhagen used to go on pilgrimage to a neighbouring spring, there to heal and strengthen themselves in the water.[2] In Spain people still bathe in the sea or roll naked in the dew of the meadows on St. John's Eve, believing that this is a sovereign preservative against diseases of the skin.[3] To roll in the dew on the morning of St. John's Day is also esteemed a cure for diseases of the skin in Normandy and Perigord. In Perigord a field of hemp is especially recommended for the purpose, and the patient should rub himself with the plants on which he has rolled.[4] At Ciotat in Provence, while the midsummer bonfire blazed, young people used to plunge into the sea and splash each other vigorously. At Vitrolles they bathed in a pond in order that they might not suffer from fever during the year, and at Saint-Maries they watered the horses to protect them from the itch.[5] A custom of drenching people on this occasion with water formerly prevailed in Toulon, Marseilles, and other towns of the south of France. The water was squirted from syringes, poured on the heads of passers-by from windows, and so

[1] Petrarch, *Epistolae de rebus familiaribus*, i. 4 (vol. i. pp. 44-46 ed. J. Fracassetti, Florence, 1859-1862). The passage is quoted by J. Grimm, *Deutsche Mythologie*,[4] i. 480 *sq.*

[2] J. Grimm, *op. cit.* i. 480.

[3] Letter of Dr. Otero Acevedo, of Madrid, *Le Temps*, September 1898.

[4] J. Lecœur, *Esquisses du Bocage Normand* (Condé-sur-Noireau, 1883-1887), ii. 8; A. de Nore, *Coutumes, Mythes et Traditions des provinces de France* (Paris and Lyons, 1846), p. 150.

[5] A. de Nore, *op. cit.* p. 20; Bérenger-Féraud, *Réminiscences populaires de la Provence* (Paris, 1885), pp. 135-141.

forth.[1]   From Europe the practice of bathing in rivers and springs on St. John's Day appears to have passed with the Spaniards to the New World.[2]

It may perhaps be suggested that this wide-spread custom of bathing in water or dew on Midsummer Eve or Midsummer Day is purely Christian in origin, having been adopted as an appropriate mode of celebrating the day dedicated to the Baptist.   But in point of fact the custom is older than Christianity, for it was denounced and forbidden as a heathen practice by Augustine,[3] and to this day it is practised at midsummer by the Mohammedan peoples of North Africa.[4]   We may conjecture that the Church, unable to put down this relic of paganism, followed its usual policy of accommodation by bestowing on the rite of a Christian name and acquiescing, with a sigh, in its observance.   And casting about for a saint to supplant a heathen patron of bathing, the Christian doctors could hardly have hit upon a more appropriate successor than St. John the Baptist.

But into whose shoes did the Baptist step?   Was the displaced deity really Adonis, as the foregoing evidence seems to suggest?   In Sardinia and Sicily it may have been so, for in these islands Semitic influence was certainly deep and probably lasting.   The midsummer pastimes of Sardinian and Sicilian children may therefore be a direct continuation of the Carthaginian rites of Tammuz.   Yet the midsummer festival seems too widely spread and too deeply rooted in Central and Northern Europe to allow us to trace it everywhere to an Oriental origin in general and to the cult of Adonis in particular.   It has the air of a native of the soil rather than of an exotic imported from the East.   We shall

The custom of bathing at midsummer is pagan, not Christian, in its origin

Old heathen festival of midsummer in Europe and the East.

---

[1] A. Breuil, "Du Culte de St. Jean Baptiste," *Mémoires de la Société des Antiquaires de Picardie*, viii. (1845) pp. 237 *sq.*   Compare *Balder the Beautiful*, i. 193 *sq.*

[2] Diego Duran, *Historia de las Indias de Nueva España*, edited by J. F. Ramirez (Mexico, 1867-1880), ii. 293.

[3] Augustine, *Opera*, v. (Paris, 1683) col. 903 ; *id.*, Pars Secunda, coll. 461 *sq.*   The second of these passages occurs in a sermon of doubtful authen-

ticity.   Both have been quoted by J. Grimm, *Deutsche Mythologie*,[4] i. 490.

[4] E. Doutté, *Magie et Religion dans l'Afrique du Nord* (Algiers, 1908), pp. 567 *sq.*; E. Westermarck, "Midsummer Customs in Morocco," *Folk-lore*, xvi. (1905) pp. 31 *sq.*; *id.*, *Ceremonies and Beliefs connected with Agriculture, Certain Dates of the Solar Year, and the Weather* (Helsingfors, 1913), pp. 84-86.   See *Balder the Beautiful*, i. 216.

do better, therefore, to suppose that at a remote period similar modes of thought, based on similar needs, led men independently in many distant lands, from the North Sea to the Euphrates, to celebrate the summer solstice with rites which, while they differed in some things, yet agreed closely in others; that in historical times a wave of Oriental influence, starting perhaps from Babylonia, carried the Tammuz or Adonis form of the festival westward till it met with native forms of a similar festival; and that under pressure of the Roman civilization these different yet kindred festivals fused with each other and crystallized into a variety of shapes, which subsisted more or less separately side by side, till the Church, unable to suppress them altogether, stripped them so far as it could of their grosser features, and dexterously changing the names allowed them to pass muster as Christian. And what has just been said of the midsummer festivals probably applies, with the necessary modifications, to the spring festivals also. They, too, seem to have originated independently in Europe and the East, and after ages of separation to have amalgamated under the sway of the Roman Empire and the Christian Church. In Syria, as we have seen, there appears to have been a vernal celebration of Adonis; and we shall presently meet with an undoubted instance of an Oriental festival of spring in the rites of Attis. Meantime we must return for a little to the midsummer festival which goes by the name of St. John.

Midsummer fires and midsummer couples in relation to vegetation.

The Sardinian practice of making merry round a great bonfire on St. John's Eve is an instance of a custom which has been practised at the midsummer festival from time immemorial in many parts of Europe. That custom has been more fully dealt with by me elsewhere.[1] The instances which I have cited in other parts of this work seem to indicate a connexion of the midsummer bonfire with vegetation. For example, both in Sweden and Bohemia an essential part of the festival is the raising of a May-pole or Midsummer tree, which in Bohemia is burned in the bonfire.[2] Again, in a Russian midsummer ceremony a straw figure of Kupalo,

---

[1] *Balder the Beautiful*, i. 100 *sqq.*
[2] *The Magic Art and the Evolution of Kings*, ii. 65 *sq.*

the representative of vegetation, is placed beside a May-pole or Midsummer-tree and then carried to and fro across a bonfire.[1] Kupalo is here represented in duplicate, in tree-form by the Midsummer-tree, and in human form by the straw effigy, just as Adonis was represented both by an image and a garden of Adonis ; and the duplicate representatives of Kupalo, like those of Adonis, are finally cast into water. In the Sardinian and Sicilian customs the Gossips or Sweethearts of St. John probably answer, on the one hand to Adonis and Astarte, on the other to the King and Queen of May. In the Swedish province of Blekinge part of the midsummer festival is the election of a Midsummer Bride, who chooses her bridegroom ; a collection is made for the pair, who for the time being are looked upon as man and wife.[2] Such Midsummer pairs may be supposed, like the May pairs, to stand for the powers of vegetation or of fertility in general : they represent in flesh and blood what the images of Siva or Mahadeo and Parvati in the Indian ceremonies, and the images of Adonis and Aphrodite in the Alexandrian ceremony, set forth in effigy.

The reason why ceremonies whose aim is to foster the growth of vegetation should thus be associated with bonfires ; why in particular the representative of vegetation should be burned in the likeness of a tree, or passed across the fire in effigy or in the form of a living couple, has been discussed by me elsewhere.[3] Here it is enough to have adduced evidence of such association, and therefore to have obviated the objection which might have been raised to my theory of the Sardinian custom, on the ground that the bonfires have nothing to do with vegetation. One more piece of evidence may here be given to prove the contrary. In some parts of Germany and Austria young men and girls leap over midsummer bonfires for the express purpose of making the hemp or flax grow tall.[4] We may, therefore, assume that in the Sardinian custom the blades of wheat and barley which are

Gardens of Adonis intended to foster the growth of vegetation, and especially of the crops.

[1] *The Dying God,* p. 262.

[2] L. Lloyd, *Peasant Life in Sweden* (London, 1870), p. 257.

[3] *Balder the Beautiful,* i. 328 sqq., ii. 21 sqq.

[4] W. Mannhardt, *Baumkultus,* p. 464 ; K. von Leoprechting, *Aus dem Lechrain* (Munich, 1855), p. 183. For more evidence see *Balder the Beautiful,* i. 165, 166, 166 sq., 168, 173, 174.

forced on in pots for the midsummer festival, and which correspond so closely to the gardens of Adonis, form one of those widely-spread midsummer ceremonies, the original object of which was to promote the growth of vegetation, and especially of the crops. But as, by an easy extension of ideas, the spirit of vegetation was believed to exercise a beneficent and fertilizing influence on human as well as animal life, the gardens of Adonis would be supposed, like the May-trees or May-boughs, to bring good luck, and more particularly perhaps offspring,[1] to the family or to the person who planted them; and even after the idea had been abandoned that they operated actively to confer prosperity, they

Modes of divination at midsummer like the gardens of Adonis.

might still be used to furnish omens of good or evil. It is thus that magic dwindles into divination. Accordingly we find modes of divination practised at midsummer which resemble more or less closely the gardens of Adonis. Thus an anonymous Italian writer of the sixteenth century has recorded that it was customary to sow barley and wheat a few days before the festival of St. John (Midsummer Day) and also before that of St. Vitus; and it was believed that the person for whom they were sown would be fortunate, and get a good husband or a good wife, if the grain sprouted well; but if it sprouted ill, he or she would be unlucky.[2] In various parts of Italy and all over Sicily it is still customary to put plants in water or in earth on the Eve of St. John, and from the manner in which they are found to be blooming or fading on St. John's Day omens are drawn, especially as to fortune in love. Amongst the plants used for this purpose are *Ciuri di S. Giovanni* (St. John's wort?) and nettles.[3] In Prussia two hundred years ago the farmers used to send out their servants, especially their maids, to gather St. John's

---

[1] The use of gardens of Adonis to fertilize the human sexes appears plainly in the corresponding Indian practices. See above, pp. 241, 242, 243.

[2] G. Pitrè, *Spettacoli e Feste Popolari Siciliane*, pp. 296 *sq.*

[3] G. Pitrè, *op. cit.* pp. 302 *sq.*; Antonio de Nino, *Usi e Costumi Abruzzesi* (Florence, 1879, 1883), i. 55 *sq.*; A. de Gubernatis, *Usi Nuziali in Italia e presso gli altri Popoli Indo-Europei* (Milan, 1878), pp. 39 *sq.* Compare

L. Passarini, "Il Comparatico e la Festa di S. Giovanni nelle Marche e in Roma," *Archivio per lo Studio delle Tradizioni Popolari*, i. (1882) p. 135. At Smyrna a blossom of the *Agnus castus* is used on St. John's Day for a similar purpose, but the mode in which the omens are drawn is somewhat different. See Teotilo, "La notte di San Giovanni in Oriente," *Archivio per lo Studio delle Tradizioni Popolari*, vii. (1888) pp. 128-130.

wort on Midsummer Eve or Midsummer Day (St. John's Day). When they had fetched it, the farmer took as many plants as there were persons and stuck them in the wall or between the beams ; and it was thought that he or she whose plant did not bloom would soon fall sick or die. The rest of the plants were tied in a bundle, fastened to the end of a pole, and set up at the gate or wherever the corn would be brought in at the next harvest. The bundle was called *Kupole* : the ceremony was known as Kupole's festival ; and at it the farmer prayed for a good crop of hay, and so forth.[1] This Prussian custom is particularly notable, inasmuch as it strongly confirms the opinion that Kupalo (doubtless identical with Kupole) was originally a deity of vegetation.[2] For here Kupalo is represented by a bundle of plants specially associated with midsummer in folk-custom ; and her influence over vegetation is plainly signified by placing her vegetable emblem over the place where the harvest is brought in, as well as by the prayers for a good crop which are uttered on the occasion. This furnishes a fresh argument in support of the view that the Death, whose analogy to Kupalo, Yarilo, and the rest I have shown else-where, originally personified vegetation, more especially the dying or dead vegetation of winter.[3] Further, my interpre-tation of the gardens of Adonis is confirmed by finding that in this Prussian custom the very same kind of plants is used to form the gardens of Adonis (as we may call them) and the image of the deity. Nothing could set in a stronger light the truth of the theory that the gardens of Adonis are merely another manifestation of the god himself.

In Sicily gardens of Adonis are still sown in spring as well as in summer, from which we may perhaps infer that Sicily as well as Syria celebrated of old a vernal festival of the dead and risen god. At the approach of Easter, Sicilian women sow wheat, lentils, and canary-seed in plates, which they keep in the dark and water every two days. The plants soon shoot up ; the stalks are tied together with red ribbons, and the plates containing them are placed on

Sicilian gardens of Adonis in spring.

---

[1] Matthäus Prätorius, *Deliciae Prus-siae* (Berlin, 1871), p. 56.

[2] *The Dying God*, pp. 261 *sq.*

[3] *The Dying God*, pp. 233 *sqq.*, 261 *sqq.*

the sepulchres which, with the effigies of the dead Christ,
are made up in Catholic and Greek churches on Good
Friday,[1] just as the gardens of Adonis were placed on the
grave of the dead Adonis.[2] The practice is not confined
to Sicily, for it is observed also at Cosenza in Calabria,[3] and
perhaps in other places. The whole custom—sepulchres, as
well as plates of sprouting grain—may be nothing but a continuation, under a different name, of the worship of Adonis.

Nor are these Sicilian and Calabrian customs the only
Easter ceremonies which resemble the rites of Adonis.
" During the whole of Good Friday a waxen effigy of the
dead Christ is exposed to view in the middle of the Greek
churches and is covered with fervent kisses by the thronging
crowd, while the whole church rings with melancholy, mono-
tonous dirges. Late in the evening, when it has grown quite
dark, this waxen image is carried by the priests into the
street on a bier adorned with lemons, roses, jessamine, and
other flowers, and there begins a grand procession of the
multitude, who move in serried ranks, with slow and solemn
step, through the whole town. Every man carries his taper
and breaks out into doleful lamentation. At all the houses
which the procession passes there are seated women with
censers to fumigate the marching host. Thus the community solemnly buries its Christ as if he had just died. At
last the waxen image is again deposited in the church, and
the same lugubrious chants echo anew. These lamentations, accompanied by a strict fast, continue till midnight on
Saturday. As the clock strikes twelve, the bishop appears
and announces the glad tidings that 'Christ is risen,' to
which the crowd replies, 'He is risen indeed,' and at once
the whole city bursts into an uproar of joy, which finds vent
in shrieks and shouts, in the endless discharge of carronades
and muskets, and the explosion of fire-works of every sort.
In the very same hour people plunge from the extremity
of the fast into the enjoyment of the Easter lamb and neat
wine." [4]

[1] G. Pitrè, *Spettacoli e Feste Popolari
Siciliane*, p. 211.

[2] Κῆπους ἐσίων ἐπιταφίους Ἀδέριδι,
Eustathius on Homer, *Od.* xi. 590.

[3] Vincenzo Dorsa, *La tradizione*
Greco-Latina negli usi e nelle credenze
popolari della Calabria Citeriore (Cosenza, 1884), p. 50.

[4] C. Wachsmuth, *Das alte Griechen-
land im neuem* (Bonn, 1864), pp. 26

In like manner the Catholic Church has been accustomed to bring before its followers in a visible form the death and resurrection of the Redeemer. Such sacred dramas are well fitted to impress the lively imagination and to stir the warm feelings of a susceptible southern race, to whom the pomp and pageantry of Catholicism are more congenial than to the colder temperament of the Teutonic peoples. The solemnities observed in Sicily on Good Friday, the official anniversary of the Crucifixion, are thus described by a native Sicilian writer. " A truly moving ceremony is the procession which always takes place in the evening in every commune of Sicily, and further the Deposition from the Cross. The brotherhoods took part in the procession, and the rear was brought up by a great many boys and girls representing saints, both male and female, and carrying the emblems of Christ's Passion. The Deposition from the Cross was managed by the priests. The coffin with the dead Christ in it was flanked by Jews armed with swords, an object of horror and aversion in the midst of the profound pity excited by the sight not only of Christ but of the Mater Dolorosa, who followed behind him. Now and then the 'mysteries' or symbols of the Crucifixion went in front. Sometimes the procession followed the 'three hours of agony' and the 'Deposition from the Cross.' The 'three hours' commemorated those which Jesus Christ passed upon the Cross. Beginning at the eighteenth and ending at the twenty-first hour of Italian time two priests preached alternately on the Passion. Anciently the sermons were delivered in the open air on the place called the Calvary: at last, when the third hour was about to strike, at the words

Resemblance of the Easter ceremonies in the Catholic Church to the rites of Adonis.

---

sq. The writer compares these ceremonies with the Eleusinian rites. But I agree with Mr. R. Wünsch (*Das Frühlingsfest der Insel Malta*, pp. 49 sq.) that the resemblance to the Adonis festival is still closer. Compare V. Dorsa, *La tradizione Greco-Latina negli usi e nelle credenze popolari della Calabria Citeriore*, pp. 49 sq. Prof. Wachsmuth's description seems to apply to Athens. In the country districts the ritual is apparently similar.

See R. A. Arnold, *From the Levant* (London, 1868), pp. 251 sq., 259 sq. So in the Church of the Holy Sepulchre at Jerusalem the death and burial of Christ are acted over a life-like effigy. See Henry Maundrell, *Journey from Aleppo to Jerusalem at Easter, A.D. 1697*, Fourth Edition (Perth, 1800), pp. 110 sqq.; id., in Th. Wright's *Early Travels in Palestine* (London, 1848), pp. 443-445.

emisit spiritum Christ died, bowing his head amid the sobs
and tears of the bystanders.   Immediately afterwards in
some places, three hours afterwards in others, the sacred
body was unnailed and deposited in the coffin.   In Castro-
nuovo, at the Ave Maria, two priests clad as Jews, representing Joseph of Arimathea and Nicodemus, with their
servants in costume, repaired to the Calvary, preceded by
the Company of the Whites.   There, with doleful verses
and chants appropriate to the occasion, they performed the
various operations of the Deposition, after which the procession took its way to the larger church. . . . In Salaparuta
the Calvary is erected in the church.   At the preaching of
the death, the Crucified is made to bow his head by means
of machinery, while guns are fired, trumpets sound, and
amid the silence of the people, impressed by the death of
the Redeemer, the strains of a melancholy funeral march
are heard.   Christ is removed from the Cross and deposited
in the coffin by three priests.   After the procession of the
dead Christ the burial is performed, that is, two priests lay
Christ in a fictitious sepulchre, from which at the mass of
Easter Saturday the image of the risen Christ issues and is
elevated upon the altar by means of machinery."[1]   Scenic
representations of the same sort, with variations of detail, are
exhibited at Easter in the Abruzzi,[2] and probably in many
other parts of the Catholic world.[3]

The Christian festival of Easter perhaps grafted on a festival of Adonis.

When we reflect how often the Church has skilfully contrived to plant the seeds of the new faith on the old stock
of paganism, we may surmise that the Easter celebration of
the dead and risen Christ was grafted upon a similar celebration of the dead and risen Adonis, which, as we have seen
reason to believe, was celebrated in Syria at the same season.
The type, created by Greek artists, of the sorrowful goddess
with her dying lover in her arms, resembles and may have

---

[1] G. Pitrè, *Spettacoli e Feste Popolari
Siciliane*, pp. 217 *sq.*

[2] G. Finamore, *Credenze, Usi e
Costumi Abruzzesi*, pp. 118-120; A.
de Nino, *Usi e Costumi Abruzzesi*,
i. 64 *sq.*, ii. 210-212.   At Roccacara-
manico part of the Easter spectacle is
the death of Judas, who, personated by
a living man, pretends to hang himself

upon a tree or a great branch, which
has been brought into the church and
planted near the high altar for the purpose (A. de Nino, *op. cit.* ii. 211).

[3] The drama of the death and resurrection of Christ was formerly celebrated at Easter in England.   See
Abbot Gasquet, *Parish Life in Mediaeval England*, pp. 177 *sqq.*, 182 *sq.*

been the model of the *Pietà* of Christian art, the Virgin with the dead body of her divine Son in her lap, of which the most celebrated example is the one by Michael Angelo in St. Peter's. That noble group, in which the living sorrow of the mother contrasts so wonderfully with the languor of death in the son, is one of the finest compositions in marble. Ancient Greek art has bequeathed to us few works so beautiful, and none so pathetic.[1]

In this connexion a well-known statement of Jerome may not be without significance. He tells us that Bethlehem, the traditional birthplace of the Lord, was shaded by a grove of that still older Syrian Lord, Adonis, and that where the infant Jesus had wept, the lover of Venus was bewailed.[2] Though he does not expressly say so, Jerome seems to have thought that the grove of Adonis had been planted by the heathen after the birth of Christ for the purpose of defiling the sacred spot. In this he may have been mistaken. If Adonis was indeed, as I have argued, the spirit of the corn, a more suitable name for his dwelling-place could hardly be found than Bethlehem, "the House of Bread,"[3] and he may well have been worshipped there at his House of Bread long ages before the birth of Him who said, "I am the bread of life."[4] Even on the hypothesis that Adonis followed rather than preceded Christ at Bethlehem, the choice of his sad figure to divert the allegiance of Christians from their Lord cannot but strike us as eminently appropriate when we remember the similarity of the rites which commemorated the death and resurrection of the two. One of the earliest seats of the worship of the new god was Antioch, and at Antioch,

---

[1] The comparison has already been made by A. Maury, who also compares the Easter ceremonies of the Catholic Church with the rites of Adonis (*Histoire des Religions de la Grèce Antique*, Paris, 1857–1859, vol. iii. p. 221).

[2] Jerome, *Epist.* lviii. 3 (Migne's *Patrologia Latina*, xxii. 581).

[3] Bethlehem is בית לחם, literally "House of Bread." The name is appropriate, for "the immediate neighbourhood is very fertile, bearing, besides wheat and barley, groves of olive and almond, and vineyards. The wine of Bethlehem ('Talḥamī') is among the best of Palestine. So great fertility must mean that the site was occupied, in spite of the want of springs, from the earliest times" (George Adam Smith, *s.v.* "Bethlehem," *Encyclopaedia Biblica*, i. 560). It was in the harvest-fields of Bethlehem that Ruth, at least in the poet's fancy, listened to the nightingale "amid the alien corn."

[4] John vi. 35.

The Morning Star, identified with Venus, may have been the signal for the festival of Adonis.

as we have seen,[1] the death of the old god was annually celebrated with great solemnity. A circumstance which attended the entrance of Julian into the city at the time of the Adonis festival may perhaps throw some light on the date of its celebration. When the emperor drew near to the city he was received with public prayers as if he had been a god, and he marvelled at the voices of a great multitude who cried that the Star of Salvation had dawned upon them in the East.[2] This may doubtless have been no more than a fulsome compliment paid by an obsequious Oriental crowd to the Roman emperor. But it is also possible that the rising of a bright star regularly gave the signal for the festival, and that as chance would have it the star emerged above the rim of the eastern horizon at the very moment of the emperor's approach. The coincidence, if it happened, could hardly fail to strike the imagination of a superstitious and excited multitude, who might thereupon hail the great man as the deity whose coming was announced by the sign in the heavens. Or the emperor may have mistaken for a greeting to himself the shouts which were addressed to the star. Now Astarte, the divine mistress of Adonis, was identified with the planet Venus, and her changes from a morning to an evening star were carefully noted by the Babylonian astronomers, who drew omens from her alternate appearance and disappearance.[3] Hence we may conjecture that the festival of Adonis was regularly timed to coincide with the appearance of Venus as

---

[1] Above, p. 227.

[2] Ammianus Marcellinus, xxii. 9. 14. "*Urbique propinquans in speciem alicujus numinis votis excipitur publicis, miratus voces multitudinis magnae, salutare sidus inluxisse eois partibus adclamantis.*" We may compare the greeting which a tribe of South American Indians used to give to a worshipful star after its temporary disappearance. "The Abipones think that the Pleiades, composed of seven stars, is an image of their ancestor. As the constellation is invisible for some months in the sky of South America, they believe that their ancestor is ill, and every year they are mortally afraid that he will die. But when the said

stars reappear in the month of May, they imagine that their ancestor is recovered from his sickness and has returned ; so they hail him with joyous shouts and the glad music of pipes and war-horns. They congratulate him on his recovery. 'How we thank you ! At last you have come back ? Oh, have you happily recovered ?' With such cries they fill the air, attesting at once their gladness and their folly." See M. Dobrizhoffer, *Historia de Abiponibus* (Vienna, 1784), ii. 77.

[3] M. Jastrow, *The Religion of Babylonia and Assyria*, pp. 370 *sqq.*; H. Zimmern, in E. Schrader's *Die Keilinschriften und das Alte Testament*,[3] p. 424.

the Morning or Evening Star. But the star which the people of Antioch saluted at the festival was seen in the East ; therefore, if it was indeed Venus, it can only have been the Morning Star. At Aphaca in Syria, where there was a famous temple of Astarte, the signal for the celebration of the rites was apparently given by the flashing of a meteor, which on a certain day fell like a star from the top of Mount Lebanon into the river Adonis. The meteor was thought to be Astarte herself,[1] and its flight through the air might naturally be interpreted as the descent of the amorous goddess to the arms of her lover. At Antioch and elsewhere the appearance of the Morning Star on the day of the festival may in like manner have been hailed as the coming of the goddess of love to wake her dead leman from his earthy bed. If that were so, we may surmise that it was the Morning Star which guided the wise men of the East to Bethlehem,[2] the hallowed spot which heard, in the language of Jerome, the weeping of the infant Christ and the lament for Adonis.

The Star of Bethlehem.

---

[1] Sozomenus, *Historia Ecclesiastica*, ii. 5 (Migne's *Patrologia Graeca*, lxvii. 948). The connexion of the meteor with the festival of Adonis is not mentioned by Sozomenus, but is confirmed by Zosimus, who says (*Hist.* i. 58) that a light like a torch or a globe of fire was seen on the sanctuary at the seasons when the people assembled to worship the goddess and to cast their offerings of gold, silver, and fine raiment into a lake beside the temple. As to Aphaca and the grave of Adonis see above, pp. 28 *sq.*

[2] Matthew ii. 1-12.

INTRODUCTION

I.—THE AUTHOR AND HIS BOOK.

NOTHING is positively known, and little can be conjectured with any degree of probability, concerning the author of the *Library*. Writing in the ninth century of our era the patriarch Photius calls him Apollodorus the Grammarian,[1] and in the manuscripts of his book he is described as Apollodorus the Athenian, Grammarian. Hence we may conclude that Photius and the copyists identified our author with the eminent Athenian grammarian of that name, who flourished about 140 B.C. and wrote a number of learned works, now lost, including an elaborate treatise *On the Gods* in twenty-four books, and a poetical, or at all events versified, *Chronicle* in four books.[2] But in modern times good reasons have been given for rejecting this identification,[3]

[1] Photius, *Bibliotheca*, p. 142a, 37 *sq.*, ed. Bekker.
[2] W. Christ, *Geschichte der griechischen Litteratur* (Nördlingen, 1889), pp. 455 *sqq.*; Schwartz, in Pauly-Wissowa, *Real-Encyclopädie der classichen Altertumswissenschaft*, i. 2855 *sqq.* The fragments of Apollodorus are collected in C. Müller's *Fragmenta Historicorum Graecorum*, i. 428 *sqq.*
[3] This was first fully done by Professor C. Robert in his learned and able dissertation *De Apollodori Bibliotheca* (Berlin, 1873). In what follows I accept in the main his arguments and conclusions.

and the attribution of the *Library* to the Athenian grammarian is now generally abandoned. For the treatise *On the Gods* appears, from the surviving fragments and references, to have differed entirely in scope and method from the existing *Library*. The aim of the author of the book *On the Gods* seems to have been to explain the nature of the deities on rationalistic principles, resolving them either into personified powers of nature [1] or into dead men and women,[2] and in his dissections of the divine nature he appears to have operated freely with the very flexible instrument of etymology. Nothing could well be further from the spirit and method of the mythographer, who in the *Library* has given us a convenient summary of the traditional Greek mythology without making the smallest attempt either to explain or to criticize it. And apart from this general dissimilarity between the works of the grammarian and of the mythographer, it is possible from the surviving fragments of Apollodorus the Grammarian to point to many discrepancies and contradictions in detail.[3]

Another argument against the identification of the mythographer with the grammarian is that the author of the *Library* quotes the chronicler Castor ;[4]

[1] Joannes Lydus, *De Mensibus*, iv. 27 ; *Fragmenta Historicorum Graecorum*, iv. 649.

[2] Athenagoras, *Supplicatio pro Christianis*, 28, p. 150, ed. Otto ; *Fragmenta Historicorum Graecorum*, i. 431, frag. 12.

[3] See C. Robert, *De Apollodori Bibliotheca*, pp. 12 *sqq.*

[4] Apollodorus, *Bibliotheca*, ii. 1. 3.

x

for this Castor is supposed to be a contemporary of Cicero and the author of a history which he brought down to the year 61 B.C.[1] If the chronicler's date is thus correctly fixed, and our author really quoted him, it follows that·the *Library* is not a work of the Athenian grammarian Apollodorus, since it cannot have been composed earlier than about the middle of the first century B.C. But there seems to be no good ground for disputing either the date of the chronicler or the genuineness of our author's reference to him; hence we may take it as fairly certain that the middle of the first century B.C. is the earliest possible date that can be assigned to the composition of the *Library*.

Further than this we cannot go with any reasonable certainty in attempting to date the work. The author gives no account of himself and never refers to contemporary events: indeed the latest occurrences recorded by him are the death of Ulysses and the return of the Heraclids. Even Rome and the Romans are not once mentioned or alluded to by him. For all he says about them, he might have lived before Romulus and Remus had built the future capital of the world on the Seven Hills.

---

[1] Suidas, *s.v.* Κάστωρ ; Strabo, xii. 5. 3, p. 568 ; W. Christ, *Geschichte der griechischen Litteratur*, p. 430. He married the daughter of King Deiotarus, whom Cicero defended in his speech *Pro rege Deiotaro*, but he was murdered, together with his wife, by his royal father-in-law. Among his writings, enumerated by Suidas, was a work Χρονικὰ ἀγνοή-ματα.

INTRODUCTION

And his silence on this head is all the more remarkable because the course of his work would naturally have led him more than once to touch on Roman legends. Thus he describes how Hercules traversed Italy with the cattle of Geryon from Liguria in the north to Rhegium in the south, and how from Rhegium he crossed the straits to Sicily.[1] Yet in this narrative he does not so much as mention Rome and Latium, far less tell the story of the hero's famous adventures in the eternal city. Again, after relating the capture and sack of Troy he devotes some space to describing the dispersal of the heroes and their settlement in many widely separated countries, including Italy and Sicily. But while he mentions the coming of Philoctetes to Campania,[2] and apparently recounted in some detail his wars and settlement in Southern Italy,[3] he does not refer to the arrival of Aeneas in Latium, though he had told the familiar stories, so dear to Roman antiquaries, of that hero's birth from Aphrodite[4] and his escape from Troy with his father Anchises on his back.[5] From this remarkable silence we can hardly draw any other inference than that the writer was either unaware of the existence of Rome or deliberately resolved to ignore it. He

---

[1] The *Library*, ii. 5. 10.   [2] *Epitome*, vi. 15.
[3] *Epitome*, vi. 15b. It is to be noted, however, that this passage is not found in our manuscripts of Apollodorus but has been conjecturally restored to his text from the *Scholia on Lycophron* of Tzetzes.
[4] The *Library*, iii. 12. 2.   [5] *Epitome*, iii. 21.

xii

cannot have been unaware of it if he wrote, as is now generally believed, under the Roman Empire. It remains to suppose that, living with the evidence of Roman power all around him, and familiar as he must have been with the claims which the Romans set up to Trojan descent,[1] he carefully abstained from noticing these claims, though the mention of them was naturally invited by the scope and tenor of his work. It must be confessed that such an obstinate refusal to recognize the masters of the world is somewhat puzzling, and that it presents a serious difficulty to the now prevalent view that the author was a citizen of the Roman empire. On the other hand it would be intelligible enough if he wrote in some quiet corner of the Greek world at a time when Rome was still a purely Italian power, when rumours of her wars had hardly begun to trickle across the Adriatic, and when Roman sails had not yet shown themselves in the Aegean.

As Apollodorus ignored his contemporaries, so apparently was he ignored by them and by posterity for many generations. The first known writer to quote him is Photius in the ninth century A.D., and the next are John and Isaac Tzetzes, the learned Byzantine grammarians of the twelfth century, who made much use of his book and often cite him by

---

[1] Juvenal repeatedly speaks of the old Roman nobility as *Troiugenae* (i. 100, viii. 181, xi. 95); and the same term is used by Silius Italicus (*Punic.* xiv. 117, xvi. 658) as equivalent to Romans.

name.[1] Our author is named and quoted by scholiasts on Homer,[2] Sophocles,[3] and Euripides.[4] Further, many passages of his work have been interpolated, though without the mention of their author's name, in the collection of proverbs which Zenobius composed in the time of Hadrian.[5] But as we do not know when the scholiasts and the interpolator lived, their quotations furnish us with no clue for dating the *Library*.

Thus, so far as the external evidence goes, our author may have written at any time between the middle of the first century B.C. and the beginning of the ninth century A.D. When we turn to the internal evidence furnished by his language, which is the only remaining test open to us, we shall be disposed to place his book much nearer to the earlier than to the later of these dates. For his Greek style, apart from a few inaccuracies or solecisms, is fairly correct and such as might not discredit a writer of the first or second century of our era. Even turns or phrases, which at first sight strike the reader as undoubted symptoms of a late or degenerate Greek, may occasionally be defended by the example of earlier writers. For example, he

[1] See *e.g.* Tzetzes, *Scholia on Lycophron*, 178, 355, 440, 1327 ; *id.*, *Chiliades*, i. 557.
[2] Scholiast on Homer, *Il.* i. 42, 126, 195 ; ii. 103, 494.
[3] Scholiast on Sophocles, *Antigone*, 981, ταῦτα δ' ἱστορεῖ Ἀπολλόδωρος ἐν τῇ Βιβλιοθήκῃ.
[4] Scholiast on Euripides, *Alcestis*, 1.
[5] As to the date of Zenobius, see Suidas, *s.v.* Ζηνόβιος.

xiv

once uses the phrase ταῖς ἀληθείαις in the sense of
" in very truth."[1]   Unquestionably this use of the
plural is common enough in late writers,[2] but it is
not unknown in earlier writers, such as Polybius,[3]
Alcidamas,[4] and even Isocrates.[5]   It occurs in some
verses on the unity of God, which are attributed to
Sophocles, but which appear to be undoubtedly
spurious.[6]   More conclusive evidence of a late date
is furnished by our author's use of the subjunc-
tive with ἵνα, where more correct writers would
have employed the infinitive;[7] and by his occasional
employment of rare words or words used in an
unusual sense.[8]   But such blemishes are comparatively
rare.   On the whole we may say that the style of
Apollodorus is generally pure and always clear,

[1] ii. 7. 7.
[2] For examples see Babrius, lxxv. 19, with Rutherford's
note ; Tzetzes, *Schol. on Lycophron*, 522 ; Scholiast on
Homer, *Il.* ix. 557 ; Scholiast on Apollonius Rhodius, ii. 178,
iv. 815.   [3] Polybius, x. 40. 5, ed. Dindorf.
[4] Alcidamas, *Odysseus*, 13, p. 179 in Blass's edition of
Antiphon. However the genuineness of the *Odysseus* is
much disputed. See Pauly-Wissowa, *Real-Encyclopädie der
classichen Altertumswissenschaft*, i. 1536.
[5] Isocrates, xv. 283, vol. ii. p. 168, ed. Benseler.
[6] *The Fragments of Sophocles*, edited by A. C. Pearson
(Cambridge, 1917), vol. iii. p. 172, frag. 1126, with Jebb's
note, p. 174.
[7] i. 4. 2, συνθεμένων δὲ αὐτῶν ἵνα . . . διαθῇ : i. 9. 15, ᾐτήσατο
παρὰ μοιρῶν ἵνα . . . ἀπολυθῇ : iii. 12. 6, ποιησαμένου εὐχὰς
Ἡρακλέους ἵνα αὐτῷ παῖς γένηται : *Epitome*, v. 17, δόξαν δὲ
τοῖς πολλοῖς ἵνα αὐτὸν ἐάσωσι.
[8] For example ἐκτροχάζειν, "to run out" (ii. 7. 3), προσ-
ανέχειν, "to favour" (ii. 8. 4).   For more instances see
C. Robert, *De Apollodori Bibliotheca*, pp. 42 *sqq.*

XV

simple, and unaffected, except in the very rare
instances where he spangles his plain prose with a
tag from one of his poetical sources.[1] But with all
his simplicity and directness he is not an elegant
writer. In particular the accumulation of participles,
to which he is partial, loads and clogs the march of
his sentences.

From a consideration of his style, and of all
the other evidence, Professor C. Robert inclines
to conclude that the author of the *Library* was a
contemporary of Hadrian and lived in the earlier
part of the first century A.D.[2] Another modern
scholar, W. Christ, even suggested so late a date
for the composition of the work as the reign of
Alexander Severus in the third century A.D.[3] To
me it seems that we cannot safely say more than
that the *Library* was probably written at some time
in either the first or the second century of our era.
Whether the author's name was really Apollodorus,
or whether that name was foisted on him by the
error or fraud of scribes, who mistook him or desired
to palm him off on the public for the famous
Athenian grammarian, we have no means of deciding. Nor, apart from the description of him by
the copyists as " Apollodorus the Athenian," have

---

[1] See for example his description of the Cretan labyrinth
as οἴκημα καμπαῖς πολυπλόκοις πλάνων τὴν ἔξοδον (iii. 1. 3,
compare iii. 15. 8) ; and his description of Typhon breathing
fire, πολλὴν δὲ ἐκ τοῦ στόματος πυρὸς ἐξέβρασσε ζάλην (i. 6. 3).

[2] C. Robert, *De Apollodori Bibliotheca*, pp. 40 *sq.*

[3] W. Christ, *Geschichte der griechischen Litteratur*, p. 571.

xvi

we any clue to the land of his birth. He himself is silent on that as on every other topic concerning himself. But from some exceedingly slight indications Professor C. Robert conjectures that he was indeed an Athenian.[1]

Turning now from the author to his book, we may describe the *Library* as a plain unvarnished summary of Greek myths and heroic legends, as these were recorded in literature ; for the writer makes no claim to draw on oral tradition, nor is there the least evidence or probability that he did so : it may be taken as certain that he derived all his information from books alone. But he used excellent authorities and followed them faithfully, reporting, but seldom or never attempting to explain or reconcile, their discrepancies and contradictions.[2] Hence his book possesses documentary value as an accurate record of what the Greeks in general believed about the origin and early history of the world and of their race. The very defects of the writer are in a sense advantages which he possessed for the execution of the work he had taken in hand. He was neither a philosopher nor a rhetorician, and therefore lay under no temptation either to recast his materials under the influence of theory or to embellish them

[1] C. Robert, *De Apollodori Bibliotheca*, pp. 34 *sq*. Amongst these indications is the author's acquaintance with the " sea of Erechtheus " and the sacred olive-tree on the Acropolis of Athens. See Apollodorus, iii. 14. 1.

[2] This is recognized by Professor C. Robert, *De Apollodori Bibliotheca*, p. 54.

for the sake of literary effect. He was a common man, who accepted the traditions of his country in their plain literal sense, apparently without any doubt or misgiving. Only twice, among the many discrepant or contradictory views which he reports without wincing, does he venture to express a preference for one over the other. The apples of the Hesperides, he says, were not, as some people supposed, in Libya but in the far north, in the land of the Hyperboreans ; but of the existence of the wondrous fruit, and of the hundred-headed dragon which guarded them, he seemingly entertained no manner of doubt.[1] Again, he tells us that in the famous dispute between Poseidon and Athena for the possession of Attica, the judges whom Zeus appointed to adjudicate on the case were not, as some people said, Cecrops and Cranaus, nor yet Erysichthon, but the twelve gods in person.[2]

How closely Apollodorus followed his authorities may be seen by a comparison of his narratives with the extant originals from which he drew them, such as the *Oedipus Tyrannus* of Sophocles,[3] the *Alcestis*[4] and *Medea*[5] of Euripides, the *Odyssey*,[6] and above all the *Argonautica* of Apollonius Rhodius.[7] The

[1] Apollodorus, ii. 5. 11.   [2] Apollodorus, iii. 14. 1.
[3] Apollodorus, iii. 3. 5. 7 *sqq.*   [4] Apollodorus, i. 9. 15.
[5] Apollodorus, i. 9. 28.   [6] Apollodorus, *Epitome*, vii.
[7] Apollodorus, ii. 9. 16–26. However, Apollodorus allowed himself occasionally to depart from the authority of Apollonius, for example, in regard to the death of Apsyrtus. See i. 19. 24 with the note ; and for other variations, see C. Robert, *De Apollodori Bibliotheca*, pp. 80 *sqq.*

xviii

154

fidelity with which he reproduced or summarized the
accounts of writers whose works are accessible to
us inspires us with confidence in accepting his
statements concerning others whose writings are
lost. Among these, perhaps, the most important
was Pherecydes of Leros, who lived at Athens in the
first half of the fifth century B.C. and composed a
long prose work on Greek myth and legend, which
more than any other would seem to have served as
the model and foundation for the *Library* of
Apollodorus. It is unfortunate that the writings of
Pherecydes have perished, for, if we may judge
of them by the few fragments which survive,
they appear to have been a treasure-house of Greek
mythical and legendary lore, set forth with that
air of simplicity and sincerity which charm us in
Herodotus. The ground which he covered, and the
method which he pursued in cultivating it, coincided
to a large extent with those of our author. Thus
he treated of the theogony, of the war of the gods
and the giants, of Prometheus, of Hercules, of the
Argive and the Cretan sagas, of the voyage of the
Argo, and of the tribal or family legends of Arcadia,
Laconia, and Attica; and like Apollodorus he
seems to have paid great attention to genealogies.[1]
Apollodorus often cites his opinion, and we cannot
doubt that he owed much to the writings of his

[1] See W. Christ, *Geschichte der griechischen Litteratur*,
p. 249; *Fragmenta Historicorum Graecorum*, ed. C. Müller,
i. 70 *sqq.*

xix

learned predecessor.[1]   Other lost writers whom our author cites, and from whose works he derived materials for his book, are the early Boeotian genealogist Acusilaus, who seems to have lived about 500 B.C., and Asclepiades of Tragilus, a pupil of Isocrates, in the fourth century B.C., who composed a treatise on the themes of Greek tragedies.[2]

Compiled faithfully, if uncritically, from the best literary sources open to him, the *Library* of Apollodorus presents us with a history of the world, as it was conceived by the Greeks, from the dark beginning down to a time when the mists of fable began to lift and to disclose the real actors on the scene.   In other words, Apollodorus conducts us from the purely mythical ages, which lie far beyond the reach of human memory, down to the borderland of history.   For I see no reason to doubt that many, perhaps most, of the legendary persons recorded by him were not fabulous beings, but men of flesh and blood, the memory of whose fortunes and family relationships survived in oral

---

[1] As to the obligations of Apollodorus to Pherecydes, see C. Robert, *De Apollodori Bibliotheca*, pp. 66 *sqq.*

[2] For the fragments of Acusilaus and Asclepiades, see *Fragmenta Historicorum Graecorum*, ed. C. Müller, i. 101 *sqq.*, iii. 301 *sqq.*   Another passage of Acusilaus, with which Apollodorus would seem to have been acquainted, has lately been discovered in an Egyptian papyrus. See *The Oxyrhynchus Papyri*, Part XIII, edited by B. P. Grenfell and A. S. Hunt (London, 1919), p. 133; and my note on Apollodorus, *Epitome*, i. 22, vol. ii. p. 151.   As to the obligations of Apollodorus to Acusilaus and Asclepiades, see C. Robert, *De Apollodori Bibliotheca*, pp. 68 *sqq.*, 72 *sqq.*

tradition until they were embalmed in Greek literature. It is true that in his book, as in legend generally, the real and the fabulous elements blend so intimately with each other that it is often difficult or impossible to distinguish them. For example, while it seems tolerably certain that the tradition of the return of the Heraclids to Peloponnese is substantially correct, their ancestor Hercules a few generations earlier looms still so dim through the fog of fable and romance that we can hardly say whether any part of his gigantic figure is solid, in other words, whether the stories told of him refer to a real man at all or only to a creature of fairyland.[1]

[1] In favour of the view that Hercules was a man of flesh and blood, a native of Thebes, might be cited the annual sacrifice and funeral games celebrated by the Thebans at one of the gates of the city in honour of the children of Hercules (Pindar, *Isthm.* iv. 61 (104) *sqq.*, with the Scholiast) ; the statement of Herodotus (v. 59) that he had seen in the sanctuary of the Ismenian Apollo at Thebes a tripod bearing an inscription in "Cadmean letters" which set forth that the tripod had been dedicated by Amphitryon, the human father of Hercules ; and again the statement of Plutarch (*De genio Socratis*, 5 ; compare *id. Lysander*, 28) that the grave of Alcmena, mother of Hercules, at Haliartus had been opened by the Spartans and found to contain a small bronze armlet, two jars with petrified earth, and an inscription in strange and very ancient characters on a bronze tablet, which Agesilaus sent to the king of Egypt to be read by the priests, because the form of the inscription was supposed to be Egyptian. The kernel round which the Theban saga of Hercules gathered may perhaps have been the delivery of Thebes from the yoke of the Minyans of Orchomenus ; for according to tradition Thebes formerly paid tribute to that ancient and once powerful people, and it was Hercules who not only freed his people from that badge of servitude, but

Again, though the record of the old wars of Thebes and Troy is embellished or defaced by many mythical episodes and incidents, we need not scruple to believe that its broad outlines are true, and that the principal heroes and heroines of the Theban and Trojan legends were real and not mythical beings.

Of late years it has been supposed that the heroes and heroines of Greek legend are "faded gods," that is, purely imaginary beings, who have been first exalted to the dignity of deities, and then degraded to a rank not much above that of common humanity. So far as I can judge, this theory is actually an inversion

gained so decisive a victory over the enemy that he reversed the relations between the two cities by imposing a heavy tribute on Orchomenus. There is nothing impossible or even improbable in the tradition as recorded by Apollodorus (ii. 4. 11). Viewed in this light, the delivery of the Thebans from the Orchomenians resembles the delivery of the Israelites from the Philistines, and Hercules may well have been the Greek counterpart of Samson, whose historical existence has been similarly dimmed by fable. Again, the story that after the battle Hercules committed a murder and went to serve Eurystheus as an exile at Tiryns (Apollodorus, ii. 4. 12) tallies perfectly with the usage of what is called the heroic age of Greece. The work of Apollodorus contains many instances of banishment and servitude imposed as a penalty on homicides. The most famous example is the period of servitude which the great god Apollo himself had to undergo as an expiation for his slaughter of the Cyclopes. (See Apollodorus, iii. 10. 4.) A homicide had regularly to submit to a ceremony of purification before he was free to associate with his fellows, and apparently the ceremony was always performed by a foreigner in a country other than that in which the crime had been committed. This of itself entailed at least temporary banishment on the homicide. (See Index, s.vv. "Exile" and "Purification.")

xxii

158

of the truth. Instead of the heroes being gods on the
downward road to humanity, they are men on the up-
ward road to divinity; in other words, they are men
of flesh and blood, about whom after their death fancy
spun her glittering cobwebs till their real humanity
was hardly recognizable, and they partook more and
more of the character of deities. When we consider
the divine or semi-divine honours paid in historical
times to men like Miltiades,[1] Brasidas,[2] Sophocles,[3]
Dion,[4] Aratus,[5] and Philopoemen,[6] whose real existence is incontestable, it seems impossible to deny
that the tendency to deify ordinary mortals was an

[1] Herodotus, vi. 38.   [2] Thucydides, v. 11.
[3] *Etymologicum Magnum, s.v.* Δεξίων, p. 256. 6; Istrus,
quoted in a life of Sophocles, *Vitarum Scriptores Graeci
Minores*, ed. A. Westermann (Brunswick, 1845), p. 131;
Fragmenta Historicorum Graecorum, ed. C. Müller, i. 425.
The poet was worshipped under the title of Dexion, and " the
sanctuary of Dexion" is mentioned in an Athenian inscription
of the fourth century B.C. See Ch. Michel, *Recueil d'Inscriptions Grecques* (Brussels, 1920), No. 966, pp. 761 *sq.*;
G. Dittenberger, *Sylloge Inscriptionum Graecarum³*, No. 1096
(vol. iii. pp. 247 *sq.*). Compare P. Foucart, *Le culte des Héros
chez les Grecs* (Paris, 1918), pp. 121 *sqq.* (from the *Mémoires
de l'Académie des Inscriptions et Belles-Lettres*, tome xlii.).
In this valuable memoir the veteran French scholar has
treated of the worship of heroes among the Greeks with
equal judgment and learning. With his treatment of the
subject and his general conclusions I am happy to find myself
in agreement.   [4] Diodorus Siculus, xvi. 20.
[5] Polybius, viii. 14; Plutarch, *Aratus*, 53; Pausanias,
ii. 8. 1, ii. 9. 4 and 6.
[6] Diodorus Siculus, xxix. 18, ed. L. Dindorf; Livy, xxxix.
50. Heroic or divine honours are not mentioned by Plutarch
in his impressive description of the funeral of Philopoemen
(*Philopoemen*, 21); but he says that the Messenian prisoners
were stoned to death at the tomb.

xxiii

operative principle in ancient Greek religion, and that the seeds of divinity which it sowed were probably still more prolific in earlier and less enlightened ages; for it appears to be a law of theological evolution that the number of deities in existence at any moment varies inversely with the state of knowledge of the period, multiplying or dwindling as the boundaries of ignorance advance or recede. Even in the historical age of Greece the ranks of the celestial hierarchy were sometimes recruited, not by the slow process of individual canonization, as we may call it, but by a levy in mass; as when all the gallant men who died for the freedom of Greece at Marathon and Plataea received the first step of promotion on the heavenly ladder by being accorded heroic honours, which they enjoyed down to the second century of our era.[1]

Yet it would be an error to suppose that all Greek heroes and heroines had once been live men and women. Many of them were doubtless purely

---

[1] As to the heroic honours accorded to the dead at Marathon, see Pausanias, i. 32. 4; *Corpus Inscriptionum Atticarum*, ii. No. 471. Remains of the sacrifices offered to the dead soldiers have come to light at Marathon in modern times. See my commentary on Pausanias, vol. ii. 433 *sq.* As to the heroic honours enjoyed by the dead at Plataea, see Thucydides, iii. 58; Plutarch, *Aristides*, 21; G. Kaibel, *Epigrammata Graeca ex lapidibus conlecta* (Berlin, 1878), No. 461, p. 183; *Inscriptiones Graecae Megaridis Oropiae Boeotiae*, ed. G. Dittenberger (Berlin, 1892), No. 53, pp 31 *sq.* In the inscription the dead are definitely styled "heroes," and it is mentioned that the bull was still sacrificed to them by the city "down to our time" (μεχρὶς ἐφ' ἡμῶν).

xxiv

160

fictitious beings, created on the model of the others to satisfy the popular craving for supernatural patronage. Such in particular were many of the so-called eponymous heroes, who figured as the ancestors of families and of tribes, as the founders of cities, and as the patrons of corporations and trade guilds. The receipt for making a hero of this pattern was simple. You took the name of the family, tribe, city, corporation, or guild, as the case might be, clapped on a masculine termination, and the thing was done. If you were scrupulous or a stickler for form, you might apply to the fount of wisdom at Delphi, which would send you a brevet on payment, doubtless, of the usual fee. Thus when Clisthenes had created the ten Attic tribes, and the indispensable heroes were wanted to serve as figure-heads, the Athenians submitted a " long leet " of a hundred candidates to the god at Delphi, and he pricked the names of ten, who entered on their office accordingly.[1] Sometimes the fictitious hero might even receive offerings of real blood, as happened to Phocus, the nominal ancestor of the Phocians, who got a libation of blood poured into his grave every day,[2] being much luckier than another hero, real or fictitious, at Phaselis in Lycia, who was kept on a low diet of fish

[1] Aristotle, *Constitution of Athens*, 21 ; *Etymologicum Magnum, s.v.* Ἐπώνυμοι ; Scholiast on Aristides, *Panathen.*, vol. iii. p. 331, ed. G. Dindorf (where for Καλλισθένης we must read Κλεισθένης). As to the fictitious heroes, see P. Foucart, *Le culte des Héros chez les Grecs*, pp. 47 *sqq.*

[2] Pausanias, x. 4. 10. As to Phocus in his character of eponymous hero of Phocis, see Pausanias, x. 1. 1.

and had his rations served out to him only once a year.[1] It is difficult to conceive how on such a scale of remuneration the poor hero contrived to subsist from one year's end to the other.

The system of Euhemerus, which resolves the gods into dead men, unquestionably suffers from the vice inherent in all systems which would explain the infinite multiplicity and diversity of phenomena by a single simple principle, as if a single clue, like Ariadne's thread, could guide us to the heart of this labyrinthine universe; nevertheless the theory of the old Greek thinker contains a substantial element of truth, for deep down in human nature is the tendency, powerful for good as well as for evil, to glorify and worship our fellow-men, crowning their mortal brows with the aureole as well as the bay. While many of the Greek gods, as Ouranos and Ge, Helios and Selene, the Naiads, the Dryads, and so on, are direct and transparent personifications of natural powers; and while others, such as Nike, Hygieia, and Tyche, are equally direct and transparent personifications of abstract ideas,[2] it is possible

---

[1] Athenaeus, vii. 51, pp. 297ʀ–298ᴀ.

[2] The personification and deification of abstract ideas in Greek and Roman religion are illustrated, with a great wealth of learning, by L. Deubner in W. H. Roscher's *Lexikon der griechischen und römischen Mythologie*, iii. 2068 *sqq.* What Juvenal says (x. 365 *sq.*) of the goddess of Fortune, one of the most popular of these deified abstractions, might be said with equal truth of many other gods and goddesses :

> *Nos te,*
> *Nos facimus, Fortuna, deam caeloque locamus.*

xxvi

162

and even probable that some members of the pantheon set out on their career of glory as plain men and 'women, though we can no longer trace their pedigree back through the mists of fable to their humble origin. In the heroes and heroines of Greek legend and history we see these gorgeous beings in the chrysalis or incubatory stage, before they have learned to burst the integuments of earth and to flaunt their gaudy wings in the sunshine of heaven. The cerements still cling to their wasted frames, but will soon be exchanged for a gayer garb in their passage from the tomb to the temple.

But besides the mythical and legendary narratives which compose the bulk of the *Library,* we may detect another element in the work of our author which ought not to be overlooked, and that is the element of folk-tale. As the distinction between myth, legend, and folk-tale is not always clearly apprehended or uniformly observed, it may be well to define the sense in which I employ these terms.

By myths I understand mistaken explanations of phenomena, whether of human life or of external nature. Such explanations originate in that instinctive curiosity concerning the causes of things which at a more advanced stage of knowledge seeks satisfaction in philosophy and science, but being founded on ignorance and misapprehension they are always false, for were they true they would cease to be myths. The subjects of myths are as numerous as the objects which present themselves to the mind

of man; for everything excites his curiosity, and of
everything he desires to learn the cause. Among
the larger questions which many peoples have
attempted to answer by myths are those which
concern the origin of the world and of man, the
apparent motions of the heavenly bodies, the regular
recurrence of the seasons, the growth and decay
of vegetation, the fall of rain, the phenomena of
thunder and lightning, of eclipses and earthquakes,
the discovery of fire, the invention of the useful arts,
the beginnings of society, and the mystery of death.
In short, the range of myths is as wide as the world,
being coextensive with the curiosity and the ignorance of man.[1]

By legends I understand traditions, whether oral
or written, which relate the fortunes of real people
in the past, or which describe events, not necessarily

[1] By a curious limitation of view some modern writers
would restrict the scope of myths to ritual, as if nothing but
ritual were fitted to set men wondering and meditating on the
causes of things. As a recent writer has put it concisely,
"*Les mythes sont les explications des rites*" (F. Sartiaux,
"La philosophie de l'histoire des religions et les origines du
Christianisme dans le dernier ouvrage de M. Loisy," *Revue
du Mois*, Septembre-Octobre, 1920, p. 15 of the separate
reprint). It might have been thought that merely to open
such familiar collections of myths as the *Theogony* of
Hesiod, the *Library* of Apollodorus, or the *Metamorphoses*
of Ovid, would have sufficed to dissipate so erroneous a conception; for how small is the attention paid to ritual in
these works! No doubt some myths have been devised to
explain rites of which the true origin was forgotten; but
the number of such myths is small, probably almost infini-
tesimally small, by comparison with myths which deal with
other subjects and have had another origin.

xxviii

human, that are said to have occurred at real places. Such legends contain a mixture of truth and falsehood, for were they wholly true, they would not be legends but histories. The proportion of truth and falsehood naturally varies in different legends; generally, perhaps, falsehood predominates, at least in the details, and the element of the marvellous or the miraculous often, though not always, enters largely into them.

By folk-tales I understand narratives invented by persons unknown and handed down at first by word of mouth from generation to generation, narratives which, though they profess to describe actual occurrences, are in fact purely imaginary, having no other aim than the entertainment of the hearer and making no real claim on his credulity. In short, they are fictions pure and simple, devised not to instruct or edify the listener, but only to amuse him; they belong to the region of pure romance. The zealous student of myth and ritual, more intent on explaining than on enjoying the lore of the people, is too apt to invade the garden of romance and with a sweep of his scythe to lay the flowers of fancy in the dust. He needs to be reminded occasionally that we must not look for a myth or a rite behind every tale, like a bull behind every hedge or a canker in every rose. The mind delights in a train of imagery for its own sake apart from any utility to be derived from the visionary scenes that pass before her, just as she is charmed by the contemplation of

a fair landscape, adorned with green woods, shining
rivers, and far blue hills, without thinking of the
timber which the woodman's axe will fell in these
green glades, of the fish which the angler's line will
draw from these shining pools, or of the ore which
the miner's pick may one day hew from the bowels
of these far blue hills. And just as it is a mistake
to search for a mythical or magical significance in
every story which our rude forefathers have bequeathed to us by word of mouth, so it is an error to
interpret in the same sad and serious sense every
carving and picture with which they decorated the
walls of their caverns. From early times, while
some men have told stories for the sheer joy of
telling them, others have drawn and carved and
painted for the pure pleasure which the mind takes
in mimicry, the hand in deft manipulation, and the
eye in beautiful forms and colours.[1] The utilitarian
creed is good and true only on condition that we
interpret utility in a large and liberal sense, and do

[1] M. Marcellin Boule has lately made some judicious
observations on the tendency to push too far the magical
interpretation of prehistoric cave paintings. Without denying
that magic had its place in these early works of art, he concludes, with great verisimilitude, that in the beginning "*l'art
n'est probablement qu'une manifestation particulière d'un
esprit général d'imitation déjà si développé chez les singes.*"
See his book, *Les Hommes Fossiles* (Paris, 1921), p. 260 note.
A similar view of the origin of art in emotional impulses
rather than in the deliberate and purposeful action of magic
and religion, is expressed by Mr. Sarat Chandra Roy in his
able work, *Principles and Methods of Physical Anthropology* (Patna, 1920), pp. 87 *sq.*

xxx

not restrict it to the bare satisfaction of those bodily instincts on which ultimately depends the continuance both of the individual and of the species.

If these definitions be accepted, we may say that myth has its source in reason, legend in memory, and folk-tale in imagination; and that the three riper products of the human mind which correspond to these its crude creations are science, history, and romance.

But while educated and reflective men can clearly distinguish between myths, legends, and folk-tales, it would be a mistake to suppose that the people, among whom these various narratives commonly circulate, and whose intellectual cravings they satisfy, can always or habitually discriminate between them. For the most part, perhaps, the three sorts of narratives are accepted by the folk as all equally true or at least equally probable. To take Apollodorus, for example, as a type of the common man, there is not the least indication that he drew any distinction in respect of truth or probability between the very different kinds of narrative which he included in the *Library*. To him they seem to have been all equally credible; or if he entertained any doubts as to their credibility, he carefully suppressed them.

Among the specimens, or rather morsels, of popular fiction which meet us in his pages we may instance the tales of Meleager, Melampus, Medea, Glaucus, Perseus, Peleus, and Thetis, which all bear traces of the story-teller's art, as appears plainly enough when we compare them with similar incidents in undoubted folk-tales. To some of these stories, with the comparisons which they invite, I have called attention in the notes and Appendix, but their number might no doubt easily be enlarged. It seems not improbable that the element of folk-tale bulks larger in Greek tradition than has commonly been suspected. When the study of folk-lore is more complete and exact than at present, it may be possible to trace to their sources many rivulets of popular fiction which contributed to swell the broad and stately tide of ancient literature.[1]

In some respects the *Library* of Apollodorus resembles the book of Genesis. Both works profess to record the history of the world from the creation, or at all events from the ordering of the material universe, down to the time when the ancestors of the author's people emerged in the land which was to be the home of their race and the scene of their

[1] Among recent works which mark a distinct advance in the study of folk-tales I would particularly mention the modestly named *Anmerkungen zu den Kinder- und Hausmärchen der Brüder Grimm* by Johannes Bolte and Georg Polívka, published in three octavo volumes, Leipsic, 1913–1918. A fourth volume, containing an index and a survey of the folk-tales of other peoples, is promised and will add greatly to the utility of this very learned work, which does honour to German scholarship. Even as it is, though it deals only with the German stories collected by the two Grimms, the book contains the fullest bibliography of folk-tales with which I am acquainted. I regret that it did not reach me until all my notes were passed for the press, but I have been able to make some use of it in the Appendix.

glory. In both works the mutations of nature and the vicissitudes of man are seen through the glamour, and distorted or magnified by the haze, of myth and legend. Both works are composite, being pieced together by a comparatively late redactor, who combined materials drawn from a variety of documents, without always taking pains to explain their differences or to harmonize their discrepancies. But there the resemblance between them ends. For whereas the book of Genesis is a masterpiece of literary genius, the *Library* of Apollodorus is the dull compilation of a commonplace man, who relates without one touch of imagination or one spark of enthusiasm the long series of fables and legends which inspired the immortal productions of Greek poetry and the splendid creations of Greek art. Yet we may be grateful to him for saving for us from the wreck of ancient literature some waifs and strays which, but for his humble labours, might have sunk irretrievably with so many golden argosies in the fathomless ocean of the past.

RICHARD F. HARDIN

"Ritual" in Recent Criticism: The Elusive Sense of Community

A READER OF modern criticism learns to live with uncertainty when encountering some of the most ordinary terms. Words like "symbol," "rhythm," or "irony" require our patience, our openness to an unpredictable set of theoretical assumptions. Not many readers are so fastidious as to demand a new word for every shade of difference from an "accepted" meaning, and this is probably a healthy condition. "The abuse of an old word, if explained, may give less trouble than the invention of a new," writes C. S. Lewis (550). The mania for new phraseology has not always helped the social sciences, and there is no reason to think it would advance the understanding of literature. Still, explanations should be forthcoming when words undergo their necessary abuse. What, for example, does it mean to call a literary work a ritual? Some of the most reputable critics over the past decade have said that Milton's *Lycidas* is "a mourning ritual" (Wittreich 98), that Goethe's *Faust* "is an exceptionally clear instance of the work of art conceived as a socializing *rite de passage*" (Hartman, *Fate* 110), that Eliot's "Love Song of J. Alfred Prufrock" ends "with a ritual drama of rolling the universe toward an overwhelming question" (Feder 221), that a minor Jacobean play exemplifies the principle that "poetry is a ritual of resurrection and rebirth" (Cope 174). For the most part these statements are illuminating when read in the context of their arguments, so it would be churlish to accuse the authors of irresponsibility. "Ritual," however, has become a wonderfully unstable and intriguing word, owing, as I hope to show, to developments in our understanding of both ritual and literature over the past ten or fifteen years.

The use of "ritual" has quite properly been associated with myth criticism, but if we examine John B. Vickery's classic collection of essays in this field, *Myth and Literature*, we may find that as late as the 1960s myth critics held certain notions about ritual that are no longer tenable. Stanley Edgar Hyman's 1958 essay in that collection stands as the most confident assertion of these beliefs. A great student of Darwin's prose, Hyman seems to view literary theory as undergoing its own modest evolution within the larger progress of the human sciences, from E. B. Tylor's *Primitive Culture* to James G. Frazer's *Golden Bough* and the applications of Frazer by the so-called Cambridge school of criticism (Jane Harrison, Gilbert Murray, A. B. Cook, and F. M. Cornford). Since the 1960s virtually every "discovery" that Hyman attributes to this movement has been seriously challenged. Few people believe that all myth, including the bulk of Homer and "the whole body of Near East sacred literature" (51), originates in ritual. Few classical scholars would now say that "the ritual view has illuminated almost the whole of Greek culture" (56) or even that "the forms of Attic tragedy arise out of sacrificial rites of tauriform or aegiform Dionysos" (57). Although the ritual origins of drama in general are not so readily assumed as they were in Hyman's day, it remains true that, as Heinrich Dörrie observes, the specialist criticism of classicists "has not sufficiently prevailed in those areas in which more than one area of scholarship connect (ethnology, religious studies, psychology). In these fields it is still true that whatever pleases is allowed" (129, n. 13). The most influential developments of Frazer and the Cambridge school came, of course, not from Hyman but from Northrop Frye, whose elegant theories of myth, genre, mode, and archetype promoted a rich harvest of myth criticism in the 1960s. Still, Frye's assumptions are not all that different from Hyman's. At least one advance in myth criticism, and in our perceptions of "ritual" in literature, has come since Frye, in the theories of René Girard, whose ideas often resemble Frye's in their comprehensiveness, though they usually lead to conclusions diametrically opposed to his.

In this essay I propose that many critics of the

last ten or fifteen years have still not come to terms with the meaning of "ritual," often because they base their assumptions on outdated notions about the origins of myth in ritual, about the connections between Greek or medieval drama and ritual, or about narrative as displaced ritual. It needs to be more generally known that these subjects have undergone serious reexamination in the last few years and that the very concept of ritual (or ceremony—I use the terms interchangeably, as indeed most scholars do) has received much scrutiny in the social sciences during the same period. One particular theory, that of Victor Turner, has received wide acceptance, and I propose it as the most adequate for criticism today. Besides its clarity and precision, the theory has the advantage of recognizing the social foundations of ritual, a characteristic that critics have often overlooked. Rites cannot exist in an aesthetic or formalist vacuum; they require the context of community. We do not invent the great ceremonies of our culture but, rather, come to them as parts of a whole. Although rites may share their symbolic nature with art, they convey the sense of satisfaction peculiar to them alone in the intense experience of community that is their chief reason for being. The first two sections of the essay summarize some important new insights into relations between literature and ritual since midcentury and some of the ideas recently brought to bear on the subject by the social sciences. The third section surveys criticism, chiefly of the 1970s, that employs ritual as a central concept. I make no pretensions to have covered all literary studies, however, and in fact have had to leave out some items that, worthwhile in themselves, are not sufficiently relevant to my essay. There are critics, I believe, who have dealt quite aptly with this subject, though they may show no signs of having read anthropology; it is from them, perhaps, that we have the most to learn.

I

We can attribute many assumptions regarding a ritual element in literature to the influence of handbooks, anthology introductions, and such widely read critical works as Francis Fergusson's *Idea of a Theater* and those of Frye. These perpetuate the view that Greek tragedy origi-

nated in primitive Greek ritual, with the corollary that other forms of drama, perhaps all drama, had such roots. Jane Harrison believed that *drama* was related to *dromenon*, "the thing done" in a rite, which had a corresponding myth or *legomenon*, "thing spoken" (Hyman, "Ritual" 48–49). Thus the ritual theory of myth arises simultaneously with the ritual theory of drama, so that discussion of one inevitably leads to the other.

Of the many classical scholars who now dispute the ritual origins of tragedy none is more convincing or more aware of the implications of the theory for criticism at large than Gerald F. Else, whose *Origins and Early Form of Greek Tragedy* takes up the cudgels where Sir Arthur Pickard-Cambridge left off.[1] From the beginning, Else is alarmed that so influential a book as *The Idea of a Theater* would depend so fully on the exploded ideas of the Cambridge school, whose theory of tragedy "is not now held, at least in its strictest form, by any leading scholar." The disrepute of this theory "appears to have been unknown to Fergusson, and it is certainly unknown to many others" (3). Else's book questions, if it does not exactly overturn, many handbook truisms about tragedy. On the "Dionysiac" element, Else claims that nothing known about the history of early tragedy implies a Dionysiac content (31); he reminds us that Aristotle's *Poetics* never mentions the god or the spirit Dionysus is supposed to represent (14). As for the later plays,

The content of the overwhelming majority of known tragedies (and we know the title and/or content of many more than are now extant) is *heroic* myth and legend, from Homer and the epic cycle. Affiliations with cult-myths and cult-rituals, especially those of Dionysos, are secondary both in extent and importance. In other words the regular source of tragic material is heroic epic, not religious cult.

(63)

The self-awareness of the Greek tragic hero as we know him "is at the opposite pole from the Dionysiac frenzy of self-abandonment" (69). Skeptical of the belief that literary forms like tragedy must "evolve," Else poses the equally credible hypothesis that tragedy was invented in two successive acts of genius: first by Thespis, who created *tragoidia* (not, in the received sense, derived from "goat-song" [25, 70]). This was a "self-presentation" by a single epic hero in his moment of pathos. After Thespis invented this recitative event, Aeschylus, adding the second character, gave us tragic drama (65, 78).

Else mentions a number of European scholars who have rejected the ritual theory, including Albin Lesky, C. del Grande, and Harold Patzer; in this country he might have added Bernard Knox (6, 71), William Arrowsmith, and Oliver Taplin, among others. Taplin is one of many classicists who have reminded us that the requirement for sameness marks ritual as distinct from dramatic art; Greek tragedies are not the same, as anyone knows who has tried to apply the Aristotelean model to, say, Sophocles' *Philoctetes*. Indeed, "The break with the repetitiousness of ritual may well have been one of the great achievements of tragedy's creators" (*Greek Tragedy* 161). Else wrote at a time when the old order was passing—Jessie Weston, William Troy, Fergusson, Theodor Gaster, Richard Chase, Hyman, and Lord Raglan—and if we are to accept his arguments we may find that to learn anything about tragedy from the examination of ritual we must, as Michael Hinden says, study the two forms as analogous, not interdependent.[2]

A notion that Else finds especially scandalous is the modern belief that Greek audiences approached tragedy in a spirit of "ritual expectancy," a critical assumption that "does serious damage to our interpretation of the plays and through them to our conception of tragedy as a whole" (4). This view, however, has influenced theatrical productions and criticism alike, as anyone knows who has seen Tyrone Guthrie's celebrated film of *Oedipus*. Bernard Knox finds fault with that production, and Oliver Taplin, in a recent survey of Greek tragedies on film, suggests that those who liked the Guthrie version "were impressed in the way that one might be by witnessing the dances and rituals of some primitive tribe, though with no notion of their significance" ("Delphic Idea" 811). The strangeness of the film creates a response in the audience, but—and the issue will recur in this discussion—it remains to be seen whether the sense of awe or transcendence is equivalent to a response to the work as drama. On the whole, Else gives us cause to rethink, if not to reject outright, the

notion of "ritual expectancy" in drama. Anthony Graham-White proposes that it is just in the matter of expectations that ritual differs from drama. Rituals are believed to be efficacious; they never exist for their own sake. It will not do, Graham-White maintains, to equate audience participation with ritual. Rites in traditional societies "usually are carried out by a clearly defined group," with the general public carefully excluded (323).[3]

On the whole it seems that the ritual hypothesis does more violence to the evidence than do some of the less exciting proposals of later classical scholarship. Furthermore, there is much to be said for the idea that the form and purpose of rites differ from those of drama, especially tragedy. A rite can be carried on by a single "actor"; the audience seldom identifies itself with a ritual celebrant in a spirit of pathos as it does when watching an actor; even when the audience knows the "fable" behind a play, it does not know how the expected end will be reached, though such familiarity is often required in ritual, and innovation is sure to arouse controversy. Victor Turner, Margaret Mead, and other anthropologists have declared the smallest unit of ritual to be the symbol.[4] If so, then perhaps in those dramas that are most frequently seen as ritualistic we focus on the symbols rather than on the hero's pathos or the development of plot (Fichte 15; quoted in Flanigan's second article, 115).[5] Although *Oedipus* is a well-plotted mimetic drama, the richness of the symbolism almost justifies Guthrie's treatment: one thinks of plague, blindness, the crossroads, the shepherd-king, the lame savior, incest, and countless other images in the language and action of the play hinting at a latent meaning of far greater consequence than the experienced events. Ritual drama is thinly plotted, but like much Greek tragedy it creates deep emotion through the use of symbols. Yeats, who called his own plays "not drama but the ritual of a lost faith," wrote with great success in this way, using incantatory language, masks, and archetypal characters "to draw the audience away from daily life and into the deeper levels of contemplation and response" (Gorsky 176). Yet because no theory of tragedy has ever elevated the symbol to so crucial a place in the genre, we may question whether the ritual hypothesis serves as useful a purpose in criticism of drama, particularly tragedy, as scholars once thought.

Although the ritual theory of myth, like that of tragedy, was already in the air during the later nineteenth century, we may trace its debut in English literary studies to the year 1890, when William Robertson Smith's *Religion of the Semites*, Jane Harrison's *Mythology and Monuments of Ancient Athens*, and Frazer's *Golden Bough* all first saw publication. To an outsider the theory that all myths derive from rituals may seem needlessly reductive, so that Clyde Kluckhohn's well-known critique of the theory in 1942 would appear to right the balance on behalf of common sense. Other serious flaws in the theory came to light during the next two decades, as in Joseph Fontenrose's book on the Delphic myth, which shows that the Babylonian myth of beginnings as told in the *Enuma elish* was recited in the Akitu festival but not enacted or symbolized in the rites of the occasion (ch. 15).[6] Such research has led us to see that although some myths are indeed "the spoken correlative of things done," as Harrison insisted, there are fundamental differences between myth and rite that obviate the ritual theory. "The truth is," G. S. Kirk has recently observed, "that myths seem to possess essential properties—like their fantasy, their freedom to develop, and their complex structure—that are not reproduced in ritual and suggest that their motive and origin are in important respects distinct" (25). Frazer himself, despite a certain positivist disdain for religion that led him to repudiate both Robertson Smith and the Cambridge group (Ackerman), is viewed by many folklorists as responsible for the confusion introduced by the ritual theory: "The fact is that he was not clear on the difference between fable and cult when he began to write *The Golden Bough*. . . . he gave cult an absolute priority over narrative, and viewed all cult from the peculiar vantage of a classicist, which does not in any case give a very full or unobstructed prospect of either cult or fable." (Bynum 158, 160; on the "ritual fallacy," see 149–254. An earlier folklorist critique is Bascom's "Myth-Ritual Theory.")

The work of Harrison and her adherents is well known for its concept of the original myth, the mono-myth from which all other myths descend and diverge: the divine king who must be sacrificed so that his society may prosper. A decisive, perhaps fatal blow to this theory came from Joseph Fontenrose in his 1966 critique of the Cambridge group and its later adherents. In its own sphere this book does what Else's nearly contemporaneous series of lectures does in the study of tragedy. Fontenrose reviews the case made by Andrew Lang in *Magic and Religion* (1901) that Frazer's theory was wholly based on misrepresentation or exaggeration of the evidence. We thus encounter a parallel between the ritual theories of myth and tragedy, in that although specialists had long ago repudiated the principal facts and assumptions supporting the theory, it nonetheless continued to be nourished by literary critics (Fontenrose singles out Lord Raglan and Stanley Edgar Hyman as principal offenders). "In all the ancient world [Greece included] we find no record, clear or obscure, of an annual or periodic sacrifice of divine kings" (8). The anecdote of the "king of the woods" in the grove at Nemi, Frazer's one clear instance of a king put to death when his strength fails, proves to have been an Italian folk custom that cannot be documented as involving the murder of a king (36–49). There is no ethnographic evidence, moreover, of any society anywhere in the world practicing the periodic sacrifice of a king. Well-known instances of a tribe's killing its kings in Africa cannot be used to support the mono-myth: these executions are not conducted periodically—they usually occur when the king is too old to govern—and they are not enacted ritually (9–13). Thus, what Frazer's early readers believed to be a truth grounded on historical and anthropological facts ought rightly to be recognized as a fiction about primitive life. Although Joyce, Eliot, and D. H. Lawrence appear to have credited Frazer's theory with as much historicity as did Harrison, Murray, and Cornford (see Vickery, *Literary Impact*), any myth critic has to admit that the assumptions behind, say, the notes to Eliot's *Waste Land* have lost much of the authority that they had a half century ago. Northrop Frye's recent apologia on the subject employs a rather qualified language compared to some of his earlier statements on the subject:

Frazer demonstrated the existence *in the human mind* of a symbolism *often latent in the uncon-*

scious, perhaps never emerging in any complete form, but revealed through many ritual acts and customs, of a divine man killed at the height of his powers whose flesh and blood are ceremonially eaten and drunk. This symbolism expresses the social anxiety for a continuity of vigorous leadership and sexual vitality, and for a constant renewal of the food supply, as the bread and wine of the vegetable crops and the bodies of eaten animals are symbolically identified with the divine-human victim.

("Expanding Eyes" 111–12; italics mine)

Divine king has become a "divine man," but the critic at least saves the appearances of consistency with his earlier opinion of Frazer and his view of *The Golden Bough* as key to the origins of drama: "it reconstructs an archetypal ritual from which the structural and generic principles of drama may be logically, not chronologically, derived. It does not matter two pins to the literary critic whether such a ritual had any historical existence or not" (*Anatomy* 109).

This tendency to dismiss the question of Frazer's historicity (certainly Frazer, Harrison, and even Murray believed that they were recovering evidence of things that had really happened) is a disturbing feature of much myth-and-ritual theory. Those who apply the theory seldom admit that it has no basis in fact. Anne Righter, in her justly acclaimed *Shakespeare and the Idea of the Play*, speaks in factual terms about the resemblance of the murdered York in *Henry VI* to Frazer's ill-fated king:

The story has reverberations that are even older than the mocking of Christ, echoes that call up the Golden Grove at Nemi and the whole problem of the temporary king. Many primitive societies, reluctant at last to slay the true king, as custom demanded, habitually elected a substitute ruler who took the ritual death upon himself in return for a brief reign. (106)

Yet Fontenrose has shown the wholly fictitious nature of Frazer's King of the Woods and the thin ethnographic evidence for the periodic sacrifice of a king (*Ritual* 36, 8–14). If this kind of thing never really happened, where does such a theory come from? If Frye's theory of drama and myth "may be" logically derived from a never-observed archetypal ritual, may it also *not* be derived? The strange, terrible specificity of the young man killed and eaten contrast sharply with the obscurity of a symbolism that according to Frye not only remains "latent in the unconscious" but has perhaps never come out of the incubator.

II

The potential fallacy of ritual origins is seriously compounded by the likelihood that "ritual" will be applied with no serious reflections on the exact meaning of the word. Critics using "mythic" to bestow value on a literary text (a practice noted well before Frye's *Anatomy*; see Wallace Douglas 127) have often done the same with "ritual." Yet the nature of ritual has evaded even social scientists and theologians during the past decade.[7] Scholars still debate, for example, whether rituals are independent of the social structure or whether they make statements about the relative status of persons in society (Crocker 48). Edmund Leach prefers to think of ritual as, narrowly, "a body of custom specifically associated with religious performance" but, more generally, "any noninstinctive predictable action or series of actions that cannot be justified by a 'rational' means-to-end type of explanation" (520–21). The latter definition has the advantage of incorporating the psychiatrist's sense of personal or private ritual, but some have doubted the appropriateness of this word to describe individual compulsive or idiosyncratic behavior, since "ritual" has traditionally referred to a social and communicative activity (Burkert 49; see also Thomas J. Scheff's critics, who are quoted on pp. 490–500 of his article). Viewed as implying compulsive behavior, the word still has connections with the rough-and-ready formulas of early twentieth-century psychiatric thought. If the study of myth and folklore has led us to understand that an apparently similar myth should not be interpreted identically for all cultures (Ferris 265), the same must be true of ritual, in which the symbols and structures are at least as arbitrary. For this reason, to associate "compulsive" or highly systematic literary structures with ritual, as Fletcher does in linking allegory and ritual, represents a straining of the word, if not a complete misapplication.[8]

Scheff has used another psychological definition of ritual—"the distanced reenactment of situations which evoke collectively held emotional distress"—to establish a theory of catharsis in drama by working from the assumption (debatable, as we have seen) that drama is in its origins ritualistic ("Distancing" 489; the theory forms the basis of Scheff's *Catharsis*). Critics of this theory have rightly noted that the definition neglects the positive, celebrative role of ritual; the theory also requires that social institutions be interpreted in terms of individual behavior, despite massive evidence that the influence is in the opposite direction. Whatever contributions psychology has made to criticism have not been made in association with ritual. It might even be said that an unexpected consequence of the whole literature-as-ritual approach has been to move literature from the province of the self, making us more aware of the "world" of the play or poem, outside the confines of the author's or reader's psyche. If only psychoanalytic critics would admit the deficiencies in their concept, much confusion on the topic would disappear.

The most widely discussed work on ritual during the last two decades approaches the subject as a purely communal act. Victor Turner has described ritual as "prescribed formal behavior for occasions, not given over to technological routine, having reference to beliefs in mystical beings or powers" (*Forest* 19; cf. Goody). This definition lies behind Geoffrey Hartman's usage quoted in the beginning of this article, and it has won many adherents. The inclusion of "beliefs" in Turner's account would seem to limit the term, more than Leach's definition does, by excluding such formal gestures as handshaking, not to mention animal and insect "rituals" (on such rituals see LaFontaine and *Discussion of Ritualization*). In this view, however, it is the *belief* that effects the communal bonding that ritual achieves. Turner, in his study of the Ndembu people in Africa, observes that rites oblige the participants to undergo a change in social status, in which they momentarily exchange their established place in the social structure for a condition of "communitas." During this state the bonds are "anti-structural in that they are undifferentiated, equalitarian, direct..." (*Dramas* 46–47). Structure, rank, and social and economic status are what hold people apart; "communitas" unites people across the barriers.

Following Arnold Van Gennep's classic *Rites of Passage*, Turner calls this state of being outside the categories of ordinary social life "liminality" —literally "thresholdness"—explaining that it can occur both in the state of communitas and in a condition of solitude away from society (*Dramas* 52–53). Acknowledging these two kinds of liminality may explain why "ritual" feelings or expectations are attributed to some literary works—feelings that can be identified with the timeless, dislocating effect that is perhaps essential, but is not peculiar, to ritual. Margaret Mead thus defines ritual as "the repetition of those symbols which evoke the feeling of that primordial event which initially called the community into being with such power that it effects our presence at that event—in other words, represents the primordial event" (127). This feeling can, however, be evoked by other than ritual means. Neither Mead nor Turner, I should note, equates ritual with the festive spirit, as scholars do in studies that follow the lead of C. L. Barber's *Shakespeare's Festive Comedy*, where "puritan" antiritualism is opposed to the natural impulse toward the celebrative and saturnalian. In the wake of the nostalgia for our primitive past developed by Mircea Eliade, Roger Callois, and others, we should keep in mind that not all primitive people indulge in saturnalian release during festivals; some behave quite otherwise, in fact (Isambert).

At the same time that rituals help us rise above personal and social limitations, even above time and space, they also work, as Mary Douglas argues, to strengthen social status and respect for authority. This function is attested in rites of passage for adolescents throughout the world. According to Turner, this paradoxical effect results from the continuing cycle of "social dramas" in which the tension between elements of the "structure" leads to redress in order to reintegrate the disturbed social group—in effect a movement from structure to communitas to (if the rite is successful) renewed structure. The superbly literate and civilized Turner himself occasionally mentions possible applications of his "ritual process" to literature (e.g., *Dramas* 265). Recently he has suggested that we might profitably think of modern activities that seem ritualistic, like sports and the theater, as "liminoid" rather than liminal. "Many of the symbolic and ludic capacities of tribal religion have, with the advancing division of labor, with massive increase in the scale and complexity of political and economic units, migrated into nonreligious genres." Liminoid events are not necessarily collective; they are usually produced by known, named individuals. Although separated from the work place, they are unrelated to "calendrical or social-structural cycles or crises in social processes." Turner leads us to consider the presence of liminal experiences in literature rather than the structure of literature as ritual:

If we focus, for example, on the liminoid genres of literature, on scenes and moments famous for the quality of their communitas and flow, such as Achilles's encounter with Priam in the *Iliad*, the episode of Raskolnikov's and Sonya's long, painful discovery of one another in *Crime and Punishment*, so well discussed by Paul Friedrich, the communitas of the liminary outcasts, Lear, Tom O'Bedlam, Kent, and the Fool in the scene on the heath in *King Lear*, in the serious vein; and the woman's communitas in Aristophanes' *Lysistrata*, and many episodes in *Tom Jones, Don Quixote*, and other "carnivalized novels," in the ludic, my hunch is that there will be key symbols which "open" up the relationship to communitas.   ("Variations" 52)[9]

Florence Falk has recently applied the theory to *A Midsummer Night's Dream*, showing how the Athens-woods-Athens sequence resembles that of structure-communitas-structure. (For other uses of Turner and Van Gennep, see Boose.) Yet in this, as in so much similar criticism, we may be left feeling that we have been told what we already knew—though no doubt our knowledge can be sharpened and clarified. Shakespeare very likely has more to teach the anthropologists about ritual than he or even his audiences could learn from them.

III

Reviewing some of the criticism that has used the concept of ritual during the past decade, we may appreciate the advantage of a precise and informed notion of the subject. Studies of drama especially can benefit from a socially grounded theory like Turner's. Often those who speak of drama as rite neglect these social implications, emphasizing instead the mere feeling of transcen-

dence or the "flow" of liminal and liminoid activities alike. Jackson Cope writes of the timeless quality inherent in both ritual and drama:

'Ritual,' I take it, is a ceremonial order of acts which at first level imitates; that is, it re-enacts an established pattern. But at its second level of definition, ritual demands that this conservative re-enactment be really efficacious, effective in its repetitions as it was in its origins. Thus ritual is a present act which historically recalls the past for the purpose of reordering—even predetermining—the future. But that present moment of re-enactment merges into the future, and so makes the efficacy of predictive action inevitable as its pattern evolves from contingency into control. In short, ritual is a prediction which, completed, fulfills itself.   (171)

This definition appears carefully designed to bring ritual into perfect accord with the aims and province of art. A tragedy of kingship, for example, will repeat the original king's moment of pathos with a view to evoking in the audience those feelings that once were or should have been. Thereafter no one will regard the king apart from the original pathos of the dream time. "Know ye not, I am Richard the Second?" Shakespeare's queen is reported to have said. Such a conception, encompassing as it does the long-acknowledged capacity of art to mediate between the historical and the ideal, is too broad to be serviceable. To further delineate the boundaries of rite and art, I have already mentioned the possibility of ritual drama, a special form that appeals to the audience chiefly in its use of symbols rather than in imitated actions. It is these symbols that evoke the necessary community of belief.

Much comment on the union of rite and drama has occurred in the field of medieval theater, especially since the influential findings of Hardison and Wickham on the subject. Confuting the idea that English religious and secular drama evolved out of Christian worship—a theory quite compatible with Frazer and the Cambridge school, as the writings of E. K. Chambers show—these two scholars have proved the existence of two distinct, largely independent dramatic traditions in the Middle Ages: "the drama of the Real Presence within the liturgy" and "the imitative drama of Christ's humanity," in Wickham's terms (314).[10] During the 1960s, however, one still encountered the view that the mystery play is based on rite, so that the audience and the actors "shared the same ritual world" during performance, "a world more real than the one which existed outside its frame" (Righter 21). We now see that although there was a shared belief in the transcendent meaning of the events enacted, the principal effect of, say, the grisly realism of the York *Crucifixion* is to draw the audience closer to the event not through symbols but through representation of recognizable human experiences, familiar human types. In an important article Martin Stevens aids our perspective on the separation of rite from drama and even raises doubts whether the Mass ought properly to be considered dramatic.[11] Following Brecht, Stevens proposes that drama, unlike rite, consists of enacted illusion; even "ritual drama" if performed in the church would lose ritual aspects entirely. Thus the sense of shared belief, the possibility for communitas, would be emptied from such "liturgical drama" as the Easter visitation at the tomb, which was performed as part of the Easter rite at a stylized sepulcher within the church. If a "play" cannot be staged without becoming representational drama, then ritual plays of the Yeatsian type would seem impossible. Although the persistence (documented by Hardison) of liturgical drama centuries after the establishment of "competing" mystery plays indicates that two entirely different sets of needs were being met (and the persistence of rites would of course add a third), many scholars still maintain, like Stevens, that rite and drama are mutually exclusive. "It is quite evident," writes Gauvin, using a concept resembling Mead's and Turner's,

that a rite is composed of both the prescribed gesture and of its theological significance, which goes far beyond that. In Catholic liturgy the gesture has a deep symbolic and mystic value: it actualizes, in the present time of the ceremony, a past or future event that is thus mysteriously recreated or anticipated. The Catholic rite par excellence is the Mass, which can be said to reconstitute systematically the mystery of the Redemption by the death and Resurrection of Christ. (131; my trans.)[12]

To equate theater with ritual is therefore to say that theater recreates in the present that which it represents. This position, Gauvin believes, entails two untenable consequences for the English mystery plays: first, that these dramas-ceremonies are truly religious, though conducted by laymen; second, that the persons represented, including the Father and the incarnate Son, are not disguised actors but themselves. Perhaps, he concludes, the cycle plays and other religious representational drama (presumably including liturgical drama, if no play can be a rite) are best classified with devotional images. They do not stand in place of the Mass or any other rite, but they do arouse devout feelings in the viewer, just as a statue or a painting does (138–39; Hanning also argues the theological impossibility of ritual drama). The dramatic element of playing or pretending, however, is quite at odds with the nature of ritual, in which participants act for a purpose (to become adults, to join in marriage, to receive the eucharistic elements).

Twenty years ago a critic struggling with the supposed ritual element in Shakespeare's plays could say, "I shall not be arguing that imaginative works *are* rituals in disguise, nor (save of course for the cases like Greek tragedy or medieval miracle plays, where it is already common knowledge) that they derive from rituals or explain or justify them. Such extravagances would be absurd" (Holloway 176). Yet at the outset we saw that some respectable scholars do speak of some literary works as rituals; we have also seen that the ritual origins of Greek and medieval theater are no longer accepted as "common knowledge," at least not among specialists in these fields. Hallett Smith's criticism of ritualist approaches to Shakespeare's late plays proceeds from a view similar to Gauvin's: that the plays inhibit the participation essential to true ritual because their theatricality distances the audience (197–202). As with studies of other literature, so with Shakespeare, the decline of myth criticism seems to have brought a waning of enthusiasm for the ceremonial element in the plays, at least as they are construed through the dubious methods of the Cambridge school.[13] The influence of the Christian liturgy is another matter, and it is the focus of Coursen's lengthy study of the tragedies (Hassel also examines drama and liturgy of the period). Coursen believes that Shakespeare conceived both comedy and tragedy in terms of the communion service, comedy working toward communion while "The tragic world divorces itself from the unifying powers expressed in communion" (34). The tragedies thus present an array of counterrituals like the murder of Caesar or Richard II's parting from his queen, which Coursen views as an "anti-marriage" (77). Since the audience is not participating in these actions, they can of course be considered rites only from the characters' standpoint. And if we reflect on Victor Turner's definition, we have to add that these moments of disunion are not prescribed or occasioned. We may compare the recent claim that the nunnery scene in *Hamlet* is an "inverted marriage ceremony," in which Ophelia "violates the ritual" by siding with her father rather than with her potential husband (Boose 329).[14] From the audience's perspective such scenes may be symbolic, but (again) the audience does not participate in them; to the characters they are not rites but quite real sets of actions. It is true that Brutus wants to make Caesar's murder an act of sacrifice, but that effort would seem the result of Brutus' special derangement.[15] An approach tying the plays to the Book of Common Prayer invites a return to earlier theories of drama and ritual as performative equivalents, a path fraught with difficulties. The tradition of the masque, however, should be sufficient to silence those who uncompromisingly separate rite from drama in this period. Jonson's masques especially disclose a sense of drama in the antimasque (when the characters show no awareness of the audience); yet they also contain a ceremonial sense in the mythological-symbolic trappings of the major figures, who mingle with the spectators in dance (see Orgel).

Criticism of narrative during the past decade has been influenced by ritual theories, though not quite as strongly as drama has been. Frazer's ideas inspired a number of modern authors to weave into their stories rites of rebirth, baptism, initiation, and so forth. Among novelists, D. H. Lawrence is especially fascinated with the idea that, as one critic puts it, "ritual as an organizing principle in the novel could link the pattern of an individual's life with that of society at large, and, beyond that, with Nature" (Ross 6). Lawrence's reading of Jane Harrison's *Ancient Art and Ritual*, Eliot's acquaintance with Jessie

Weston, and of course the widespread interest in Frazer led to that deliberate infusion of ritual into fiction which John B. Vickery explores amply in *The Literary Impact of The Golden Bough*. Critics of such myth-dominated fiction would probably gain from careful thought about its ritual content. It is well to see John Updike's *The Centaur* as a series of mythic and timeless moments experienced by a father and relived by his son; but is it true that "By its transformation of a particular situation into a paradigm, myth makes rite dynamic and meaningful" (Vargo 459)? This statement implies that rites consist of details that cannot be "meaningful" without a mythic content. Yet we have seen that rites often exist without myths and that rites, being constituted of symbols, still convey meaning. We shall return later to this widely held assumption that ritual is inferior to myth, often because it is supposed prior to myth. In one of Faulkner's stories, the fact that a cardplayer throws the game supposedly signifies the victory of ritual as "a formal agent of hidden necessity" over game, the "formal agent of apparent freedom" (Zender 59; in fact, game is often defined in terms of social necessity [see n. 2, below]). Faulkner, the critic says, "is concerned with the tension between the predetermined movement of characters through a pattern analogous to a traditional myth or ritual, and their free movement in an invented dramatic action" (53). Zender seems to mean that the freedom we exercise contrasts with the predetermined part of our lives, which is a ritual. But the card game is "analogous" to ritual at best, for the program of fated action is like a rite only in that it is prescribed. There is no sense that the one who throws the game does so for communal purposes—to guarantee the harvest or restore the vitality of his community. In all likelihood the claimed association of ritual with "hidden necessity" was suggested by the role of the Fates in a ritualist theory of Greek tragedy. Even in the most familiar kind of fiction involving rites—stories of initiation like Faulkner's *The Bear* or Dickey's *Deliverance*—we should ask whether the stories *are* "rites of passage" when in fact they are *about* human lives in which initiation occurs.[16] By contrast, in many real initiation rites there is no myth or story involved, only a series of arbitrarily chosen and ordered symbols for the initiate.

In summary, despite the careful work of anthropologists, classical scholars, and others who aim to disentangle the term from irrelevant and dubious associations, much criticism has continued to tie literature with an imprecise concept of ritual. The major problems seem to be the tendencies to equate rite with literature because of literature's emotional effects, its use of the symbol, its performative features, and its creation of a sense of kinship with fictional characters and hence with humanity at large. An uninformed, Cambridge-style ritualism also continues despite the efforts of Fontenrose, Else, and others. A 1981 study of the Soviet novel assumes a ritual theory of myth to show that the triteness and predictability of these novels shape them into "a sort of parable for the working-out of Marxism-Leninism in history" (Clark 9).[17] Especially in view of the communal roots of ritual, one may ask whether it makes sense to think of the lonely novel reader entering into a ritual of anything.

We should not deny the usefulness of some recent criticism aimed at the discovery of ritual content. I have already noted the rites embedded in Lawrence's stories. One recent study proposes that the setting of Joyce's "The Dead" is not a New Year's party but a funeral celebration featuring the "dance of the dead," a rite noted by Van Gennep and mentioned in one of Joyce's poems (J. W. Foster). John Vickery analyzes the pattern of the scapegoat ritual in the work of several authors whom we have every reason to believe were fully aware of this material ("Scapegoat"). (In the same collection, however, a recanting ritualist offers a caveat on interpreting quest narratives like *Gawain and the Green Knight* as rites of passage [Moorman, "Comparative"].)[18] The demonstrable influence of Nietzsche moved André Gide to construct *L'Immoraliste* around "symbolic rituals of death and revival" and to have his hero pass through rebirth and "a pagan-like cleansing ceremony in which sun, water, and a variation of tonsuring are used" (O'Reilly). Frazer's influence may also have indirectly moved Christian authors to incorporate their ceremonies into their works. In one of Charles Williams' "liturgical novels," *The Greater Trumps*, a character discovers that the Christian service in her village is part of a hidden cosmic dance, a means to participate in the universal delight that leads to mystic ecstasy (Manlove 169).[19] Such narratives not only contain rituals, they are about them, about the feelings they generate and the needs they serve, so that we may justly speak of a ritual ambience in these works, if not quite a ritual form.

It need hardly be said that this projection into narrative and drama of details suggesting religious worship owes much to the nineteenth-century dream of a cult of art that would supplant traditional religion. This familiar theme takes various forms in Arnold, Nietzsche, and Joyce, who has Stephen Dedalus expound such a theory near the end of *Portrait of the Artist*. Renouncing Catholicism, Mallarmé nevertheless tries as Joyce does to retain a sense of the sacred through invented rites in his work (see, e.g., Danahy). Karl Beckson traces the course of British religious aestheticism in Yeats's "infallible church of poetic tradition," in the poets Lionel Johnson (who believed that "Life should be a ritual") and Ernest Dowson, and in the novels of Walter Pater (*Marius the Epicurean*) and Frederick Rolfe (*Hadrian the Seventh*). So many scholars still believe that "literature in man's historical evolution was once religious liturgy and dance, charms and oracles" (Ruland 119), that the "mythology of aestheticism" is often taken for granted by both the religious and the nonreligious.[20] Such assumptions are evident in the typical late twentieth-century observation that *A Midsummer Night's Dream*, although a secular play, embodies "more successfully than the religious and folk traditions, an extra-temporal moment of achieved harmony in human life, a triumph formerly shared with ritual, now in the sole possession of the work of art" (Vlasopolos 29).

A major voice of the past decade, questioning older theories regarding literature, especially drama, and the ritual process, has been René Girard. Following Freud in *Totem and Taboo*, Girard proposes that a primal killing threatened to destroy human community through successive retributions. This violence could be avoided only by the appointment of a scapegoat who would receive the full force of the community's wrath. The sacrificial victim becomes a characteristic human expedient and "constitutes a major means, perhaps the sole means, by which men expel from their consciousness the truth about their violent nature—that knowledge of past violence which, if not shifted to a single 'guilty' figure, would poison both the present and the future" (*Violence* 83). In all human relations, Girard sees three figures locked in a circle of "mimetic desire": the subject, the rival, and the object. "The subject desires the object because the rival desires it" (146). A telling instance is Shakespeare's *Troilus and Cressida*, in which the Greeks want Helen back because the Trojans have taken her away and the Trojans want to keep her because the Greeks want her back ("Shakespeare's Theory" 113). Mimetic desire is "the immediate interplay of imitating and imitated desire. Mimesis generates rivalry, which in turn reinforces mimesis" (*Double Business* 53).

The scapegoat process gives birth to a vast array of myths and rituals, all of which serve merely to conceal the ugly facts of the surrogate victim sacrificed to this mimetic, desire-caused violence. Since myths exist to rationalize the scapegoat mechanism, mythology is little more than "a text of persecution" that rituals exist to enact ("Interview" 40): "Ritual is nothing more than the regular exercise of 'good' violence" (*Violence* 37), that is, violence that will prevent the spread of retribution or revenge and similar kinds of hostility throughout the community. Like almost all culture, drama originates in violence: "All religious rituals spring from the surrogate victim, and all the great institutions of mankind, both secular and religious, spring from ritual. Such is the case . . . with political power, legal institutions, medicine, the theater, philosophy and anthropology itself" (*Violence* 306). By "religion" Girard here means primitive religion as opposed to the beliefs of the Hebrew prophetic books and the Gospels (a point he makes clear in *Des choses* 178).

Although to skeptics his theory must seem a quaint throwback to mono-myth, Girard, like Frye, has built his hypothesis on an intricate theoretical structure. A fundamental principle is social differentiation: "Order, peace, and fecundity depend on cultural distinctions," the loss of which gives birth to rivalries and violence (*Violence* 49). Thus in *Troilus*, "degree" is what "permits individuals to find a place for themselves in society" (50). The final annihilation of differences can only lead to the triumph of the

strong over the weak in a Hobbesian state of nature (51). This view accounts for the frequent concern in Girard's work with myths of twins or doubles (Cain and Abel, Romulus and Remus, Eteocles and Polyneices). Our modern loss of differences is attested by the change from these ancient myths of warring twins to the modern concept of affectionate family relations (61). Girard attacks the structuralist notion, shared by Lévi-Strauss and Frye, that literature and myth deal with differentiation, while ritual searches for an "undifferentiated immediacy." In fact both ritual and myth tend to destroy difference ("Shakespeare's Theory" 109, "Lévi-Strauss"). "The sacred concerns itself above all with the destruction of differences, and this nondifference cannot appear as such in structure" (*Violence* 241). Thus what Nietzsche called the "Dionysiac" state must aim to "erase all manner of differences: familial, cultural, biological, and natural" (160).

When the sacrificial rites disappear, at a time coinciding with the loss of the difference between "good" and "bad" violence, difference cannot be reasserted as it was each time on completion of the old rites. We then have a "sacrificial crisis," a time of deterioration for the system by which reciprocal violence is channeled off. When we "demystify" religion, our doing so "necessarily coincides with the disintegration of that system. . . . In fact, demystification leads to constantly increasing violence, a violence less 'hypocritical' than the violence it seeks to expose, but more energetic . . . a violence that knows no bounds" (24–25). Euripides' *Bacchae* concerns just such a crisis (126–42). Thus, while for Turner rites exist to instill a sense of communitas, of values shared across social boundaries (especially when violence threatens), Girard believes that rites are used to redirect violence. Violence, however, is the inescapable condition of society.

These ideas have particular relevance to drama, since drama, especially the great tragedies of the Greeks, "is by its very nature a partial deciphering of mythological motifs" (64). In Sophocles and Euripides (as later in Shakespeare), the poet at certain moments "lifts the veil long enough for you to glimpse the long hidden historical truth that lies at the origin" ("Interview" 35; this is the interviewer's paraphrase). Even though tragedy originated in ritual, the inspiration of a play like *Oedipus Rex* is "essentially antimythical and antiritualistic" (*Violence* 95). In "Myth and Ritual in Shakespeare's *A Midsummer Night's Dream*," Girard warns Shakespearean critics of the myth-ritual school to reconsider their assumptions: "Instead of viewing myth as a humanization of nature, as we always tend to do, Shakespeare views it as the naturalization as well as the supernaturalization of a very human violence. Specialists on the subject might be well advised to take a close look at this Shakespearean view; what if it turned out to be less mythical than their own!" (200–01; the word "ritual," although it appears in the title, scarcely appears in the essay itself). In the same essay, Girard proposes that *A Midsummer Night's Dream* is a drama of mimetic desire in which the self idolizes the "other" for the sake of the self—in effect, the self mythologizes the other. This play shows that the myth always captivates sooner than the truly human does; thus, in *The Merchant of Venice*, where the same rules operate, Bassanio falls in love with Portia's picture, not with Portia.

It is in a recent essay on this play, in fact, that Girard offers by implication a way of resolving some of the confusion inherited from the past about ritual and literature. Ritual may inhere thematically, structurally, or, in certain special cases, affectively, by a deliberate appeal to audience participation. Girard sees *The Merchant of Venice* as a play about revenge and retribution, with Shylock as the "grotesque double" ("To Entrap" 105) of Antonio. He points out the telling evidence of Portia's question when she enters the courtroom, "Which is the merchant and which is the Jew?" The classic Jew of European anti-Semitism, Shylock is widely recognized as a scapegoat, hence his doubling in the play. Yet, Girard asks, should we see scapegoat as theme or structure here? If scapegoat is theme, the author will actually realize the evil of the scapegoat mechanism, as did the Greek tragic dramatists; if structure, though, the scapegoat ritual will be "a passively accepted delusion" of the author (109). In Girard's view Shakespeare, like the Greeks, fully intends his meaning—scapegoat is theme; but for those unable to be reached by Shakespeare's meaning, there is also a scapegoat structure. Finally a special quality of *The Mer-*

chant of Venice that evokes the audience's wishful participation gives the play what Turner would call its "liminoid" characteristics. "The crowd in the theater becomes one with the crowd on the stage. The contagious effect of scapegoating extends to the audience" during the trial scene, when "the presence of the silent Magnificoes, the elite of the community, turns the trial into a rite of social unanimity" (111). The crowd involvement in *Julius Caesar* is similar; in all such examples drama merges almost totally with ritual.

In Girard's view, the great tragedies signal a reaction against the excess of communality in ritual by asserting the claims of the suffering individual compelled by a socially determined necessity. Girard is always careful to admit that his hypothesis about human desire and the scapegoat mechanism is just that, and he denies that he is working toward a universally applicable "theory of literature." Although I cannot offer here a critique of his hypothesis, I might suggest that the equation of ritual with sacrifice (and therefore with the scapegoat process) narrows the concept excessively. Nevertheless, Girard's position does furnish a serviceable alternative to the familiar view that all literature gains profundity or beauty from a touch of the ritualistic.

IV

If there have been great authors who found the ritual sense dangerous or irrelevant (in *Madame Bovary* it is even a refuge for banality and superstition) there have always been those who have sought to recover that sense. Charting this recovery in the novels of George Eliot, Barbara Hardy calls to our attention a passage from *Daniel Deronda*:

The most powerful movement of feeling within a liturgy is the prayer which seeks for nothing special, but is the yearning to escape from the limitations of our own weakness and an invocation of all Good to enter and abide with us; or else a self-oblivious lifting-up of gladness, a *Gloria in Excelsis* that such Good exists; both the yearning and the exultation gathering their utmost force from the sense of communion in a form which has expressed them both, for long generations of struggling fellowmen. (5)

What George Eliot conveys here is an appreciation of the flow and communitas that Turner finds in ritual, for the worshiper joins both other human beings and his or her ancestors in a momentary "time out of time." "Human feeling," Barbara Hardy observes, "is given clarity and definition by ritual, and shown at crucial moments to feel itself a part of a larger tradition" (14). Instead of attempting to bring ritual and literature together, she suggests reasons for appreciating their difference. Ritual is really "the ground, the bass," in much fiction, while "counterpointed against it is the change in feeling and circumstance" necessary in a novel or play (9).

Geoffrey Hartman's description of *Faust* as a ritual may be ascribable to the "liminoid" relation between the sacred and secular that Turner discusses. Art "seems generically and ambiguously involved with the sacred and profane . . ."; "it is always inauthentic vis-à-vis a thoroughgoing realism" (*Beyond Formalism* 21–22). Elsewhere in the same book, thinking of the romantic period, Hartman says, "There clearly comes a time when art frees itself from subordination to religion or religiously inspired myth and continues or even replaces them." He sees *Faust*, in fact, as attempting to "bridge the gap between the myth-centered age of romance and the modern spirit" (305, 310). Hartman proposes the evolutionary continuum in a critique of the "structuralist adventure," the program that in many respects includes Frye and that would reject Hartman's distinction between ancient and modern art, primitive and civilized mind. Understanding the testament of ancient art has been a task of modern civilization since the inception of the "modern," and a share of the task has been to discover the place of ritual in art. In literary thought, this enterprise begins not with Frazer's admirers but with the young Nietzsche's *Birth of Tragedy*. Nietzsche's book met with outrage from his fellow classical scholars, especially from the future prince of *Altertumswissenschaft*, Ulrich von Wilamowitz-Moellendorff. Twenty-five years later Nietzsche would agree with Wilamowitz in many respects: his first book was "badly written, ponderous, embarrassing, image-mad and image-confused, sentimental, . . . an arrogant and rhapsodic book." He particularly regretted that "the Dionysiac" remained as obscure and elusive a concept as ever. (Silk and Stern 95, 119–20. See also J. B. Foster on Gide, Lawrence, Malraux, and Mann.) The Dionysiac-Apolline polarity, so persistent in ritual conceptions of drama during our century, retains a certain hold on contemporary theater, but in criticism it has been reduced to an instance of the "radical indeterminacy" supposedly at the heart of literary discourse (de Man). The prospects for a fuller understanding of ritual in relation to literature might be improved if we could agree that both these features of cultural life exist in an ecology not unlike what George Eliot proposed, in which subject and object, worshiper and cult, reader (writer) and text acquire meaning only in the context of a community.[21]

University of Kansas
Lawrence

Notes

[1] The posthumous 1962 edition of Pickard-Cambridge's book omits much of the rebuttal of the Cambridge school.

[2] Using terminology borrowed from Richard Schechner, Hinden proposes that classical tragedy moves toward community—from the arena of play and the self-assertive "I" to that of game (the social "we") to the self-transcendent "other" of ritual.

[3] Graham-White cites a number of theater critics who use "ritual" imprecisely. Yet one of these, Richard Schechner, has since developed his ideas impressively in a study of the common features of ritual and theater as recreations of past events or "restored behavior." Jerzy Grotowski is among the more recent experimenters in the ritualizing of theater (see Findlay).

[4] Yet Herbert Weisinger restricts symbol to art alone: "To speak of symbolic meaning is already to have made the leap from myth to art" (152). I agree with Ernst Cassirer that symbolism is an inevitable human response, whether in art, religion, or politics (41–62).

[5] See C. Clifford Flanigan's comprehensive discussions of Christian liturgical drama, which have considerable relevance to my subject.

[6] Reviewing this book, Hyman says Fontenrose is "proudly enrolled under Henri Frankfort's obscurantist banner, in a crusade to undo the last seventy years of

generalization in comparative mythology by the denial of the ancient Near East as a unified culture area" (127).

⁷ See Robert Goodin's strictures on this point (281). Various definitions are proposed in Moore and Meyerhoff, and Roy A. Rappaport's "Obvious Aspects of Ritual" is of great importance.

⁸ Also questionable is Fletcher's association of "contagious magic" with ritual form (195–99). For the distinction between religion and magic in ritual, see Goody. Wittgenstein remarks that such an act as burning in effigy "is obviously *not* based on a belief that it will have a definite effect on the object which the picture represents. It aims at some satisfaction and it achieves it. Or rather, it does not *aim* at anything; we act in that way and then feel satisfied" (4e).

⁹ "Flow" is a term borrowed from the social psychologist Mihali Csikszentmihalyi, meaning the "holistic sensations present when we act with total involvement," as in religious or creative experience or in sports ("Variations" 48).

¹⁰ Francis Edwards' guide for students still speaks of drama as moving "from the confines of the church to the open air" (64).

¹¹ Blandine-Dominique Berger argues against Hardison's view that the Mass is drama. She sees liturgical drama "at the heart of a new type of liturgy" in the Middle Ages (132) but believes that liturgy was not the simple source for Western drama.

¹² Mary and Max Gluckman, two social scientists, make a similar point: "When an ancient myth is reenacted in a drama, there is no idea that the events are in any way occurring then and there, with the actors becoming the heroes and heroines of that distant event, and the audience participating in the event itself. The drama is presentation, not a representation as ritual is" (235).

¹³ Cambridge-style criticism has persisted, however. See Isaacs and Reese and Bryant. The opening section of Robert Weimann's *Shakespeare and the Popular*

Tradition (1–6) does not inspire confidence when it cites Frazer, E. K. Chambers, and Christopher Caudwell as its principal authorities on the alliance of ritual and theater. Weimann concurs with Hardison's doubts about the evolutionary view but claims that Hardison underestimates "the historical element of change" that links liturgy to Shakespearean drama (271, n. 23). Yet Weimann's opening section, entitled "Ritual and Mimesis," seems to treat "the gradual movement from myth to realism" (3) in evolutionary terms.

¹⁴ Boose discusses several such "rituals." Although she cites anthropological studies, she is much influenced by psychological conceptions of ritual, as when she asserts that "What the church service is actually all about is the separation of the daughter from the interdicting father" (326).

¹⁵ Ritualist readings of Caesar's murder have continued since Brents Stirling and Ernest Schanzer; see, e.g., de Gerenday's study, which shows the influence of Freud and Erik Erikson.

¹⁶ William Stephenson argues the primacy of the inner rite of Drew the artist over the initiation of the "antinomian" rugged hero Lewis. Cf. Lindberg.

¹⁷ Clark also observes that "The majority of initiating ordeals more or less clearly imply a ritual death—or at least some token mutilation—followed by a resurrection or new birth. In the Stalinist novel, death and token mutilation have a predominantly mythic function" (178).

¹⁸ Moorman reconsiders his earlier "Myth and Medieval Literature."

¹⁹ The entire issue of *Mosaic* in which Manlove's article appears (Winter 1979) is devoted to liturgy and literature.

²⁰ Ruland's bibliographical survey is well informed from the standpoint of both religious and literary studies.

²¹ This study was supported by a grant from the General Research Fund of the University of Kansas.

Works Cited

Ackerman, Robert. "Frazer on Myth and Ritual." *Journal of the History of Ideas* 36(1975):115–34.

Arrowsmith, William. Introd. *The Bacchae.* In *Euripides V.* Ed. David Grene and Richmond Lattimore. Chicago: Univ. of Chicago Press, 1959, 142–53.

Bascom, William. "The Myth-Ritual Theory." *Journal of American Folklore* 70(1957):103–14.

Beckson, Karl. "A Mythology of Aestheticism." *English Literature in Transition* 17(1974):233–49.

Berger, Blandine-Dominique. *Le Drame liturgique de Pâques.* Paris: Editions Beauchesne, 1976.

Boose, Lynda E. "The Father and the Bride in Shakespeare." *PMLA* 97(1982):325–47.

Bryant, J. A., Jr. "Falstaff and the Renewal of Windsor." *PMLA* 89(1974):296–301.

Burkert, Walter. *Structure and History in Greek Mythology and Ritual.* Berkeley: Univ. of California Press, 1979.

Bynum, David E. *The Daemon in the Wood: A Study of Oral Narrative Patterns.* Cambridge, Mass.: Center for the Study of Oral Literature, 1978.

Cassirer, Ernst. *An Essay on Man.* 1944; rpt. New York: Doubleday, 1954.

Clark, Katerina. *The Soviet Novel: History as Ritual.* Chicago: Univ. of Chicago Press, 1981.

Cope, Jackson I. *The Theater and the Dream: From*

Metaphor to Form in Renaissance Drama. Baltimore: Johns Hopkins Univ. Press, 1973.

Coursen, Herbert N., Jr. *Christian Ritual and the World of Shakespeare's Tragedies.* Lewisburg, Pa.: Bucknell Univ. Press, 1976.

Crocker, Christopher. "Ritual and the Development of Social Structure: Liminality and Inversion." In *The Roots of Ritual.* Ed. James D. Shaughnessy. Grand Rapids, Mich.: Eerdmans, 1973, 47–86.

Danahy, Michael. "The Drama of Herodiade: Liturgy and Irony." *Modern Language Quarterly* 34(1973): 292–311.

de Gerenday, Lynn. "Play, Ritualization, and Ambivalence in *Julius Caesar.*" *Literature and Psychology* 24(1976):24–33.

de Man, Paul. "Genesis and Genealogy in Nietzsche's *The Birth of Tragedy.*" *Diacritics* 2.4(1972):44–53.

A Discussion of Ritualization of Behaviour in Animals and Man. Philosophical Transactions of the Royal Society of London. Series B. Biological Series 251. London: Royal Society of London, 1966.

Dörrie, Heinrich. "The Meaning and Function of Myth in Greek and Roman Literature." *Yearbook of Comparative Criticism* 9(1980):109–31.

Douglas, Mary. *Natural Symbols: Explorations in Cosmology.* New York: Random, 1973.

Douglas, Wallace. "The Meanings of Myth" (1953). In *Myth and Literature: Contemporary Theory and Practice.* Ed. John B. Vickery. Lincoln: Univ. of Nebraska Press, 1966, 119–28.

Edwards, Francis. *Ritual and Drama: The Medieval Theatre.* London: Lutterworth, 1976.

Else, Gerald F. *Origins and Early Form of Greek Tragedy.* Martin Classical Lectures, vol. 20. Cambridge: Harvard Univ. Press, 1967.

Falk, Florence. "Drama and Ritual Process in *A Midsummer Night's Dream.*" *Comparative Drama* 14(1980):263–79.

Feder, Lillian. *Ancient Myth in Modern Poetry.* Princeton: Princeton Univ. Press, 1971.

Ferris, William R., Jr. "Myth and the Psychological School: Fact or Fantasy." *New York Folklore Quarterly* 30(1974):254–66.

Fichte, Jörg O. *Expository Voices in Medieval Drama.* Nürnberg: Hans Karl, 1975.

Findlay, Robert. "Grotowski's 'Cultural Explorations Bordering on Art, Especially Theatre.'" *Theatre Journal* 32(1980):349–56.

———. "Grotowski's Laboratorium after Twenty Years: Theory and Operation." *Kansas Quarterly* 12(Fall 1980):133–39.

Flanigan, C. Clifford. "The Liturgical Drama and Its Tradition: A Review of Scholarship 1965–1975." *Research Opportunities in Renaissance Drama* 18(1975):81–102.

———. "The Liturgical Drama and Its Tradition: A Review of Scholarship (Part II)." *Research Opportunities in Renaissance Drama* 19(1976):109–36.

Fletcher, Angus. *Allegory: The Theory of a Symbolic Mode.* Ithaca, N.Y.: Cornell Univ. Press, 1964.

Fontenrose, Joseph. *Python: A Study of Delphic Myth and Its Origins.* Berkeley: Univ. of California Press, 1959.

———. *The Ritual Theory of Myth.* Folklore Studies, no. 18. Berkeley: Univ. of California Press, 1966.

Foster, John Burton, Jr. *Heirs to Dionysos: A Nietzschean Current in Literary Modernism.* Princeton: Princeton Univ. Press, 1981.

Foster, John Wilson. "Passage through 'The Dead.'" *Criticism* 15(1973):91–108.

Frye, Northrop. *Anatomy of Criticism: Four Essays.* 1957; rpt. New York: Atheneum, 1967.

———. "Expanding Eyes." In his *Spiritus Mundi: Essays on Literature, Myth, and Society.* Bloomington: Indiana Univ. Press, 1976, 99–122.

Gauvin, C. "Rite et jeu dans le théâtre anglais du Moyen Age." *Revue d'Histoire du Théâtre* 29 (1977):128–40.

Girard, René. *Des choses cachées depuis la fondation du monde.* Paris: Bernard Grasset, 1978.

———. "Interview." *Diacritics* 8.1(1978):31–54.

———. "Lévi-Strauss, Frye, Derrida, and Shakespearean Criticism." *Diacritics* 3.3(1973):34–38.

———. "Myth and Ritual in Shakespeare's *A Midsummer Night's Dream.*" In *Textual Strategies: Perspectives in Post-Structuralist Criticism.* Ed. Josué Harari. Ithaca, N.Y.: Cornell Univ. Press, 1979, 189–212.

———. "Shakespeare's Theory of Mythology." *Proceedings of the Comparative Literature Symposium* 11(1980):107–24.

———. *To Double Business Bound: Essays on Literature, Mimesis, and Anthropology.* Baltimore: Johns Hopkins Univ. Press, 1978.

———. "'To Entrap the Wisest': A Reading of *The Merchant of Venice.*" In *Literature and Society: Selected Papers of the English Institute.* Ed. Edward W. Said. Baltimore: Johns Hopkins Univ. Press, 1978, 100–19.

———. *Violence and the Sacred.* Trans. Patrick Gregory. Baltimore: Johns Hopkins Univ. Press, 1977.

Gluckman, Mary, and Max Gluckman. "On Drama, and Games and Athletic Contests." In *Secular Ritual.* Ed. Sally Moore and Barbara C. Meyerhoff. Assen, Neth.: Van Gorcum, 1977, 227–43.

Goodin, Robert. "Rites of Rulers." *British Journal of Sociology* 29(1978):281–99.

Goody, Jack R. "Religion and Ritual: The Definitional Problem." *British Journal of Sociology* 12(1961): 142–64.

Gorsky, Susan R. "A Ritual Drama: Yeats's Plays for Dancers." *Modern Drama* 17(1974):165–78.

Graham-White, Anthony. "'Ritual' in Contemporary Theatre Criticism." *Educational Theater Journal* 28(1976):318–24.

Hanning, R. W. "'You Have Begun a Parlous Playe': The Nature and Limits of Dramatic Mimesis as a Theme in Four Middle English 'Fall of Lucifer' Cycle Plays." *Comparative Drama* 7(1973):22–50.

Hardison, O. B. *Christian Rite and Christian Drama in the Middle Ages.* Baltimore: Johns Hopkins Univ. Press, 1965.

Hardy, Barbara. *Rituals and Feeling in the Novels of George Eliot.* W. D. Thomas Memorial Lecture. Swansea, Wales: University College of Swansea, 1973.

Hartman, Geoffrey H. *Beyond Formalism.* New Haven: Yale Univ. Press, 1970.

———. *The Fate of Reading and Other Essays.* Chicago: Univ. of Chicago Press, 1975.

Hassel, R. Chris. *Renaissance Drama and the English Church Year.* Lincoln: Univ. of Nebraska Press, 1979.

Hinden, Michael. "Ritual and Tragic Action: A Synthesis of Current Theory." *Journal of Aesthetics and Art Criticism* 32(1974):357–73.

Holloway, John. *The Story of the Night: Studies in Shakespeare's Major Tragedies.* Lincoln: Univ. of Nebraska Press, 1961.

Hyman, Stanley Edgar. "The Ritual View of Myth and the Mythic" (1958). In *Myth and Literature: Contemporary Theory and Practice.* Ed. John B. Vickery. Lincoln: Univ. of Nebraska Press, 1966, 47–58.

———. Rev. of Joseph Fontenrose's *Python. Carleton Miscellany* 1(1960):124–27.

Isaacs, Neil D., and Jack E. Reese. "Dithyramb and Paean in *A Midsummer Night's Dream.*" *English Studies* 55(1974):351–57.

Isambert, F. A. "Feasts and Celebrations: Some Critical Reflections on the Idea of Celebration." Trans. Bernd Jager. *Humanitas* 5(1969):29–42.

Kirk, G. S. *Myth: Its Meaning and Function in Ancient Greece and Other Cultures.* Cambridge: Cambridge Univ. Press, 1970.

Kluckhohn, Clyde. "Myth and Ritual: A General Theory." *Harvard Theological Review* 35(1942):45–79.

Knox, Bernard. *Word and Action: Essays on the Ancient Theater.* Baltimore: Johns Hopkins Univ. Press, 1979.

LaFontaine, J. S., ed. *The Interpretation of Ritual.* London: Tavistock, 1972.

Leach, Edmund. "Ritual." *International Encyclopedia of the Social Sciences.* New York: Macmillan, 1968, 13:520–26.

Lewis, C. S. *English Literature in the Sixteenth Century excluding Drama.* New York: Oxford Univ. Press, 1954.

Lindberg, Henry J. "James Dickey's *Deliverance*: The Ritual of Art." *Southern Literary Journal* 6(1974):83–90.

Manlove, C. N. "The Liturgical Novels of Charles Williams." *Mosaic* 12(Winter 1979):161–81.

Mead, Margaret. *Twentieth Century Faith: Hope and Survival.* New York: Harper, 1972.

Moore, Sally, and Barbara G. Meyerhoff, eds. *Secular Ritual.* Assen, Neth.: Van Gorcum, 1977.

Moorman, Charles. "Comparative Mythography: A Fungo to the Outfield." In *The Binding of Proteus: Perspectives on Myth and the Literary Process.* Ed. Marjorie W. McCune et al. Lewisburg, Pa.: Bucknell Univ. Press, 1980, 63–77.

———. "Myth and Medieval Literature: *Sir Gawain and the Green Knight.*" In *Myth and Literature: Contemporary Theory and Practice.* Ed. John B. Vickery. Lincoln: Univ. of Nebraska Press, 1966, 171–86.

O'Reilly, Robert F. "Ritual, Myth and Symbol in Gide's *L'Immoraliste.*" *Symposium* 28(1974):346–55.

Orgel, Stephen. *The Jonsonian Masque.* Cambridge: Harvard Univ. Press, 1967.

Pickard-Cambridge, Arthur. *Dithyramb, Tragedy and Comedy.* Oxford: Clarendon, 1927.

Rappaport, Roy A. "The Obvious Aspects of Ritual." In his *Ecology, Meaning, and Religion.* Richmond, Calif.: North Atlantic, 1979, 173–221.

Righter, Anne. *Shakespeare and the Idea of the Play.* 1962; rpt. Harmondsworth, Eng.: Penguin, 1967.

Ross, Charles L. "D. H. Lawrence's Use of Greek Tragedy: Euripides and Ritual." *D. H. Lawrence Review* 10(1977):1–19.

Ruland, Vernon. *Horizons of Criticism: An Assessment of Religious-Literary Options.* Chicago: American Library Assn., 1975.

Schechner, Richard. "Collective Reflexivity: Restoration of Behavior." In *A Crack in the Mirror: Reflexive Perspectives in Anthropology.* Ed. Jay Ruby. Philadelphia: Univ. of Pennsylvania Press, 1982, 39–81.

Scheff, Thomas J. *Catharsis in Healing, Ritual, and Drama.* Berkeley: Univ. of California Press, 1979.

———. "The Distancing of Emotion in Ritual." *Current Anthropology* 18(1977):483–505.

Silk, M. S., and J. P. Stern. *Nietzsche on Tragedy.* Cambridge: Cambridge Univ. Press, 1981.

Smith, Hallett. *Shakespeare's Romances: A Study of Some Ways of the Imagination.* San Marino, Calif.: Huntington Library, 1972.

Stephenson, William. "*Deliverance* from What?" *Georgia Review* 28(1974):114–20.

Stevens, Martin. "Illusion and Reality in the Medieval Drama." *College English* 32(1971):448–64.

Taplin, Oliver. "The Delphic Idea and After: Greek Tragedy on Film." *TLS,* 17 July 1981, 811–12.

———. *Greek Tragedy in Action.* Berkeley: Univ. of California Press, 1978.

Turner, Victor. *Dramas, Fields, and Metaphors: Symbolic Action in Human Society.* Ithaca, N.Y.: Cornell Univ. Press, 1974.

———. *The Forest of Symbols: Aspects of Ndembu Ritual.* Ithaca, N.Y.: Cornell Univ. Press, 1967.

———. "Variations on a Theme of Liminality." In *Secular Ritual.* Ed. Sally Moore and Barbara G. Meyerhoff. Assen, Neth.: Van Gorcum, 1977, 36–52.

Vargo, Edward P. "The Necessity of Myth in Updike's *The Centaur.*" *PMLA* 88(1973):452–60.

Vickery, John B. *The Literary Impact of* The Golden Bough. Princeton: Princeton Univ. Press, 1973.

———. "The Scapegoat in Literature: Some Kinds and Uses." In *The Binding of Proteus: Perspectives on Myth and the Literary Process.* Ed. Marjorie W.

McCune et al. Lewisburg, Pa.: Bucknell Univ. Press, 1980, 264–78.

———, ed. *Myth and Literature: Contemporary Theory and Practice.* Lincoln: Univ. of Nebraska Press, 1966.

Vlasopolos, Anca. "The Ritual of Midsummer: A Pattern for *A Midsummer Night's Dream.*" *Renaissance Quarterly* 31(1979):21–29.

Weimann, Robert. *Shakespeare and the Popular Tradition.* Baltimore: Johns Hopkins Univ. Press, 1978.

Weisinger, Herbert. "The Myth and Ritual Approach to Shakespeare." In *Myth and Literature: Contemporary Theory and Practice.* Ed. John B. Vick-

ery. Lincoln: Univ. of Nebraska Press, 1966, 149–60.

Wickham, Glynne. *Early English Stages.* London: Routledge, 1959.

Wittgenstein, Ludwig. *Remarks on Frazer's* Golden Bough. Ed. and trans. R. Rhees and A. C. Miles. Retford, Eng.: Brynmill, 1979.

Wittreich, Joseph A., Jr. *Visionary Poetics: Milton's Tradition and His Legacy.* San Marino, Calif.: Huntington Library, 1979.

Zender, Karl F. "A Hand of Poker: Game and Ritual in Faulkner's 'Was.'" *Studies in Short Fiction* 11(1974):53–60.

INTRODUCTION

The title of this book and its relation to my *Prolegomena* may call for a word of explanation.

In the *Prolegomena* I was chiefly concerned to show that the religion of Homer was no more primitive than his language. The Olympian gods—that is, the anthropomorphic gods of Homer and Pheidias and the mythographers—seemed to me like a bouquet of cut-flowers whose bloom is brief, because they have been severed from their roots. To find those roots we must burrow deep into a lower stratum of thought, into those chthonic cults which underlay their life and from which sprang all their brilliant blossoming.

So swift has been the advance in science or rather in historical imagination, so complete the shift of standpoint, that it has become difficult to conceive that, in 1903, any such protest was needed. Since the appearance of Professor Murray's *Rise of the Greek Epic* we realize how late and how enlightened was the compromise represented by these Olympians. We can even picture to ourselves the process by which their divinity was shorn of each and every 'mystical or monstrous' attribute.

When in 1907 a second edition of my book was called for, its theories seemed to me already belated. My sense of the superficiality of Homer's gods had deepened to a conviction that these Olympians were not only non-primitive, but positively in a sense non-religious. If they were not, for religion, starting-points, they were certainly not satisfactory goals. On the other hand, the cultus of Dionysos and Orpheus seemed to me, whatever its errors and licenses, essentially religious. I was therefore compelled reluctantly to face the question, what meaning did I attach to the word *religion*? My instinct was to condemn the Olympians as *non*-religious, because really the products of art and literature

187

though posing as divinities. Could this instinct stand the test of examination, or was it merely a temperamental prejudice masquerading as a reasoned principle ?

The problem might have continued ineffectively to haunt me, and probably to paralyse my investigations, had not light come rather suddenly from unexpected quarters, from philosophy and social psychology. To France I owe a double debt, indirect but profound, and first and foremost to Professor Henri Bergson.

It is characteristic always of a work of genius that it casts, as it were, a great search light into dark places far beyond its own immediate province. Things unseen before or insignificant shine out in luminous projection. The sudden flash may dazzle, the focus be misleading or even false ; but the light is real. New tracks open out before us, and we must needs set forth through the long uncharted shadows.

It is no part of Professor Bergson's present programme, so far as I understand it, to analyse and define the nature and function of religion. But when, four years ago, I first read his *L'Évolution Créatrice*, I saw, dimly at first, but with ever increasing clearness, how deep was the gulf between Dionysos the mystery-god and that Olympos he might never really enter. I knew the reason of my own profound discontent. I saw in a word that Dionysos, with every other mystery-god, was an instinctive attempt to express what Professor Bergson calls *durée*, that life which is one, indivisible and yet ceaselessly changing. I saw on the other hand that the Olympians, amid all their atmosphere of romance and all their redeeming vices, were really creations of what Professor William James called ' monarchical deism.' Such deities are not an instinctive expression, but a late and conscious representation, a work of analysis, of reflection and intelligence. Primitive religion was not, as I had drifted into thinking, a tissue of errors leading to mistaken conduct ; rather it was a web of practices emphasizing particular parts of life, issuing necessarily in representations and ultimately dying out into abstract conceptions. A statement like this when condensed is necessarily somewhat cryptic. In the concrete instances to be adduced from Greek religion, it will become I hope abundantly clear. I may add that, save perhaps for a few sentences in the last two chapters, every word of my book is, I hope, intelligible without any understanding of Professor Bergson's philosophy.

My second debt is to a thinker whose temperament, manner and method are markedly different, and whose philosophy is, I believe, in France, accounted as alien to that of Professor Bergson, Professor Émile Durkheim.

In the light of *L'Évolution Créatrice*, *Matière et Mémoire* and *Les Données Immédiates de la Conscience* I had come to see the real distinction between the mystery-god Dionysos and the Olympians. In the light of Professor Durkheim's *De la Définition des Phénomènes Religieux*, *Représentations Individuelles et Représentations Collectives* and *Sociologie Religieuse et Théorie de la Connaissance*, I saw why Dionysos, the mystery-god, who is the expression and representation of *durée*, is, alone among Greek divinities, constantly attended by a thiasos, a matter cardinal for the understanding of his nature. The mystery-god arises out of those instincts, emotions, desires which attend and express life; but these emotions, desires, instincts, in so far as they are religious, are at the outset rather of a group than of individual consciousness. The whole history of epistemology is the history of the evolution of clear, individual, rational thought, out of the haze of collective and sometimes contradictory representations. It is a necessary and most important corollary to this doctrine, that the form taken by the divinity reflects the social structure of the group to which the divinity belongs. Dionysos is the Son of his Mother because he issues from a matrilinear-group.

These two ideas, (1) that the mystery-god and the Olympian express respectively, the one *durée*, life, and the other the action of conscious intelligence which reflects on and analyses life, and (2) that, among primitive peoples, religion reflects *collective* feeling and *collective* thinking, underlie my whole argument and were indeed the cause and impulse of my book. I felt that these two principles had altered my whole outlook on my own subject, and that, in the light of them, I must needs reexamine the whole material—a task at present only partially achieved.

I am however no philosopher and still more no sociologist.

All this intellectual stir and ferment might for me have remained sterile or at least have taken no definite form, but for an archaeological discovery, the finding at Palaikastro of the *Hymn of the Kouretes.* In commenting on this Hymn, discovered in the temple of Diktaean Zeus, I found to my delight that we had in it a text that embodied this very group-thinking, or rather group-emotion towards life, which I had begun to see must underlie all primitive religious representations. The Hymn sung by the Kouretes invoked a daimon, the greatest Kouros, who was clearly the projection of a thiasos of his worshippers. It accompanied a magical dance and was the vehicle of a primitive sacramental cult. In the detailed analysis of the Hymn we should come, I felt, to understand the essence of a mystery-religion and incidentally the reason also why the Olympians failed to satisfy the religious instinct. The Hymn of the Kouretes furnished for my book its natural and necessary plot.

In the pages that follow, subjects apparently unconnected will come in for discussion. We shall have to consider, for example, magic, *mana, tabu,* the Olympic games, the Drama, Sacramentalism, Carnivals, Hero-worship, Initiation Ceremonies and the Platonic doctrine of Anamnesis. All these matters, seemingly so disparate, in reality cluster round the Hymn, and can really only be understood in connection with the two principles already laid down. If the reader will be good enough to hold these two clues firmly in his hand, the windings of the labyrinth will be to him no perplexity. The course is plain before us as follows.

Chapter I is devoted to the analysis of the Hymn. The Kouretes are found to represent the initiated young men of a matrilinear group. The Daimon they invoke is, not the Father of Gods and Men, but the Greatest Kouros. He springs from the social emphasis of the rite of initiation, the central ceremony of which was a *dromenon* or enaction of the New Birth into the tribe. Among primitive peoples the child, by his first natural birth, belongs to his mother, his life is of her life. By his Second Birth at Initiation, he is made one with the life of his group, his 'soul is congregationalized,' he is received into his church, his thiasos. The new life emphasized is group life. The unity of the group is *represented* by the figure of the Daimon. The Kouros stands for the unity of the Kouretes, the Bacchos for the thiasos of Bacchoi.

Since the religious conception of a Daimon arises from a *dromenon*, it is of the first importance to be clear as to what a *dromenon* is. The second chapter is devoted to its psychological analysis. The *dromenon* in its sacral sense is, not merely a thing done, but a thing *re*-done, or *pre*-done with magical intent. The magical dance of the Kouretes is a primitive form of *dromenon*, it commemorates or anticipates, in order magically to induce, a New Birth. The Dithyramb, from which the drama arose, was also a *dromenon* of the New Birth. In the drama then we may expect to find survivals of a ritual akin to that of the Kouretes. Further, the *dromenon* is a thing which, like the drama, is collectively performed. Its basis or kernel is a *thiasos* or *choros*.

So far attention has been concentrated on Professor Durkheim's principle that religious representation arises from *collective* action and emotion. This emotion necessarily has its objects, and they prove to be such as occur in other primitive societies. I have studied especially two rites: (1) the Rite of the *Thunders* and (2) the *Omophagia* (Chapters III, IV, and V). The Thunder-Rite emphasizes man's reaction towards, and, in a sense, his desire for union with, the most striking manifestation of force in the universe around him. The emotions that arise out of similar reactions are expressed in such savage terms and conceptions as *Mana*, *Orenda*, *Wa-kon'-da*. In Greek religion this stage, owing to the Greek tendency to swift impersonation, is much obscured, but traces of it survive in such conceptions as Kratos and Bia, Styx, Horkos, μένος, θυμός and the like. Such sanctities, such *foci* of attention precede divinities and even daimones, and it is the manipulation of such sanctities that issues in the notions and practices of magic and *tabu* discussed in Chapter IV.

Magic, it is seen, though it may imply a large amount of mistaken science, arises primarily from a *dromenon*, a rite which emphasizes, and aims at inducing, man's collective desire for union with or dominion over outside powers. The kernel and essence of magic is best seen in the second Kouretic rite of initiation, the sacramental feast of the Omophagia. Sacraments lie at the heart of religion and sacraments can only be understood in the light of totemistic thinking, which may long survive any definite totemistic social structure. To the meaning of the word *sacrament* Chapter V is devoted.

Totemism, it is found, is the utterance of two kinds of unity and solidarity, that of man with his group of fellow men, and that of the human group with some group of plants or animals. Sacramentalism stands for the absorption by man of the *mana* of non-man. Gift-sacrifice implies the severance of man from that outside *mana* which man has externalized, objectified into a god. Totemistic thinking knows no god; it creates sanctities but not divinities. These animal and plant group-sanctities live on in the plant and animal forms the mystery-god can assume at will.

The Omophagia was a *dais* or communal meal. Since food is the main source or at least support of life, sacraments among primitive peoples tend to take the form of meals, though other means of contact, such as rubbing and washing, are in use. As food was primitive man's main focus of interest, it was soon observed that most food-supplies were seasonal and therefore recurrent. Hence arose the seasonal *dromenon* with its attendant sacrifice. In Greece the chief seasonal *dromenon* seems to have been in the spring; its object, the magical inducement of fresh life, for man, for other animals and for plants. A particular form of this spring rite was the Dithyramb. In Chapter VI this is discussed in connection with the famous Hagia Triada sarcophagos.

From the spring *dromenon* with its magical intent of the renewal of the year, arose two of the main factors in Greek religious life and indeed in Greek civilization: (1) the *agones* or athletic contests, and (2) that other contest significantly bearing the same name, the *agon* of the drama. Different though they seem, and different as in fact they became, they arose from the same root, the spring *dromenon* conceived of as a conflict, a dramatic setting forth of the natural happening of the spring. This *drama* might with equal appropriateness be represented as a Death followed by a Rebirth or as a contest followed by a victory. Chapter VII, by Mr Cornford, deals with the greatest of the athletic *agones* of Greece, the Olympic Games, as arising from a race of the Kouretes. The victor in the race became the daimon of the year, or, to give him a Greek name, the Eniautos-Daimon. In the victor is incarnate at once the daimon of the group and the 'luck' of the year. It is this δαίμων γέννης who is the real object of commemoration in Pindar's *Odes*; hence the prominence of mythical elements. The particular hero is commemorated rather as functionary than as individual personality.

And here I owe to the reader an apology, or at least an explanation, for the introduction of a new term. I am well aware that no such conjunction as Eniautos-Daimon exists in Greek. I did not set out to invent any such word, nor did I even foresee its employment; it simply grew on my hands from sheer necessity. Dr Frazer, following Mannhardt, gave us 'Tree-Spirit, Corn-Spirit, Vegetation Spirit,' and the use of these terms has incalculably enlarged our outlook. My own debt to Dr Frazer is immeasurable. But even 'Vegetation Spirit' is inadequate. A word was wanted that should include not only vegetation, but the whole world-process of decay, death, renewal. I prefer 'Eniautos' to 'year' because to us 'year' means something definitely chronological, a precise segment as it were of spatialized time; whereas *Eniautos*, as contrasted with *etos*, means a *period* in the etymological sense, a cycle of waxing and waning. This notion is, I believe, implicitly though not always explicitly, a cardinal factor in Greek religion. Beyond it, to anything like our modern notion of non-recurrent evolution, the Greek never advanced. I prefer the word *daimon* to 'spirit' because, as I try to show (in Chapter VIII), *daimon* has connotations unknown to our English 'spirit.'

At this point, before passing to the second great development from the spring-festival, the drama, recent controversy compelled a halt. Euhemerists of all dates, and quite recently Professor Ridgeway, have maintained that agonistic festivals and drama alike take their rise, not in magical ceremonial nor in the worship of a god or daimon, but in funeral ceremonies at the grave of some historical individual, a dead hero or chieftain. Totemism, vegetation spirits and the like are, according to Professor Ridgeway, secondary phenomena; the primary principle is the existence of the individual soul after death and the necessity for placating it. Now it is indisputable that, at agonistic festivals and in the drama,

heroes are commemorated.   For his emphasis of this fact and its
relations to the *origines* of drama we all owe a deep debt to
Professor Ridgeway.   But the analysis of the term *hero* goes
to show that the main factor in a hero is that very being whom
Professor Ridgeway would reject or ignore, the Eniautos-Daimon
himself.   Chapter VIII is devoted to the analysis of the term
hero, with results as follows.

The *hero* on examination turns out to be, not a historical great
man who happens to be dead, but a dead ancestor performing his
due functions as such, who may in particular cases happen to have
been a historical great man.   As hero he is a functionary; he
wears the mask and absorbs the ritual of an Eniautos-Daimon.
The myths of the *heroes* of Athens, from Cecrops to Theseus, show
them as kings, that is as functionaries, and, in primitive times,
these functionaries assume snake-form.   The daimon-functionary
represents the permanent life of the group.   The individual dies,
but the group and its incarnation the king survive.   *Le roi est
mort, vive le roi.*   From these two facts, of group permanency and
individual death, arose the notion of reincarnation, *palingenesia.*
Moreover, since the group included plants and animals as well as
human members, and these were linked by a common life, the
rebirth of ancestors and the renewed fertility of the earth went on
pari passu.   Hence the *Intichiuma* ceremonies of Central Aus-
tralians, hence the Revocation of ghosts at the Athenian
Anthesteria.   Gradually, as the group focussed on its king, the
daimones of fertility, the collective ancestors, focussed on to an
Agathos Daimon, a spirit of fertility, again figured as a snake.

The later Attic heroes Ion and Theseus, unlike the earlier
Cecrops and Erechtheus, do not assume snake-form.   None the
less they are functionaries rather than individual personalities—
Ion a mere eponym, a group projection of the Ionians, and Theseus
a *hero* because, as his mythology makes manifest, he took on the
ritual and functions of the Eniautos-Daimon.   This is clearly
evidenced by his festival the Oschophoria, which can be reconstructed, partly from the recorded *mythos*, partly from the *dromena.*
The principal factors are the *agon* or contest, the *pathos* a defeat or
death, the triumphant reappearance or rebirth, the Epiphany.   In
a word the ritual of the Eniautos-Daimon is substantially the

same as the ceremony of death and resurrection enacted as a rite of tribal initiation. This ritual with its attendant *mythos* lives on in the Mummers' Play and Carnival festivals still performed at spring time all over modern Europe. At Athens, reinvigorated by the Homeric saga, it issued in the splendid human diversity of the Attic drama.

What then is the relation between the Homeric saga, which furnishes obviously the plots of Attic dramas, and the ancient ritual of the Eniautos-Daimon as embodied in the Dithyramb or Spring-Dance ? The answer is given in Prof. Murray's Excursus. A detailed examination of the plays and fragments extant shows that, while the content of the plots comes from the saga, the ritual forms in which that content is cast derive straight from the *dromena* of the Eniautos-Daimon. Such forms are the Prologue, the Agon, the Pathos, the Messenger's Speech, the Threnos, the Anagnorisis and the final Theophany. Certain of these ritual forms also survive in shadowy fashion in the Games, but here they are well-nigh submerged by a growing athleticism. In the drama literary art by some blind yet happy instinct felt their value and held to them tenaciously.

Thus the ritual of the Eniautos-Daimon, who was at once the representation of the life of the group and the life of nature, issued in agonistic festivals and in the drama. We have now to watch another process, by which the daimon is transformed into a god and finally, for the Greeks, into that form of godhead which we call Olympian. To an analysis of this process the three concluding chapters are devoted.

In Chapter IX the case of Herakles who tried and failed to be a god is examined. The reason of his failure is found to be instructive. Spite of all efforts to make him *athanatos* he remains an Eniautos-Daimon, doomed by function and attributes to a yearly death and resurrection. He is also doomed to eternally recurrent Labours and cannot join the Olympians who ' dwell at ease.' He remains, like Asklepios, the typical half human *Saviour*. Asklepios, from the extraordinary spread of his cult, took rank as a god, but his snake-form enshrines his old daimon nature and prevents his becoming an Olympian. His younger form, Telesphoros, marks him clearly as Eniautos-Daimon.

195

Having seen how and why two daimones failed to become Olympians we have next to watch the transformation of one who succeeded, Apollo.

In the evolution of the Eniautos-Daimon we noted the influence of periodicity; the succession of the seasons was always important because they brought food to man. So far man's eyes are bent on earth as the food-giver. In his social structure the important features are Mother and Son, and, projecting his own emotions into nature round him, he sees in the earth the Mother as food-giver, and in the fruits of the earth her Son, her Kouros, his symbol the blossoming branch of a tree. The first divinity in the sequence of cults at Delphi is Gaia.

But before long he notices that Sky as well as Earth influences his food supply. At first he notes the 'weather,' rain and wind and storm. Next he finds out that the moon measures seasons, and to her he attributes all growth, all waxing and waning. Then his goddess is Phoibe. When later he discovers that the Sun really dominates his food supply, Phoibe gives place to Phoibos, the Moon to the Sun. The shift of attention, of religious focus, from Earth to Sky, tended to remove the gods from man; they were purged but at the price of remoteness. Apollo begins on earth as Agueius and ends in heaven as Phoibos.

Ritual at Delphi, as elsewhere, lagged behind myth and theology. Of the three great Ennaeteric Festivals, two, the *Charila* and the *Herois*, are concerned with the death and resurrection, the Kathodos and Anodos, of the Earth; they are essentially Eniautos Festivals. The third festival, the *Stepterion*, speaks still more clearly. It is the death of the Old Year envisaged as a snake, followed by the birth of the New as a Kouros carrying a branch. The same Kouros, representing Apollo in the *Daphnephoria*, carries a pole from which are hung the moon and sun. The God is thus manifestly a year-daimon. As the Son of his Father and as the god to whom the *epheboi* offered the first-fruits of their hair, he is also the Greatest Kouros. But unlike Dionysos, the other Greatest Kouros, he is a complete Olympian. Wherein lies the difference? An answer is attempted in Chapter X.

It is characteristic of an Olympian, as contrasted with a mystery-god like Dionysos, that his form is rigidly fixed and always human. The Zeus of Pheidias or of Homer cannot readily shift his shape and become a bird, a bull, a snake, a tree. The Olympian has come out from the natural facts that begot him, and has become 'idealized.' The mystery-god was called a bull because he really was a bull—a bull full of vital *mana*, eaten at a communal feast. He died and was re-born, because the world of life which he embodies really dies and is re-born. But as the reflecting worshipper began to idealize his god, it seemed a degradation, if not an absurdity, to suppose that the god was a beast with the brute vitality of a beast. He must have human form and the most beautiful human form; human intellect and the highest human intellect. He must not suffer and fail and die; he must be ever blessed, ageless and deathless. It is only a step further to the conscious philosophy which will deny to God any human frailties, any emotions, any wrath or jealousy, and ultimately any character whatever except dead, unmeaning perfection, incapable of movement or change.

Then at last we know these gods for what they are, intellectual conceptions merely, things of thought bearing but slight relation to life lived. Broadly speaking, these Olympians represent that tendency in thought which is towards reflection, differentiation, clearness, while the Eniautos-Daimon represents that other tendency in religion towards emotion, union, indivisibility. It might almost be said that the Olympians stand for articulate consciousness, the Eniautos-Daimon for the sub-conscious.

Chapter XI brings us back to the Hymn. Whatever the difference between the religion of the Eniautos-Daimon and that of the Olympians, the forms of both these religions depend on, or rather express and represent, the social structure of the worshippers. Above the gods, supreme, eternally dominant, stands the figure of Themis. She is social ordinance, the collective conscience projected, the Law or Custom that is Right.

Una superstitio superis quae reddita divis.

The social structure represented by the Olympians is the same as that of the modern family, it is patrilinear. The figure of Dionysos, his thiasos, and his relation to his mother and the

Maenads, is only to be understood by reference to an earlier social structure, that known as matrilinear. But the all-important point is not *which* particular structure is represented, but the general principle that social structure and the collective conscience which utters itself in social structure, underlie all religion. Themis conditions not only our social relations, but also our whole relation with the outside world. The Kouretes bid their daimon come 'for the Year'; they also bid him, that crops and flocks may prosper, 'leap for fair Themis.'

Ancient faith held, and in part modern religion still holds, that moral excellence and material prosperity must go together, that man by obeying Themis, the Right, can control the Way of Nature. This strange faith, daily disproved by reason, is in part the survival of the old conviction, best seen in totemism, that man and nature form one indivisible whole. A breach of Themis would offend your neighbours and produce quarrels; quite equally it would offend the river or the earth and produce floods or famine. His emotion towards this unity the Greek uttered at first in the vague shape of a daimon, later, more intellectually, in the clear-cut figure of an Olympian god. But behind Gaia the Mother, and above even Zeus the Father, stands always the figure of Themis.

Such in brief is the argument. And here it would be perhaps discreet to pause. I have neither desire nor aptitude for confessional controversy. As my main object is to elucidate Greek religion, it would be both safe and easy to shelter myself behind the adjective 'primitive' and say that with modern religion I have no concern. But I abhor obscurantism. It is to me among the deadliest of spiritual sins. Moreover, the human mind is not made in water-tight compartments. What we think about Greek religion affects what we think about everything else. So I cannot end a book on Greek religion without saying simply how the writing of it has modified my own views.

I have come to see in the religious impulse a new value. It is, I believe, an attempt, instinctive and unconscious, to do what Professor Bergson bids modern philosophy do consciously and with the whole apparatus of science behind it, namely to apprehend life as one, as indivisible, yet as perennial movement and change.

But, profoundly as I also feel the value of the religious impulse, so keenly do I feel the danger and almost necessary disaster of each and every creed and dogma. For the material of religion is essentially the uncharted, the ungrasped, as Herbert Spencer would say, though with a somewhat different connotation, the 'unknowable.' Further, every religious dogma errs in two ways. First, it is a confident statement about something unknown and therefore practically always untrustworthy; secondly, if it were right and based on real knowledge, then its subject-matter would no longer belong to the realm of religion; it would belong to science or philosophy. To win new realms for knowledge out of the unknown is part of the normal current of human effort; but to force intellectual dogma upon material which belongs only to the realm of dim aspiration is to steer for a backwater of death. In that backwater lies stranded many an ancient galley, haunted by fair figures of serene Olympians, and even, it must be said, by the phantom of Him—the Desire of all nations—who is the same yesterday, to-day and for ever. The stream of life flows on, a saecular mystery; but these, the *eidola* of man's market-place, are dead men, hollow ghosts.

As to religious ritual, we may by degrees find forms that are free from intellectual error. The only intelligible meaning that ritual has for me, is the keeping open of the individual soul—that bit of the general life which life itself has fenced in by a separate organism—to other souls, other separate lives, and to the apprehension of other forms of life. The avenues are never closed. Life itself, physical and spiritual, is the keeping of them open. Whether any systematized attempt to remind man, by ritual, of that whole of life of which he is a specialized fragment can be made fruitful or not, I am uncertain.

My other debts are many.

To Dr Verrall, who in a single sentence gave me material for my second chapter. The reader will probably feel more grateful for his single sentence—an inspired bit of translation—than for the commentary that attends it.

To Mr Arthur Bernard Cook, who has spared time from his own valuable work to read through the greater part of my proofs. He has also, with a generosity as rare as it is characteristic, allowed me to borrow many suggestions from his forthcoming book *Zeus*, the appearance of which will, I know, mark an epoch in the study of Greek Religion.   My sense of Mr Cook's great kindness is the deeper, because on some fundamental points we see differently.

Mr Francis Macdonald Cornford has again carried through for me the tedious task of proof-correcting.   My chief debt to him is however for his chapter on *The Origin of the Olympic Games*.   The conclusions he had independently arrived at in a course of lectures on Pindar, given at Trinity College during the Michaelmas Term of 1910, came as a quite unlooked for confirmation of my own views. This confirmation was the more valuable since it reached me at a time when my own argument was still inchoate and my conviction halting.   My whole book—especially its last two chapters—owes much to Mr Cornford's constant help on points which will be developed more fully in his forthcoming work, *From Religion to Philosophy*.

My thanks are also offered to

Mrs Hugh Stewart and Miss Ruth Darwin for much kind help in the drawing of illustrations and the making of the index ;

My College, which, by releasing me from teaching work, has given me the leisure necessary for writing ;

The British School of Athens for permission to republish some part of my article on *The Kouretes and Zeus Kouros*, which appeared in the Annual, 1908–1909 ;

The German Archaeological Institute, the École Française of Berlin and Athens, and the Hellenic Society for permission to reproduce plates, and Messrs Macmillan for kindly allowing me the use of blocks from my *Mythology and Monuments of Ancient Athens*, now out of print ;

The University Press for undertaking the publication of my book, and especially their skilful proof-reader, whose care has saved me from many errors.

And last I would thank my critics.

They have kindly warned me that, in the study of Alpha there is danger lest I lose sight of Omega.   Intent on *origines*, on the roots of things, I fail to gather in, they tell me, the tree's fair, final fruit and blossom.   I thank them for the warning, but I think they have not read my *Prolegomena,* or at least its preface. I there confess, and still confess, that I have little natural love for what an Elizabethan calls ' ye Beastly Devices of ye Heathen.' Savages, save for their reverent, totemistic attitude towards animals, weary and disgust me, though perforce I spend long hours in reading of their tedious doings. My good moments are when, through the study of things primitive, I come to the better understanding of some song of a Greek poet or some saying of a Greek philosopher.

It is because he has taught me to perceive, however faintly, this 'aroma of mysterious and eternal things' that I have asked leave to dedicate my most unworthy book to a scholar who is also a poet.

JANE ELLEN HARRISON.

NEWNHAM COLLEGE, CAMBRIDGE.
New Year's Eve, 1911.

THE MYTH AND RITUAL PATTERN OF THE ANCIENT EAST

The meaning of the terms 'myth' and 'ritual'—Early ritual concerned with practical problems of daily life—Myth the spoken part of ritual—The spread of culture patterns from one country to another—The three processes accompanying the spread of culture patterns—Adaptation—Disintegration—Degradation—The king the central feature of the ritual—The annual festival the centre and climax of the ritual—Its main elements—Dramatic representation of the death and resurrection of the god—Symbolic representation of the myth of creation—The ritual combat—The sacred marriage—The triumphal procession—Influence of this ritual pattern upon the religious practices of the Hebrews—The Hebrew prophets and the conception of the King-god—Moses as the originator of Hebrew hostility to this conception—Features of the Hebrew Seasonal Feasts which imply the influence of the ritual pattern—The Creation Myth and the ritual combat—The implications of early ritual prohibitions—Sun- and Moon-cults dealt with in later Essays, not of the essence of the pattern.

SINCE the terms 'myth' and 'ritual' will be constantly used in the following pages, it will be well to state briefly the particular sense in which they will be so used. In his recent book, *Myths of the Origin of Fire*, Sir James Frazer defines mythology as the philosophy of primitive man: 'It is his first attempt to answer those general questions concerning the world which have doubtless obtruded themselves on the human mind from the earliest times and will continue to occupy it to the last.' He also describes myths as 'documents of human thought in the embryo'.[1] Now the expression 'primitive man' is almost as vague as the phrase 'the man in the street'. To describe the myths and practices of Australian aborigines or Polynesian islanders as representing the behaviour and mentality of primitive man is a question-begging process.

The term 'primitive' is a purely relative one. The only

[1] Op. cit., p. vi.

B

kind of behaviour or mentality which we can recognize as 'primitive' in the strict sense is such as can be shown to lie historically at the fountain-head of a civilization. The earliest civilizations known to us are those of Egypt and Mesopotamia, and the earliest evidence which we can gather concerning the beliefs and practices there prevalent constitutes for us what is 'primitive' in the historical sense.

To the educated reader the word 'myth' probably suggests familiar and often very beautiful Greek stories, the themes of poet and dramatist, such as the myths of Zeus and Semele, Theseus and the Minotaur, Perseus and the Gorgon Medusa. But as soon as these stories are examined we find that they all contain some thread which, like the clue which Ariadne gave to Theseus, leads back to the centre, to the original or primitive significance of the story, to the home of the myth. From Perseus we find a thread leading back to the Canaanite god, Resheph. Sir Arthur Evans, in *The Palace of Minos*, has said: 'We see the Minotaur himself on the way to Crete, but if he reached the Island from the Delta, his starting-point was still the Euphrates.'[1] In both Dionysiac myth and ritual we find clues pointing back to Egypt and Osiris. Hence behind the myths of Greece, in the region of the world's most ancient civilizations, there lie those modes of behaviour which are primitive for us in the sense that they are the source of the great body of myth and ritual characteristic of ancient culture.

When we examine these early modes of behaviour we find that their originators were not occupied with general questions concerning the world but with certain practical and pressing problems of daily life. There were the main problems of securing the means of subsistence, to keep the sun and moon doing their duty, to ensure the regular flooding of the Nile, to maintain the bodily vigour of the king

[1] Op. cit., vol. ii, pt. i, p. 28.

who was the embodiment of the prosperity of the community. There were also individual problems, how to ward off disease and ill fortune, how to acquire a knowledge of the future. In order to meet these needs the early inhabitants of Egypt and Mesopotamia developed a set of customary actions directed towards a definite end. Thus the coronation of a king, both in Egypt and Babylon, consisted of a regular pattern of actions, of things prescribed to be done, whose purpose was to fit the king completely to be the source of the well-being of the community. This is the sense in which we shall use the term 'ritual'.

Moreover, we find that these early ritual patterns consisted not only of things done but of things said. The spoken word had the efficacy of an act, hence the magic value of the many punning allusions which we find in early Egyptian ritual texts, a point which will be abundantly illustrated by Dr. Blackman in his essay. In general the spoken part of a ritual consists of a description of what is being done, it is the story which the ritual enacts. This is the sense in which the term 'myth' is used in our discussion. The original myth, inseparable in the first instance from its ritual, embodies in more or less symbolic fashion, the original situation which is seasonally re-enacted in the ritual.

Thus in the Egyptian Coronation ritual contained in the Ramesseum Papyrus, with which Dr. Blackman will deal in his essay, the spoken part of the ritual embodies the myth of Osiris. Again, to take an example from the Babylonian New Year ritual, when Marduk is lying dead in the 'mountain', the recitation of the Creation myth, the *enuma elish*, is an essential part of the ritual for restoring life to the dead god. But the *enuma elish* contains the description of the situation which is being enacted in the ritual, the triumph of Marduk over his enemies, and the fixing of destinies.[1]

[1] See Mr. Gadd's description of this, pp. 50–2, 61–2 below.

Accordingly the origin of such actions as may be classed as ritual lies in the attempt to deal with or control the unpredictable element in human experience. Since in the early stages of man's knowledge of the universe the realm of the unpredictable was almost co-extensive with human life, and even the simplest acts might have unforeseen and undesirable consequences, the range of ritual activities was far larger than it is to-day. As far back as evidence for such activities in Egypt or Mesopotamia exists, that is, between three and four millenniums before Christ, we find that they had assumed a pattern which was adapted to the needs of an urban civilization and a social structure of which the king was the centre. This pattern will be discussed at a later stage.

In the myths of Greece, as we have already observed, there is a clue, a connecting thread, which leads back to this ancient myth and ritual pattern just referred to. This raises the question of the transmission of such patterns from one culture area to another. Since Goblet d'Alviella's pioneer work on the subject, the fact of the migration of symbols has been generally accepted. But a symbol is merely a detached fragment of myth or ritual which has acquired a separate life of its own. If it be recognized that a fragment of a myth or ritual may travel far from its original setting, as has happened, for instance, in the case of the familiar winged disk (see Fig. 1), it is also possible to conceive of the carrying of the larger ritual pattern with its associated myth from one country to another by one of the various ways of 'culture spread', such as commerce, conquest, or colonization.

We are on sure ground in asserting that there is abundant evidence for the interchange of many culture elements throughout the ancient East. In *The Palace of Minos*[1] Sir Arthur Evans repeatedly stresses the cultural interchange

[1] Cf. op. cit., vol. ii, pt. i, pp. 24–8.

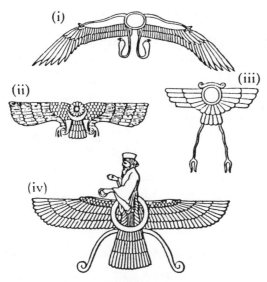

(i)

(ii)

(iii)

(iv)

FIG. 1. Examples of Winged Disks: (i) Egypt, (ii) Assyria
(iii) Cappadocia, (iv) Persia

FIG. 2. Seal from Jerusalem. The God in his Sacred Bark

between Crete, Egypt, and Mesopotamia. The relation between Hittite, Elamite, and early Babylonian seals, as indeed between most of the early seals from the culture area which we are considering, is very striking both in technique and content. The new material from Mohendjodaro[1] increases the possible range of such a 'culture spread'.

Now it may be said that in general, when such a transmission of culture patterns takes place, three processes are set in motion, namely, adaptation, disintegration, and degradation.

In the first place there is always an adaptation of borrowed cultural elements to their new environment. The bold and original way in which Minoan artists dealt with Egyptian culture motifs abundantly illustrates the principle. A simple and familiar example is furnished by the winged solar disk already referred to. In Assyria the place of the solar disk is taken by the figure of Asshur, in Persia by that of Ahura Mazda. Indeed, the presence of a cultural element which is clearly alien to its environment is often a sure indication of borrowing. For example, the representation of the god in his sacred bark is at home in Egypt, where the funeral procession of Osiris by river to Abydos was part of the regular ritual pattern.[2] We also find it in Babylon where it is not alien to the conditions of a river-valley culture, and where, even if it was originally borrowed, it has been completely assimilated. But when we find a Hebrew seal from Jerusalem, depicting a god in his sacred bark, we have a clear case of a borrowed cultural element in an alien environment, for that of Palestine is least of all a riverine civilization (see Fig. 2).

Next we have another process, one which is specially illustrated in the field of Canaanite and Hebrew culture, but

[1] See Sir John Marshall, *Mohendjodaro*, 1932.
[2] Cf. Dr. Blackman's essay, pp. 32–4.

is found throughout the world, the process of disintegration. In the first place it is clear that a very large part of Egyptian ritual was based on the practice of mummification. Hence, when the ritual was carried to an environment where mummification was the exception, much of it would tend to disappear as meaningless or be adapted to altered conditions. It would disintegrate. Mr. A. M. Hocart's valuable book *Kingship* contains overwhelming evidence of the way in which the original pattern of the elaborate ritual of coronation could be broken up in the course of its migration into various parts of the world.

Mummification was not practised in Sumer and Akkad; hence the general ritual pattern which developed there was more readily adaptable to the Semitic environment of Canaan, and its influence there is more easily traced. But the same process of disintegration took place, though to a lesser degree. The theory of culture-borrowing which we are endeavouring to establish in no way conflicts with the fact that borrowing may exist side by side with the development of independent ideas and institutions. Hence we get the peculiar mingling of cultures which is characteristic of Canaanite civilization.

But the process, that of disintegration, appears even more clearly in the breaking up of myth. The Greek myths, as we know them, are fragments of an original pattern which have taken on a separate existence as literary forms. Both the Minotaur and the Perseus myths involve an underlying ritual pattern of human sacrifice, and take us back to a stage in which the myth and ritual were united. In Mr. Hartland's *Perseus* we can see the gradual disintegration and dispersion of the severed members of the myth.

The third process, of degradation, often takes place simultaneously with adaptation and disintegration. Though it is more noticeable in the material and artistic side of culture, it is not without influence upon the content of myth and ritual. The gods and their representations in any cultural area are not isolated conceptions but form part, and indeed are the product, of the original ritual pattern.

Hence the borrowing and interchange of gods, their names and attributes, is an important part of the process we are discussing. But it is here that degradation is particularly observable. Degradation may appear as actual loss of skill and artistic feeling, as for instance, in the representation of the Hathor head-dress in the many figurines of Astarte found in Canaanite excavation.[1] It may also consist of loss of meaning, as when a symbol or a fragment of ritual persists after its original meaning has been lost. In Canaan, the region with which we are specially concerned, the pervading influence of the culture of Egypt and Babylon was bound to be felt in a marked degree owing to the fact that Canaan was a dependency of one or other of these two powers from 2000 to 1000 B.C. This is fully discussed below in the fourth essay.

The distinctive features of the Egyptian and Babylonian ritual systems are described in the next two essays. Hence it is only necessary here to give an account of the pattern assumed by the common elements of all these early rituals.

The central feature is the importance of the king for the well-being of the community—it may be a coincidence, it may be more than a coincidence, that some of the finest descriptions of the Golden Age to Come, written by Hebrew prophets and apocalyptists, had as their essential point the figure of a king, now only human, now semi-divine or more.[2] It lies beyond the scope of our inquiry to discuss the origin of this conception. But in the earliest ritual material at our disposal from Egypt and Babylon, the king is already the

[1] See Gressmann, *Texte und Bilder zum Alten Testament*, 1927, vol. ii, pl. 118, figs. 279–84.   [2] See further pp. 123–4 and pp. 156–7 below.

focus of those activities which we have described as ritual. In both Egypt and Babylon the king is regarded as divine. He represents the god in the great seasonal rituals.

The annual festival which was the centre and climax of all the religious activities of the year contained the following elements:

(*a*) The dramatic representation of the death and resurrection of the god.

(*b*) The recitation or symbolic representation of the myth of creation.

(*c*) The ritual combat, in which the triumph of the god over his enemies was depicted.

(*d*) The sacred marriage.

(*e*) The triumphal procession, in which the king played the part of the god followed by a train of lesser gods or visiting deities.

These elements might vary in different localities and at different periods, some being more strongly stressed than others, but they constitute the underlying skeleton, so to speak, not only of such seasonal rituals as the great New Year Festivals, but also of coronation rituals, initiation ceremonies, and may even be discerned in occasional rituals such as spells against demons and various diseases.

We have seen that the origin of ritual in general lies in the attempt to control the unpredictable element in human experience. The ritual pattern represents the things which were done to and by the king in order to secure the prosperity of the community in every sense for the coming year. Behind the dramatic representation of the death and resurrection of the king lies the original custom of killing the king when his physical vigour showed signs of diminishing, a custom which still survives among the Shilluk of the Upper Nile.[1]

The widespread occurrence of the myth of creation in

[1] Sir James Frazer, *The Golden Bough*, abridged ed., 1923, pp. 293–5.

connexion with this ritual pattern suggests the recall or re-enactment of the original situation out of which the civilization of the community, with its institutions, its customs, and its gods, came into existence. This situation always involved a struggle of some kind, either against material difficulties, river-floods, drought, or early political conflicts, such as the struggle between the North and the South of Egypt before the united monarchy came into existence. In the ritual this struggle is represented by the ritual combat. In the inscription of I-kher-nofret, a high Egyptian official of the time of the Twelfth Dynasty, occurs the passage: 'I avenged Un-Nefer on the day of the Great Battle, I overthrew all his enemies on the dyke (?) of Netit.'[1] In the Babylonian New Year Festival the ritual takes the form of a foot-race between Zu and Ninurta, in which Zu is defeated and afterwards, apparently, slain. In the myth the counterpart of the ritual is the story of the struggle between Horus and Set, between Marduk and Tiamat, or between Jahweh and the dragon.

One of the earliest elements in the ritual pattern was the sacred marriage. Sir James Frazer has interpreted the processional scene in the rock sculpture of Boghaz Keui as the representation of a sacred marriage:

'We may conjecture that it is the rite of the Sacred Marriage, and that the scene is copied from a ceremony which was periodically performed by human representatives of the deities. . . . If this was so at Boghaz Keui, we may surmise that the chief pontiff and his family annually celebrated the marriage of the divine powers of fertility, the Father God and the Mother Goddess, for the purpose of ensuring the fruitfulness of the earth and the multiplication of men and beasts.'[2]

[1] Sir E. A. Wallis Budge, *Osiris and the Egyptian Resurrection*, 1911, vol. ii, p. 10.
[2] *Adonis, Attis, Osiris*, 1906, pp. 58–9.

3909 C

The cylinder inscription B of Gudea contains an account of the sacred marriage of the god Ningirsu with the goddess Bau, the daughter of heaven. The text describes how the warrior Ningirsu enters like a whirlwind into his temple, and how Bau, like the rising sun, comes in to him to his couch, and how their union, like the Tigris in flood, brings prosperity to Lagash.[1]

Not the least important part of the ritual, and one of the most widespread, was the triumphal procession, the epiphany of the god, his public manifestation as risen, triumphant, possessing all power to determine the destinies of his people for the coming year.

There are many other features of early ritual. We have not mentioned them since our purpose has been simply to give the general outline of the central elements of the myth and ritual characteristic of the ancient East.

There now arises the question whether the religious practices of the Hebrews show traces of this prevalent ritual pattern. More detailed discussions of the problem and fuller statements of the evidence will be found in the later essays of this volume. We confine ourselves here to a general statement of the position.

At the outset a fact is evident which might seem at first sight fatal to the suggestion that Hebrew religion received the imprint of this ancient ritual pattern. It is the fact that the theory of divine kingship was definitely rejected by the prophets who gave to Hebrew religion its permanent form and character.[2] That the conception of a king-god was not unknown to them we learn from a remarkable passage in the

---

[1] F. Bohl, *Z.A.*, Oct. 1929, p. 91.

[2] For a discussion of this subject see C. R. North, *The Old Testament Estimate of the Monarchy*, in *The American Journal of Semitic Languages and Literature*, vol. xlviii, pp. 1 ff.

book of Ezekiel. Here is a part of his description of the king-god of Tyre:

'Son of man, say unto the prince of Tyre, Thus saith the Lord God: Because thine heart is lifted up, and thou hast said, I am a god, I sit in the seat of God, in the midst of the seas; yet thou art man, and not God, though thou didst set thine heart as the heart of God . . . thou sealest up the sum, full of wisdom, and perfect in beauty. Thou wast in Eden the garden of God; every precious stone was thy covering . . . Thou wast the anointed cherub that covereth: and I set thee, so that thou wast upon the holy mountain of God; thou hast walked up and down in the midst of the stones of fire.' (Ezek. xxviii. 1–14.)

It is clear that the prophet and, no doubt, his readers, were familiar with the conception of a king-god and with the ritual of the deification of the king.[1] Doubtless we should have had many more references to this circle of ideas but for its partial eclipse—though no more than a *partial* one—at a comparatively early period. This latter may well be attributed to the influence of Moses himself. There does not seem to be any reason for rejecting the tradition that Moses, the traditional founder of Hebrew religion, spent the first part of his life in the environment of the Egyptian Court. Here he would be familiar with the ritual pattern of which the divine king was the centre in its most elaborate form. When he was obliged to leave Egypt, he spent some years among the pastoral tribes who occupied the steppes of Midian. Here he passed through the experience which is symbolized by the story of the burning bush. This seems to have impressed upon his mind a conception of the nature of God wholly incompatible with the conception of the Egyptian divine king. This might well have produced in him a strong revulsion against the whole ritual system of Egypt and especially

[1] C. R. North, *The Religious Aspects of Hebrew Kingship*, Z.A.W., 1932, pp. 21–38.

against everything in it that implied the idea of making a man into a god.

Hebrew ritual, more especially early Hebrew ritual, is dealt with in the sixth and seventh essays. Hence it is only necessary here to refer to certain features of the early Seasonal Feasts which seem to imply the influence of the ritual pattern discussed above.

(*a*) We find a parallel to the double observance of the New Year Festival in Babylonia—in Nisan and in Tishrit—in the existence in the Hebrew Festival Calendar of the double New Year celebration of Passover and Unleavened Bread in Nisan, and of *Rosh Hashshanah* in Tishri.

(*b*) The Feast of Ingathering, later called the Feast of Tabernacles, was also clearly a New Year Festival, as is shown by the expression 'at the out-going of the year'.[1]

(*c*) A characteristic feature of the Feast of Tabernacles was the booths of greenery. This, although it belongs to the priestly account of the feast, may very well be of far earlier origin. It is probably connected with the conception of the sacred marriage and the ceremony of decorating the *gigunu*, or bridal-chamber, of the god in the *ziqqurat* with greenery.[2]

(*d*) The slaying of the first-born in Egypt, which in Exodus appears as an aetiological myth explaining Jahweh's claim to all first-born, probably goes back to the ritual of the slaying of the king; in its Hebrew form it may be connected with the night of slaughter referred to in the inscription of I-kher-nofret mentioned above, as part of the Osiris ritual.

There are many features of the early Seasonal Feasts which suggest that we have to do here with the phenomenon already referred to, namely, the breaking up of the ritual pattern in

[1] See G. B. Gray, *Sacrifice in the Old Testament*, 1925, pp. 300–1.
[2] See the article by Mr. Sidney Smith in *The Journal of the Royal Asiatic Society*, 1928, pp. 849–68.

the course of its passage into a fresh environment. The ritual pattern was probably transmitted indirectly to the Hebrews through the medium of the Canaanites—whatever may have been added afterwards.

It has long been recognized that in the various references to the fight between Jahweh and the dragon preserved in Hebrew literature,[1] we have the survival of the Creation Myth and the fight between Marduk and Tiamat.[2] But what has not been so generally recognized is that the myth thus preserved is the counterpart of the ritual combat, and constitutes a vital part of the whole ritual pattern—hence the importance of all that Mr. Gadd has written on pp. 50-2 below.

Old Testament scholars have been rather reluctant to accept Mowinckel's theory that the Processional Psalms imply the existence among the Hebrews of a New Year Festival of the enthronement of Jahweh. But the existence of such a ceremony in the earlier stages of Hebrew religion seems to be extremely probable,[3] when it is recognized that the epiphany of the god and his triumphal procession attended by a train of lesser gods is also a part of this general ritual pattern of which we have seen traces in other elements of early Hebrew ritual.

It seems possible to draw similar conclusions from an examination of a number of ritual prohibitions in early Hebrew religious legislation. We have merely indicated its general trend. While a large number of such prohibitions are evidently due to the later prophetic attack on every religious custom which bore the stamp of Canaanite origin, there is a group of ritual prohibitions, some of which belong to the earliest stage of Hebrew religious legislation, pointing to the existence of the king-god ritual pattern. This group

[1] See pp. 175-8 below.
[2] For this see, p. 128 and pp. 177-8 below.
[3] See further pp. 132-4 and pp. 188-9 below.

includes certain laws which have offered considerable difficulty to commentators, but which appear in a new light when they are related to the ritual system which sprang from the conception of the divine king. Such, for example, are the prohibitions against steps up to the altar, against seething a kid in its mother's milk, against incest, sacred prostitution, interchange of clothing between the sexes, and a number of similar instances. This point is dealt with in the fourth essay.

Lastly a word must be said about Sun-worship and Moon-worship. These cults were very prevalent throughout the cultural areas with which we are concerned. But here they can only be mentioned in passing since neither of them exercised a formative influence upon the main outlines of the ritual pattern which has been the chief subject of this essay. Those cults, however, in their relation to Jahwism, are by no means neglected in the essays which follow.

S. H. HOOKE.

THE RITUAL VIEW OF MYTH AND THE MYTHIC

By Stanley Edgar Hyman

T HE ritual approach comes directly out of Darwin, and thus, I suppose, ultimately from Heraclitus, whose *panta rei* seems to be the ancestor of any dynamic account of anything. When Darwin concluded *The Origin of Species* (1859) with a call for evolutionary treatment in the sciences of man, he opened the door to a variety of genetic studies of culture, and when he showed in *The Descent of Man* (1871) that human evolution was insignificant organically although vastly speeded up culturally (we might not be so quick to say "ethically" as he was), he made cultural studies the legitimate heirs of evolutionary biology. The same year as *The Descent,* in response to *The Origin,* E. B. Tylor's *Primitive Culture* appeared, drawing an immediate fan letter from Darwin. It staked off quite a broad claim to cultural studies in its subtitle "Researches into the Development of Mythology, Philosophy, Religion, Language, Art, and Custom." Tylor's general principle, almost his law, is that survivals are significant because they embody, sometimes in trivial or playful form, the serious usages of earlier stages. In material culture, it meant that such important tools as the bow and arrow, the fire drill, and the magician's rattle evolved into the toys of children; in non-material culture, it meant that myths were based on rites, although, like many rationalists before him, Tylor believed that they had been consciously devised as explanations.

Tylor's evolutionary anthropology, carried on by such successors as R. R. Marett and Henry Balfour, became the central tradition of British anthropology, but the emphasis gradually shifted from Tylor's concern with belief and custom to the more tangible areas of social organization, economics, and material culture. Meanwhile, at Cambridge, a classicist named James G. Frazer had found *Primitive Culture* a revelation, and his interest in ancient survivals was broadened and extended by his friend William Robertson Smith's studies of religion, in which Smith made use of the comparative method, invented by Montesquieu and developed by German philology. Weaving together the two main strands of Tylor's evolutionary survivals and Smith's comparative method, in 1885 Frazer began publishing a series of periodical articles on custom. When one of them, on a curious priesthood at Nemi in Italy, tied in with Smith's ideas about the slain god and outgrew article size, he kept working on it and in 1890 published it as the first edition of *The Golden Bough* in two volumes, dedicated to Smith. For Frazer in *The Golden Bough,* myth is still Tylor's rationalist "a fiction devised to explain an old custom, of which the real meaning and origin had been forgotten,"[1] and the evolution of custom is still Tylor's "to dwindle from solemn ritual into mere pageant and pastime,"[2] but Frazer constantly approaches, without ever quite stating, a synthesis of the two, with myths not consciously-devised rational

[1] J. G. Frazer, *The Golden Bough,* IV (London, 1915), 153.
[2] Frazer, *The Golden Bough,* IV, 214.

explanations, but the actual dwindling or later form of the rite. Long before 1915, when the third and final edition of *The Golden Bough* appeared, that synthesis had been arrived at.

Since 1882, Jane Ellen Harrison, Frazer's contemporary at Cambridge, had been writing on Greek mythology and art, and in 1903, after she had seen a clay seal at Cnossos with its sudden revelation that the Minotaur was the king of Crete in a bull mask, she published *Prolegomena to the Study of Greek Religion,* which clearly stated the priority of ritual over myth or theology. Her book acknowledged the cooperation of Gilbert Murray at Tylor's Oxford, and Frazer, F. M. Cornford, and A. B. Cook at Cambridge. Cook, whose book, *Zeus,* did not begin to appear for another decade, began publishing parts of it in periodicals about that time, and his important series "Zeus, Jupiter, and the Oak" in the *Classical Review* (1903) took an approach similar to Harrison's. By the time Murray published *The Rise of the Greek Epic* (1907), reading such mythic figures as Helen and Achilles as ritual concretizations, he was able to draw on some of this Cambridge work his earlier writings had influenced. By 1908, when the Committee for Anthropology at Oxford sponsored six lectures, published under Marett's editorship later that year as *Anthropology and the Classics,* with the aim of interesting students of the humanities in "the lower culture,"[3] students of the humanities at the sister university had been turning their attention to the lower cultures for two decades, and the seed Tylor planted had flowered elsewhere.

The watershed year was 1912, when Harrison published *Themis,* a full and brilliant exposition of the chthonic origins of Greek mythology, including an excursus on the ritual forms underlying Greek tragedy by Murray (to whom the book is dedicated), a chapter on the ritual origin of the Olympic Games by Cornford, and copious material from Cook's forthcoming work. (Curiously, this book too had been inspired by a visit to Crete, where Harrison encountered the "Hymn of the Kouretes," which suggested that ritual magic, specifically the rite of a year-daimon, was the central element in early Greek religion.) In *Themis,* Harrison made three important points with great clarity: that myth arises out of rite, rather than the reverse;[4] that it is "the spoken correlative of the acted rite, the thing done; it is *to legomenon* as contrasted with or rather as related to *to dromenon*"[5] (a Greek definition of myth is *ta legomena epi tois dromenois* 'the things said over a ritual act'); and that it is not anything else nor of any other origin.[6]

Basic to this view, as Harrison makes clear, is a dynamic or evolutionary conception of process whereby rites die out, and myths continue in religion, literature, art, and various symbolic forms with increased misunderstanding of the ancient rite, and a compensatory transformation for intelligibility in new terms. Thus myths are never the record of historical events or people, but freed from their ritual origins they may attach to historical events or people (as Alexander was believed to be, or claimed to be, a god and the son of a snake, because mythic Greek kings like Cecrops had been ritual snake gods); they never originate as scientific or aetiological explanations of nature, but freed from their ritual origins may be so used (as stars have their positions

[3] *Anthropology and the Classics,* ed. R. R. Marett (Oxford, 1907), p. 5.
[4] J. E. Harrison, *Themis* (Cambridge, 1912), p. 13.
[5] Harrison, *Themis,* p. 328.
[6] Harrison, *Themis,* p. 331.

in the sky because the mythic hero threw them there, but *his* origin is in rite, not primitive astronomy).

The ritual approach to mythology, or any form based on myth, thus cannot limit itself to genetic considerations. In the artificial division I have found most handy, it must deal with the three related problems of Origin, Structure, and Function. If the origin is the ancient anonymous collective one of ritual, the structure is intrinsically dramatic, the *dromenon* or thing done, but that form ceaselessly evolves in time in the chain of folk transmission. Here the considerations are not historic nor anthropological, but formal in terms of literary structure, principles of *Gestalt* organization, and dynamic criteria. In folk transmission, the "folk work" involves operations comparable to those Freud found in the "dream work"—splitting, displacement, multiplication, projection, rationalization, secondary elaboration, and interpretation—as well as such more characteristically aesthetic dynamics as Kenneth Burke's principle of "completion" or the fulfillment of expectations, in the work as well as in the audience. In regard to function, as the myth or text alters, there is at once a changing social function, as the work satisfies varying specific needs in the society along Malinowskian lines, and an unchanging, built-in function best described by Aristotle's *Poetics* and Freudian psychology, carrying with it its own context, taking us through its structural rites. In other words, the book of Jonah in the reading satisfies our need to be reborn in the belly of the great fish as efficiently as the initiatory rites from which it presumably derived satisfied the same need in the initiates. If these are now as then "fantasy gratifications," they are the charismatic experiences of great art now, as they were the charismatic experiences of organic religion then.

In a relatively short time, the ritual approach to folk study has met with remarkable success. There had of course been individual ritual studies in various areas long before 1912. Most of them were in the field of children's lore, where ritual survivals, after Tylor had called attention to them, were readily apparent. Some of the earliest studies were William Wells Newell's *Games and Songs of American Children* (1883), Henry Carrington Bolton's *The Counting-Out Rhymes of Children* (1888), Alice Gomme's *The Traditional Games Of England, Scotland and Ireland* (1894), and Lina Eckenstein's *Comparative Studies in Nursery Rhymes* (1906). Much of this work has never been superseded, and similarly, the most impressive ritual studies we have of the Bible appeared at the turn of the century: for the Old Testament, William Simpson's *The Jonah Legend* (1899), and for the New, John M. Robertson's series of books on the mythic Jesus, beginning with *Christianity and Mythology* (1900). All of these people seem to have operated in relative isolation, independently working through to conclusions about their own material without knowing what was going on in other areas or recognizing the general application of their conclusions.

With the appearance of *Themis,* a powerful general statement of the theory buttressed by a prodigy of scholarship in several complicated areas of Greek culture, a "Cambridge" or "ritual" approach became generally available. Within a few years, its application to Greek studies had been enormously widened: Cornford's *From Religion to Philosophy* (1912), traced the ritual origins of some basic philosophic ideas; Harrison's *Ancient Art and Ritual* (1913), turned her theory on Greek plastic and pictorial arts; Murray tested his ritual forms on one tragic dramatist in *Euripides and His Age* (1913), (both it and *Ancient Art and Ritual* as popularizations for the

Home University Library); Cornford tested the same forms on Greek comedy in *The Origin of Attic Comedy* (1914); and the first volume of Cook's enormous storehouse of ritual interpretation, *Zeus,* appeared (1914).

The first application of the theory outside Greek studies was Murray's 1914 Shakespeare Lecture, "Hamlet and Orestes,"[7] a brilliant comparative study in the common ritual origins of Shakespeare and Greek drama. 1920 saw the appearance of Jessie Weston's *From Ritual to Romance,* treating the Grail romances as the "misinterpreted" record of a fertility rite, and Bertha Phillpotts' *The Elder Edda and Ancient Scandinavian Drama,* tracing the ritual sources of Northern epic poetry. The next year Margaret Murray's *The Witch-Cult in Western Europe* appeared, claiming a real "Dianic cult," the survival of the old pagan religion, persecuted by Christianity as witchcraft, the book constituting the first substantial excursion of the theory into history. In 1923, the widening ripples took in fairy tales, in P. Saintyves' *Les Contes de Perrault et les Récits Parallèles;* folk drama, in R. J. E. Tiddy's editing *The Mummers Play;* and law, in H. Goitein's *Primitive Ordeal and Modern Law.* In 1927, A. M. Hocart's *Kingship* appeared, tracing a great variety of material to a basic royal initiatory ceremony, and in 1929 Scott Buchanan's *Poetry and Mathematics* (the first American work along these lines in the third of a century since Bolton) boldly proposed a treatment of experimental science in ritual terms, and imaginatively worked some of it out.

In the thirties, S. H. Hooke edited two important symposia, *Myth and Ritual* (1933) and *The Labyrinth* (1935), in which a number of prominent scholars studied the relationships of myth and ritual in the ancient Near East; Lord Raglan published *Jocasta's Crime,* a ritual theory of taboo (1933), and his enormously influential *The Hero* (1937), which broadly generalized the ritual origins of all myth, as against the historical; Enid Welsford investigated the sources of an archetypal figure in *The Fool* (1935); Allen, Halliday, and Sikes published their definitive edition of *The Homeric Hymns* (1936), extending previous considerations of Greek epic and dramatic poetry into sacred lyric; and in the late thirties William Troy began publishing his as yet uncollected ritual studies of such writers as Lawrence, Mann, and Fitzgerald.

By the forties, old subjects could be gone back over with greatly augmented information. George Thomson combined a ritual and Marxist approach in *Aeschylus and Athens* (1941) and *Studies in Ancient Greek Society* (the first volume of which appeared in 1949); Rhys Carpenter amplified Murray's earlier treatment of Homer in *Folk Tale, Fiction and Saga in the Homeric Epics* (1946); Lewis Spence brought Newell, Bolton, and Lady Gomme somewhat up to date in *Myth and Ritual in Dance, Game, and Rhyme* (1947); and Hugh Ross Williamson expanded Margaret Murray's brief account (in *The God of the Witches,* 1933) of the deaths of Thomas à Becket and William Rufus as Dianic cult sacrifices in *The Arrow and the Sword* (1947). Venturing into fresh fields, Gertrude Rachel Levy in *The Gate of Horn* (1948), traced some ritual sources of culture down from the stone age, paying considerable attention to plastic and pictorial art; and in 1949 there were two important literary applications: Francis Fergusson's *The Idea of a Theater,* a reading of modern drama in terms of the ritual patterns exemplified in Sophocles' *Oedipus the King,*

[7] In Gilbert Murray, *The Classical Tradition in Poetry* (Cambridge, Mass., 1927), pp. 205-240.

and John Speirs' "Sir Gawain and the Green Knight," in *Scrutiny*, Winter 1949, the first of an important series of ritual studies of medieval English literature.

So far in the fifties half a dozen new territories have been explored and to some extent colonized. Theodor H. Gaster's *Thespis* (1950) generalized a ritual origin for the whole body of Near East sacred literature; Gertrude Kurath's articles on dance in the Funk and Wagnalls' *Dictionary of Folklore* the same year embraced a body of primitive and folk dance forms in the same approach; Cornford's luminous "A Ritual Basis for Hesiod's *Theogony*" was published posthumously in *The Unwritten Philosophy* (1950, although it had been written in 1941); and C. L. Barber published an ambitious exploration of Shakespeare in "The Saturnalian Pattern in Shakespeare's Comedy" in *The Sewanee Review*, Autumn 1951. Since then we have had the publication of Levy's second volume, *The Sword from the Stone* (1953), a ritual genesis of epic; Herbert Weisinger's *Tragedy and the Paradox of the Fortunate Fall* (1953), a similar treatment of tragedy; and Margaret Murray's third book on the Dianic cult, *The Divine King in England* (1954). In this listing I have made no attempt at completeness, confining it to those writers with whose work I am most familiar, and only one or two titles by each (Murray, Cornford, and Harrison have written about a dozen books each), but the breadth and variety of even this truncated list should make it obvious that the "Cambridge" view has gone far beyond the confines of Greek mythology, and that it is apparently here to stay.

Since the ritual approach to myth and literature does not claim to be a theory of ultimate significance, but a method of study in terms of specific significances, it can cohabit happily with a great many other approaches. If its anthropology has historically been Frazerian, the comparative generalization across many cultures, many of its most successful works, from *Themis* to Speirs on Gawain, have stayed narrowly within one area, and where it deals with social function, its anthropology is most profitably Malinowskian (if an unusually historical Malinowskian). The Boas tradition in American anthropology, with its bias against cross-cultural generalization and evolutionary theory, in favor of empirical cultural studies and known history, has often seemed inimical to the ritual approach at those key points. Many of the Boas rigidities, however, seem to have softened in the decade since his death: the new culture and personality anthropology from Ruth Benedict's *Patterns of Culture* (1934) to E. Adamson Hoebel's *The Law of Primitive Man* (1954) seems as cheerfully comparative as *The Golden Bough;* we are all neo-evolutionists once again; and *Primitive Heritage* (1953), Margaret Mead's anthology with Nicholas Calas, calls for "the restoration of wonder," and means, apparently, let us take Frazer and Crawley more seriously. If out of this comes a neo-Frazerian generalizing anthropology, based, not on dubious material wrenched out of its configuration, but on detailed and accurate field studies done with Boasian rigor, no one would welcome it more than the ritualists.

In regard to psychology, the ritual approach can draw centrally on Freudian psychoanalysis, informed by new knowledge and less circumscribed by ethnocentric patterns. This requires modernization without the loss of Freud's central vision, which is tragic where such rebels as Adler and Jung and such revisionists as Fromm and Horney are cheery faith-healers; unshrinking where they bowdlerize; stubbornly materialist where they are idealist and mystic; and dynamic, concerned with process, where they are static and concerned with one or another variety of timeless *élan vital*. After we have brought the Frazerian anthropology of *Totem and Taboo* up to date and restored Freud's "vision" of the Primal Horde, in Burke's terms, to its place as "essence" rather than "origin," the book remains our most useful and seminal equation of primitive rite with neurotic behavior, and thus the bridge to Burke's own "symbolic action," the private, individual symbolic equivalent for the ancient collective ritual. In the form of "symbolic action," psychoanalytic theory gives us the other dimension of function, the wish-fulfillment or fantasy gratification, and can thus answer some of our questions about the origins of origins.

As Jung's work increasingly seems to move toward mystic religion and away from analytic psychology, it appears to be of increasingly little use to a comparative and genetic approach. Strong as Jungian psychology has been in insisting on the universal archetypal identity of myth and symbol, its explanation of this identity in terms of the collective unconscious and innate awareness militates directly against any attempt to study the specific forms by which these traits are carried and transmitted in the culture (as did Freud's own "memory traces"). As Jung is used in the work of Maud Bodkin[8] or Joseph Campbell, as a source of suggestive insights, it seems far more to our purposes, and we can readily utilize Campbell's universal "great myth" or "monomyth," a concept itself derived from Van Gennep's *rites de passage:* "a separation from the world, a penetration to some source of power, and a life-enhancing return."[9] We must first, however, put the Jungian myth back on its roots, either a specific myth and text (literary study) or a specific culture and rite (anthropology). The ritual approach is certainly compatible with varieties of mysticism, as the conclusions of Weston's *From Ritual to Romance* or Harrison's *Epilegomena to the Study of Greek Religion* (1921) make clear, and Harrison was herself strongly drawn to Jung as well as to Bergson. Despite their examples, and the opinions of even so impressive a ritual poet as William Butler Yeats, the job of mythic analysis would seem to require a basic rational materialism, and a constant pressure in the direction of science and scholarship, away from mysticism and the occult. Within these limits of naturalism, and on the frame of this central concern with ritual, all possible knowledge and all approaches to myth, from the most meticulous motif-classification to the most speculative reconstruction of an *ur*-text, can be useful, with pluralism certainly the desirable condition.

There are only two varieties of approach, I think, with which the ritual view cannot usefully coexist. One is the euhemerist, the idea that myths are based on historic persons or events. This theory has been driven back from rampart to rampart over the years, but it stubbornly holds to each new defensive position: if it is forced to give up a historic William Tell, it retreats to a historic Robin Hood; if the historic Orpheus even Harrison's *Prolegomena* accepted in 1903 seems no longer tenable, perhaps Moses is; if there was no Leda and no egg, could there not have been a real Helen? By now, in regard to the great myths, we know that none of these is possible, even at those key points the Trojan War and the figure of Jesus. With stories unquestionably made up about real people, whether fictions about Napoleon or Eleanor Roosevelt jokes, it becomes a simple matter of definition, and if the euhemerists of

[8] Maud Bodkin, *Archetypal Patterns in Poetry* (London, 1934), and *Studies of Type-Images in Poetry, Religion, and Philosophy* (London, 1951).

[9] Joseph Campbell, *The Hero with a Thousand Faces* (New York, 1949), pp. 10, 35.

our various schools want to call those stories myths, they are welcome to them. We find it more useful to apply some other term, insofar as the distinction between myth and history is a real and a basic one.[10]

The other approach to mythology that seems to offer no point of juncture with the ritual view is the cognitionist idea that myths derive from a quest for knowledge. In its nineteenth century forms, the theories that myths were personifications of nature, or the weather, or the sun and moon, it seems substantially to have died out; in various insidious twentieth century forms, the theories that myths are designed to answer aetiological questions about how death came into the world or how the bunny' got his little furry tail, or that taboo is primitive hygiene or primitive genetics, it is still pervasive. Again, all one can say is that myths do not originate in this fashion, that primitive peoples are speculative and proto-scientific, surely, but that the lore they transmit is another order of knowledge. If they knew that the tabooed food carried trichinosis or that the tabooed incestuous marriage deteriorated the stock, they would not save the first for their sacred feasts and the second for their rulers. Once more, if our various cognitionists want to call myth what is unquestionably primitive proto-science, like techniques for keeping a pot from cracking in the firing or seasonal lore for planting and harvesting, that is their privilege. The Alaskan Eskimos who took the Russian explorers for cuttlefish "on account of the buttons on their clothes," as Frazer reports,[11] obviously had speculative minds and a sense of continuity between the animal and human orders not unlike that informing Darwin's theory, but the difference between their myth of "The Great Cuttlefish That Walks Like a Man" (if they had one) and *The Origin of Species* is nevertheless substantial.

If we keep clearly in mind that myth tells a story sanctioning a rite, it is obvious that it neither means nor explains anything; that it is not science but a form of independent experience, analogous to literature. The pursuit of cognition in myth or folk literature has led to all the worst excesses of speculative research, whether the political slogans and events Katherine Elwes Thomas found hermetically concealed in nursery rhymes in *The Real Personages of Mother Goose* (1930), the wisdom messages, deliberately coded and jumbled, that Robert Graves uncoded in *The White Goddess* (1948), or, most recently, the secret fire worship Flavia Anderson discovered hidden behind every myth in *The Ancient Secret* (1953).

Among the important problems facing the ritual view at present is an adequate working-out of the relationship between ritual, the anonymous regular recurrence of an action, and history, the unique identifiable experience in time. The problem is raised dramatically in the latest book by Margaret Murray, one of the pioneers of ritual studies. Called *The Divine King in England,* it is the third in her series on the Dianic cult and easily her wildest. Where *The Witch-cult in Western Europe* named two historical figures, Joan of Arc and Gilles de Rais, as voluntary sacrificial figures in the cult, and her second book, *The God of the Witches,* added two more, Thomas à Becket and William Rufus, the new book makes the bold claim on English history

---

[10] Myth must also be distinguished from all the other things we loosely call by its name: legend, tale, fantasy, mass delusion, popular belief and illusion, and plain lie.

[11] Frazer, "Some Primitive Theories of the Origin of Man," *Darwin and Modern Science,* ed. A. C. Seward (Cambridge, 1909), p. 159.

that "at least once in every reign from William The Conqueror to James I the sacri-fice of the Incarnate God was consummated either in the person of the king or in that of his substitute,"[12] generally in a regular seven-year cycle. Since I have already reviewed the book at length for a forthcoming issue of *Midwest Folklore,* I can here only briefly summarize the problem. Murray's historical excursion is not only dubious history (as reviewers have pointed out, showing the errors of dates and durations by which she gets her seven-year victims, the number jugglery by which she gets her covens of thirteen), it is totally unnecessary history. She is certainly right about sur-vivals of the old religion into modern times, but she seems to be basically in error about the manner in which it survives, to be confusing origins with events. As the ancient rites die out in literal practice, their misunderstood and transformed record passes into myth and symbol, and that is the form in which they survive and color history, without being themselves the events of history. In English history, assuming as she does that the primitive divine king was once slain every seven years, the monarch and his subjects might very well feel an ominousness about each seventh anniversary, and might welcome the death of the king or some high personage, but the step from that to the idea that the dead man was therefore the voluntary victim of a sacrificial cult is the unwarranted one. Murray's witch cult was a genuine wor-ship of the old gods, surviving into modern times in a distorted form, but her Royal Covens are only the travesty of historical scholarship.

If the fallacy of historicity is still with us, the fallacy of aetiology may finally be on its way out. In *Themis,* as far back as 1912, Harrison wrote:

The myth is not at first aetiological, it does not arise to give a reason; it is representative, another form of utterance, of expression. When the emotion that started the ritual has died down and the ritual though hallowed by tradition seems unmeaning, a reason is sought in the myth and it is regarded as aetiological.[13]

In his recent posthumous volume edited by Lord Raglan, *The Life-Giving Myth* (1952), A. M. Hocart finally shows the process whereby myth goes beyond explaining the ritual to explaining other phenomena in nature, thus functioning as general aetiology. In Fiji, he reports, the physical peculiarities of an island with only one small patch of fertile soil are explained by a myth telling how Mberewalaki, a culture hero, flew into a passion at the misbehavior of the people of the island and hurled all the soil he was bringing them in a heap, instead of laying it out properly. Hocart points out that the myth is used aetiologically to explain the nature of the island, but did not originate in that attempt. The adventures of Mberewalaki originated, like all mythology, in ritual performance, and most of the lore of Hocart's Fijian in-formants consisted of such ritual myths. When they get interested in the topography of the island or are asked about it, Hocart argues, they do precisely what we would do, which is ransack their lore for an answer. Our lore might include a body of geo-logical process, and we would search through it for an explanation; theirs has no geology but tells the acts and passions of Mberewalaki, and they search through it similarly and come up with an explanation. It should take no more than this one pointed example, I think, to puncture that last survival of the cosmological origin theories, the aetiological myth, except as a category of function.

[12] M. A. Murray, *The Divine King in England* (London, 1954), p. 13.
[13] Harrison, *Themis,* p. 16.

After the relationship to history and to science or cognition, we are left with the relationship of ritual theory to belief. For Harrison, as for Frazer, ritual studies were part of comparative religion, and a hoped-for result, if not the ultimate aim, was finding a pattern in which a person of sense or sensibility could believe. Harrison concludes her essay in the Darwin centenary volume: "It is, I venture to think, towards the apprehension of such mysteries, not by reason only, but by man's whole personality, that the religious spirit in the course of its evolution through ancient magic and modern mysticism is ever blindly yet persistently moving."[14] In the course of his researches, Darwin himself lost most of his faith, but for Asa Gray, as for some. Darwinians since, the doctrine of evolution celebrated God's powers and strengthened Christian faith. For John M. Robertson, the demolition of the historicity of Jesus was a blow against Christianity on behalf of free-thought; for W. B. Smith and Arthur Drews it was a way of purifying Christianity by purging it of legendary accretions. William Simpson seems to have hit on the idea of Jonah as an initiation ritual because he was preoccupied with such matters as a Freemason. There is apparently no necessary correlation between knowledge and belief; to know all is to believe all, or some, or none.

Most contemporary ritual students of myth, I should imagine, are like myself unbelievers, and it would seem to get progressively more difficult to acknowledge the essential identity of religious myths, and their genesis from the act of worship itself, the god out of the machinery, while continuing to believe in the "truth" of any one of them (or of all of them, except in the woolliest and most Jungian fashion). On the other hand, in *Cults and Creeds in Graeco-Roman Egypt* (1953), we saw Sir Harold Idris Bell, a professional papyrologist, produce a learned and impressive study of the pragmatic competition of religions in Hellenistic Egypt, with the constant proviso that one of those systems, Christianity, was not only morally superior to the others, but was the divinely inspired true faith. So perhaps to know all *is* to believe all.

Finally, then, a number of technical problems remain. In its brief history, the ritual view has illuminated almost the whole of Greek culture, including religion, philosophy, art, many of the forms of literature, and much else. It has done the same for the games, songs, and rhymes of children; the Old and New Testaments, epic and romance, edda and saga, folk drama and dance, folktale and legend, Near East religion, modern drama and literature, even problems in history, law, and science. A few forms of folk literature have not yet been explored in ritual terms, prominent among them the English and Scottish popular ballads (the present writer has made a tentative foray in that direction)[15] and the American Negro blues. A ritual origin for the ballads presumes a body of antecedent folk drama, from which they evolve as narrative songs (as it in turn derives from ritual sacrifice), which hardly exists except in a few late poor fragments such as Robin Hood plays, and which must consequently be conjectured. Such conjecture is not impossible, but it is a hard job involving heavy reliance on that frail reed analogy, and it still awaits its doer. The blues raise serious problems. If they are a true folksong of ancient anonymous collective ritual origin,

[14] Harrison, "The Influence of Darwinism on the Study of Religions," *Darwin and Modern Science,* ed. A. C. Seward, p. 511.

[15] S. E. Hyman, "The Raggle-Taggle Ballads O," *The Western Review,* XV (1951), 305-313.

rather than a folk-transmitted song of modern composition, then they precede any American conditions experienced by the Negro and must have an African source. No trouble here, except that nothing like them has ever been found in Africa, perhaps because it does not exist, perhaps because it would look so different before its sea change that no one has yet identified it. In any case, a ritual origin for the blues constitutes a fascinating problem, although not a critical issue (too much obviously convincing ritual interpretation has been produced for the theory to stand or fall on any single form). A ritual account of the ballads and the blues would close two large chinks, and might keep out drafts even in the coldest climate of opinion.

The relationship of ritual and ritual myth to formal literature has hardly yet been touched. The brilliant work that should have inaugurated such a movement in literary criticism was Murray's 1914 Shakespeare Lecture, "Hamlet and Orestes," in which he showed the essential identity of the two dramatic heroes, not as the result of any direct linkage between the two, but because Shakespeare's Hamlet, through a long Northern line of Amlethus, Amlodi, and Ambales, derived from precisely the same myth and rite of the Winter King—cold, mad, death-centered, bitter, and filthy—that Orestes derived from in his warmer clime. The plays are neither myth nor rite, Murray insists, they are literature, but myth and rite underly their forms, their plots, and their characters. (Greek drama itself represents a fusion of two separate derivations from ritual: the forms of Attic tragedy arise out of the sacrificial rites of tauriform or aegiform Dionysos, the plots of Attic tragedy come mostly from Homer; and the bloody plots fit the ritual form so well, as Rhys Carpenter showed most fully, because the Homeric stories themselves derive from similar sacrificial rites far from Mount Olympus.) In the four decades since Murray's lecture, literary criticism has scarcely noticed it. A student of Murray's, Janet Spens, published a ritual treatment of Shakespeare, *An Essay on Shakespeare's Relation to Tradition* (1916), which I have never seen, but which Barber describes with serious reservations, and until his own essay almost nothing had been done along that line. Troy and Fergusson have dealt with a handful of novels and plays in ritual terms, Carvel Collins has written several essays on Faulkner, and the present writer has similarly tackled Thoreau and a few others, but there has been very little else.

The chief difficulty seems to lie in the need to recognize the relationship of literature to folk tradition, while at the same time drawing Murray's sharp line between them. Literature is analogous to myth, we have to insist, but is not itself myth. There has been a great deal of confusion on this point, best exemplified by Richard Chase's *Quest for Myth* and *Herman Melville* (both in 1949). Chase simply equates the two, defining myth in the former as "the aesthetic activity of a man's mind,"[16] turning Melville's works in the latter into so many myths or mythic organizations. Here we ought to keep in mind a number of basic distinctions. Myth and literature are separate and independent entities, although myth can never be considered in isolation, and any specific written text of the protean myth, or even fixed oral text, can fairly be called folk literature. For literary purposes, all myths are not one, however much they may be one, the monomyth or ur-myth, in essence or origin. What such modern writers as Melville or Kafka create is not myth but an individual fantasy expressing a

[16] Richard Chase, *Quest for Myth* (Baton Rouge, La., 1949), p. vii.

symbolic action, equivalent to and related to the myth's expression of a public rite. No one, not even Melville (let alone Moritz Jagendorf) can invent myths or write folk literature.

The writer can use traditional myths with varying degrees of consciousness (with Joyce and Mann perhaps most fully conscious in our time), and he often does so with no premeditated intention, working from symbolic equivalents in his own unconscious. Here other arts closer to origins, like the dance, where the ritual or symbolic action is physically mimed, can be profoundly instructive. Just as there are varying degrees of consciousness, so are there varying degrees of fruitfulness in these uses of traditional patterns, ranging from dishonest fakery at one extreme to some of the subtlest ironic and imaginative organizations in our poetry at the other. The aim of a ritual literary criticism would be the exploration of all these relations, along with missionary activity on behalf of some of the more fruitful ones.

What begins as a modest genetic theory for the origin of a few myths thus eventually comes to make rather large claims on the essential forms of the whole culture. If, as Schroedinger's *Nature and the Greeks* (1954) shows, the patterns of Greek myth and rite have been built into all our physics until the last few decades, perhaps ritual is a matter of some importance. Raglan and Hocart argue that the forms of social organization arise out of it, Goitein throws in the processes of law, Cornford and Buchanan add the forms of philosophic and scientific thinking (perhaps all our thinking follows the ritual pattern of *agon* or contest, *sparagmos* or tearing apart, then *anagnorisis* or discovery and *epiphany* or showing-forth of the new idea). Even language itself suggests at many points a ritual origin. From rites come the structures, even the plots and characters, of literature, the magical organizations of painting, the arousing and fulfilling of expectation in music, perhaps the common origin of all the arts. If ritual is to be a general theory of culture, however, our operations must get more tentative and precise in proportion as our claims become more grandiose. We then have to keep distinctions even clearer, know so much more, and use every scrap of fact or theory that can be used. Having begun so easily by explaining the myth of the Sphinx, we may yet, working humbly in cooperation with anyone who will and can cooperate, end by reading her difficult riddle.

Bennington College
Bennington, Vermont

MYTH AND RITUAL: SOME RECENT THEORIES

by   Phyllis M. Kaberry

The subject of myth and ritual[1] is one in which students of the classics, ancient history and social anthropology have a common interest; in which anthropology owes much to the work of such classical scholars as Sir James Frazer, Jane Harrison and Fustel de Coulanges.   Since the field is a wide one, I shall in this paper confine myself to the analysis of studies made by British anthropologists and to the development of new concepts and hypotheses over the last two or three decades.

Most anthropologists, at least the honest ones, would admit that myth and ritual have an intrinsic interest as an object of study; and most would admit that in the field there is always the temptation to devote more time to the witnessing of ceremonies and the collecting of myths than to the more mundane but equally important tasks of taking a village census, measuring farms, counting baskets of yams or fish, or recording the details of house construction. Malinowski, himself a student of Frazer, confessed to the fascination of ceremonial life as compared with the observation of merely technological activities; and, although he did not neglect the latter, it is worth noting that his first monograph on the Trobriand Islands was called *Argonauts of the Western Pacific* (1922) and dealt with the elaborate ceremonial exchanges that are a feature of that region of Melanesia.   There is a mass of material on the economic aspects of this institution; but, in describing the sequence of activities in ceremonial exchanges, Malinowski introduces the rituals associated with them and fills in their background of myth and religious belief.   Nevertheless, despite the appearance of several important essays on magic, religion and myth by Malinowski, Radcliffe-Brown, Evans-Pritchard and Firth during the 1920's, [2] and despite the influence of French sociologists such as Durkheim, Mauss, Van Gennep and Loisy on British social anthropologists, the number of full-length monographs on primitive religion that appeared between 1922 and 1952 are surprisingly few. Such titles as Fortune's *Sorcerers of Dobu* (1932), Malinowski's *Coral Gardens and their Magic* (1935), Fortune's *Manus Religion* (1935), Evans-Pritchard's *Witchcraft, Oracles and Magic among the Azande* (1937), Firth's *The Work of the Gods in Tikopia* (1940), and Williams's *Drama of Orokolo* (1940), are as it were rare exotics among a host of other books which deal with the bread and butter of living and the intricacies of kinship and political organization.

It is only within the last few years that British anthropologists have published full-length accounts of religion or specific rituals, among which we may mention R. Berndt, *Kunapipi*, 1951, and *Djanggawul*, 1952 (both interpretations of fertility cults of the Aborigines of north-eastern Arnhem Land); S. F. Nadel, *Nupe Religion*, 1954; E. E. Evans-Pritchard, *Nuer Religion*, 1956; Audrey I. Richards, *Chisungu*, 1956, and Monica Wilson, *Rituals of Kinship among the Nyakyusa*, 1957.   These books were preceded by studies of the social organization of the peoples concerned; in this we have the key to the modern approach.   The anthropologist does not analyse myth and ritual in a spiritual vacuum, divorced from the realities of day-to-day existence.   His first task is to describe the relation of the community to environment and natural resources, the main economic

42

activities, the pattern of settlement, the structure of social relationships, the distribution of authority, and the range of rights and obligations which link individual to individual and group to group. An account of the economic and social organization is regarded as a basis for the study of cosmology and rite, providing a meaningful context for the interpretation of the symbolism of religious belief and practice and of their functions in society and in the life of the individual as a member of society. Underlying this approach is the assumption that religion is, to quote Durkheim, something eminently social: it has a foundation in social life, in part mirrors social organization and expresses certain social values. Few anthropologists would go as far as Durkheim in postulating that the empirical reality underlying religion is society, that God or gods are merely symbols of society or social groups, and that the dependence of the individual on the supernatural is, in the last resort, the dependence of the individual on his society. But most would admit that the structure of society and its essential activities affect the conception of relations between members of society and the supernatural; and that where important kin or local groups exist there is a widespread tendency for them to be associated with spiritual beings, to have their own rituals, and to play a specific role in rituals at the tribal or national level.

Now in saying that few books on primitive religion have been published until recently, I do not wish to imply that in studies of economy and social organization material on myth and ritual has been excluded. On the contrary, if we take a monograph such as Firth's *Primitive Polynesian Economy* (1939), we find that accounts of economic activities are punctuated by details of rites _ associated with them, and that in a chapter on "Ritual in Productive Activity" there is a careful analysis of what the Tikopia expect ritual to achieve, how far it is believed to be part of the technique of production, at what points it enters into production and how far it affects efficiency (p.174). In the manufacture of fishing nets the Tikopia explicitly place reliance on the choice of good materials and technical knowledge. The accompanying ritual is believed to help the net in fulfilling its proper function of attracting fish to it. It gives an atmosphere of significance to the task of production, provides explanations for failure, may allay anxiety, and serves as a stimulus to activity in so far as it and the underlying religious dogma give a sanction for assembly and co-operation under a priest-leader. In the periodic rebuilding of sacred canoes, in yam-planting, turmeric manufacture, and shark fishing we have examples of relatively large-scale production in association with the belief that the ancestors and gods have certain needs and are interested in seeing that those needs are met (pp.179-181). There is thus a ritual incentive to undertake the work at the appropriate time and for all to fulfil their obligations. Such rituals, performed under the aegis of the chief and others in authority, reinforce political status and reaffirm certain common values.

Another example of the analysis of religious beliefs and practices within the context of social organization may be taken from *The Dynamics of Clanship among the Tallensi* (1945) by Fortes. The book is primarily an account of lineage organization and a demonstration of the importance of the lineage as a residential, economic, legal and political unit of society. Fortes shows us the way in which ties of kinship provide the basic qualification for individuals to come together in ritual activity in relation to the ancestors and earth spirit.

43

231

At first glance such analyses may suggest a parallel to those made by Frazer in *Psyche's Task* (1913) where he put forward the proposition that among certain races and at certain times "superstition has strengthened the respect" for government, private property and marriage. But in demonstrating his thesis Frazer culled examples from many parts of the world and abstracted them from their ethnographic context. Now while it is true that sexual morality and marriage are frequently associated with certain religious beliefs and practices, an understanding of their interrelationships in any one society demands an analysis of the system of descent, the rights and obligations of marriage, and the role of marriage and the family in the economic and political structure. If, however, Frazer's methods and the validity of the generalizations based upon them are open to criticism, he directed attention to the positive functions of what he termed 'superstition'; his writings contain many fruitful hypotheses which anthropologists have been able to examine and test in the light of evidence obtained from intensive field work among particular communities.

These intensive field studies have profoundly modified the anthropologist's concept of society and culture. Culture is no longer viewed as a collection of customs, but as a system of interlocking institutions or formalized patterns of purposive behaviour which regulate the social relationships between individuals and between groups of individuals. When he selects any set of related institutions for study, the anthropologist attempts to place them within the context of social life, and examines them in terms of social structure, norms and values. Some of the problems with which we anthropologists have been concerned are what are the main patterns of behaviour in society, what are the mechanisms of social control in securing conformity to such patterns, what are the values towards which conduct is oriented, and how these values are expressed in the symbolism of ceremony, rite and myth.

Another consequence of intensive field research has been the growing recognition of the complexity of religious phenomena in even the most simple societies and of the futility of seeking to establish a single line of development. We have no grounds for assuming that totemism is the most 'primitive' form of religion or that in the earliest stages of human society magical beliefs controlled all forms of social activity. For example, field studies of Australian tribes have shown that the Aborigines possess a body of empirical knowledge on which they explicitly rely for existence. As for totemism itself, which at one time Frazer equated with magic, it is now seen to be a complex set of cosmological beliefs and practices which give expression to the conception of society and nature as a spiritual and moral order.

The native is no longer thought of as a creature who is incapable of distinguishing the animate from the inanimate, who is continually ridden by superstitious fears, and who is unable to make rational choices and rely on commonsense, on himself and his fellows. It is true that in many societies there is more ritual than in our own secular society; and that in some there is a belief in witchcraft and sorcery or a conviction that some offences are sins and bring supernatural punishment. But the latter belief is also current in many advanced civilizations. From my own experience in New Guinea and West Africa, I have found that life goes on in a native village very much as it does here. Marriage is monogamous for most; few can afford polygyny. Much of the time is spent by husband and wife in caring for the needs of the family, in gardening, fishing, cooking, and so forth. Plots are carefully prepared for

44

232

planting, fenced and weeded; decisions are made about the allocation of time
and labour to tasks; goods are distributed and stored; obligations to kin
and neighbours are fulfilled and sometimes evaded. Indeed, day-to-day activities, attitudes and values have so much in common with our own that the
feeling of strangeness soon wears off; one begins to weary of taking notes
of what seems obvious; and one may be weeks or even months in a village before
one witnesses a ritual or records a myth.

If the native does not resort to ritual on the slightest provocation,
neither is he a person who invariably thinks in mythological terms or who may
be accredited with a prelogical mentality. There are some societies which
have few myths and/or ceremonies: the Fort Jameson Ngoni are a case in point,
and the same is true of the cattle-herding Nuer of the Sudan who lack a developed
religious cult and mythology.[3] Among peoples whom I myself have studied, the
Nsaw of Bamenda in the British Cameroons represent another instance of a society
with little in the way of myths, though they do possess an elaborate ancestor
cult. They number just under 60,000, practise a subsistence agriculture and
inhabit high upland country in the east of Bamenda. They are one of a number
of Tikar tribes who migrated from what is now the French Cameroons perhaps 250
years ago. Since there are no written records my assignment of a date is
arbitrary, but in many of the Tikar groups chiefly genealogies contain the names
of 20 to 25 chiefs, and in Nsaw itself there have been at least 18 rulers. The
King of Nsaw is called the *Fon*, and he with a titled nobility and palace-officials
constitutes the council of state; with the assistance of the Great Councillor
(Ndzendzef), priests and priestesses, he performs sacrifices for the welfare of
the country.

The Nsaw possess little in the way of myths, and if pressed for an account
of the origin of the world they are apt to reply that either they do not know or
that God made it. If asked about the origin of Nsaw institutions, they
frequently narrate details of how the first Fon and a small band of followers
arrived from Rifem (in what is now the French Cameroons) and established themselves
at Kovifem, the seat of the ancient capital in the north-east of Nsaw. Djing
(the first Fon) and Le (the first queen mother) are alleged to have taught the
people how to hoe and make porridge. They were, said one sophisticated pagan,
just like Adam and Eve. In the country to the south and west of Kovifem there
were already other small communities speaking somewhat different dialects. The
most powerful of these was Nkar, but initially relationships seem to have been
peaceful.

The Fon and his people prospered, multiplied, attracted adherents from
neighbouring settlements, and established their own villages over the territory
to the south. However, a Fulani raid occurred and the Fon with some of his
followers moved south to Tauvisa, where he and his successor died. For various
reasons, a return was made to Kovifem but there were more Fulani raids, a son
and daughter of the Fon were captured and sold as slaves to the tribe to the
tribe to the north of Nsaw. A man of the Ndzendzef lineage subsequently redeemed
them, installed the boy as Fon, and in return for his services was elevated to
the position of Great Councillor and given important privileges. Round about
the beginning of the nineteenth century the Fulani again attacked, the Fon fled,
and after many vicissitudes reached Kimbaw (south of Tauvisa) which he decided
to make his capital. He conquered the chief of Nkar, subjugated alien groups
to the north-west, and created a centralized state. Kimbaw has remained the
capital, five kings have been buried there, but every year the King makes a

45

journey to Kovifem to carry out the annual sacrifices on the twelve graves of the kings who ruled there.

The account which I have given was held to be true by the reigning Fon, his predecessor, a number of the titled nobility, and the commonalty of Nsaw; but the Great Councillor had his own version which differed in important details and I shall discuss these later, since they have some bearing on existing political alignments.   Here two points should be noted   In the first place, the legend contains certain mythological elements.   The prevailing type of economy in this region of Africa is one of subsistence agriculture and it is highly improbable that the Nsaw arrived in their present territory as a band of of hunters and collectors, and even more unlikely that the first Fon wielded a hoe and the first queen mother cooked porridge.   But the attribution of the origin of agriculture to the founder of the Nsaw state and the tendency to regard the first ruler as a source of good has parallels in the legends of many African peoples.   In the second place, it should be noted that the people are not interested in the history of the Nsaw when they formed part of a kingdom at Tibati or Ndobo in the French Cameroons.   The 'history' of Nsaw begins when three disgruntled princes of the kingdom of Tibati broke away with small bands of followers, travelled to Rifem, separated and eventually reached their present habitats.   In other words, the interest of the Nsaw in their past is highly selective and is focussed on the period when the Nsaw king became a ruler in his own right, was powerful in war, attracted allies, and established the Nsaw state. Furthermore, there is obviously a telescoping of events.   Apart from some account of the secession of two sons of a Fon at Kovifem and their success in creating two small chiefdoms to the south and south-west, the details of the struggle for power which most probably occurred in the initial stages of settlement have been forgotten.   Legend validates the present political system, the power of the king and the structure of authority.   Reference is often made to the graves of the twelve or sixteen kings buried at Kovifem, but this is produced not as an item of genealogical information but as evidence of the antiquity of settlement and of a long line of triumphant rulers.

So far I have confined my comments to the legend of settlement given me by some of the most important dignitaries in Nsaw; but Ndzendzef, the Great Councillor, had his own version which he stated dogmatically was the true one. He, like his two predecessors in office, had a long-standing quarrel with the Fon and he no longer performed his priestly functions at the annual sacrifices to the Fon's ancestors and to God, though this was believed by the people to affect the welfare of the country adversely.   He claimed to be the sole king-maker and sole intermediary between the king and the rest of the populace, including the titled nobility.   And in validation of this claim he produced his account of Nsaw history.   He alleged that his ancestors had been living near Kovifem long before the Nsaw arrived; that the first ruler of Nsaw went direct from Rifem to Tauvisa; and that the first ruler at Kovifem was the prince who had been sold as a slave by the Fulani to the tribe to the north and who was subsequently rescued by Ndzendzef's ancestor.   In return for this service, Ndzendzef was elevated above the other councillors and given all the privileges which his descendant now claimed, but some of which the present Fon refused to recognize.

Ndzendzef's version was acceptable only to his own clan, to a few disgruntled persons who had their own private quarrels with the Fon and, lastly, to an anthropologist who had preceded me in my investigations and who seems to

46

234

have used Ndzendzef as his principal informant.[4]   Apart from anything else,
Ndzendzef's version pointed to a relatively recent occupation by the Nsaw of
their present territory and failed to account for the existence of the twelve
graves of kings who had ruled at Kovifem before the capital was transferred to
Kimbaw.   Nevertheless, in the absence of documents, there was really no way of
reconciling these rival versions though for many months I was naive enough to
think that if my enquiries were only sufficiently intensive and comprehensive
I should somehow arrive at the truth.   I was faced with a problem that must
frequently confront the ancient historian who attempts to reconstruct the history
of a tribe and who has few or no reliable documents.   I came to realise that,
although some of the events recorded in the legend had probably occurred, it
was likely that what had first been a chronicle, no doubt with its own distortions
and omissions, had become a legend and eventually something of a myth.

My investigations were conducted in an atmosphere of some tension, since
the reigning Fon was senile and the question of the rights of individuals to
appoint a successor was no academic issue.   Not only was I given accounts of the
causes of the quarrel between the Fon and Ndzendzef, but individuals, competing
for power, sometimes volunteered their own version of the founding of the Nsaw
state and interpreted the legend to validate their own claims.   From this point
of view the legend fulfilled one of the functions of certain types of myth;   it
presented a model of Nsaw society in terms of key political statuses and their
interrelationship;   it was a commentary on the present or near-present rather than
on the past;   and it had a different significance for various sections of the
population.   The commoner who was not directly involved in palace factions usually
knew little beyond the bare outline of the history of settlement, though he might
claim that the ancestor of his clan had early on become an ally of a king at the
ancient capital of Kovifem.   Such claims were not always consistent with other
details of clan history, but they revealed the mystical importance of Kovifem in
Nsaw ideology.

Now while this disagreement was particularly frustrating to me in the course
of my investigations in the field, it also directed my attention to new aspects of
factionalism in the state and helped me to understand the existing social structure
and the way in which it was envisaged by the members of the society.   You may say
that, strictly speaking, this legend is not a myth or at most only a myth in the
making;   but the manipulation of the legend and the inclusion of what are obviously
fictitious elements will suggest parallels with the early Greek reconstructions of
their own history.[5]   Many other examples might be cited from Africa and Polynesia
in illustration of the way in which myths are used to validate authority and link
a line of rulers with supernatural beings.

In a recent study of Kachin communities, *Political Systems of Highland Burma*,
1954, Dr. Leach has analysed the relation between myth and ritual on the one hand
and political organization on the other.   He has shown that while rivals for
precedence are all agreed as to what the principles of seniority are, they either
disagree about the crucial mythological incidents which are supposed to sanction
present-day social status, or disagree about the interpretation of the 'ethic' of
the myth itself (p.275 *et passim*).   This book is an important contribution to
anthropological theory and a good example of the 'structuralist' approach to the
analysis of social phenomena.   Dr. Leach suggests that the models which the
people have of their own society are expressed in myth and ritual, and that these
models are constructed from symbols which are of an imprecise kind as compared with
those used in scientific models.   It is because of the multivalency of such

47

symbols that rival and even contradictory interpretations of meaning can be found
in the same society; and it is because of this fluidity of meaning that myths
and rituals frequently persist even when there has been much social and cultural
change. New meanings are attached to the symbols to fit the contemporary situation. Cosmological beliefs and myths do not therefore mirror exactly society as
it is in the present or as it was in the past; but they do reflect certain aspects
of it and they tend to express socially approved or proper relations; to that
extent they provide a guide and sense of continuity without which there would be
anarchy.

I have given you in summary form some of the main hypotheses of Dr. Leach's
book and cannot do justice here to a close-knit and cogent argument based on Kachin
ethnographic material. It is an example of one of the approaches adopted by
modern social anthropologists to the study of myth, and it should be clear from
what I have already said that we no longer conceive of myths as a species of badly
recorded history, or as figments of a prelogical mentality or as "a disease of
language." Nor do we regard myths as the first attempts by natives to provide
a scientific explanation of nature and the creation. Those of us who have done
fieldwork know from experience that the native has different sets of criteria for
truth and that he applies these in different circumstances. Some are based on
experience and are phrased in terms of observed cause and effect; in some there
is an appeal to tradition; in others, again, to religious dogma or myth. And
it is rare to find these criteria confused. The anthropologist by studying
social organization and by observing the occasions when myths are recounted is
made aware that while myths do in part provide an 'explanation' of certain phenomena for the native, they also have a relevance for him in relation to the present.
In this the native is no mere antiquarian.

Now the approach which I have illustrated by reference to Nsaw and Kachin
material goes back in part to Radcliffe-Brown and Malinowski. In his *Andaman
Islands* (1922), Radcliffe-Brown rejected the idea that myths are merely a primitive
substitute for scientific explanation: he suggested that myths express sentiments
and attitudes held by the people in relation to the social and natural order; that
the meaning of many details of myth is to be found in present-day social life.
Malinowski, in an essay on "Myth in Primitive Psychology", 1926 (and in earlier
writings), reached a similar position, but independently of Radcliffe-Brown. He
claimed that "myth expresses, enhances and codifies belief; safeguards and
enforces morality, and vouches for the efficacy of ritual". And he illustrated
these generalizations from the way in which myths were cited by the Trobriand
Islanders to establish claims to the ownership of land and rituals; to sanction
certain moral rules of behaviour, laws of marriage, the supremacy of the paramount
chief, the ranking of clans and sub-clans, and so on.

While admitting that history must have left its imprint on the myths and that
some historical reconstruction is possible by a careful comparison of versions and
the use of other information, Malinowski's considered opinion was that "myth taken
as a whole cannot be sober dispassionate history, since it is always made *ad hoc*
to fulfil a certain sociological function, to glorify a certain group or to justify
an anomalous status. It also means that, to the native, immediate history, semi-
historic legend and unmixed myth flow into one another, form a continuous sequence
and fulfil really the same sociological function" (p.102). "Myth then is a retro-
spective but ever present live actuality. It is neither a fictitious story, nor
an account of a dead past. It is also clear that myth functions especially where
there is sociological strain, such as matters of great difference in rank and power,
matters of precedence and subordination, and unquestionably where profound historical

48

changes have taken place.   So much can be asserted as a fact, though it must always remain doubtful how far we can carry out historical reconstruction from myth" (pp.102-3).

Malinowski did not himself pursue further his hypothesis that myths may express sectional interests as well as common values, but social anthropologists have continued to investigate the secular and ritual contexts in which myths are narrated to justify claims to authority and privilege.   Myths are a way of thinking about reality in symbolic terms and whether the figures in them are supernatural beings, culture heroes or great men is from one point of view irrelevant.   History or legend, a place, person or thing may assume a mythological character in so far as it comes to symbolize qualities or values;   in so far as it endows the present with significance, creates a sense of ordered and meaningful relationships for the individual, the group or the community. The mythopoeic mode of thought is a universal feature of human life, and most individuals, unless they lead a mole-like existence focussed on immediate limited ends (and it is conceivable that even moles have myths), have their myth or myths, though these differ in consistency, coherence, sophistication and in the range and kind of the relationships which are knit together into a meaningful whole.   Myth is thus a means of integrating different levels or orders of experience in symbolic terms;   and logic and imagination are both involved.

Myths may be taken over from the historian, poet, theologian, politician, or scientist and given some particular slant or new emphasis to meet the needs of the individual.   The scientist like anyone else is apt to have his own preconceptions or assumptions and is rarely content to meet his facts as they come.   Once the scientist steps outside the narrow range of experimental situations with which he is concerned and makes the assumption that scientific methods are the only valid ones for establishing truth, and that ultimately the universe can be explained in terms of scientific principles, he is creating a model of the universe which has a mythological character.   Equally the anthropologist who believes that the study of 'social structure' provides the key to the understanding of society has his own myth about society.[6]

In discussing the general nature of myth and the universality of the mythopoeic mode of thought, I have put on one side the analysis of the types of social institutions which certain myths validate or explain, although reference has already been made to such secular institutions as political organization, rank and land tenure.   In many societies myth is intimately connected with ritual. This is not to say that every myth has a rite associated with it or that there is no rite without its attendant myth.   Research has shown that in some communities there may be a rich ceremonialism without an extensive mythological counterpart, and in others there may be many myths but little ritual.   The long-standing controversy over the primacy of myth or rite is now largely an academic one: on the one hand, there are well documented cases of historical personages who have instituted new ceremonies on the basis of visionary experiences, which have then become part of the validating myth;   and, on the other, there are cases where uniformity of a ritual over a wide area and diversity of mythological explanations would seem to indicate that either the ritual was a stimulus for the origin of a myth or that a ritual from one group was taken over by another group and linked to a pre-existing myth.[7]   The multivalency of the symbols of myth and rite facilitates such processes

49

of diffusion and would in part explain why it is possible for a myth and rite
formerly unconnected to become associated in a new cultural context.   A particularly good example is the diffusion of the *Kunapipi* fertility cult from the
tribes in the region of the Roper River to those at Yirrkalla in north-eastern
Arnhemland.   The latter already possessed a myth about two sisters called
Wauwalak who symbolized fertility.   After the adoption of the cult, the sisters
came to be regarded as the daughters of *Kunapipi*, the Great Mother.   In his
book, *Kunapipi* (1951), Dr. Berndt describes how parts of the myth are sung
during the ceremony, and certain incidents in the myth enacted by the men.   He
gives native texts and translations of the chants, and also the interpretation
of the symbolism offered by the natives themselves.   What is of particular
interest is the natives' awareness that they are using symbols and that a number
of meanings are possible.

The problem of the interpretation of ritual is one that should be tackled
at a number of levels, and a prerequisite is not only an adequate knowledge of
the native language, but also the collection of commentaries made by the natives
themselves on the ceremonies and the meaning of the symbolism.[8]   As I have
indicated earlier, anthropologists who have been influenced by Malinowski have,
on the whole, adopted an eclectic approach and have taken into account the
purpose of rites as formulated by the people themselves, the effect of performance on the individual participants, the relationship between ritual and secular
institutions and, lastly, the extent to which ritual expresses and serves to
maintain social statuses and structure.   But, from about 1936 onwards, the
followers of Radcliffe-Brown and of the French sociologists, such as Durkheim
and Van Gennep, have been primarily concerned with the structural implications
of myth and ritual.   The method has been fruitful in its results and has focused
attention on aspects overlooked by those who have confined themselves to a purely
cultural analysis; in its extreme form, however, it has led to the neglect of
many aspects of ritual and has sometimes involved the anthropologist in circular
arguments, such as 'social structure is reflected in ritual, and ritual maintains the solidarity of the social structure'.   Latterly, anthropologists have
begun to examine some of these assumptions more critically.   Leach has shown
that Kachin society is not fully integrated; and he poses the question of the
relation between the model of a society at peace, as expressed in the symbols
of ritual, and the empirical society with its conflicts, factions and feuds.

Other anthropologists, such as Gluckman, have drawn attention to the
occurrence in some rituals of what appear to be symbolic protests against the
social order: subjects express hatred for the king; women swagger, don male
ornaments, taunt the men and indulge in acts of obscenity; two inter-marrying
groups insult one another at a wedding ceremony, and so on.   Yet the complete
ritual is believed to create unity and bring peace and prosperity to the wider
community.[9]   Gluckman, while admitting that psychological, sociological and
even physiological interpretations are required for a full analysis of religion,
is concerned in his essay with the sociological and suggests that conflicts
which are latent or overt in social life are expressed and even exaggerated in
ritual; such 'ritual rebellion' is effective because while it provides a
catharsis it does not threaten the belief that the existing social order is
morally right.   He then puts forward the hypothesis that "conflicts can be
stated openly wherever the social order is unquestioned and indubitable - where
there are rebels and not revolutionaries".(p.134).[10]   "The acceptance of the
established order as right and good, and even sacred, seems to allow unbridled

50

238

license, very rituals of rebellion, for the order itself keeps this rebellion within bounds. Hence to act the conflicts, whether directly or by inversion or in other symbolical forms, emphasizes the social cohesion within which the conflicts exist" (p.125).

Gluckman's interesting hypothesis has redirected attention to the ambivalence in social attitudes which is sometimes expressed in ritual; this, is, in some cases, demonstrably connected with open conflict and hostility in the relationships concerned. Ritual may sometimes give a clue to latent tensions hitherto undetected by the anthropologist, who can then investigate them. But the interpretation of ritually-expressed tensions is chancy. Terms like 'structural tension' and 'cleavage' merely disguise conjectural psychological explanations. Even when, in one society, information about tensions drawn from ritual and secular life is mutually consistent, it does not provide a basis for generalizations about other societies. There may, in some societies, be hostility and dissension between rulers and subjects, or between husbands and wives, which is not symbolically expressed in ritual. One cannot predict whether the existing status, or the normal status, or the desired status will be reflected in ritual. Indeed, Gluckman's hypothesis that the symbolic enactment of conflict emphasizes social cohesion is beyond verification. It is one thing to say that, after the ritual is over, subjects continue to obey their rulers and wives their husbands; another to demonstrate that such rituals have no harmful effect on social relations; and yet another to demonstrate that they actually reinforce cohesion.[11]

In sounding a note of scepticism, I do not wish to minimize the recent sociological contributions of anthropologists, who are now no longer content with the facile assumption that myth and ritual mirror only what is socially valuable or structurally important. A broadening of approach is also evident in the writings of anthropologists who, while admitting the need for structural analysis, do not consider it to be exhaustive. Structure is, after all, only one framework of reference: to regard it as anything more is to project upon the individuals of a given society the anthropologist's own intense preoccupation with social relationships.[12] As I have said earlier, myth is a means of integrating different orders of experience in symbolic terms; systems of cosmological belief and ritual prefigure a transcendent reality which encompasses both society and physical environment and, from the point of view of the individual, defines a man's place in the world as well as in society.[13]

Firth has been one of the anthropologists to put the individual back into the centre of the picture; and, in his Myers Lecture on "Religious Belief and Personal Adjustment" (*J.Roy.Anthrop.Inst.*1948), he suggests that variations in religious belief are attempts on the part of individuals to secure a coherent view of their universe, both physical and social. Religious belief, apart from its wider sociological functions, has a role in securing personal integration, especially in conditions of rapid change. This may not strike the reader as novel; and, indeed, Malinowski was himself concerned with the effects of belief and religious practice on the individual as well as on society. But over the last two decades there has been what is almost a ritual avoidance by anthropologists of explanations which take account of individual satisfactions.

An eclectic approach is also to be found in two full-length studies of religion by Nadel and Evans-Pritchard. In *Nupe Religion* (1954), Nadel has suggested that a comparative study of religions may be made in terms of their capacities to furnish certain supplements to the view of the world of experience which our intelligence is driven to demand; to announce and maintain moral values;

51

to hold together societies and sustain their structure; and to furnish individuals
with specific experiences and stimulations (pp. 259-60). Evans-Pritchard, in his
monograph, deals with Nuer religion as a system of ideas and practices, in its own
right. He admits that collective beliefs and rites tell us something about the
social order and are in part co-ordinated to the social structure, but he denies
that religious conceptions can be reduced to or explained by the social order
alone (p. 320 *et passim*).

Lastly, Dr. Audrey Richards and Professor Monica Wilson have recently published
detailed accounts of rituals. I cannot discuss within the scope of this article
Professor Wilson's book, which describes and analyses the symbolic patterns of the
rituals of kinship among the Nyakyusa; but those who wish to learn something of
the concepts and methods of analysis employed by contemporary social anthropologists
should read it and also Dr. Richards's *Chisungu: A girls' initiation ceremony
among the Bemba of Northern Rhodesia*(1956). Chisungu is performed at puberty and
is both a nubility and fertility ceremony. Dr. Richards places this rite firmly
within the context of social and economic activities: she gives a brief outline
of environment and economics, of the main religious beliefs of the Bemba, especially
in so far as they refer to sex, marriage and fertility; and, lastly, an account
of the main features of the social structure. This is followed by a detailed
description of the ritual and of the clay figurines, which have a symbolic significance and are specially made for the occasion. She includes the texts of songs
and a translation, along with the interpretation of their symbolism made by participants, bystanders and other Bemba informants. The ceremony was witnessed in
1931 and lasted a month; in the old days it would have taken six months to perform.

Having given us the ethnographic data, Dr. Richards then discusses the expressed
purposes of Chisungu, as formulated by the Bemba themselves in terms of primary and
secondary motives; the deduced attitudes based on the anthropologist's observation
of the effects of the ceremony on the girls and other participants; the part occupied
by either moral instruction or the affirmation of the rights and duties of marriage;
and the relation of Chisungu to the tribal dogma and values in general. In this last
stage of analysis, Dr. Richards is not content with vague generalizations: she
systematically sets out the relevant data on a chart. In one column she lists the
special features of Bemba society in terms of environment and activities, aspects of
social structure, and salient values; in a second column she gives the dogmas underlying such features; in a third she documents the extent to which these are expressed
in the Chisungu rites; and, in a fourth, their expression in other important Bemba
rites, e.g. those connected with agriculture and those surrounding chieftainship (pp. 141-13
145).

One of the most fascinating parts of this book is the diversity of interpretations offered by the Bemba themselves of the meaning of ritual acts and objects.
After discussing the various emblematic devices used in the ritual, Dr. Richards puts
forward an interesting hypothesis on the nature of symbols. "An interesting feature
of the emblem mechanism is that it provides a fixed form, a model, and a song with
the possibility of multiple meanings in each case. It is in the nature of symbols,
whether they occur in dreams, speech or action, to become the centre of a cluster of
different associations. The efficacy of ritual as a social mechanism depends on this
very phenomenon of central and peripheral meanings and on their allusive and evocative
powers. It makes possible interpretations that vary with the age, knowledge and
even the temperament of individual performers. The essential fact about *mbusa*
(clay figurines) is not their exact meaning but the fact that they are what they

52

are - 'things handed down'.   Hence they act as signs that things will go on as they have gone on, and that powers given to mankind before will be given to them again.   They are used as the basis of rites of charter maintenance.   All symbolic objects make it possible to combine fixity of form with multiple meanings, of which some are standardized and some highly individual" (164-5).

I have taken a very broad field for my subject and have been able to discuss briefly only those theories developed by British anthropologists.   It is obvious that there is still considerable disagreement among them, and considerable diversity in their approach to the analysis of religious phenomena.   Frazer, in his *Lectures on the Early History of Kingship*, spoke of two repellant features of anthropological books: the apparently disproportionate space occupied by bare description and the cataloguing of facts;   and the unstable, shifting, discordant nature of the theories put forward to explain the facts.   He regretted both features, but regarded them as unavoidable in 1905.   They can hardly be avoided at the present stage of inquiry in 1957.   Nevertheless, some advances have been achieved over the last three decades.   There is a rich and growing body of ethnographic material on which to base generalizations;   there has been a continual effort to clarify concepts and to apply them more rigorously;   there has been some re-examination of assumptions about the nature of society.   The analysis of myth and ritual within the framework of social structure has been productive of many fruitful hypotheses and has illumined aspects which were disregarded or overlooked in some of the earlier studies of religion.   Along with this, there has been an increasing recognition of the need for a plurality of approaches, especially in relation to symbolism and values. Already several anthropologists have made one or two excursions into this field, and they will be followed by others.

University College London

NOTES

1 This article is based on a paper read at a Colloquium at the Institute of Classical Studies on the 29th January, 1957.

2 B. Malinowski, *Magic, Science and Religion and Other Essays*, Free Press, 1948;   A. R. Radcliffe-Brown, "The Sociological Theory of Totemism", 1929, reprinted in *Structure and Function in Primitive Society*, London, 1952;   E. E. Evans-Pritchard, "The Intellectualist (English) Interpretation of Magic", *Bull.Fac.of Arts*, Egyptian Univ., Vol.1 1933-35; R. Firth, "Totemism in Polynesia", *Oceania*, Vol.1, 1930-31.

3 Such examples are of theoretical interest in view of the emphasis placed by Fustel de Coulanges on the role of religious belief and cult in the emergence or establishment of secular institutions.   *Vide,La Cité Antique*.

4 For a brief account of these rival versions see M. D. W. Jeffreys and P. Kaberry, "Nsaw History and Social Categories", *Africa*, XXII, 1952.   For a detailed account of Nsaw social organization and economy, see my *Women of the Grassfields*, Colonial Res.Pubs., No.14, H.M.S.O., 1952.

5 cf. J. B. Bury, *A History of Greece*, London, 3rd ed. 1956, pp.78-84.   Bury in discussing what the Greeks thought of their own early history makes the point that the Greek "belief in their legendary past was thoroughly practical;   mythic events were often the basis of diplomatic transactions;   claims to territory might be founded on the supposed conquests or dominions of ancient heroes of divine birth' (p.78).

53

6 The view advanced here would not be acceptable to some of my colleagues, and it would be regarded as heretical by the philosopher, Professor David Bidney, who has written: "To regard myth as a neutral term beyond truth or falsity (like belief) and to interpret the culture of scientific rationalism as if it were also based on myth is to undermine the basis of scientific thought' (*Theoretical Anthropology*, 1953, ch. on 'The Concept of Myth', p.296). However, I think few anthropologists would be satisfied to define myth as he does in terms of its truth or falsity for believers or non-believers respectively (op.cit. p.295); or to define it negatively as a "belief, usually expressed in narrative form, that is incompatible with scientific and rational knowledge" (p.295). A more fruitful approach to the study of myth has recently been made by another philosopher, Professor Alan Watts, in his *Myth and Ritual in Christianity*, London, 1954.

7 Clyde Kluckhohn, "Myths and Rituals: A General Theory", *Harvard Theological Rev.*, Vol.XXXV, 1942, pp.48-52.

8 Good examples of meticulous documentation of native interpretations are *The Work of the Gods in Tikopia* by R. Firth; *Chisungu*, by A. I. Richards; and *Rituals of Kinship among the Nyakyusa* by Monica Wilson.

9 M. Gluckman, "The Licence in Ritual" in *Custom and Conflict in Africa*, Blackwell, 1955. See also his *Rituals of Rebellion in South-east Africa* (Frazer Lecture, 1952), Manchester U.P., 1954. Frazer was of course one of the first to examine such 'rites of reversal' in *The Golden Bough*.

10 However, Professor Schapera, in his *Government and Politics in Tribal Societies* (Watts, 1956), has pointed out that among the Zulu and Swazi there were civil wars and that these frequently resulted in the flight or secession of one section (pp.175-176).

11 Monica Wilson, who has recorded the expression of anger and hostility in some rituals among the Nyakyusa, draws attention to the emphasis placed by the people themselves on the need for confession. The rites not only provide for the public expression of anti-social attitudes and tendencies, but also for their public rejection (op.cit. pp.227-8). She is, however, much more cautious than Gluckman in predicating the effects of such catharsis.

12 For the anthropologist concerned only with a structural analysis, the customary distinction between rite and ceremony is largely irrelevant since for him they both express or symbolize social relationships. But, in making a comprehensive study of religion, the distinction between *rites* - socially sanctioned activities which are believed to achieve desired ends through the manipulation of symbols, having a supernatural referent - and *ceremonies* - socially sanctioned activities which are expressive of the importance of an event and of social statuses - cannot be ignored.

13 For a symposium on the cosmological beliefs of a selected number of African peoples, see *African Worlds*, O.U.P., 1954, ed. by Daryll Forde.

54

MYTHS AND RITUALS:[1] A GENERAL THEORY

CLYDE KLUCKHOHN
HARVARD UNIVERSITY

I

NINETEENTH century students strongly tended to study mythology apart from associated rituals (and indeed apart from the life of the people generally). Myths were held to be symbolic descriptions of phenomena of nature.[2] One prominent school, in fact, tried to find an astral basis for all mythic tales. Others, among whom Andrew Lang was prominent, saw in the myth a kind of primitive scientific theory. Mythology answered the insistent human HOW? and WHY? How and why was the world made? How and why were living creatures brought into being? Why, if there was life must there be death? To early psychoanalysts such as Abraham[3] and Rank[4] myths were "group phantasies," wish-fulfillments for a society strictly analogous to the dream and day-dream of individuals. Mythology for these psychoanalysts was also a symbolic structure par excellence, but the symbolism which required interpretation was primarily a sex symbolism which was postulated as universal and all-pervasive. Reik[5] recognized a connection between rite and myth, and he, with Freud,[6] verbally agreed to

[1] Based upon a paper read at the Symposium of the American Folklore Society at Chicago in December, 1939. My thanks are due to W. W. Hill, Florence Kluckhohn, A. H. Leighton, Arthur Nock, E. C. Parsons, and Alfred Tozzer for a critical reading and a number of suggestions, to Ruth Underhill and David Mandelbaum for supplying unpublished material on the Papago and Toda respectively.

[2] Professor Nock has called my attention to the fact that the naturalistic theory actually works very well for the Vedic material.

[3] See Traum und Mythus (Vienna, 1909). Rank's final conclusion was that "myths are relics from the infantile mental life of the people, and dreams constitute the myths of the individual" (Selected Papers of Karl Abraham, London, 1927, p. 32). Cf. also Traum und Mythus, pp. 69, 71.

[4] See Otto Rank, Psychoanalytische Beiträge zur Mythenforschung (Vienna and Leipzig, 1919) and Der Mythus von der Geburt des Helden (2nd edition, Leipzig and Vienna, 1922). Rank attempts to show that hero myths originate in the delusional structures of paranoiacs.

[5] Theodor Reik, Das Ritual (Leipzig, Vienna, Zurich, 1928).

[6] Cf. Freud's statement in his introduction to Reik, op. cit., p. 11.

Robertson Smith's proposition that mythology was mainly a description of ritual. To the psychoanalysts, however, mythology was essentially (so far as what they did with it is concerned) societal phantasy material which reflected impulse repression.[7] There was no attempt to discover the practical function of mythology in the daily behaviors of the members of a society [8] nor to demonstrate specific interactions of mythology and ceremonials. The interest was in supposedly pan-human symbolic meanings, not in the relation of a given myth or part of a myth to particular cultural forms or specific social situations.[9]

To some extent the answer to the whole question of the relationship between myth and ceremony depends, of course, upon how wide or how restricted a sense one gives to "mythology." In ordinary usage the Oedipus tale is a "myth," but only some Freudians believe that this is merely the description of a ritual! The famous stories of the Republic are certainly called "μῦθος," and while a few scholars [10] believe that Plato in *some* cases had reference to the Orphic and/or Eleusinian mysteries there is certainly not a shred of evidence that all of Plato's immortal "myths" are "descriptions of rituals." To be sure, one may justifiably narrow the problem by saying that in a technical sense these are "legends," and by insisting that "myths" be rigorously distinguished from "legends," "fairy-

[7] Many psychoanalysts today consider myths simply "a form of collective daydreaming." I have heard a prominent psychoanalyst say "Creation myths are for culture what early memories (true or fictitious) are to the individual."

[8] This has been done, even by anthropologists, only quite recently. Boas, as early as 1916 (Tsimshian Mythology, Bureau of American Ethnology, Annual Report for 1909–10, vol. 31, pp. 29–1037), did attempt to show how the origin of all folklore must be sought in imaginings based upon the ordinary social life of the society in question. But in this (as in his later publication on the Kwakiutl) he showed how mythology reflected social organization — *not* how mythology preserved social equilibrium or symbolized social organization.

[9] Dr. Benedict in her Zuni Mythology (New York, 1935) follows a form of explanation which draws heavily from psychoanalytic interpretations. Thus, (p. xix) in discussing the compensatory functions of mythology, she speaks of "folkloristic daydreaming." But her treatment lacks the most objectionable features of the older psychoanalytic contributions because she does not deal in universalistic, *pan*-symbolic "meanings" but rather orients her whole presentation to the richly documented Zuni materials and to the specific context of Zuni culture.

[10] Cf. e.g., R. H. S. Crossman, Plato Today (London, 1937), p. 88.

tales," and "folk-tales." If, however, one agrees that "myth" has Durkheim's connotation of the "sacred" as opposed to the "profane" the line is still sometimes hard to draw in concrete cases. What of "creation myths"? In some cases (as at Zuni) these are indeed recited [11] during ritual performances (with variations for various ceremonies). In other cases, even though they may be recited in a "ritual" attitude, they do not enter into any ceremonial. Nevertheless, they definitely retain the flavor of "the sacred." Moreover, there are (as again at Zuni) exoteric and esoteric forms of the same myth. Among the Navaho many of the older men who are not ceremonial practitioners know that part of a myth which tells of the exploits of the hero or heroes but not the portion which prescribes the ritual details of the chant. Granting that there are sometimes both secular and sacred versions of the same tale and that other difficulties obtrude themselves in particular cases, it still seems possible to use the connotation of the sacred as that which differentiates "myth" from the rest of folklore.[12] At least, such a distinction appears workable to a rough first approximation and will be followed throughout this paper.

But defining "myth" strictly as "sacred tale" does not

[11] There are Aranda, Fijian, and Winnebago chants which are almost purely recitals of an origin myth.

[12] This covers the differentia which is often suggested: namely, that myth is distinguished from legend or folktale by the circumstance that some (or perhaps most) of the actors in a myth must be supernatural beings — not simply human beings of however great a legendary stature. There are, of course, other distinctions which could — for other purposes — profitably be entered into. Thus, Professor Nock has suggested to me that there are differences of some consequence between an oral mythology and a written theology. "A true myth," he says, "never takes form with an eye to the pen or to the printed page."

These refinements are undoubtedly interesting and important, but they do not seem directly relevant to the issues dealt with in this paper. Here only the major contrast of sacred and profane appears crucial. Any segregation of myth from folktale, legend, fairytale, etc. which rests upon hair-splitting or upon special premises must be avoided. Thus Roheim's recent stimulating discussion (Myth and Folk-Tale, American Imago, vol. 2, 1941, pp. 266–279) is acceptable only insofar as one grants the major postulates of orthodox Freudian psychoanalysis. Roheim says: "A folktale is a narrative with a happy end, a myth is a tragedy; a god must die before he can be truly divine" (p. 276). "In the folk tale we relate how we overcome the anxiety connected with the 'bad parents' and grew up, in myth we confess that only death can end the tragic ambivalence of human nature. Eros triumphs in the folk-tale, Thanatos in the myth" (p. 279).

carry with it by implication a warrant for considering mythology purely as a description of correlative rituals. Rose [13]
quite correctly says "among myths there are many whose
connection with any rite is a thing to be proved, not assumed."
What is needed is a detailed comparative analysis of actual associations. Generally speaking, we do seem to find rich ritualism and a rich mythology together. But there are cases (like
the Toda)[14] where an extensive ceremonialism does not appear
to have its equally extensive mythological counterpart and
instances (like classical Greece) where a ramified mythology
appears to have existed more or less independent of a comparatively meagre rite-system.[15] For example, in spite of the many
myths relating to Ares the rituals connected with Ares seem
to have been few in number and highly localized in time and
space.[16] The early Romans, on the other hand, seemed to
get along very well without mythology. The poverty of the
ritual which accompanies the extremely complex mythology of
the Mohave is well known.[17] Kroeber indeed says "Public
ceremonies or rituals as they occur among almost all native
Americans cannot be said to be practised by the Mohave." [18]

[13] H. J. Rose, Review of "The Labyrinth" (Man, vol. 36, 1936, no. 87, p. 69).

[14] Dr. Mandelbaum writes me: "For the Todas do not have complex myths; myth
episodes which take hours and days in the telling among Kotas, are told by Todas in
less than three minutes." Cf. M. Emeneau, The Songs of the Todas (Proceedings of
the American Philosophical Society, vol. 77, 1937, pp. 543–560); " . . . the art of story-
telling is almost non-existent. In fact, imaginative story-telling hardly exists and the
stories of traditional events in the life of the tribe do not seem to be popular. . . . Some
of the songs are based on legendary stories, but even in the case of these some of my
informants knew the songs without knowing the stories" (p. 543).

[15] I am thinking here of public (non-cultist) mythology and of official and public
ritual. Orphic ritual may have been more closely connected to the complicated Orphic
myth. Cf. W. K. C. Guthrie, Who Were the Orphics? (Scientia, vol. 67, 1937, pp. 110–
121), esp. pp. 119–120.

[16] Cf. L. R. Farnell, The Cults of the Greek States, vol. IV (Oxford, 1909), pp. 396–
407.

[17] A. L. Kroeber, Handbook of the Indians of California (Washington, 1925), p. 660.

[18] Ibid., p. 755. The Mohave are, of course, also a classic case where myths, at least
according to cultural theory, are dreamed. But even though we recognize the cultural
patterning of the "dreaming" this in no sense justifies the inference that the myths are
derived from the meagre rituals. Indeed Kroeber points out (p. 770) that some myths
are not sung to — i.e. are not even ritualized to the extent of being connected with song
recitals.

The Bushmen likewise had many myths and very little ritual. On the other hand, one can point to examples like the Central Eskimo, where every detail of the Sedna myth has its ritual analogue in confessional, other rites, or hunting tabus, or, for contrast, to the American Indian tribes (especially some Californian ones) where the creation myth is never enacted in ceremonial form. In different sectors of one culture, the Papago, all of these possibilities are represented. Some myths are never ceremonially enacted. Some ceremonies emphasize content foreign to the myth. Other ceremonies consisting only of songs have some vague place in the mythological world; between these and the myths "there is a certain tenuous connection which may be a rationalization made for the sake of unity. . . ." [19]

The anthropology of the past generation has tended to recoil sharply from any sort of generalized interpretation. Obsessed with the complexity of the historical experience of all peoples, anthropologists have (perhaps over-much) eschewed the inference of regularities of psychological reaction which would transcend the facts of diffusion and of contacts of groups. Emphasis has been laid upon the distribution of myths and upon the mythological patterning which prevailed in different cultures and culture areas. Study of these distributions has led to a generalization of another order which is the converse of the hypothesis of most nineteenth century classical scholars [20] that a ritual was an enactment of a myth. In the words of Boas: [21] "The uniformity of many such rituals over large areas and the diversity of mythological explanations show clearly that the ritual itself is the stimulus for the origin of the myth. . . . The ritual existed, and the tale originated from the desire to account for it."

[19] Personal communication from Dr. Ruth Underhill.

[20] Certain contemporary classical scholars take a point of view which is very similar to that adopted in this paper. Thus H. J. Rose (Modern Methods in Classical Mythology, St. Andrews, 1930, p. 12) says " . . . I postulate . . . a reciprocal influence of myth and ceremony. . . ." Cf. also L. R. Farnell, The Value and the Methods of Mythologic Study (London, 1919), p. 11, " . . . occasionally myth is the prior fact that generates a certain ritual, as for instance the offering of horses to St. George in Silesia was suggested by the myth of St. George the horseman. . . ."

[21] F. Boas and others, General Anthropology (New York, 1938), p. 617.

While this suggestion of the primacy of ritual over myth is probably a valid statistical induction and a proper statement of the modal tendency of our evidence, it is, it seems to me, as objectionably a simple unitary explanation (if pressed too far) as the generally rejected nineteenth century views. Thus we find Hocart [22] recently asking: "If there are myths that give rise to ritual where do these myths come from?" A number of instances will shortly be presented in which the evidence is un-equivocal that myths did give rise to ritual. May I only re-mark here that — if we view the matter objectively — the Christian Mass, as interpreted by Christians, is a clear illus-tration of a ritual based upon a sacred story. Surely, in any case, Hocart's question can be answered very simply: from a dream or a waking phantasy or a personal habit system of some individual in the society. The basic psychological mechanisms involved would seem not dissimilar to those whereby individu-als in our own (and other) cultures construct private rituals [23] or carry out private divination [24] — e.g. counting and guessing before the clock strikes, trying to get to a given point (a traffic light, for instance) before something else happens. As DuBois[25] has suggested, "the explanation may be that personal rituals have been taken over and socialized by the group." These "personal rituals" could have their genesis in idiosyncratic habit [26] formations (similar to those of obsessional neurotics in our culture) or in dreams or reveries. Mrs. Seligman [27] has con-

[22] A. M. Hocart, Myth and Ritual (Man, vol. 36, no. 230), p. 167.

[23] Cf. A. M. Tozzer, Social Origins and Social Continuities (New York, 1934), pp. 242–267, esp. p. 260 ff.

[24] R. R. Willoughby gives good examples and discussions of these culturally un-formalized divinatory practices. See Magic and Cognate Phenomena: An Hypothesis (In: A Handbook of Social Psychology, Carl Murchison, ed., Worcester, Mass., 1935, pp. 461–520), pp. 480–482.

[25] C. DuBois, Some Anthropological Perspectives on Psychoanalysis (Psychoana-lytic Review, vol. 24, 1937, pp. 246–264), p. 254.

[26] In other words, in terms of patterns of behavior which are distinctive of an in-dividual, not as a representative of a particular cultural tradition, but as a differen-tiated biological organism who — either because of inherited constitutional differences or because of accidents of the conditioning process — behaves differently in major respects from most individuals of the same age, sex, and status acculturated in the same culture.

[27] B. Z. Seligman, The Part of the Unconscious in Social Heritage (In: Essays Pre-sented to C. G. Seligman, London, 1934, pp. 307–319).

vincingly suggested that spontaneous personal dissociation is a frequent mechanism for rite innovations. The literature is replete with instances of persons "dreaming" that supernaturals summoned them, conducted them on travels or adventures, and finally admonished them thereafter to carry out certain rites (often symbolically repetitive of the adventures).

Moreover, there are a number of well documented actual cases where historical persons, in the memory of other historical persons, actually instituted new rituals. The ritual innovations of the American Indian Ghost Dance cult [28] and other nativistic cults of the New World [29] provide striking illustration. In these cases the dreams or phantasies — told by the innovators before the ceremonial was ever actualized in deeds — became an important part of traditionally accepted rite-myths. Lincoln [30] has presented plausible evidence that dreams are the source of "new" rituals. Morgan,[31] on the basis of Navaho material, says:

> . . . delusions and dreams . . . are so vivid and carry such conviction that any attempt to reason about them afterwards on the basis of conscious sense impressions is unavailing. Such experiences deeply condition the individual, sometimes so deeply that if the experience is at variance with a tribal or neighborhood belief, the individual will retain his own variation. There can be no doubt that this is a very significant means of modifying a culture.

Van Gennep [32] asserts that persons went to dream in the sanctuary at Epidaurus as a source for new rites in the cult of Asclepius. To obtain ceremony through dream is, of course, itself a pattern, a proper traditional way of obtaining a ceremony or power. I do not know of any cases of a society where dreaming

[28] I am, of course, well aware that the rites of the Ghost Dance were not by any means identical in all tribes. But in spite of wide variations under the influence of pre-existent ideal and behavioral patterns *certain* new ritual practices which must be connected with the visions of the founder may be found in almost every tribe.

[29] See A. F. Chamberlain, New Religions among the North American Indians (Journal of Religious Psychology, 1913, vol. 6, pp. 1–49).

[30] J. S. Lincoln, The Dream in Primitive Cultures (Baltimore, 1935).

[31] William Morgan, Human Wolves Among the Navaho (Yale University Publications in Anthropology, No. 11, 1936), p. 40. Dr. Henry A. Murray of the Harvard Psychological Clinic informs me that there is clinical evidence that an individual can be conditioned (in the technical psychological sense) by a dream.

[32] A. van Gennep, La Formation des Légendes (Paris, 1910), p. 255. The peyote cult is, of course, an outstanding case where dreams determine variation in ritual.

is generally in disrepute, as at Zuni, and where ceremony has yet demonstrably originated through dream. But where dreaming is accepted as revelation it must not be assumed that the content (or even, entirely, the structure) of a new myth and its derived ceremony will be altogether determined by preexistent cultural forms. As Lowie [33] has remarked, "That they themselves (dreams) in part reflect the regnant folklore offers no ultimate explanation." Anthropologists must be wary of what Korzybski calls "self-reflexive systems" — here, specifically, the covert premise that "culture alone determines culture."

The structure of new cultural forms (whether myths or rituals) will undoubtedly be conditioned by the pre-existent cultural matrix. But the rise of new cultural forms will almost always be determined by factors external to that culture: pressure from other societies, biological events such as epidemics, or changes in the physical environment. Barber [34] has recently shown how the Ghost Dance and the Peyote Cult represent alternative responses of various American Indian tribes to the deprivation resultant upon the encroachment of whites. The Ghost Dance was an adaptive response under the earlier external conditions, but under later conditions the Peyote Cult was the more adaptive response, and the Ghost Dance suffered what the stimulus-response psychologists would call "extinction through non-reward." At any rate the Ghost Dance became extinct in some tribes; in others it has perhaps suffered only partial extinction.

There are always individuals in every society who have their private rituals; there are always individuals who dream and who have compensatory phantasies. In the normal course of things these are simply deviant behaviors which are ridiculed or ignored by most members of the society. Perhaps indeed one should not speak of them as "deviant" — they are "deviant" only as carried to extremes by a relatively small number of individuals, for everyone probably has some

[33] R. H. Lowie, The History of Ethnological Theory (N. Y., 1937), p. 264.

[34] Bernard Barber, Acculturation and Messianic Movements (American Sociological Review, vol. 6, 1941, pp. 663–670); A Socio-Cultural Interpretation of the Peyote Cult (American Anthropologist, 1941, vol. 43, pp. 673–676).

private rituals and compensatory phantasies. When, however, changed conditions happen to make a particular type of obsessive behavior or a special sort of phantasy generally congenial, the private ritual is then socialized by the group, the phantasy of the individual becomes the myth of his society. Indeed there is evidence [35] that when pressures are peculiarly strong and peculiarly general, a considerable number of different individuals may almost simultaneously develop substantially identical phantasies which then become widely current.

Whether belief (myth) or behavior (ritual) changes first will depend, again, both upon cultural tradition and upon external circumstances. Taking a very broad view of the matter, it does seem that behavioral patterns more frequently alter first. In a rapidly changing culture such as our own many ideal patterns are as much as a generation behind the corresponding behavioral patterns. There is evidence that certain ideal patterns (for example, those defining the status of women) are slowly being altered to harmonize with, to act as rationalizations for, the behavioral actualities. On the other hand, the case of Nazi Germany is an excellent illustration of the ideal patterns ("the myth") being provided from above almost whole cloth and of the state, through various organizations, exerting all its force to make the behavioral patterns conform to the standards of conduct laid down in the Nazi mythology.

Some cultures and sub-cultures are relatively indifferent to belief, others to behavior. The dominant practice of the Christian Church, throughout long periods of its history, was to give an emphasis to belief which is most unusual as seen from a cross-cultural perspective. In general, the crucial test as to whether or not one was a Christian was the willingness to avow belief in certain dogmas.[36] The term "believer" was almost synonymous with "Christian." It is very possibly because of this cultural screen that until this century most European scholars selected the myth as primary.

[35] See Marie Bonaparte, Princess of Greece, The Myth of the Corpse in the Car (The American Imago, 1941, vol. 2, pp. 105–127).

[36] Ruth Benedict in the Article "Myth" (Encyclopaedia of the Social Sciences, vol. IX, 1933) makes a similar point but distorts it by the implication that belief in a certain *cosmology* was the single crucial test of Christianity.

II

To a considerable degree, the whole question of the primacy of ceremonial or mythology is as meaningless as all questions of. "the hen or the egg" form. What is really important, as Malinowski has so brilliantly shown, is the intricate interdependence of myth (which is one form of ideology) with ritual and many other forms of behavior. I am quite aware that I have little to add conceptually to Malinowski's discussion in "The Myth in Primitive Psychology." [37] There he examines myths not as curiosa taken out of their total context but as living, vitally important elements in the day to day lives of his Trobrianders, interwoven with every other abstracted type of activity. From this point of view one sees the fallacy of all unilateral explanations. One also sees the aspect of truth in all (or nearly all) of them. There are features which seem to be explanatory of natural phenomena.[38] There are features which reveal the peculiar forms of wish fulfillments characteristic of the culture in question (including the expression of the culturally disallowed but unconsciously wanted). There *are* myths which are intimately related to rituals, which may be descriptive of them, but there are other myths which stand apart. If these others are descriptive of rituals at all, they are, as Durkheim (followed by Radcliffe-Brown and others) suggested, descriptions of rituals of the social organization. That is, they are symbolic representations of the dominant configurations [39] of the particular culture. Myths, then, may ex-

[37] London, 1926.

[38] Radcliffe-Brown's explanation, though useful, strikes me as too narrow in that it seems to deny to nonliterate man *all* bare curiosity and any free play of fancy, undetermined by societal necessities. He says (Andaman Islanders, Cambridge, England, 1933, pp. 380–381): "Natural phenomena such as the alternation of day and night, the changes of the moon, the procession of the seasons, and variations of the weather, have important effects on the welfare of the society . . . a process of bringing within the circle of the social life those aspects of nature that are of importance to the well-being of the society."

[39] "Configuration" is here used as a technical term referring to a structural regularity of the covert culture. In other words, a configuration is a principle which structures widely varying contexts of culture content but of which the culture carriers are minimally aware. By "configuration" I mean something fairly similar to what some authors have meant by "latent culture pattern" as distinguished from "manifest

press not only the latent content of rituals but of other culturally organized behaviors. Malinowski is surely in error when he writes [40] " . . . myth . . . is not symbolic. . . ." Durkheim and Mauss [41] have pointed out how various non-literate groups (notably the Zuni and certain tribes of southeastern Australia) embrace nature within the schema of their social organization through myths which classify natural phenomena precisely according to the principles that prevail in the social organization. Warner[42] has further developed this type of interpretation.

Boas,[43] with his usual caution, is sceptical of all attempts to find a systematic interpretation of mythology. But, while we can agree with him when he writes ". . . mythological narratives and mythological concepts should not be equalized; for social, psychological, and historical conditions affect both in different ways," [44] the need for scrupulous inquiry into historical and other determinants must not be perverted to justify a repudiation of all attempts to deal with the symbolic processes of the all-important covert culture. At all events, the factual record is perfectly straightforward in one respect: neither myth nor ritual can be postulated as "primary."

This is the important point in our discussion at this juncture, and it is unfortunate that Hooke and his associates in their otherwise very illuminating contributions to the study of the relations between myth and ritual in the Near East have emphasized only one aspect of the system of interdependences which Malinowski and Radcliffe-Brown have shown to exist. When Hooke [45] points out that myths are constantly used to

culture pattern." The concept is also closely akin to what Sumner and Keller call a cultural "ethos." For a fuller discussion of "configuration" and "covert culture" see Clyde Kluckhohn, Patterning as Exemplified in Navaho Culture (In: Language, Culture, and Personality, L. Spier, ed., Menasha, 1941, pp. 109–131), esp. pp. 109, 124–129.

[40] Op. cit., p. 19.

[41] De Quelques formes primitives de classification (L'Année Sociologique, vol. 6).

[42] W. L. Warner, A Black Civilization (New York, 1937), esp. pp. 371–411.

[43] See especially F. Boas, Review of G. W. Locher, "The Serpent in Kwakiutl Religion: a Study in Primitive Culture" (Deutsche Literaturzeitung, 1933, pp. 1182–1186; reprinted in Race, Language, and Culture, New York, 1940, pp. 446–450).

[44] Ibid., p. 450.

[45] S. H. Hooke, The Origins of Early Semitic Ritual (London, 1938), pp. 2, 3, 8. See also Myth and Ritual (London, 1933).

justify rituals this observation is quite congruent with the observed facts in many cultures. Indeed all of these data may be used toward a still wider induction: man, as a symbol-using animal, appears to feel the need not only to act but almost equally to give verbal or other symbolic "reasons" for his acts.[46] Hooke [47] rightly speaks of "the vital significance of the myth as something that works," but when he continues "and that dies apart from its ritual" he seems to imply that myths cannot exist apart from rituals and this, as has been shown, is contrary to documented cases. No, the central theorem has been expressed much more adequately by Radcliffe-Brown: [48] "In the case of both ritual and myth the sentiments expressed are those that are essential to the existence of the society." This theorem can be regarded as having been well established in a general way, but we still lack detailed observations on change in myths as correlated with changes in ritual and changes in a culture generally.[49] Navaho material gives certain hints that when a culture as a whole changes rapidly its myths are also substantially and quickly altered.

In sum, the facts do not permit any universal generalizations as to ritual being the "cause" of myth or vice versa. Their relationship is rather that of intricate mutual interdependence, differently structured in different cultures and probably at different times in the same culture. As Benedict [50] has pointed out, there is great variation in the extent to which mythology conditions the religious complex — "the small role of myth in Africa and its much greater importance in religion in parts of North America." Both myth and ritual satisfy the needs of a
ɛ

[46] This statement is not to be interpreted as credence in "the aetiological myth" if by this one means that a myth "satisfies curiosity." We are not justified, I believe, in *completely* excluding the aetiological (in this sense) motive in every case, but Whitehead's statement (Religion in the Making, New York, 1926) probably conforms to a rough induction: "Thus the myth not only explains but reinforces the hidden purpose of the ritual which is emotion" (p. 25).

[47] S. H. Hooke (ed.) The Labyrinth (New York, 1935), p. ix.

[48] Op. cit., p. 405.

[49] The best documentation of the fact that myths are constantly undergoing revision is probably to be found in various writings of Boas. See, for example, Race, Language, and Culture (New York, 1940), pp. 397–525, passim.

[50] Op. cit., p. 180.

society and the relative place of one or the other will depend upon the particular needs (conscious and unconscious) of the individuals in a particular society at a particular time. This principle covers the observed data which show that rituals are borrowed without their myths,[51] and myths without any accompanying ritual. A ritual may be reinforced by a myth (or vice versa) in the donor culture but satisfy the carriers of the recipient culture simply as a form of activity (or be rationalized by a quite different myth which better meets their emotional needs).[52] In short, the only uniformity which can be posited is that there is a strong tendency for some sort of interrelationship between myth and ceremony and that this interrelationship is dependent upon what appears, so far as present information goes, to be an invariant function of both myth and ritual: the gratification (most often in the negative form of anxiety reduction) of a large proportion of the individuals in a society.

If Malinowski and Radcliffe-Brown (and their followers) turned the searchlight of their interpretations as illuminatingly upon specific human animals and their impulses as upon cultural and social abstractions, it might be possible to take their work as providing a fairly complete and adequate general theory of myth and ritual. With Malinowski's notion of myth as "an active force" which is intimately related to almost every other

[51] This appears to be the Papago case. (Underhill, personal communication.)

[52] There are many striking and highly specific parallels between Navaho and Hopi ceremonial practices. For example, the mechanical equipment used in connection with the Sun's House phase of the Navaho Shooting Way chants has so much in common with similar gadgets used in Hopi ceremonials that one can hardly fail to posit a connection. Dr. Parsons has documented the intimate resemblances between the Male Shooting Way chant and Hopi Flute and Snake-Antelope ceremonies (A Pre-Spanish Record of Hopi Ceremonies; American Anthropologist, 1940, vol. 42, pp. 541–543, fn. 4, p. 541). The best guess at present would be that the Hopi was the donor culture, but the direction of diffusion is immaterial here: the significant point is that the supporting myths in the cases concerned show little likeness. For instance, Dr. Parsons regards the Flute Ceremony as a dramatization of the Hopi emergence myth, but the comparable ritual acts in Navaho culture are linked to chantway legends of the usual Holy Way pattern and not to the emergence story. In contrast, the White Mountain Apache seem to have borrowed *both* Snake myth and ritual from the Hopi. See E. C. Parsons, Pueblo Indian Religion (Chicago, 1939), p. 1060 and G. Goodwin, Myths and Tales of the White Mountain Apache (Memoirs of the American Folklore Society, vol. 33, New York, 1939), p. vii.

aspect of a culture we can only agree. When he writes: [53] "Myth is a constant by-product of living faith which is in need of miracles; of sociological status, which demands precedent; of moral rule which requires sanction," we can only applaud. To the French sociologists, to Radcliffe-Brown, and to Warner we are indebted for the clear formulation of the symbolic principle. Those realms of behavior and of experience which man finds beyond rational and technological control he feels are capable of manipulation through symbols. [54] Both myth and ritual are symbolical procedures and are most closely tied together by this, as well as by other, facts. The myth is a system of word symbols, whereas ritual is a system of object and act symbols. Both are symbolic processes for dealing with the same type of situation in the same affective mode.

But the French sociologists, Radcliffe-Brown, and — to a lesser extent — Malinowski are so interested in formulating the relations between conceptual elements that they tend to lose sight of the concrete human organisms. The "functionalists" do usually start with a description of some particular ritualistic behaviors. Not only, however, do the historical origins of this particular behavioral complex fail to interest them. Equally, the motivations and rewards which persons feel are lost sight of in the preoccupation with the contributions which the rituals make to the social system. Thus a sense of the specific detail is lost and we are soon talking about myth in general and ritual in general. From the "functionalist" point of view specific details are about as arbitrary as the phonemes of a language are with respect to "the content" of what is communicated by speech. Hence, as Dollard [55] says, "What one sees from the cultural angle is a drama of life much like a puppet show in which 'culture' is pulling the strings from behind the scenes." The realization that we are really dealing with "animals struggling in real dilemmas" is lacking.

From this angle, some recent psychoanalytic interpretations

[53] Op. cit., p. 92.

[54] That is, forms of behavior whose value or meaning is assigned by human beings — not inherent in the intrinsic properties of the words or acts.

[55] John Dollard, Culture, Society, Impulse, and Socialization (American Journal of Sociology, vol. 45, pp. 50–64), p. 52.

of myth and ritual seem preferable. We may regard as unconvincing Roheim's [56] attempts to treat myths as historical documents which link human phylogenetic and ontogenetic development, as we may justly feel that many psychoanalytic discussions of the latent content of mythology are extravagant and undisciplined. Casey's [57] summary of the psychoanalytic view of religion " . . . ritual is a sublimated compulsion; dogma and myth are sublimated obsessions" may well strike us as an over-simplified, over-neat generalization, but at least our attention is drawn to the connection between cultural forms and impulse-motivated organisms. And Kardiner's [58] relatively sober and controlled treatment does "point at individuals, at bodies, and at a rich and turbulent biological life" — even though that life is admittedly conditioned by social heredity: social organization, culturally defined symbolic systems, and the like.

In a later section of this paper, we shall return to the problem of how myths and rituals reinforce the behavior of individuals. But first let us test the generalities which have been propounded thus far by concrete data from a single culture, the Navaho.[59]

III

The Navaho certainly have sacred tales which, as yet at all events, are not used to justify associated rituals. A striking case, and one where the tale has a clear function as expressing a sentiment "essential to the existence of the society," is known from different parts of the Navaho country.[60] The tales

[56] G. Roheim, The Riddle of the Sphinx (London, 1934), esp. pp. 173–174.

[57] R. P. Casey, The Psychoanalytic Study of Religion (Journal of Abnormal and Social Psychology, vol. 33, 1938, pp. 437–453), p. 449.

[58] A. Kardiner, The Individual and His Society (New York, 1939), esp. pp. 182–194, 268–270.

[59] Some Navaho material has, of course, already been presented. See pp. 47, 51, 57, supra.

[60] E. L. Hewett (The Chaco Canyon and Its Monuments, Albuquerque, 1936, p. 139) records the dissemination of this tale among the Chaco Canyon Navaho. Drs. A. and D. Leighton and I have obtained independent evidence that the same story was told, and believed by many, among the Ramah Navaho (two hundred odd miles away) at the same time. Those who believed the tale carried out ceremonials but not new ceremonials. Rather the old ceremonials (especially Blessing Way rites) were carried out in unusual frequency. In 1936 in the Huerfano country a young woman reported that she had been visited by White Shell Woman who had been given instructions for

differ in detail but all have these structural elements in common: one of "the Holy People" visits one or more Navahos to warn them of an impending catastrophe (a flood or the like) which will destroy the whites — but believing Navahos will be saved if they retire to the top of a mountain or some other sanctuary. It is surely not without meaning that these tales became current at about the time that the Navahos were first feeling intensive and sustained pressure (they were not just prisoners of war as in the Fort Sumner epoch) from the agents of our culture.[61]

Father Berard Haile [62] has recently published evidence that

Blessing Ways to be held — but with special additional procedures. These rites were widely carried out in the northeastern portion of the Navaho area. (See article by Will Evans in the Farmington, N. M., Times Hustler, under date-line of February 21, 1937.) Also in 1936 a woman in the Farmington region claimed to have been visited by Banded Rock Boy (one of the Holy People) and a similar story spread over the Reservation. A famous singer, Left-handed, refused to credit the tale and many Navahos attributed his death (which occurred soon thereafter) to his disbelief. See Mesa Verde Notes, March, 1937, vol. 7, pp. 16–19. F. Gilmor (Windsinger, New York, 1930) has used a story of the same pattern, obtained from the Navaho of the Kayenta, Arizona region as a central episode in a novel.

[61] Jane Harrison (Themis, Cambridge, England, 1912) says: "It is this collective sanction and solemn purpose that differentiate the myth alike from the historical narrative and the mere conte or fairy-tale . . ." (p. 330), and many agreeing with her will doubtless assert that my argument here is invalid because these tales though unquestionably having "solemn purpose" lack "collective sanction." Some would also contend that since living persons claim to have seen the supernatural beings these stories must be called "tales" or, at any rate, not "myths." I see these points and, since I wish to avoid a purely verbal quarrel, I would agree, so far as present data go, that Navaho myths (in the narrow sense) are uniformly associated with ritual behaviors. Actually, the myth which most Navaho call their most sacred (the emergence story) is associated with rites only in a manner which is, from certain points of view, tenuous. The emergence myth is not held to be the basis for any single ceremonial, nor is it used to justify any very considerable portion of ceremonial practice. The emergence myth (or some part of it) is often prefaced to the chantway legend proper. In any case, I must insist (granting always that the line between secular and sacred folk literature must not be drawn too sharply) that the stories dealt with above are not part of the "profane" folklore of the Navaho in the sense in which the Coyote tales, for example, are. The origin legends of the various clans are certainly not secular literature, but I imagine that a purist would maintain that we must call these "legends" as lacking "solemn purpose" (in Harrison's sense). Nevertheless I repeat that "myths" in the broad sense of "sacred tale" are, among the Navaho, found quite dissociated from ritual.

[62] A Note on the Navaho Visionary (American Anthropologist, vol. 42, 1940, p. 359). This contains still another reference to the flood motif.

Navaho ceremonials may originate in dreams or visions rather than being invariably post hoc justifications for existent ritual practices. A practitioner called "son of the late Black Goat" instituted a new ceremonial "which he had learned in a dream while sleeping in a cave." Various informants assured Father Berard that chantway legends originated in the "visions" of individuals.[63] We have, then, Navaho data for (a) the existence of myths without associated rituals, (b) the origin of both legends and rituals in dreams or visions.

It is true that all ceremonial practice among the Navaho is, in cultural theory, justified by an accompanying myth. One may say with Dr. Parsons [64] on the Pueblos: "Whatever the original relationship between myth and ceremony, once made, the myth supports the ceremony or ceremonial office and may suggest ritual increments." One must in the same breath, however, call attention to the fact that myth also supports accepted ways of secular behavior. As Dr. Hill [65] has pointed out, "Women are required to sit with their legs under them and to one side, men with their legs crossed in front of them, because it is said that in the beginning Changing Woman and the Monster Slayer sat in these positions." Let this one example suffice for the many which could easily be given.[66] The general point is that in both sacred and secular spheres myths give some fixity to the ideal patterns of cultures where this is not attained by the printed word. The existence of rituals has a similar effect.

[63] The assertion that ceremonials sometimes have their genesis in dreams and the like does not imply that this, any more than that between myth and ritual, is a one-way relationship. One can by no means dispose of the matter simply by saying "dreams cause myths and myths cause ceremonies." William Morgan (Navaho Dreams, American Anthropologist, vol. 34, 1932, pp. 390–406), who was also convinced that some Navaho myths derive from dreams (p. 395), has pointed out the other aspect of the interdependence: " . . . myths . . . influence dreams; and these dreams, in turn, help to maintain the efficacy of the ceremonies. . . . Repetitive dreams do much to strengthen the traditional beliefs concerning dreams" (p. 400).

[64] E. C. Parsons, Pueblo Indian Religion (Chicago, 1939), p. 968, footnote.

[65] W. W. Hill, The Agricultural and Hunting Methods of the Navaho Indians (New Haven, 1938), p. 179.

[66] Dr. Parsons has suggested (personal communication) an analogue from our own culture: "It was argued that because Eve was made from Adam's rib women should not have the vote."

Although I cannot agree with Wissler [67] that "the primary function" of rituals is "to perpetuate exact knowledge and to secure precision in their application," there can be no doubt that both myths and rituals are important agencies in the transmission of a culture and that they act as brakes upon the speed of culture change.

Returning to the connections between myth and rite among the Navaho, one cannot do better than begin by quoting some sentences from Washington Matthews: [68] "In some cases a Navajo rite has only one myth pertaining to it. In other cases it has many myths. The relation of the myth to the ceremony is variable. Sometimes it explains nearly everything in the ceremony and gives an account of all the important acts from beginning to end, in the order in which they occur; at other times it describes the work in a less systematic manner. . . . Some of the myths seem to tell only of the way in which rites, already established with other tribes, were introduced among the Navajos. . . . The rite-myth never explains all of the symbolism of the rite, although it may account for all the important acts. A primitive and underlying symbolism which probably existed previous to the establishment of the rite, remains unexplained by the myth, as though its existence were taken as a matter of course, and required no explanation."

To these observations one may add the fact that knowledge of the myth is in no way prerequisite to carrying out of a chant. Knowledge does give the singer or curer prestige and ability to expect higher fees, and disparaging remarks are often heard to the effect "Oh, he doesn't know the story," or "He doesn't know the story very well yet." And yet treatment by a practitioner ignorant of the myth [69] is regarded as efficacious.

[67] C. Wissler, The Function of Primitive Ritualistic Ceremonies (Popular Science Monthly, vol. 87, pp. 200–204), p. 203.

[68] Washington Matthews, Some Illustrations of the Connection between Myth and Ceremony (International Congress of Anthropology, Memoirs, Chicago, 1894, pp. 246–251), p. 246.

[69] How much a practitioner knows of both legend and ceremonial depends upon the demands he made upon his instructor during his apprenticeship. The instructor is not supposed to prompt his pupil. Many practitioners are satisfied with quite mechanical performances, and there is no doubt that much information (both legendary and ritualistic) is being lost at present owing to the fact that apprentices do not question their instructors more than superficially.

Navahos are often a little cynical about the variation in the myths. If someone observes that one singer did not carry out a procedure exactly as did another (of perhaps greater repute) it will often be said "Well, he says *his* story is different." Different forms of a rite-myth tend to prevail in different areas of the Navaho country and in different localities. Here the significance of the "personality" of various singers may sometimes be detected in the rise of variations. The transvestite [70] "Left-handed" who died a few years ago enjoyed a tremendous reputation as a singer. There is some evidence [71] that he restructuralized a number of myths as he told them to his apprentices in a way which tended to make the hermaphrodite be?gočidí a kind of supreme Navaho deity — a position which he perhaps never held in the general tradition up to that point. [72] I have heard other Navaho singers say that sandpaintings and other ceremonial acts and procedures were slightly revised to accord with this tenet. If this be true, we have here another clear case of myth-before-ritual.

Instances of the reverse sort are also well documented. From a number of informants accounts have been independently obtained of the creation (less than a hundred years ago) of a new rite: Enemy Monster Blessing Way. All the information agreed that the ritual procedures had been devised by one man who collated parts of two previously existent ceremonials and added a few bits from his own fancy. And three informants independently volunteered the observation "He didn't have any story. But after a while he and his son and another fellow made one up." [73] This is corroborated by the fact that none of Father Berard's numerous versions of the Blessing Way myth mention an Enemy Monster form. [74]

Besides these notes on the relations between myth and rite

[70] A transvestite is an individual who assumes the garb of the other sex. Transvestites are often, but apparently not always, homosexuals.

[71] See W. W. Hill, The Status of the Hermaphrodite and Transvestite in Navaho Culture (American Anthropologist, vol. 37, 1935, pp. 273–280), p. 279.

[72] For a hint, however, that be?gočidí was so considered at an earlier time, see W. Matthews, Navaho Legends (New York, 1897), p. 226, footnote 78.

[73] Cf. Clyde Kluckhohn and Leland C. Wyman, An Introduction to Navaho Chant Practice (Memoir 53, American Anthropological Association, 1940), pp. 186–187.

[74] Personal communication.

I should like to record my impression of another function of myth — one which ranges from simple entertainment to "intellectual edification." Myth among the Navaho not only acts as a justification, a rationale for ritual behavior and as a moral reinforcement for other customary behaviors. It also plays a role not dissimilar to that of literature (especially sacred literature) in many literate cultures. Navahos have a keen expectation of the long recitals of myths (or portions of them) around the fire on winter nights.[75] Myths have all the charm of the familiar. Their very familiarity increases their efficacy, for, in a certain broad and loose sense, the function of both myths and rituals is "the discharge of the emotion of individuals in socially accepted channels." And Hocart [76] acutely observes: "Emotion is assisted by the repetition of words that have acquired a strong emotional coloring, and this coloring again is intensified by repetition." Myths are expective, repetitive dramatizations — their role is similar to that of books in cultures which have few books. They have the (to us) scarcely understandable meaningfulness which the tragedies had for the Greek populace. As Matthew Arnold said of these, "their significance appeared inexhaustible."

IV

The inadequacy of any simplistic statement of the relationship between myth and ritual has been established. It has likewise been maintained that the most adequate generalization will not be cast in terms of the primacy of one or the other of these cultural forms but rather in terms of the general tendency

[75] Why may the myths be recited only in winter? In Navaho feeling today this prohibition is linked in a wider configuration of forbidden activities. There is also, as usual, an historical and distributional problem, for this same prohibition is apparently widely distributed in North America. For example, it is found among the Berens River Salteaux (see A. I. Hallowell, Fear and Anxiety as Cultural and Individual Variables in a Primitive Society, Journal of Social Psychology, vol. 9, 1938, pp. 25–48, p. 31) and among the Iroquois (Dr. William Fenton: personal conversation). But I wonder if in a certain "deeper" sense this prohibition is not founded upon the circumstance that only winter affords the leisure for telling myths, that telling them in summer would be unfitting because it would interfere with work activities?

[76] A. M. Hocart, Ritual and Emotion (Character and Personality, vol. 7, 1939, pp. 201–211), p. 208.

for the two to be interdependent. This generalization has been arrived at through induction from abstractions at the cultural level. That is, as we have sampled the evidence from various cultures we have found cases where myths have justified rituals and have appeared to be "after the fact" of ritual; we have also seen cases where new myths have given rise to new rituals. In other words, the primary conclusion which may be drawn from the data is that myths and rituals tend to be very intimately associated and to influence each other. What is the explanation of the observed connection?

The explanation is to be found in the circumstance that myth and ritual satisfy a group of identical or closely related needs of individuals. Thus far we have alluded only occasionally and often obliquely to myths and rituals as cultural forms defining individual behaviors which are adaptive or adjustive [77] responses. We have seen how myths and rituals are adaptive from the point of view of the society in that they promote social solidarity, enhance the integration of the society by providing a formalized statement of its ultimate value-attitudes, afford a means for the transmission of much of the culture with little loss of content — thus protecting cultural continuity and stabilizing the society. But how are myth and ritual rewarding enough in the daily lives of individuals so that individuals are instigated to preserve them, so that myth and ritual continue to prevail at the expense of more rational responses?

A systematic examination of this question, mainly again in terms of Navaho material, will help us to understand the prevailing interdependence of myth and ritual which has been documented. This sketch of a general theory of myth and ritual as providing a cultural storehouse of adjustive responses for individuals is to be regarded as tentative from the writer's point of view. I do not claim that the theory is proven — even in the context of Navaho culture. I do suggest that it provides a series of working hypotheses which can be tested by specifically pointed field procedures.

[77] This useful distinction I owe to my colleague, Dr. Hobart Mowrer. "Adaptation" is a purely descriptive term referring to the fact that certain types of behavior result in survival. "Adjustment" refers to those responses which remove the motivation stimulating the individual. Thus suicide is adjustive but not adaptive.

We can profitably begin by recurring to the function of myth as fulfilling the expectancy of the familiar. Both myth and ritual here provide cultural solutions to problems which all human beings face. Burke has remarked, "Human beings build their cultures, nervously loquacious, upon the edge of an abyss." In the face of want and death and destruction all humans have a fundamental insecurity.[78] To some extent, all culture is a gigantic effort to mask this, to give the future the simulacrum of safety by making activity repetitive, expective — "to make the future predictable by making it conform to the past." From one angle our own scientific mythology is clearly related to that motivation as is the obsessive, the compulsive tendency which lurks in all organized thought.

When questioned as to why a particular ceremonial activity is carried out in a particular way, Navaho singers will most often say "because the diɣin diné — the Holy People — did it that way in the first place." The *ultima ratio* of non-literates [79] strongly tends to be "that is what our fathers said it was." An Eskimo said to Rasmussen: [80] "We Eskimos do not concern ourselves with solving all riddles. We repeat the old stories in the way they were told to us and with the words we ourselves remember." The Eskimo saying "we keep the old rules in order that we may live untroubled" is well-known. The Navaho and Eskimo thus implicitly recognize a principle which has been expressed by Harvey Ferguson [81] as follows:

... man dreads both spontaneity and change, ... he is a worshipper of habit in all its forms. Conventions and institutions are merely organized and more or less sanctified habits. These are the real gods of human society, which transcend and outlive all other gods. All of them originate as group expedients which have some social value at some time, but they remain the objects of a passionate adoration long after they have outlived their usefulness. Men fight and die for them. They have their high priests, their martyrs, and their rituals. They are the working gods, whatever the ostensible ones may be.

[78] Cf. Malinowski (op. cit., p. 78): "They would screen with the vivid texture of their myths, stories, and beliefs about the spirit world, the vast emotional void gaping beyond them."

[79] There is, to be sure, at least a rough parallel in our own culture in "the Bible says so" and similar phrases.

[80] Knud Rasmussen, Intellectual Culture of the Hudson Bay Eskimos (Copenhagen, 1938), p. 69.   [81] Modern Man (New York, 1936), p. 29.

These principles apply as well to standardized overt acts as to standardized forms of words. Thus Pareto considered the prevalence of ritual in all human cultures as perhaps the outstanding empirical justification for his thesis of the importance of non-logical action. Merton [82] writes:

... activities originally conceived as instrumental are transmuted into ends in themselves. The original purposes are forgotten and ritualistic adherence to institutionally prescribed conduct becomes virtually obsessive. . . Such ritualism may be associated with a mythology which rationalizes these actions so that they appear to retain their status as means, but the dominant pressure is in the direction of strict ritualistic conformity, irrespective of such rationalizations. In this sense ritual has proceeded farthest when such rationalizations are not even called forth.

Goldstein, [83] a neurologist, recognizes a neurological basis for the persistence of such habit systems and writes: "The organism tends to function in the accustomed manner, as long as an at least moderately effective performance can be achieved in this way."

Nevertheless, certain objections to the position as thus far developed must be anticipated and met. It must be allowed at once that the proposition "man dreads both spontaneity and change" must be qualified. More precisely put, we may say "most men, most of the time, dread both spontaneity and change in most of their activities." This formulation allows for the observed fact that most of us *occasionally* get irked with the routines of our lives or that there are certain sectors of our behavior where we fairly consistently show spontaneity. But a careful examination of the totality of behavior of any individual who is not confined in an institution or who has not withdrawn almost completely from participation in the society will show that the larger proportion of the behavior of even the greatest iconoclasts is habitual. This must be so, for by very definition a socialized organism is an organism which behaves mainly in a predictable manner. Even in a culture like contemporary American culture which has made an institutionalized value of change (both for the individual and for society), conformity

[82] R. K. Merton, Social Structure and Anomie (American Sociological Review, vol. 3, 1938, pp. 672–683), p. 673.
[83] Kurt Goldstein, The Organism (New York, 1939), p. 57.

is at the same time a great virtue. To some extent, this is phrased as conformity with the latest fashion, but Americans remain, by and large, even greater conformists than most Europeans.

Existence in an organized society would be unthinkable unless most people, most of the time, behaved in an expectable manner. Rituals constitute a guarantee that in certain societally organized behaviors touching upon certain "areas of ignorance" which constitute "tender spots" for all human beings, people can count upon the repetitive nature of the phenomena. For example, in Zuni society (where rituals are highly calendrical) a man whose wife has left him or whose crops have been ruined by a torrential downpour can yet look forward to the Shalako ceremonial as something which is fixed and immutable. Similarly, the personal sorrow of the devout Christian is in some measure mitigated by anticipation of the great feasts of Christmas and Easter. Perhaps the even turn of the week with its Sunday services and mid-week prayer meetings gave a dependable regularity which the Christian clung to even more in disaster and sorrow. For some individuals daily prayer and the confessional gave the needed sense of security. Myths, likewise, give men "something to hold to." The Christian can better face the seemingly capricious reverses of his plans when he hears the joyous words "lift up your hearts." Rituals and myths supply, then, fixed points in a world of bewildering change and disappointment.

If almost all behavior has something of the habitual about it, how is it that myths and rituals tend to represent the maximum of fixity? Because they deal with those sectors of experience which do not seem amenable to rational control and hence where human beings can least tolerate insecurity. That very insistence upon the minutiae of ritual performance, upon preserving the myth to the very letter, which is characteristic of religious behavior must be regarded as a "reaction formation" (in the Freudian sense) which compensates for the actual intransigeance of those events which religion tries to control.

To anticipate another objection: do these "sanctified habit systems" show such extraordinary persistence simply because they are repeated so often and so scrupulously? Do myths and rituals constitute repetitive behavior par excellence not merely as reaction formations but because the habits are practiced so insistently? Perhaps myths and rituals perdure in accord with Allport's "principle of functional autonomy" [84] — as interpreted by some writers? No, performances must be rewarded in the day to day lives of participating individuals. Sheer repetition in and of itself has never assured the persistence of any habit. If this were not so, no myths and rituals would ever have become extinct except when a whole society died out. It is necessary for us to recognize the somewhat special conditions of drive and of reward which apply to myths and rituals.

It is easy to understand why organisms eat. It is easy to understand why a defenceless man will run to escape a charging tiger. The physiological bases of the activities represented by myths and rituals are less obvious. A recent statement by a stimulus-response psychologist gives us the clue: [85] "The position here taken is that human beings (and also other living organisms to varying degrees) can be motivated either by organic pressures (needs) that are currently felt or by the mere anticipation of such pressures and that those habits tend to be acquired and perpetuated (reinforced) which effect a reduction in either of these two types of motivation." That is, myths and rituals are reinforced because they reduce the anticipation of disaster. No living person has died — but he has seen others die. The terrible things which we have seen happen to others may not yet have plagued us, but our experience teaches us that these are at least potential threats to our own health or happiness.

If a Navaho gets a bad case of snow-blindness and recovers after being sung over, his disposition to go to a singer in the event of a recurrence will be strongly reinforced. And, by the

[84] As a matter of fact, Allport has made it plain (Motivation in Personality: Reply to Mr. Bertocci, Psychological Review, 1940, vol. 47, pp. 533–555) that he contends only that motives may be autonomous in respect to their origins but never in respect to the satisfaction of the ego (p. 547).

[85] O. H. Mowrer, A Stimulus-Response Analysis of Anxiety and its Role as a Reinforcing Agent (Psychological Review, vol. 46, 1939, pp. 553–566), p. 561.

principle of generalization, he is likely to go even if the ailment is quite different. Likewise, the reinforcement will be reciprocal — the singer's confidence in his powers will also be reinforced. Finally, there will be some reinforcement for spectators and for all who hear of the recovery. That the ritual treatment rather than more rational preventatives or cures tends to be followed on future occasions can be understood in terms of the principle of the gradient of reinforcement. Delayed rewards are less effective than immediate rewards. In terms of the conceptual picture of experience with which the surrogates of his culture have furnished him, the patient *expects* to be relieved. Therefore, the very onset of the chant produces some lessening of emotional tension — in technical terms, some reduction of anxiety. If the Navaho is treated by a white physician, the "cure" is more gradual and is dependent upon the purely physicochemical effects of the treatment. If the native wears snow goggles or practices some other form of prevention recommended by a white, the connection between the behavior and the reward (no soreness of the eyes) is so diffuse and so separated in time that reinforcement is relatively weak. Even in those cases where no improvement (other than "psychological") is effected, the realization or at any rate the final acceptance that no help was obtained comes so much later than the immediate sense of benefit [86] that the extinction effects are relatively slight.[87]

Navaho myths and rituals provide a cultural storehouse of adjustive [88] responses for individuals. Nor are these limited to

[86] I have attended hundreds of Navaho ceremonials and I have never yet seen a case where the patient at some point, at least, during the ceremonial did not profess to feel an improvement. This applies even to cases where the patient was actually dying.

[87] The theory of this paragraph has been stated in the language of contemporary stimulus-response psychology. But it is interesting to note that E. S. Hartland (Ritual and Belief, New York) expressed essentially the same content in 1916: "Recurrence of the emotional stress would tend to be accompanied by repetition of the acts in which the reaction has been previously expressed. If the recurrence were sufficiently frequent, the form of the reaction would become a habit to be repeated on similar occasions, even where the stress was less vivid or almost absent. It can hardly be doubted that many rites owe their existence to such reactions" (pp. 116–117).

[88] It is not possible to say adaptive here because there are not infrequent occasions on which ceremonial treatment aggravates the condition or actually brings about death (which would probably not have supervened under a more rational treatment or even

the more obvious functions of providing individuals with the possibility of enhancing personal prestige through display of memory, histrionic ability, etc. Of the ten "mechanisms of defence" which Anna Freud [89] suggests that the ego has available, their myths and rituals afford the Navaho with institutionalized means of employing at least four. Reaction-formation has already been briefly discussed. Myths supply abundant materials for introjection and likewise (in the form of witchcraft myths) suggest an easy and culturally acceptable method of projection of hostile impulses. Finally, rituals provide ways of sublimation of aggression and other socially disapproved tendencies, in part, simply through giving people something to *do*.

All of these "mechanisms of ego defence" will come into context only if we answer the question "adjustive with respect to what?" The existence of motivation, of "anxiety" in Navaho individuals must be accounted for by a number of different factors. In the first place — as in every society — there are those components of "anxiety," those "threats" which may be understood in terms of the "reality principle" of psycho-analysis: life *is* hard — an unseasonable temperature, a vagary of the rainfall does bring hunger or actual starvation; people *are* organically ill. In the second place, there are various forms of "neurotic" anxiety. To some extent, every society tends to have a type anxiety. In our own society it is probably sexual, although this may be true only of those segments of our society who are able to purchase economic and physical security. In most Plains Indians sexual anxiety, so far as we can tell from the available documents, was insignificant. There the basic anxiety was for life itself and for a certain quality of that life (which I cannot attempt to characterize in a few words).

---

if the patient had simply been allowed to rest). From the point of view of the society, however, the rituals are with little doubt adaptive. Careful samples in two areas and more impressionistic data from the Navaho country generally indicate that the frequency of ceremonials has very materially increased concomitantly with the increase of white pressure in recent years. It is tempting to regard this as an adaptive response similar to that of the Ghost Dance and Peyote Cult on the part of other American Indian tribes.

[89] Anna Freud, The Ego and the Mechanisms of Defence (London, 1937).

Among the Navaho the "type anxiety" is certainly that for health. Almost all Navaho ceremonials (essentially every ceremonial still carried out today) are curing ceremonials. And this apparently has a realistic basis. A prominent officer of the Indian Medical Service stated that it was his impression that morbidity among the Navaho is about three times that found in average white communities. In a period of four months' field work among the Navaho Drs. A. and D. Leighton found in their running field notes a total of 707 Navaho references to "threats" which they classified under six headings.[90] Of these, sixty per cent referred to bodily welfare, and are broken down by the Leightons as follows:

Disease is responsible for sixty-seven per cent, accidents for seventeen per cent, and the rest are attributed to wars and fights. Of the diseases described, eighty-one per cent were evidently organic, like smallpox, broken legs, colds, and sore throats; sixteen per cent left us in doubt as to whether they were organic or functional; and three per cent were apparently functional, with symptoms suggesting depression, hysteria, etc. Of all the diseases, forty per cent were incapacitating, forty-three per cent were not, and seventeen per cent were not sufficiently specified in our notes to judge. From these figures it can easily be seen that lack of health is a very important concern of these Navahos, and that almost half of the instances of disease that they mentioned interfered with life activities.

While I am inclined to believe that the character of this sample was somewhat influenced by the fact that the Leightons were white physicians — to whom organic illnesses, primarily, would be reported — there is no doubt that these data confirm the reality of the health "threat." In terms of clothing and shelter which are inadequate (from our point of view at least), of hygiene and diet which similarly fail to conform to our health standards, it is not altogether surprising that the Navaho need to be preoccupied with their health.[91] It is unequivocally true in my experience that a greater proportion of my Navaho friends are found ill when I call upon them than of my white friends.

[90] See A. H. and D. C. Leighton, Some Types of Uneasiness and Fear in a Navaho Indian Community (to appear in the American Anthropologist, April, 1942).

[91] It remains amazing that their population could have increased at such an extraordinary rate if health conditions have been so poor. Dr. A. Leighton suggests to to me that it is conceivable that when the land was less crowded their health was better.

The Navaho and Pueblo Indians live in essentially the same physical environment. But Pueblo rituals are concerned predominantly with rain and with fertility. This contrast to the Navaho preoccupation with disease cannot (in the absence of fuller supporting facts) be laid to a lesser frequency of illness among the Pueblos, for it seems well documented that the Pueblos, living in congested towns, have been far more ravaged by endemic diseases than the Navaho. The explanation is probably to be sought in terms of the differing historical experience of the two peoples and in terms of the contrasting economic and social organizations. If one is living in relative isolation and if one is largely dependent (as were the Navaho at no terribly distant date) upon one's ability to move about hunting and collecting, ill health presents a danger much more crucial than to the Indian who lives in a town which has a reserve supply of corn and a more specialized social organization.

That Navaho myths and rituals are focussed upon health and upon curing has, then, a firm basis in the reality of the external world. But there is also a great deal of uneasiness arising from inter-personal relationships, and this undoubtedly influences the way the Navaho react to their illnesses. Then, too, one type of anxiousness always tends to modify others. Indeed, in view of what the psychoanalysts have taught us about "accidents" and of what we are learning from psychosomatic medicine about the psychogenic origin of many "organic" diseases we cannot regard the sources of disease among the Navaho as a closed question.[92]

Where people live under constant threat from the physical environment, where small groups are geographically isolated and "emotional inbreeding" within the extended family group is at a maximum, inter-personal tensions and hostilities are inevitably intense. The prevalence of ill health which throws additional burdens on the well and strong is in itself an additional socially disrupting force.[93] But if the overt expression

[92] It does not seem implausible that some disorders (especially perhaps those associated with acute anxieties) are examples of what Caner has called "superstitious self-protection." See G. C. Caner, Superstitious Self-Protection (Archives of Neurology and Psychiatry, 1940, vol. 44, pp. 351–361).

[93] Dr. A. Leighton has pointed out to me that these disruptive tendencies are re-

of aggressive impulses proceeds very far the whole system of "economic" co-operation breaks down and then sheer physical survival is more than precarious. Here myths and rituals constitute a series of highly adaptive responses from the point of view of the society. Recital of or reference to the myths re-affirms the solidarity of the Navaho sentiment system.[94] In the words of a Navaho informant: "Knowing a good story will protect your home and children and property. A myth is just like a big stone foundation — it lasts a long time." Per-formance of rituals likewise heightens awareness of the common system of sentiments. The ceremonials also bring individuals together in a situation where quarrelling is forbidden. Prepara-tion for and carrying out of a chant demands intricately ramified co-operation, economic and otherwise, and doubtless thus rein-forces the sense of mutual dependency.

Myths and rituals equally facilitate the adjustment of the individual to his society. Primarily, perhaps, they provide a means of sublimation of his anti-social tendencies. It is surely not without meaning that essentially all known chant myths take the family and some trouble within it as a point of de-parture. Let us look at Reichard's [95] generalization of the chant myth:

A number of chant legends are now available and all show approximately *the same* construction. People are having a hard time to secure *subsistence or have some grievance. A boy of the family is forbidden* to go somewhere or to do some particular thing. He does not observe the warnings and does that

inforced by one of the techniques for survival which those Navahos who have intimate and competitive relations with whites have developed. He writes: "A group threatened by a stronger group can swing to one of two poles. (*a*) They can coalesce and form a highly efficient, highly integrated unit that can act with swiftness, power, and pre-cision, and in which all individuals stand or fall together. (*b*) They can disperse like a covey of quail so as never to present a united target to the foe. This is the Navaho method of dealing with the whites. It is every man for himself, and though individuals may fall, enough escape to survive. You don't rush to help your tribesman when trouble comes, you stay out of it, you 'let it go.' Such an attitude, however, does lead to mutual mistrust."

[94] Cf. Radcliffe-Brown (op. cit., p. 330): " . . . tales that might seem merely the products of a somewhat childish fancy are very far indeed from being merely fanciful and are the means by which the Andamanese express and systematize their fundamental notions of life and nature and the sentiments attaching to those notions."

[95] Gladys Reichard, Navajo Medicine Man (New York, 1939), p. 76. Italics mine.

which was forbidden, whereupon he embarks upon a series of adventures which keep him away from home so long that *his family despairs of his return.* . . . After the dramatic episodes, the hero returns to his home bringing with him the ritualistic lore which he teaches to *his brother.* He has been away so long and has become so accustomed to association with deity that *his own people seem impure* to him. He corrects that fault by teaching them the means of purification. . . . He has *his brother* conduct the ritual over *his sister* . . . he vanishes into the air.

While as a total explanation the following would be over-simple, it seems fair to say that the gist of this may be interpreted as follows: the chant myth supplies a catharsis for the traumata incident upon the socialization of the Navaho child. That brother and sister are the principal *dramatis personae* fits neatly with the central conflicts of the Navaho socialization process. This is a subject which I hope to treat in detail in a later paper.

Overt quarrels between family members are by no means infrequent, and, especially when drinking has been going on, physical blows are often exchanged. Abundant data indicate that Navahos have a sense of shame [96] which is fairly persistent and that this is closely connected with the socially disapproved hostile impulses which they have experienced toward relatives. It is also clear that their mistrust of others (including those in their own extended family group) is in part based upon a fear of retaliation (and this fear of retaliation is soundly based upon experience in actual life as well as, possibly, upon "unconcious guilt"). Certain passages in the myths indicate that the Navaho have a somewhat conscious realization that the ceremonials act as a cure, not only for physical illness, but also for anti-social tendencies. The following extract from the myth of the Mountain Top Way Chant will serve as an example: "The ceremony cured Dsiliyi Neyani of all his strange

[96] This is significantly reflected in ceremonial lore. Torlino, a singer of Beauty Way, said to Washington Matthews: "I am ashamed before the earth; I am ashamed before the heavens; I am ashamed before the dawn; I am ashamed before the evening twilight; I am ashamed before the blue sky; I am ashamed before the sun; *I am ashamed before that standing within me which speaks with me* (*my conscience*). Some of these things are always looking at me. I am never out of sight." Washington Matthews, Navaho Legends (American Folklore Society, Memoirs, 5, 1897), pp. 58–59. Italics are mine.

feelings and notions. The lodge of his people no longer smelled unpleasant to him." [97]

Thus "the working gods" of the Navaho are their sanctified repetitive ways of behavior. If these are offended by violation of the culture's system of scruples, the ceremonials exist as institutionalized means of restoring the individual to full rapport with the universe: nature and his own society.[98] Indeed "restore" is the best English translation of the Navaho word which the Navaho constantly use to express what the ceremonial does for the "patient." The associated myths reinforce the patient's belief that the ceremonial will both truly cure him of his illness and also "change" him so that he will be a better man in his relations with his family and his neighbors. An English-speaking Navaho who had just returned from jail where he had been put for beating his wife and molesting his stepdaughter said to me: "I am sure going to behave from now on. I am going to be changed — just like somebody who has been sung over."

Since a certain minimum of social efficiency is by derivation a biological necessity for the Navaho, not all of the hostility and uneasiness engendered by the rigors of the physical environment, geographical isolation, and the burdens imposed by illness is expressed or even gets into consciousness. There is a great deal of repression and this leads, on the one hand, to projection phenomena (especially in the form of phantasies that others are practicing witchcraft against one[99]) and, on the other hand, the strong feelings of shame at the conscious level are matched by powerful feelings of guilt at the unconscious level. Because a person feels guilty by reason of his unconscious hostilities toward members of his family (and friends and neighbors generally), some individuals develop chronic anxie-

[97] W. Matthews, The Mountain Chant (Annual Report of the Bureau of American Ethnology, vol. 5, Washington, 1887, pp. 379–467), p. 417.

[98] Cf. A. R. Radcliffe-Brown, Taboo (Cambridge, England, 1939), p. 44. "The primary value of ritual . . . is the attribution of ritual value to objects and occasions which are either themselves objects of important common interests linking together the persons of a community or are symbolically representative of such objects."

[99] This view is developed with full documentation in a forthcoming publication to be issued by the Peabody Museum of Harvard University in the spring of 1942.

ties. Such persons feel continually uncomfortable. They say they "feel sick all over" without specifying organic ailments other than very vaguely. They feel so "ill" that they must have ceremonials to cure them. The diagnostician and other practitioners, taking myths as their authority, will refer the cause of the illness to the patient's having seen animals struck by lightning, to a past failure to observe ritual requirements or to some similar violation of a cultural scruple. But isn't this perhaps basically a substitution of symbols acceptable to consciousness, a displacement of guilt feelings?

It is my observation that Navahos other than those who exhibit chronic or acute anxieties tend characteristically to show a high level of anxiety. It would be a mistake, however, to attribute all of this anxiety to intra-familial tensions, although it is my impression that this is the outstanding pressure. Secondary drives resultant upon culture change and upon white pressure are also of undoubted importance. And it is likewise true, as Mr. Homans [100] has recently pointed out, that the existence of these ritual injunctions and prohibitions (and of the concomitant myths and other beliefs) gives rise to still another variety of anxiety which Homans has well called secondary anxiety. In other words, the conceptual picture of the world which Navaho culture sets forth makes for a high threshold of anxiety in that it defines all manner of situation as fraught with peril, and individuals are instigated to anticipate danger on every hand.

But the culture, of course, prescribes not only the supernatural dangers but also the supernatural means of meeting these dangers or of alleviating their effects. Myths and rituals jointly provide systematic protection against supernatural dangers, the threats of ill health and of the physical environment, anti-social tensions, and the pressures of a more powerful society. In the absence of a codified law and of an authoritarian "chief" or other father substitute, it is only through the myth-ritual system that Navahos can make a socially supported, unified response to all of these disintegrating threats.

[100] G. C. Homans, Anxiety and Ritual (American Anthropologist, vol. 43, 1941), pp. 164–173.

The all-pervasive configurations of word symbols (myths) and of act symbols (rituals) preserve the cohesion of the society and sustain the individual, protecting him from intolerable conflict. As Hoagland [101] has recently remarked:

Religion appears to me to be a culmination of this basic tendency of organisms to react in a configurational way to situations. We must resolve conflicts and disturbing puzzles by closing some sort of a configuration, and the religious urge appears to be a primitive tendency, possessing biological survival value, to unify our environment so that we can cope with it.

V

The Navaho are only one case.[102] The specific adaptive and adjustive responses performed by myth and ritual will be differently phrased in different societies according to the historical experience of these societies (including the specific opportunities they have had for borrowing from other cultures), in accord with prevalent configurations of other aspects of the culture, and with reference to pressures exerted by other societies and by the physical and biological environment. But the general nature of the adaptive and adjustive responses performed by myth and ritual appears very much the same in all human groups. Hence, although the relative importance of myth and of ritual does vary greatly, the two tend universally to be associated.

For myth and ritual have a common psychological basis. Ritual is an obsessive repetitive activity — often a symbolic dramatization of the fundamental "needs" of the society, whether "economic," "biological," "social," or "sexual." Mythology is the rationalization of these same needs, whether they are all expressed in overt ceremonial or not. Someone has said "every culture has a type conflict and a type solution."

[101] Hudson Hoagland, Some Comments on Science and Faith (In: Conference on Science, Philosophy, and Religion, New York, 1941, mimeographed), p. 5.

[102] But I was very much struck in reading Dr. Hallowell's recent article (A. I. Hallowell, The Social Function of Anxiety in a Primitive Society, American Sociological Review, vol. 6, December, 1941, pp. 869–882) — which I read only when this paper was in proof — at the similarity not only in the interpretations he reached but at that in the data from the Saulteaux, when he says "fear of disease is a major social sanction" (p. 871) that fits the Navaho case precisely — as does "illness due to having done bad things or to transgression of a parent" (p. 873).

Ceremonials tend to portray a symbolic resolvement of the conflicts which external environment, historical experience, and selective distribution of personality types [103] have caused to be characteristic in the society. Because different conflict situations characterize different societies, the "needs" which are typical in one society may be the "needs" of only deviant individuals in another society. And the institutionalized gratifications (of which rituals and myths are prominent examples) of culturally recognized needs vary greatly from society to society. "Culturally recognized needs" is, of course, an analytical abstraction. Concretely, "needs" arise and exist only in specific individuals. This we must never forget, but it is equally important that myths and rituals, though surviving as functioning aspects of a coherent culture only so long as they meet the "needs" of a number of concrete individuals, are, in one sense, "supra-individual." They are usually composite creations; they normally embody the accretions of many generations, the modifications (through borrowing from other cultures or by intra-cultural changes) which the varying needs of the group as a whole and of innovating individuals in the group have imposed. In short, both myths and rituals are cultural products, part of the social heredity of a society.

[103] This selective distribution of personality types may become established biologically, through the operation of genetic mechanisms, or through the processes of child socialization operative in the particular culture.

MYTH AND RITUAL IN EARLY GREECE

By A. N. MARLOW, M.A.

SENIOR LECTURER IN LATIN IN THE UNIVERSITY OF MANCHESTER

THE words Myth and Ritual taken by themselves include practically the whole of the activities that we call religious ; but in the decade before the second World War there came into prominence a school of interpreters of ancient religious belief which gave to the phrase Myth and Ritual a particular significance, namely, the existence in all early religious symbolism of a divine kingship, a sacred marriage, a combat between the king and the the forces of evil, a death and resurrection of the divine king and a typifying by his myth of the death and rebirth of the seasons and crops. A predominant element in all religious myth is thus seen to be the securing by ritual of the means of subsistence, the regular cycle of the seasons and the return of life to the dead earth. This theory obviously owes much to the material collected by Sir James Frazer, and particularly to *Adonis, Attis, Osiris*, published in 1906 ; and of course it also owes much to the work of people like Jane Harrison and Gilbert Murray who in books such as *Prolegomena* (1903) and *Five Stages of Greek Religion* (1912) [1] examined early religious beliefs with the theory in their minds that in most myths could be detected a " year δαίμων ", and, as some now think, overstated their case. The work of scholars such as Cumont, Wendland and Reitzenstein [2] in showing the affinity of Christianity to the saviour religions of the Near East must also have created an expectancy of finding these elements universally.

The popularization of the " Myth and Ritual " theory of religious interpretation is, however, due in the main to the work of S. H. Hooke and his followers who were particularly anxious

[1] This work, originally delivered as lectures in 1912, first appeared as *Four Stages of Greek Religion.*

[2] See, for example, Cumont, *Les Religions Orientales dans l'Empire Romain* (Paris, 1906) ; P. Wendland, *Hellenistisch-Römische Kultur* (Tübingen, 1912) ; Reitzenstein, *Die hellenistischen Mysterienreligionen* (Leipzig, 1910) ; Dieterich, *Eine Mithrasliturgie* (Leipzig, 1903).

to save Christianity for themselves by showing that its central doctrines were fundamental to a good deal of existing religious belief and that its historical claims could be accepted as a unique example of the heightening and tension integral to all religions.[1] In two volumes of essays, *Myth and Ritual*, published in 1933, and *The Labyrinth*, published in 1935, the " Myth and Ritual " theory is applied, first to the religions of Egypt, Babylon and Palestine and then to the later religious developments of the Near East, and an attempt is made, with only partial success, to show its profound influence on the history of civilization.

The purpose of this essay is to examine what evidence, if any, is provided by the literature and beliefs of early Greece for the myth of a sacral kingship, a ritual combat, a sacred marriage and a ritual death and rebirth. In all hitherto-published works on Myth and Ritual Greek myth is either treated superficially [2] or interpreted with absurd eccentricity as in Lord Raglan's book *The Hero* (London, 1936), the whimsical interpretations in which were largely responsible for my own essay, since I had to dispel for myself the mental fog in which the book left me ; but of this more later.

Professor Hooke and his school see, or saw, in religious texts the myth which accompanied the ritual enactment of the sacred combat and marriage, and some of his disciples see in what appear to be manifestly secular poems and songs nothing more than a spoken myth which accompanied a ritual. The curious thing is that although many scholars gave general assent to this theory, they have almost with one voice found its particular application unsatisfactory. Professor Brandon has dealt effectively with the theory as applied to Egypt,[3] Professor Fish sees no justification

[1] I leave undiscussed the question whether, even had they established their thesis, Professor Hooke and his school could be said to have enhanced the claims of Christianity.

[2] See, for example, E. O. James's *Myth and Ritual in the Ancient Near East* (London, 1958), which says nothing of the Athenian *archon basileus*, nothing of the *pharmakos* or scapegoat and of many other elements.

[3] In a further symposium entitled *Myth, Ritual and Kingship* (1958), pp. 261 ff. It must be noted that in this symposium Professor Hooke reaffirms the claims of the Myth and Ritual school, though other contributors are guarded in their adherence to it, while at the same time reaffirming its great influence on religious thought.

whatsoever for applying it to Babylonian religious texts, [1] and these two religions were originally the principal witnesses for the theory. As we shall see, the close examination of the Greek evidence also raises grave doubts. In fact, the Myth and Ritual School could now almost be said to be in decline, were it not that new books have appeared in which the original scope of the term Myth and Ritual has been widened to include practically all ritual *mimesis*, and its origins have been traced back to Palaeolithic cave art ; and incidentally the originally sharp outlines of the theory have been blurred, until what we now see is a series of disquisitions with much material but few conclusions, on some common elements of primitive religious belief. Notable here are the works of Professor E. O. James, of which the most recent are *Myth and Ritual in the Ancient Near East* (1958) and *The Ancient Gods* (1960). Before narrowing our attention to the specifically Greek evidence it is relevant to see briefly on what lines the investigation has run in other religions.

In the widest sense all art is *mimesis*, imitation ; when one makes toy soldiers a Greek would say that he " imitated soldiers with tin " [2] ; so that Homer and Virgil and Ovid and Shakespeare are practising *mimesis*, and it becomes easier to maintain that their writings are particular examples of the myth that accompanies a ritual. This is really a false aetiology : all art is *mimesis*, but not of the special kind which the " Myth and Ritual " school need to support their theory.

Professor James takes us back to the caves of Lascaux, Altamira and Les Trois-Frères, and sees in the wonderful cave-paintings of the Old Stone Age the foreshadowing of the ritual themes of later times ; the ritual control of the chase, increase rites, the mimetic sacred dance, the funerary ritual, the vegetation cultus.[3] It is true that much cave art from all over the world seems to have significant features in common: the representations of the hunt, with the actual killing of the animal, the lifelike drawings of the animals themselves, the scenes of war and sex and

[1] Professor Fish expressed his views in a paper read to a seminar in the University of Manchester some years ago.

[2] I owe this idea to a brilliant essay by Gilbert Murray on *Poesis and Mimesis*, reprinted in his *Essays and Addresses* (London, 1921), pp. 107-24.

[3] E. O. James, *Myth and Ritual in the Ancient Near East*, pp. 21-37.

death ; the strange way in which these drawings were reproduced in the inmost recesses of caves, sometimes as much as half a mile from daylight, which suggests that they were part of a secret cult, particularly as some of them appear near to ledges and tunnels quite out of reach of the floor, and only accessible by devious passages ; and the equally strange way in which some pictures are a kind of palimpsest, with two or three figures superimposed when there is plenty of available wall space, as if one particular spot had a special importance. Recent investigations in North Africa, East Africa, South Africa and India have shown how many of these features are common to all cave art. The witch-doctor or sorcerer—the man disguised as an animal—is also found in many places, a most pronounced and suggestive example of *mimesis*, and even the styles are consistent : there is, for example, a kind of drawing which reduces men and animals to elongated sticks, and this is found in Europe, Africa and India.[1]

The theory is that the chase, the marriage, the killing, the birth, were all enacted in mime before the actual incident took place, a ritual seen so commonly in rites for fertility, rain-increase and the like and which forms a part of so many children's games. This theory has been abundantly argued and demonstrated, but already in the Palaeolithic period we are confronted with mysteries which we cannot wholly explain, and this sense of bafflement will, or should, persist when we are dealing with material which is relatively of yesterday, i.e. within the compass of recorded history. We cannot be sure that we know the purpose of any of the

[1] From a voluminous literature on cave art the following seem to cover most of the ground : The Abbé Breuil, *Quatre cents siècles d'art pariétal* (Montaignac, 1952) ; H. Alimen, *The Prehistory of Africa* (London, 1957), pp. 352-98 ; D. H. Gordon, *The Prehistoric Background of Indian Culture* (Bombay, 1958), pp. 98-117 ; H. Kuhn, *The Rock Pictures of Europe* (London, 1956). There is useful material in three recent Pelican books : C. B. M. McBurney, *The Stone Age of Northern Africa* (1960), pp. 258-71 ; Sonia Cole, *The Prehistory of East Africa* (1954), pp. 247-70 ; and Desmond Clark, *The Prehistory of Southern Africa* (1959), pp. 253-80. M. C. Burkitt in *The Old Stone Age* (3rd edn., London, 1955), pp. 178-232, was among the first to examine the whole question of Palaeolithic cave art, and Professor S. G. F. Brandon has recently published an illuminating study of what he calls " the ritual perpetuation of the past " in which he traces most, if not all, man's religious activities to the preoccupation with death ; he deals at length with the question of the well-known Sorcerer of Les Trois-Frères (*Numen*, vol. vi., fasc. 2, Dec. 1959, pp. 112-29).

cave-paintings, and although it is very naïve to assume that Stone Age man whiled away the long dark evenings by drawing bison and rhinoceros, it is humourless to see in every drawing evidence of a cult, so that a man throwing a spear is made to have a dim and esoteric significance. The trouble here as everywhere is that professors cannot help riding their theories to death.

Moving swiftly down the ages, the next cultures to occupy the attention of Professor James [1] are the village settlements in Baluchistan and Iran which preceded the city-civilization of Mohenjo-daro and Harappā, and whose pottery has been so exhaustively discussed by Stuart Piggott, their dates being roughly in the end of the fourth millennium B.C. and the beginning of the third. Here there is insufficient evidence on which to base a theory. In the Zhob valley in particular in northern Baluchistan there have been found female figurines with holes for eyes and a generally terrifying appearance in spite of their small size of a few inches, and these, says Professor Piggott, were probably images of the dread goddess of death and rebirth—in fact one might say Persephone in her earliest known guise. Again, in the Kulli culture of southern Baluchistan we find, as in Anatolia, Mesopotamia, Egypt and elsewhere, figurines with exaggerated breasts and bodies, sometimes in association with objects thought to be *phalli*, and on occasion bearing traces of red paint, which was used on statues to enhance life-giving powers in Egypt, Mesopotamia and Malta. If, as is becoming a widespread belief, civilization as we know it originally sprang from Iran or near it, these village-cultures are of great importance for the primitive forms of religious belief and ceremony ; but being prehistoric they cannot help us much. If every long and narrow stone that has been identified as a phallus were really a phallus, then every mountainside would give evidence of Priapean orgies.

When we reach the city-civilizations of Harappā and Mohenjo-daro, there seems at first sight much more evidence for a priest-kingship with its accompanying rites and ceremonies. These twin cities bore many points of resemblance to the cities of Sumeria and Egypt ; in all three countries the dominant feature

[1] E. O. James, op. cit. pp. 132 ff.; Stuart Piggott, *Prehistoric India* (London, 1950), pp. 66-131.

of the landscape was a great river or rivers, which in all three countries irrigated an arid desert. The two great Indus cities are dominated by great citadels, where Marshall, Mackay, Wheeler and others have shown the great baths, the colleges of priests, the signs of serfdom of the masses and many other features denoting the absolute mastery of the priesthood. Unfortunately no one has deciphered the Indus script, although we have several thousand seals on which its four hundred or so characters are clearly stamped. Many of these scenes could plausibly be argued to show sacrifice of animals or even human beings at some ceremony, and we can see what seem to be traces of a scapegoatritual [1] ; but there are several features of the Indus seals which defy explanation, as for instance the sacred brazier or manger which appears on so many of them, and here again the only possible attitude is one of qualified scepticism.

While still in India let us look for a moment at the Vedas and at Brahmanic ritual, since here at last our evidence is literary and we have texts to deal with. To what extent are the Vedic hymns texts to accompany a ritual ? The obvious answer is, to a very great extent indeed, but of the myth we are looking for there is very little evidence among the Brahmins. Their myths were originally personifications of natural forces, the fire, the stormcloud, the heavens, the lightning, the sun. There is an almost Milesian ring about some of the earlier Vedic speculations, as for example in Rig Veda, x. 129 :

Nor Aught nor Naught existed, yon bright sky
Was not, nor heaven's broad roof outstretched above.
What covered all? What sheltered? What concealed?
Was it the water's fathomless abyss?

There was not death—yet was there naught immortal,
There was no confine betwixt day and night ;
The only One breathed breathless by Itself,
Other than It there nothing since has been.

[1] See R. E. M. Wheeler, *The Indus Age* (Cambridge, 1953), pp. 82 ff., and D. H. Gordon, op. cit. pp. 57-76. James, op. cit. pp. 106-7, has really very little to contribute on this point except to stress the importance attached to ritual bathing at Mohenjo-daro, and the frequent occurrence of figurines akin to those of Kulli and the Zhob valley.

Darkness there was, and all at first was veiled
In gloom profound—an ocean without light—
The germ that still lay covered in the husk
Burst forth, one nature, from the fervent heat.

Who knows the secret? Who proclaimed it here?
Whence, whence this manifold creation sprang?
The gods themselves came later into being—
Who knows from whence this great creation sprang?

He, from whom all this great creation came,
Whether His will created was or mute,
The Most High Seer that is in highest heaven,
He knows it—or perchance even He knows not.[1]

The Brahmanic priesthood is probably a more or less faithful reflection of the priesthood in the Indus cities, where the priest was himself a kind of king and mediated with the gods on behalf of the people. The Brahmins themselves always retained something of this mysterious power, and although for some time after north-west India had succumbed to the Aryan invaders the king, the warrior, *kshatriya*, took precedence over the priest, by the time the Brahmanas, the prose commentaries on the Vedic hymns, were composed, the Brahmins had re-established their supremacy as the power behind the throne, since they had succeeded in persuading the kings that nothing, not even the rising daily of the sun, could take place without an elaborate and lengthy ritual, the proper performance of which was possible only to the Brahmins themselves. In the coronation ceremony of the ancient Indian kings we find of course much symbolism : lustrations, sacrifices, a token cattle-raid, a stepping in the direction of the cardinal points, the throwing of dice and so on ; and of course the king is the patron and father of his people, responsible for moral as well as social law. But much of this must have been a perfunctory conformity with tradition, since it was the Brahmins themselves who held all spiritual power and whose incantations made the world go round. Again, the horse-sacrifice, by which a horse is turned loose and the king claims all the ground covered by it, has faint resemblances, in the actual turning-loose, to scapegoat-ritual, but nothing more. Of the sacred marriage, of the death and

[1] Trans. Max Müller.

rebirth of the king-god and of the other central features of " myth and ritual " as it is professedly found elsewhere, there is not a trace. Nor are the Vedic hymns themselves at all like " myth and ritual " texts.[1]   Some of them much resemble, in length and even in sentiment, hymns in the Ancient and Modern collection. Finally, the whole tendency of Upanishadic interpretation of Vedic hymns was latent from the start in the hymns themselves. They imply a much more abstract and philosophical approach to the deity than that of sympathetic magic.

Turning now to the protreptic ritual of the Near East, the king was here represented as himself divine or given divine status as champion and representative of the people, though it is impossible to get a clear picture how in the myth the human king merges into the divine figure or the god descends to become the human king. The details vary in different cults and the texts themselves are of a varying state of completeness, coherence and intelligibility. The texts which we have are the words or story of the king-god or hero, recited periodically as an accompaniment to the ritual, which is held to be a re-enactment of the combat of the hero-king with the personified forces of darkness and evil, his death and resurrection.

It is important here to stress again that this is a theory imposed on the facts, not the facts themselves. Admittedly, like Lyell's geological theories and Darwin's *Descent of Man*, it has thrown much light on all kinds of obscure points ; but, as we shall see, the thoroughgoing application of the theory has its dangers.

In early Egypt the general picture seemed fairly clear, though the texts are obscure and often fragmentary. Hooke listed the essential features of the annual festival which was observed to symbolize the death and rebirth of the year as follows :[2]

(1) The dramatic representation of the death and resurrection of the god.

(2) The recitation or symbolic representation of the myth of creation.

---

[1] " The *Rigveda* is much more than an adjunct to ritual.   It might be called a literary anthology, drawn from family traditions.   The religious expressions found in it are poetic exordia to the cult and are not designed as the direct accompaniment of ceremonies" (L. Renou, *The Religions of Ancient India* (London, 1953), p. 10).

[2] S. H. Hooke, *Myth and Ritual*, p. 8.

(3) The ritual combat, in which the triumph of the god over his enemies was depicted.

(4) The sacred marriage.

(5) The triumphal procession, in which the king played the part of the god followed by a train of lesser gods or visiting deities.

All these elements are to be found in Egypt, where the earliest mythology bears in certain details a striking resemblance to that of Greece.[1] We find the emergence of the sun-god from the primeval waters, the creation of the god of the atmosphere and the goddess of moisture, who in turn create the earth-god and the sky-goddess,[2] and the emergence of their offspring, Osiris, Isis, Seth and Nephthys. Osiris weds Isis but is ousted from the throne of Egypt by Seth and killed ; later he is miraculously brought to life and Isis bears him a son Horus, who in combat with Seth emasculates him just as Zeus emasculates his father Cronos. Some features of this story, notably the incestuous union of Osiris and Isis and the preoccupation with virility and its symbols, are of course common to a number of ancient myths. So far as can be discovered, Horus is identified in pre-dynastic Egypt with the reigning monarch of Heliopolis who is also the high priest of Osiris, and every year in the spring month of Khoiakh a most elaborate festival was held in which an effigy of Osiris was ritually buried in a funerary chamber and sprinkled with water, barley and sand, after which various weird and intricate ceremonies took place to symbolize the revivification of the god. This indeed seems a drastic over-simplification of the ceremony, which seems to be a mingling of reminiscences of two if not three festivals, and is found only in texts in which even the sequence of scenes is in dispute.[3] In fact, a reading of the literature of the subject leaves one with a feeling of utter bewilderment that any sense whatever can be made out of the apparently nonsensical beliefs implied in the rites and ceremonies of early Egypt, and that we really understand little more about them than did Plutarch or Herodotus. So ardent an Egyptologist

[1] A. M. Blackman, *Myth and Ritual in Ancient Egypt*, in S. H. Hooke, op. cit. pp. 15-39 ; and authorities there cited.

[2] Cf. *Iliad*, xiv. 201, 246 ; Hesiod, *Theogony*, 155, 176, 337 ff.

[3] See H. W. Fairman, " The Kingship Rituals of Egypt ", in *Myth, Ritual and Kingship*, p. 83.

as S. G. F. Brandon challenges the whole conception of Osiris as a yearly champion of good against evil or a yearly fighter on behalf of the crops.   He draws attention to the striking fact that the Egyptian mind was directed towards death and the life after death and that its mythology was all oriented in this way.[1] This involves the whole question of diffusion *versus* evolution as the explanation of the widespread occurrence of Myth and Ritual themes in the Near East.   To the evolutionists who claim that at a given stage in the evolution of an agricultural community these beliefs are bound to occur, he quotes the example of ancient China, where in a community based on agriculture and with the same dependence on the seasons that we find in Egypt, there is no trace of a sacred marriage or of a dying god or of a ritual combat.[2] If diffusion is the explanation, then it no longer seems clear, as it once did, that Egypt is the birthplace of these rites.   Professor Blackman, for example, considered that the original myth and ritual pattern came, not from Egypt, but from Syria.[3]   Finally, Professor Brandon emphasizes that from earliest times Osiris was not primarily " a vegetation deity, with whose being the king was intimately associated and whose life-cycle constituted critical points in the course of the year ; rather Osiris was the saviour to whom men and women turned for the assurance of immortality and before whom they believed that they would be judged in the next world.".[4]

Babylonia provides us with another example of the kingly combat and the sacred marriage, and equal doubt attaches here too to the interpretation of the texts.   There must have been a belief in prehistoric times that the king-god was responsible for the state of agricultural land and even for the regular recurrence of the seasons.   The great festival was the New Year festival, at which the Creation Epic was twice recited, and the substance of the epic is Marduk's career and the annual triumph of order over Chaos.   Marduk was a kind of year $\delta\alpha i\mu\omega\nu$ and is identified with

[1] S. G. F. Brandon, " The Myth and Ritual Position Critically Considered " (*Myth, Ritual and Kingship*, pp. 265 ff.).

[2] Op. cit., p. 273.

[3] *Myth and Ritual*, p. 39.

[4] *Myth, Ritual and Kingship*, pp. 276-7, where Professor Brandon in a note adduces evidence from vignettes in *The Book of the Dead*.

the various heavenly bodies during the course of the year, but a feature of the myth that is conspicuously lacking is the sacred marriage. "Babylonian myths had a similar cycle for all kinds of year-gods ; that is why it can be argued that the Marduk myth as we know it was an adaptation of an earlier Enurta myth. Other gods had their New Year festivals, in which the ritual apparently ressembled that of Babylon. It is to be presumed that the ritual of the bridal of Marduk and Sarpanitum was celebrated at the same time as a seasonal festival, the sacred marriage, elsewhere. Definite evidence that it was celebrated at the New Year festival is lacking, the best witness is the statement that implies a bridal after the festival." [1]

There is definite evidence for a sacred marriage, but it seems to have been connected with an autumn festival ; but the Babylonian calendar is imperfectly known, and the whole body of evidence about the myth and ritual of that country is an incomprehensible jumble to which we lack a large number of the most important clues. Professor Smith in the article just quoted sums up his conclusions as follows : "What can legitimately be regarded as established is that the marriage rite was a state institution, that kings in practice could not, during some periods, neglect it, and that it belonged to a ' pattern ', the sequence of festivals throughout a year." [2]   After some of the confident assertions previously made about myth and ritual in Babylonia, this is a very negative conclusion indeed.

The same caution prevails in the approach to the problem in the religion of the Hittites, in the Ras Shamra tablets and in the origins of Hebrew religion. O. R. Gurney and others see in the *purulli* festival at Nerik, with its ritual dragon-slaying, a weather-ritual very like that which can be surmised in Egypt and Babylonia, but we cannot really be sure at what season the Hittite New Year began ; and in any case the reconstruction and interpretation of parts of the Hittite texts is conjectural, while the texts themselves, particularly those relating to festival rituals, are fragmentary.[3]   The Ras Shamra tablets are even more conjectural

[1] Emeritus Professor S. Smith, " The Practice of Kingship in Early Semitic Kingdoms " in *Myth, Ritual and Kingship*, p. 53.   [2] Op. cit. p. 71.
[3] O. R. Gurney, " Hittite Kingship " in *Myth, Ritual and Kingship*, pp. 107 ff.

in meaning, and R. de Langhe enters the same *caveat* as do Messrs. Brandon, Smith, Gurney and others on excessive theorizing.[1] Here, too, aesthetic considerations begin to creep in. De Langhe's sober scepticism of the theories of Gaster and Kapelrud is an excellent and most readable example of a sane and unbiased approach to a difficult text.[2]

In the realm of Hebrew religion, once again the enthusiasm of Engnell and Mowinckel and Haldar and others is toned down very drastically by scholars such as H. H. Rowley, who perceive the value of the Myth and Ritual theory in establishing the importance and status of the Israelitic king and the existence of traces of cultic hymns in the Psalter, but who cannot detect a true Myth and Ritual pattern in the Old Testament.[3]

We can now approach our Greek material knowing to some extent what we can expect. There should be a mass of evidence for the various constituents of the Myth and Ritual pattern— kingship, the sacred marriage, the combat with the forces of evil, the dying and rising of a god and so forth ; this evidence should come from primitive strata of belief and should survive unexplained or drastically modified and occasionally uncritical application of the Myth and Ritual theory to writings which will not support that theory (this would happen, one supposes, in the mid-thirties, when the Myth and Ritual school was really getting under way) ; and we should expect to find that in spite of attempts to make all the evidence cohere in support of a theory, the facts simply will not fit in to the theory without jagged edges—there are either not enough pieces to complete the puzzle or there are some left over. And that is in fact what we do find.

In 1936 Lord Raglan published a book entitled *The Hero*, which surveyed Norse saga, English and Irish folklore, and Greek mythology in an attempt to prove that all were merely myths that accompanied a ritual drama of the expected kind. The oddities of the theory stand out most conspicuously in his treatment of the Homeric saga.[4] Here we are expected to believe that Achilles and Hector never in fact existed, that the siege of

[1] R. de Langhe, " Myth, Ritual and Kingship in the Ras Shamra Tablets ", in *Myth, Ritual and Kingship*, pp. 130-1.
[2] Op. cit. pp. 122-48.   [3] See H. H. Rowley in *MRK*, pp. 236-60.
[4] Lord Raglan, *The Hero* (London, 1936), pp. 102 ff.

Troy is a fiction and that the *Iliad* and the *Odyssey* were a sung or spoken accompaniment of a mock king-killing. It would seem that no one could read either epic and ever come to a conclusion of this kind.

To begin with, where and at what sort of Greek festival would we expect to find these tales ? Admittedly the first text of Homer seems to date back to the *Panathenaia*, the five-yearly festival of rejoicing and renewal which was restored and re-invigorated by Peisistratus in the sixth century, but even if our present Homer were of that date, there is ample evidence that it incorporates far earlier lays and traditions, and Homer incorporates so much that is quite irrelevant to a ritual drama, and omits so much that would be necessary to it, that the theory must fall down on that account alone.

As to the date of Homer, opinion seems to be hardening in assigning him to the very end of the eighth or the beginning of the seventh century.[1] This agrees very well with literary and archaeological evidence : for example, the first scenes from the Iliad on Athenian vases are of about the middle of the sixth century,[2] and the elegiac and lyric poets of the seventh century, such as Archilochus and Mimnermus, obviously knew him. Recent archaeological work in the Troad continues to confirm the topographical accuracy of the Iliad on points of detail, which it would be absurd to suppose were accidentally and irrelevantly correct in a ritual poem composed in Athens.[3] Even if one were to grant that the *Iliad* and *Odyssey* were composed specially for the *Panathenaia*, they are in no way composed for a ritual in the sense that Lord Raglan intends.

But we have left entirely out of consideration another very powerful argument, that from literary excellence. In Homer for the first time we are confronted with a poem of the very highest quality, which bears every mark of a personally and individually creative mind. The Sumerian and Ugaritic and Babylonian and Egyptian

---

[1] See Wade-Gery, *The Poet of the Iliad* (Oxford, 1952) ; and, for a summary of recent work on Homer, see *Fifty Years of Classical Scholarship* (ed. Platnauer, Oxford, 1954), pp. 1-37.

[2] J. D. Beazley, *The Development of Attic Black-Figure* (Berkeley, California, 1951).

[3] Professor J. M. Cook reported the results of a further exploration of possible sites for the Greek camp at Troy in a paper read to the Archaeological Society of the University of Manchester in November 1960.

ritual texts take us back into a dim semi-articulate world, where formulae are repeated and incantations spelt out, where ugly proper names form the major content of many verses, where, in a word, no one ever seems to show any literary sensibility whatsoever. Contrast the *mleccha*-like grunts of a Ras-Shamra text with the rapidity, the nobility, the simplicity of any passage from the Iliad. The authorship of Homer remains an enigma, but on the evidence for design in both poems examined by Bowra, Nilsson, Schadewaldt, Focke and others [1] ; from the fact that the *Odyssey* never overlaps the *Iliad*, though it fills several gaps in that story ; that both poems show a narrative strategy unsurpassed in any literature, it seems that, whether or not the same person composed them, each was given its present form by a single person with all the resources of a professional bard at his finger-tips, and that the author of the *Odyssey* was intimately acquainted with the *Iliad*.

This point has not indeed been given its due weight by Homeric scholars from Wolf onwards : the art of selection, for instance, is well exampled by the plot of the *Iliad*, which takes one single episode of the Trojan war, the wrath of Achilles over the stealing by Agamemnon of the slave-girl Briseis, and skilfully interweaves events so that the whole panorama of the long-drawn-out war is before us. Again, the poet's delight in his art, his love of storytelling for its own sake, come out in a score of places. Lord Raglan confessed that he could read little or no Greek, and implies that textual scholars, brought up on textual and linguistic training, utterly misunderstand the underlying meaning of Homer. And what of the opinions of a critic who cannot even read the language ?

Even the Norse sagas, which with the Hindu epics form the nearest parallel to Homer, cannot compare with him in literary art ; but there is an instructive parallel here, nevertheless. Both the Norse sagas and the Greek epics were in a sense a case of supply and demand. Both were based on lays written for declamation at the carousals of a warrior clan, with no more concern for myth and ritual than the man in the moon. In *Odyssey* viii,

[1] See Bowra, *Tradition and Design in the Iliad* (Oxford, 1930) ; Nilsson, *Homer and Mycenae* (London, 1953) ; Schadewaldt, *Iliasstudien* (Liepzig, 1938) ; Focke, *Die Odyssee* (Stuttgart, 1943). The most recent study of the problem is by D. L. Page, *History and the Homeric Iliad* (Berkeley, California, 1959).

62 ff. we see an actual banquet portrayed for us, at which the blind bard is led in and placed on a seat of honour, where he proceeds to declaim the mighty deeds of the past—who can doubt the possibility that Homer had himself in mind ?   Everywhere the Aryan invaders went, from Troy to Mohenjo-daro, we see their brutal indifference to the cults and rites of the native popu-lation—*Semisepulta virum curvis feriuntur aratris Ossa* as Ovid says (*Heroides* i. 55-6).[1]   They are utterly outside the influence of the nexus of Near-Eastern religions where alone we find evidence of a sacred kingship and the rest.

The serious and considered judgement of classical scholars, as of the Greeks themselves, has been that the *Iliad* is the epic of a distant campaign with at least a foundation in history ; the exact period does not matter.   Archaeology continues to justify this view ; and Lord Raglan's dictum that no author of a cultic text was ever allowed to invent anything rather hamstrings him in seeking to trace the origins of the Trojan myth.

Why should we not assume that Agamemnon was king and leader of the Greek hosts, each of which comes with its prince, e.g. Achilles and Odysseus, to besiege Troy either because of the rape of some princess or just for the sake of war as the Norsemen invaded our shores ?   That after ten years of intermittent fight-ing, probably including long periods when nothing was happening, Troy was sacked and the conquerors returned home ?   Admit-tedly there are some queer features in the story, but are they made any less queer by treating the whole story as a fairy tale made up to accompany some rite?   Or by seeing a sinister significance in certain items such as the frequent occurrence of the figure ten ?

What objections does Lord Raglan put forward to the simple, straightforward interpretation of the story ?   Or rather, what are his main contentions on this whole question ?   He puts the case in its extreme form, whereas nearly all other writers on the subject of myth and ritual treat the Greek evidence as a weak link in a long chain.   His views are to be found in chapters IX and XV of *The Hero.*

[1] Sir Mortimer Wheeler strongly believes that it was the Aryans who were responsible for the last massacre at Mohenjo-daro. See *The Indus Age*, p. 92 ; " On circumstantial evidence such as this, considered in the light of the chron-ology as now inferred, Indra stands accused."

(1) The details of the siege of Troy, such as the leadership of Agamemnon, the motives for the siege and its duration, are all unlikely ; nothing is known to history of any of the characters in the epic. Therefore it is a myth.

(2) Greek religion in the eighth century B.C. consisted of sacrificial worship of heroes at local shrines combined with the periodic performance of more important and more generalised rites. These, especially the games and contests associated with them, as in *Iliad* xxiii, are survivals from a primitive state of society in which the king was an all-important figure.

(3) The status of the victors in the Olympic games, the title of ἄρχων βασιλεύς at Athens and other signs, suggest that this kingship was of a purely ritual character ; and this attitude to kingship is implicit in Homer and in early Greek myth.

(4) The dramatic ritual represented the death and resurrection of a king who was also a god, performed by priests and members of the royal family. There was a sacred combat followed by a triumphal procession in which the neighbouring gods took part, an enthronement, a ceremony to determine the destinies of the state for the year, and a sacred marriage.[1]

(5) The story of Helen is a myth to explain the worship of Helen in different parts of Greece. Several Homeric heroes were likewise the objects of a cult.

(6) Early peoples have little sense of time and therefore would not picture the events in the *Iliad* as taking place in a remote past, but as something recreated by a rite.

(7) The attacks on Troy and Thebes are so alike that they are probably identical in origin.

(8) The parting of Hector from Andromache and the slaying of Hector are paralleled in the mythology of Java and elsewhere, various incidents in the *Iliad* correspond with known features of maze ritual (Lord Raglan falls into the trap of instancing the entry of the wooden horse, which of course does not occur in Homer), Odysseus visits the dead as part of his progress towards divine kingship (in fact, of course, Odysseus does not visit the dead, but entices the shades to earth), and various incidents in the story of Ajax son of Oileus which again do not occur in Homer (e.g. his violation of Cassandra at the sack of Troy) have a ritual and sacrificial ring.

(9) Therefore the *Iliad* and presumably the *Odyssey* are myths to accompany the ritual enactments of the death and rebirth of a king-god.

Most of these statements would be quite irrelevant even if true ; but many of them, such as (4), are mere assertion un-accompanied by any evidence whatever. Let us take them *seriatim* :

(1) It is misleading to assert that we know nothing historically of Agamemnon and his fellow princes. What little we can gather from Linear B texts shows that at least some Homeric names were known in the fifteenth century B.C., and although it is scarcely fair to urge Linear B against Lord Raglan, yet Mycenae

[1] Here Lord Raglan is obviously following the article by S. H. Hooke, in. *Myth and Ritual*, pp. 8 ff.

is surely circumstantial enough.   Lord Raglan is sceptical because a Dark Age succeeded to that of Homer, which is he says unlikely ; one does not see why.   As to the details of the siege, its motives and its duration being improbable, that is purely a matter of opinion and quite extraneous to the issue.

(2) This is true, but what has it to do with Homer ?   Does Lord Raglan mean that Homer cannot have come from such a background ?   One may refer him once more to the findings of archaeology.

(3) The status of the victors in the games proves nothing, since the games in the *Iliad* are a late and, as some think, extraneous part of the story.   As to the ἄρχων βασιλεύς at Athens, more of him in a moment.   There is little or no evidence that Agamemnon was a ritual king.

(4) This is merely a list of the chief features of the Myth and Ritual pattern in the ancient Near East, with the unsupported assertion that these features are found in Greek religious practice.

(5) The story of the siege of Troy does anything but explain the worship of Helen in various parts of Greece, particularly in Sparta.

(6) Again, there seem no grounds whatever for such a rash assertion.

(7) Even if the stories of Troy and Thebes were very similar (and their likeness has been exaggerated) this would only show that sieges are apt to be alike anyway, and that similar legends accrued in a similar situation.

(8) This contention is sufficiently refuted by the fact that several of the chief incidents which support it are not found in Homer, and that they occur in the Homeric Cycle is not the point.

An obvious difficulty at the outset is, who is the hero or god-king commemorated in the presumed ritual ?   I should have thought Agamemnon or Achilles ; but no, it is now Hector and now Odysseus.   But they cannot both be god-kings celebrated in the same ritual poem, and if the two poems are for separate rituals, why is it that so many incidents are completely irrelevant to the main theme ; e.g. the catalogue of ships, the innumerable battles, the exploits of Odysseus and Diomede, and above all the slaying of Patroclus ?

This is not to say that Homer does not obviously embody primitive tradition in which Myth and Ritual features may have been present. The sacral kingship is the most important element in the whole Myth and Ritual theory, and it can be argued very plausibly that the epic kings had to perform rituals, and had certain characteristics, which may be explained on the theory that they were originally king-gods, champions of the people. It is now certain that the Cretan Zeus, whose name was taken over by the Olympian supreme god, was actually a pre-Greek deity. Furumark argues that it was the Mycenaean Greeks who made the identification when they established themselves in Knossos in about 1475 B.C., and that they simply identified the Cretan supreme god with their own. He adds that the Palai-kastro hymn, which is a true ritual text, shows the μέγιστος κοῦρος to be an annually returning god who by his act of begetting brings fertility, prosperity, peace and justice, and is identified with the Cretan Zeus through his cult-myth. " Birth (the Divine Child motive), death (ridiculed by Callimachus), and resurrection (annual return) belong to the characteristics of this god." [1] Both Furu-mark and E. O. James see in the magnificence of the palace and of the Temple Tomb, the carved throne, the frescoes of griffins (the guardians of the gods), the sacred furnishings, strong evidence that the Minoan king was divine, and infer the rest of his functions as a ritual champion and promoter of fertility and the like.[2] Zeus was in the earliest myth miraculously born and has a body-guard or θίασος of dancers in which Jane Harrison saw evidence of an initiation rite.[3] He kills his father Kronos and usurps his throne, but although at times in the *Iliad* he appears omnipotent, yet τύχη is stronger than he, and it may be that he originally main-tained his power only by some ritual purification or atonement.[4]

[1] Furumark, " Was there a Sacral Kingship in Minoan Crete ? " in *La Regalità Sacra*, a series of papers read at the 8th International Congress of the History of Religions, Rome, 1955 (Leiden, 1959), pp. 369-70.

[2] See E. O. James, *Myth and Ritual in the Ancient Near East*, pp. 101 ff.

[3] Jane Harrison, *Themis* (Cambridge, 1912), pp. 1-29.

[4] A. B. Cook, *Zeus*, vol. iii (Cambridge, 1940), collects a large amount of material, but his conclusions are not universally accepted.

Yet these scholars seem in their busy collection of odd ritual facts and bits of archaeological evidence to overlook entirely certain simple common-sense considerations which would instantly occur to a layman not weighed down with learning.   What do we expect of a king, or what was the character of kingship in the ancient world ?   Some of the exponents of Myth and Ritual seem to think that the ritual came first and that the mysterious Melchizedek-like figures of kings came later-and played the part assigned to them in the ritual.   But it is in human nature to love power and to seek it by conquest and maintain it by cruelty.   We do not need the bland sophistries of Herodotus [1] to tell us that in the long run things tend to revert to dictatorship, and there was certainly nothing mythical or ritual about the atrocities committed by the Sultans of Delhi or by Adolf Hitler.   Once an ancient despot was established on his throne it was natural that he should be regarded as divine : he was the embodiment of supreme power and simple minds would think he could command the weather as well ; so he would find it convenient to accept worship as omnipotent and even to go through the motions of offering sacrifice for fertility and increase in order to keep his subjects contented.   In this sense there may have been a sacral kingship in early Greece, but it has left very few influences of any note on the Greece of the classical period.

In this connection Professor H. J. Rose read an illuminating paper, full of healthy scepticism, to the International Congress for the History of Religions in Rome in 1955.[2]   Archaeology, he says, gives us no warrant for seeing in the Minoan king any sort of ritual figure ; all we know is that he had a magnificent palace which contained a chapel full of sacred emblems and the like. Minoan art never shows us the king in company with the gods or even sacrificing to them, as Oriental art often does.   In any case, we learn from Minos very little about Greece proper.

The gods in Homer are immortal, ἀθάνατοι.   They lead a life in the empyrean, far from care, and amuse themselves by allotting ills to mankind (cf. the Epicurean picture of the gods

---

[1] See his discourse on the three forms of government, iii. 80-2.
[2] H. J. Rose, " The Evidence for Divine Kings in Greece ", in *La Regalità Sacra*, pp. 371-8.

given by Achilles to Priam, *Iliad* xxiv, 525-6). They are completely above even kings, so there can be no question here of identifying a king with a god, for the essence of the Myth and Ritual theory is that the king shall undergo death and revivification in his combat with evil, and so the king and the god are both mortal. Admittedly Homer has Graecized and rationalized the myths, but there is a limit to what would be found acceptable innovation in an epic, and it would be truer to say that the Greek spirit is too rational to tolerate such identification for long. In the *Iliad* Agamemnon receives a good deal of homage on occasion, and no prince speaks in the assembly without holding the sceptre which symbolizes power, but Achilles can speak as sharply as a bargee to Agamemnon as in *Iliad* i. 225 ff. (or is this ritual reviling? I have seen equally absurd suggestions seriously mooted). Possibly Alcinous comes nearest to the ancient conception of a divine king: he married a goddess or at least the daughter of a goddess (*Od.* vii, 66-72) and the devotion which Arete enjoyed is described so emphatically that I am surprised that no one has detected here traces of a *hieros gamos* ; Arete was his cousin, which again suggests the divine in-breeding characteristic of ritual kingship [1] ; Alcinous himself is the " idol " of his people (*Od.* vii. 11), he is divine (167). But he appears quite ignorant of the will of the gods and speaks of placating them with sacrifices like any ordinary human being (vii. 199 ff). No one would dream that he might be a ritual figure without being steeped previously in Myth and Ritual so as to be morbidly vigilant for clues. Rose [2] sees the possibility of a Frazerian king in *Od.* xix. 109 ff, where Odysseus likens Penelope to " a perfect king, ruling a populous and mighty state with the fear of god in his heart, and upholding the right, so that the dark soil yields its wheat and barley, the trees are laden with ripe fruit, the sheep never fail to bring forth their lambs, nor the sea to provide its fish—all as a result of his good government—and his people prosper under him " ; but he adds that there is nothing here more than would be expected of a good and just earthly king.

[1] Among the Incas this was carried so far that a king could only marry his sister ; see P. Radin, " The Sacral Chief among American Indians " in *La Regalità Sacra*, p. 94.   [2] *La Regalità Sacra*, p. 373.

Turning to history, the two kings at Sparta originally had priestly functions, but the duality of kingship, like the duality of the Roman consulship, may have originally been as much military as religious. Kings are often priests in the ancient world, but the division between priest and layman is not so great in some communities as in others—in Greece a priest had no separate status at all apart from honorary offices except as part of the official duty devolving upon a high magistrate. We now come to the Athenian ἄρχων βασιλεύς, who by his title seems at first sight to be the very person we are looking for. The duties of *archon* or ruler in Athens were shared by a body of nine, of whom the first was later called ἐπώνυμος as giving his name to the year, the second βασιλεύς or king and the third πολέμαρχος or war-leader ; the remaining six were called θεσμόθεται or legislators. It used to be thought that the title βασιλεύς referred to the legendary days when kings ruled Athens, but later scholarship seems to run counter to this view and to regard the title as almost wholly connected with religion. For example, the philosopher Heraclitus was made βασιλεύς of Ephesus. The duties of the ἄρχων βασιλεύς at Athens were to preside at the Dionysia, to superintend the Mysteries and to offer up sacrifices at both Athens and Eleusis. Indictments for impiety and controversies about the priesthood were laid before him ; and in cases of murder he brought the trial before the Areopagus and voted with its members. His wife, called queen, βασίλισσα, had to offer certain sacrifices and it was therefore required that she be a citizen of pure stock and previously unmarried.[1] She had to take part in a remarkable sacred marriage with Dionysus at the Anthesteria,[2] but whatever significance there may have been in this was the wrong way round for the Myth and Ritual theorists. The βασιλεύς was merely a magistrate annually elected, and no special significance was attached to his office.

Kings were often called by cult-titles in early Greece as in other Near-Eastern communities. Rose discusses this whole problem in the article already quoted, and makes two important points : firstly, that as regards divine titles the evidence has often

[1] See Pauly's *Real-Encyclopädie*, s.v. Archontes.
[2] Aristotle, Ἀθ. πολ., 3. 5.

been late and uncritically used (he instances Periphas, a king supposedly so ancient that Kekrops had not yet been produced from the earth, yet who appears only in Hellenistic sources and in authors like Ovid who copied them) ; and secondly, that no one theory will account for the numerous kings and prominent figures to whom the name Zeus is at one time or another appended.[1] To this one might add that the important point is whether there are any traces of cult accompanying the myth (in the case of Periphas there are none—Rose sees in him a " faded god whose cult was later absorbed by Zeus or perhaps by Apollo "), and also that such considerations as time and place are significant. Rose explains some of the cult-titles by syncretism : " For example since Zeus is (among other titles) Soter and Soter is also a favourite title of Asklepios, I see no reason why the minor, but enormously popular, god should not have been on occasion identified with the greater one. "   If this explanation sounds a little too verbal, yet by our own experience we can concede that it would be easy to imagine each god in turn as the only true and great god, of whom all the other god-kings and god-men are aspects.

There are legends in Greek epic which conform to the requirements of a ritual myth, but it seems that a hero is more often than a king looked upon as the champion of a people against the forces of destruction. Glaucus in *Iliad* vi. 152 ff tells Diomede how queen Anteia, the wife of Proetus king of Ephyre in Argos, fell in love with the young nobleman Bellerophon, was repulsed and forthwith lied to her husband with the result that Bellerophon was sent to Lycia with sealed tablets instructing the king of Lycia to kill him.   Bellerophon is set a number of superhuman tasks, all of which he accomplishes.   This familiar theme, which recurs in the stories of Jason and Heracles, is taken by Raglan and others to indicate a struggle between a hero-king and the forces of destruction, which was ritually enacted for the purpose of securing the fertility of the land for another year. The old charioteer Phoenix tells a similar story about himself in *Iliad* ix. 434 ff., the chief features of which are that he obtains the love of his father's paramour, is driven away by his father in consequence and entertains thoughts of murdering him.   This

[1] *La Regalità Sacra*, pp. 373-4.

looks like an even more primitive form of the story with elements akin to the legend of Oedipus. Yet with all this I cannot help the suspicion that these tales are told for their own sake to a delighted audience who have no interest whatever in myth and ritual.

Did the hero-cult, which reached its peak in the Games, originate in a sacred combat for the renewal of fertility? In its essentials we have a young man such as Theseus or Jason or Heracles, himself of divine or semi-divine parenthood, undergoing various labours for various peoples in the course of which he comes near to losing his life. A noteworthy feature here, and one which militates somewhat against the Myth and Ritual interpretation of the story, is the vagrancy of the hero, who appears as a kind of strong man out of the West, the kind of champion who in a diluted form enjoys much popularity nowadays in such incarnations as the Lone Ranger (and incidentally the Lone Ranger is a good test case—is he or is he not a cult figure? And if he is, who cares about this when watching his exploits on television?)

Of this kind of hero the outstanding example is of course Heracles, the son of Zeus and Alcmene according to Homer. As he lies in his cradle Hera sends two serpents to destroy him, but he strangles them with his bare hands. Throughout his career he is liable to outbursts of primitive violence ; thus he is instructed by the youth Linos in lyre-playing, but kills him after receiving a rebuke, and is then sent by Amphitryon, who is instructing him in chariot-driving, to look after cattle. After various pugilistic adventures he is driven mad by Hera and kills his own children. As a purification he is ordered by the Delphic priestess to serve Eurystheus of Tiryns for twelve years. During this time he performs his twelve labours, all of which involve the destruction of a national scourge, and one of which includes a journey to the underworld to bring back Cerberus. Heracles marries Deianeira the daughter of Oineus after fighting with the river Achelous for her (I do not know if there is a ritual significance in fighting with rivers). He accidentally kills a lad Eunomus and goes into exile, in the course of which the centaur Nessus attacks Deianeira and is killed by a poisoned arrow. The dying centaur calls to Deianeira to take his blood with her as a sure means of retaining the love of her husband ; Heracles carries off Iole the daughter of Eurytus of Oechalia and comes to Euboea whence he sends his companion Lichas to Trachis for a white garment which he intends to put on for sacrifice. Deaineira, thinking it is for Iole, steeps the garment in the blood of Nessus, and when he puts it on Heracles suffers the most excruciating agony. He immolates himself on a pyre on Mount Oeta and is received into Olympus where he marries Hebe the daughter of Hera. And yet he is not at home on Olympus, for Homer makes Odysseus see him in Hades and be puzzled thereat : " Next I observed the mighty Heracles—that is, his shade, since he himself banquets with the immortal gods and has for consort Hebe " (*Od.* xi. 601 ff).[1]

One obvious fact emerging from all this is that the Heracles legend is in reality a collection of stories of various dates and places all gathered round the one name, and, one may suspect, often merely variants of the same story. The descent into Hades is very like the sacred combat, but it is also told of Theseus and Orpheus, and the point that matters is, Had the story any ritual significance at the time of our literary sources ? The answer is surely very little. Euripides uses in the *Alcestis* a primitive myth about Heracles fighting with death, and here it does seem that there is a very strong cultic flavour about the story, which was almost certainly taken over by Euripides from a very early source, as was his wont. Jane Harrison collected evidence to show that Heracles was originally a year *daimon*.[2] His labours are twelve, a significant number for astronomy and the calendar. His club was originally a bough from a living tree, and in an Orphic hymn is referred to as banishing the Keres or fates ; in the left hand he is sometimes represented with a cornucopia which he broke off from the river Achelous when it fought him in the shape of a bull. The wooing of Deianeira may be a *hieros gamos* or ritual marriage. Herodotus remarks (ii. 44) that his researches prove Heracles to be a figure of great antiquity and quotes with approval those

[1] A convenient summary of the legends about Heracles will be found in the *Oxford Classical Dictionary*, s.v.

[2] Harrison, *Themis*, chap. ix.

Greeks who see him as a dual figure, both god and hero, and who worship these aspects of him in separate temples. Diodorus Siculus (iv. 39) says that at Opous the inhabitants were ordered to make a yearly sacrifice in honour of the hero Heracles. It seems, then, that Heracles is more of a Myth and Ritual figure than Agamemnon.

The origin of the Olympic Games has been dealt with by F. M. Cornford in a separate chapter of *Themis*. His conclusions are that the games were originally an annual or quadrennial sacrifice ritual, and in essence a New Year festival, the inauguration of a year. The traditional myth was that Pelops beat Oenomaus in a chariot race in which Oenomaus had been wont to pursue and slay all suitors for his daughter Hippodameia. At the funeral of Oenomaus Pelops held magnificent games. Here one can recognize the contest between young and old kings, so central a feature of the myth and ritual of death and rebirth, a theme which has been carried to such lengths by Margaret Murray that she sees in the deaths of William Rufus, John, Edward II and Richard II the ritual slaying of a king of declining powers.[1] There is also the *harpage* or carrying-off of the bride, possibly some survival of a sacred marriage.

A. B. Cook once suggested that in mythical times the Olympic contest was a means of deciding who should be king of the district and champion of the local tree-Zeus.[2] In historic times the victor was treated with divine honours, feasted in the prytaneum, crowned with a spray of olive like the wreath of Zeus, and when he returned to his native city he was dressed in royal purple and drawn by white horses through a breach in the walls (honours almost as extravagant are paid to the winning football team in the cup final at Wembley). In some cases he was worshipped after death as a hero ; and this may be because he was once thought to be incarnate god. Plutarch (*Symposium*, v. 2. 675) says : " I hesitate to mention that in ancient times there was also held at Pisa a contest consisting of a single combat, which ended only with the slaughter and death of the vanquished."

---

[1] Margaret Murray, " The Divine King ", in *La Regalità Sacra*, pp. 595-608.

[2] See *Classical Review*, xvii. 268 ff. Professor Cook's views have, of course, been elaborated, and an immense amount of material collected, in his *Zeus*.

The word " year " does not necessarily denote a solar year, for Servius on *Aen*. iii. 284 remarks that " the ancients computed their time by the heavenly bodies and at first called a period of thirty days a lunar year ". There is little evidence of the variation of meaning of the Greek word ἔτος, but it is possible that the four-year period constituting an Olympiad may be a survival of a longer year. The difficulty here is to reconcile a longer year with the renewal of fertility in men, animals and crops, a ceremony which would necessarily take place each year. A fifth-century *krater* in Chicago [1] shows Salmoneus, a weather-king arrayed with the attributes of an Olympic victor, wearing a fetter on his left ankle, and there are traces of a κρόνος πεδητής who was released annually at the winter festival. Cornford's explanation, if it can be called such, is that the single combat and possibly the whole festival may have originally taken place in midwinter, but that every forty-nine or fifty months the lunar year of 354 days and the solar year of 365¼ days coincided by the addition of intercalary months, and that at some time a fresh " great year " was inaugurated, beginning in midsummer.

Other features in the development of the Games may be briefly noted : Pausanias (v, 7, 6) sees in the games a celebration of the birth of the Cretan Zeus, at which the Kouretes danced ; Pindar relates in this connection the legend of Tantalus serving up to the gods the body of his son Pelops boiled in a cauldron ; Zeus' miraculous restoring of the child is taken by Cornford as an ritual of new birth preceded by a symbolic and counterfeit death. This gives us, he says, the ritual needed to complete the religion of the mother and child and the Kouretes in the Idaean cave beneath the hill of Kronos. There are several myths of the eating of children, Thyestes, Kronos, Zeus, and Cornford connects this with the succession to an annual or periodic kingdom.

To sum up, Cornford's conclusions about the Victor and the Hero : the triumphal procession, with its sacrifice and eating of a bull, the hymn to the hero and the concluding feast in the banqueting chamber, was the central rite and the foot-race was a preliminary. The race was originally run to determine who should be the greatest Kouros or king of his year, but developed

[1] See Harrison, *Themis*, p. 80.

into the vast sports of classical times. Even in historic times there is evidence that the person of the victor was not of primary importance. The earliest salute to the victor was " Hail, king Heracles ! " and even in Pindar's Odes there is a personal reference only at the beginning and the end. The rest is occupied with the deeds of ancestors and the δαίμων γενέθλιος or genius of his house, and it is this δαίμων incarnate which is the real subject of commemoration. Cornford draws the analogy here between the victory ode and tragedy. Both—and this is even more true of early tragedy—begin with a ritual to which the accompanying myth is secondary.

At least part of the expiation for past sins in Greece as in Israel and other countries devolved upon the φαρμακός or scape-goat, literally " remedy ".[1] In *Iliad*, ii. 217 ff., 258 ff., we come across a man who might have been drawn for the part, Thersites. He was the ugliest man to come to Ilium. He had a game foot and was bandy-legged. His rounded shoulders almost met across his chest ; and above them rose an egg-shaped head, which sprouted a few short hairs. Achilles and Odysseus were his favourite butts. He rails at Agamemnon, and Odysseus threatens to strip him naked and cast him out of the assembly to blubber by the ships.

In various Greek states the φαρμακός was loaded with insults and driven forth from men. In Harpocration's lexicon we read that in Athens at the Thargelia (the harvest of first-fruits in May and June) they led out two men as καθάρσια or purifications for the city, one for the men and one for the women ; he gives an explanation involving a φαρμακός who had stolen cups from Apollo and was killed in consequence, and adds καὶ τὰ τοῖς θαργηλίοις ἀγόμενα τούτων ἀπομίμηματά ἐστιν, the ceremony at the Thargelia was an imitation of this. Helladius in the lexicon of Photius agrees with this account. The ceremony of casting out the φαρμακός may at one time have involved human sacrifice, and Rohde thought that several allusions in the lyric and comic poets of the classical period showed that this was still true, but Murray argued that the language involved no more than a mimetic ceremony.[2] The

[1] See J. G. Frazer, *The Golden Bough*, part vi (*The Scapegoat*) ; G. Murray, *The Rise of the Greek Epic* (3rd edn., Oxford, 1924), Appendix A.
[2] Rohde, *Psyche* (4th edn., Tubingen, 1907), pp. 406 ff.

significance of the φαρμακός is that he is a sin-offering to a god who is not wholly but at least partly " other ", and cannot very well exist side by side with a king-god who dies and is reborn as champion of his people and the expiator of their sins. The motive may have been the same but the conception was quite different.

There were two strains in the blood of the Greek : the indigenous, pastoral strain, reflected in myths such as that of Demeter, and the nomadic, active strain evidenced in the Achaean invasions and reflected in Homer. In the legend of Demeter and Persephone we find another variant of the myth of the mother-goddess which, as we have seen, is evidenced as early as the fourth millennium B.C. There are many representations of this goddess in Minoan and Mycenaean art. The general opinion, held, e.g. by Nilsson, Farnell and Picard,[1] is that the goddess represents the earth and the young god who is seen with her is sacrificed and born again. The goddess appears under a variety of names, Rhea, Britomartis, Dictynna, Aphaia, and in various guises as divine mother, as protectress of animals and as a warrior goddess. Sir Arthur Evans gives representatives of her worship by Zeus or Zagreus,[2] and Axel W. Persson claims to detect a cycle in the worship of this deity from Mycenaean rings.[3] He affects to find on these rings mourning ceremonies connected with a burial in which dying vegetation is portrayed ; dances and the giving of gifts ; various forms of thanksgiving at the return of spring, budding flowers, rain and decorated shrines ; bull games ; a summer festival showing both god and goddess ; and the goddess of fertility departing over the sea in a divine boat. Aphaia, Aphrodite, Ariadne, Artemis, Demeter, Eileithuia, Helen, Persephone—all are worshipped under this guise ; and we find Dionysos, Erichthonios, Eros, Glaukos, Hyacinthos, Cronos and the Cretan Zeus at times in the rôle of the youthful god.

[1] L. R. Farnell, *Cults of the Greek States* (Oxford, 1921), chaps. i-iv ; M. P. Nilsson, *Minoan-Mycenaean Religion* (London, 1927), chap. i ; Picard, *Les Religions Préhelléniques* (Paris, 1948), 74-80, 111 ff.

[2] Evans, *The Palace of Minos*, vols. iii and iv.

[3] A. W. Persson, *The Religion of Greece in Prehistoric Times* (Berkeley, California, 1942), pp. 25-104.

The Eleusinian mysteries are a vast subject and do not afford much help to the seeker after the conventional Myth and Ritual pattern. They originated in a festival of the sowing, which took place in Boedromion (Sept./Oct.), and if the Homeric Hymn to Demeter is a cult-text, as it very well may be, we are presented with a goddess-figure, Persephone, to typify the death and re-birth of the year. She is a very ancient figure, almost as terrifying as the Zhob figurines which Stuart Piggott found in Baluchistan ; in Homer she is always the " dread goddess " whose name is coupled with that of Hades as passing judgement on the dead when they reached the underworld.[1] In the Homeric Hymn all this primitive awe is dispelled and we find an innocent maiden who reminds us of *The Winter's Tale*. The whole hymn is full of forward-looking allusions to the Mysteries, but we are still in ignorance of what was disclosed to initiates. It may be that one might seek an analogy with the democratization of Egyptian religion associated with Osiris in the assurance of personal im-mortality, which was the greatest gift conferred at Eleusis. A young god or goddess dies, is lamented and rises again by mira-culous means, and the rejoicing over his resurrection may include a sacred marriage between the god and a mortal, in this case the wife of the *archon basileus*. But whether this is a marriage of the " Myth and Ritual " kind, what significance it had for the participants, to what extent it was influenced by foreign cults, are questions to which there is no final answer.

One important point to stress in conclusion is that the myth of the king-god, though it left certain traces in older Greek legend, had no lasting or deep influence on Greek religion and certainly not on its literature. The *Iliad* remains a great poem ranking with the *Aeneid*, *Paradise Lost* and *La Divina Commedia*, and its morality and outlook are to be classed with theirs. A malady of our present age is that we now know about the Subconscious and that, brought up on Freud, we see in religion no more than " beastly devices of the heathen ". There is something alien and repellent about the Sumerian gods, about Marduk and the Pharaonic king-god, about the Eye-Goddess and Moloch and Baal ; we do not regard them any the more favourably for

[1] E.g. *Od.* xi. 213, 635.

knowing more about them. The nineteenth-century interpreters of the Classics got more out of them than we do because they went straight to the noble and rational and uplifting things which are the real legacy of Greek literature and did not probe into the primeval slime from which it emerged. The same is true of the Christian religion ; it was once said of Frazer that the worst kind of Polynesian superstition would fare better at his hands than evangelical Christianity, and his school of interpretation has certainly done harm as well as good in focussing attention on the often degrading and worthless cults of remote tribes instead of on the central phenomena of religion in contemporary society. It is pleasing to think that a sober and sceptical judgement finds little to justify wild theories about the presence of the Myth and Ritual pattern in Greek literature.

PRINTED IN GREAT BRITAIN AT
THE UNIVERSITY PRESS
ABERDEEN

HAMLET AND ORESTES

A STUDY IN TRADITIONAL TYPES

By GILBERT MURRAY, LL.D., D.LITT.

FELLOW OF THE ACADEMY

June 23, 1914

I

I AM no Shakespearian scholar; and if I have ventured, at the invitation of the Academy, to accept the perilous honour of delivering its Annual Shakespeare Lecture in succession to lecturers, and in the presence of listeners, whose authority on this subject is far greater than mine, it is for a definite reason. In studying the general development of Tragedy, Greek, English, French and Mediaeval Latin, I have found myself haunted by a curious problem, difficult to state in exact terms and perhaps impossible to answer, which I should much like to lay before an audience such as this. It concerns the inter-action of two elements in Literature, and especially in Drama, which is a very primitive and instinctive kind of literature: I mean the two elements of tradition and invention, or the unconscious and the conscious. The problem has been raised in three quite recent discussions: I mention them in chronological order. My own note on the *Ritual Forms in Greek Tragedy*, printed in Miss Harrison's *Themis*; Mr. F. M. Cornford's book on the *Origin of Attic Comedy*; and a course of lectures given at Oxford by Miss Spens of Lady Margaret Hall on *The Scapegoat in Tragedy*, which I hope to see published next year. I am not proposing to-night to argue in favour of the theories propounded in any of these treatises. I am rather considering, in one salient instance, a large question which seems to underlie them. As for my own tentative answer to the problem, I will only mention that it has received in private two criticisms. One friend has assured me that every one knew it before; another has observed that most learned men, sooner or later, go a little mad on some subject or other, and that I am just about the right age to begin.

My subject is the study of two great tragic characters, Hamlet and Orestes, regarded as Traditional Types.   I do not compare play with play, but simply character with character, though in the course of the comparison I shall of course consider the situations in which my heroes are placed and the other persons with whom they are associated.

Orestes in Greek is very clearly a traditional character.   He occurs in poem after poem, in tragedy after tragedy, varying slightly in each one but always true to type.   He is, I think, the most central and typical tragic hero on the Greek stage ; and he occurs in no less than seven of our extant tragedies—eight if we count the *Iphigenia in Aulis,* where he is an infant—whereas Oedipus, for instance, only comes in three and Agamemnon in four.   I shall use all these seven plays as material : viz. Aeschylus, *Choephori* and *Eumenides* ; Sophocles, *Electra* ; and Euripides, *Electra, Orestes, Iphigenia in Tauris,* and *Andromache.*   And before any of these plays was written Orestes was firmly fixed both in religious worship and in epic and lyric tradition.

As for Hamlet, I note in passing the well-known fragments of evidence which indicate the existence of a *Hamlet*-tragedy before the publication of Shakespeare's Second Quarto in 1604.

These are, counting backwards : a phrase in Dekker's *Satiromastix,* 1602, ' My name 's Hamlet : Revenge ! '

1598. Gabriel Harvey's remarks about Shakespeare's *Hamlet.* The true date of this entry is disputed.

1596. Lodge, *Wit's Miserie and the World's Madness* : ' he looks as pale as the ghost which cried so miserally at the theator like an oysterwife, Hamlet, revenge.'

1594. Henslowe's Diary records a play called *Hamlet* as acted at Newington Butts Theatre on June 9.

The earliest reference seems to be in Nash's *Epistle* prefixed to Greene's *Menaphon* : it is dated 1589, but was perhaps printed in 1587. ' Yet English Seneca read by candle light yeeldes many good sentences, as Bloud is a beggar, and so foorth : and if you intreate him faire in a frosty morning, he will affoord you whole Hamlets, I should say handfulls of tragicall speeches.'

The play of *Hamlet* is extant in three main forms :

The First Quarto, dated 1603 but perhaps printed in 1602.   It is entitled ' *The Tragicall Historie of Hamlet Prince of Denmark* by William Shake-speare, As it hath been at divers times acted by his Highnesse servants in the Cittie of London : as also in the two Vniversities of Cambridge and Oxford and else-where '.   It is much shorter than the *Hamlet* which we commonly read, having only 2,143 lines, many of them incomplete, as against the 3,891 of the Globe edition. It differs from our version also in the order of the scenes and to some extent in plot. For instance, the Queen's innocence of her husband's murder is made quite explicit: when she hears how it was wrought she exclaims:

> But, as I have a soul, I swear by Heaven
> I never knew of this most horride murder;

and thereafter she acts confidentially with Hamlet and Horatio. Also some of the names are different: for Polonius we have Corambis, and for Reynaldo Montano.

The Second Quarto, dated 1604, describes itself as 'enlarged to almoste as much againe as it was, according to the true and perfecte coppie'.

Thirdly, there is the Folio of 1623. This omits a good deal that was in the Second Quarto, and contains some passages which are not in that edition but have their parallels in the First Quarto.

Thus *Hamlet*, like most of the great Elizabethan plays, presents itself to us as a whole that has been gradually built up, not as a single definitive creation made by one man in one effort. There was an old play called *Hamlet* extant about 1587, perhaps by Kyd or another. It was worked over and improved by Shakespeare; improved doubtless again and again in the course of its different productions. We can trace additions; we can even trace changes of mind or repentances, as when the Folio of 1623 goes back to a discarded passage in the First Quarto. It is a live and growing play; apt no doubt to be slightly different at each performance, and growing steadily more profound, more rich, and more varied in its appeal.

And before it was an English play, it was a Scandinavian story: a very ancient Northern tale, not invented by any one, but just living, and doubtless from time to time growing and decaying, in oral tradition. It is recorded at length, of course with some remodelling, both conscious and unconscious, by Saxo Grammaticus in his great *History of the Danes*, *Gesta Danorum*, Books III and IV. Saxo wrote about the year 1185; he calls his hero Amlethus, or Amloði, prince of Jutland, and has worked in material that seems to come from the classical story of Brutus—Brutus the Fool, who cast out the Tarquins—and the deeds of Anlaf Curan, king of Ireland. But the story of Hamlet existed long before Saxo; for the Prose Edda happens to quote a song by the poet Snaebjørn, composed about 980, with a reference to 'Amloði'. And it must mean our Amloði; for our Amloði in his pretended madness was a great riddle-maker, and the song refers to one of his best riddles. He speaks in Saxo of the sand as meal ground by the sea; and Snaebjørn's song calls the sea 'Amloði's meal-bin'.

Besides Saxo we have a later form of the same legend in the Icelandic *Ambales Saga*. The earliest extant manuscripts of this belong to the seventeenth century.

Thus our sources for Hamlet will be (1) the various versions of the play known to us, (2) the story in Saxo Grammaticus and the *Ambales Saga*, and (3) some occasional variants of these sagas.[1]

II

Now to our comparison.

1. The general situation. In all the versions, both Northern and Greek, the hero is the son of a king who has been murdered and succeeded on the throne by a younger kinsman—a cousin, Aegisthus, in the Greek; a younger brother, Feng or Claudius, in the Northern. The dead king's wife has married his murderer. The hero, driven by supernatural commands, undertakes and carries through the duty of vengeance.

In Shakespeare the hero dies as his vengeance is accomplished; but this seems to be an innovation. In Saxo, *Ambales*, and the Greek he duly succeeds to the kingdom. In Saxo there is no mention of a ghost; the duty of vengeance is perhaps accepted as natural. In *Ambales*, however, there are angels; in the English, a ghost; in the Greek, dreams and visions of the dead father, and an oracle.

2. In all versions of the story there is some shyness about the mother-murder. In Saxo the mother is not slain; in Shakespeare she is slain by accident, not deliberately murdered; in *Ambales* she is warned and leaves the burning Hall just in time. In one of the variants the mother refuses to leave the Hall and is burnt with her husband.[2] In the Greek versions she is deliberately slain, but the horror of the deed unseats the hero's reason. We shall consider this mother more at length later on.

3. In all the versions the hero is in some way under the shadow of madness. This is immensely important, indeed essential, in his whole dramatic character. It is present in all the versions, but is somewhat different in each.

[1] There are, of course, numerous variants and offshoots of the Hamlet story. See *Corpus Hamleticum* by Professor Josef Schick of Munich. Only vol. i, *Das Glückskind mit dem Todesbrief* (1912), seems to be out.

[2] Halfdan is killed by his brother Frodi, who also takes his wife. Halfdan's sons Helgi and Hroar eventually burn Frodi at a feast. See Professor Elton's appendix to his translation of Saxo, edited by York Powell.

In *Hamlet* the madness is assumed, but I trust I am safe in saying that there is something in the hero's character which at least makes one wonder if it is entirely assumed. I think the same may be said of Amloði and Ambales.

In the Greek the complete madness only comes as a result of the mother-murder; yet here too there is that in the hero's character which makes it easy for him to go mad. In the *Choephori*, where we see him before the deed, he is not normal. His language is strange and broken amid its amazing eloquence; he is a haunted man. In other plays, after the deed, he is seldom actually raving. But, like Hamlet, in his mother's chamber he sees visions which others cannot:

> You see them not: 'tis only I that see

(*Cho.* 1061, cf. *Or.* 255–79); he indulges freely in soliloquies (*I. T.* 77–94, *El.* 367–90; cf. *I. T.* 940–78; *Cho.* 268–305 and last scene); especially, like Hamlet, he is subject to paralysing doubts and hesitations, alternating with hot fits. For instance, once in the *Iphigenia* he suddenly wishes to fly and give up his whole enterprise and has to be checked by Pylades (*I. T.* 93–103):

> O God, where hast thou brought me? what new snare
> Is this?—I slew my mother, I avenged
> My father at thy bidding. I have ranged
> A homeless world, hunted by shapes of pain. . . .
> . . . We still have time to fly for home,
> Back to the galley quick, ere worse things come.

> PYLADES
> To fly we dare not, brother: 'tis a thing
> Not of our custom.

Again, in the *Electra* he suspects that the God who commands him to take vengeance may be an evil spirit in disguise:

> How if some fiend of Hell
> Hid in God's likeness spake that oracle?

(*El.* 979; cf. *Hamlet*, II. 2:

> The spirit that I have seen
> May be the devil).

At the moment before the actual crisis he is seized with horror and tries to hold back. In the *Choephori* this is given in a line or two: 'Pylades, what am I do? Let me spare my mother!'—or 'Shall I spare', if we put a query at the end of the line (*Cho.* 899). In the *Electra* it is a whole scene, where he actually for the moment forgets what it is that he has to do; he only remembers that it has something to do with his mother.

313

The scene is so characteristic that I must quote several lines of it. Aegisthus has just been slain: Clytemnestra is seen approaching (*Electra*, 962–87).

ORESTES

What would we with our mother? . . . Didst thou say
Kill her?

ELECTRA

What? Is it pity? . . . Dost thou fear
To see thy mother's shape?

ORESTES

'Twas she that bare
My body into life. She gave me suck.
How can I strike her?

ELECTRA

Strike her as she struck
Our father!

ORESTES (*to himself, brooding*)

Phoebus, God, was all thy mind
Turned unto darkness?

ELECTRA

If thy God be blind,
Shalt thou have light?

ORESTES (*as before*)

Thou, Thou, didst bid me kill
My mother: which is sin.

ELECTRA

How brings it ill
To thee, to raise our father from the dust?

ORESTES

I was a clean man once. . . . Shall I be thrust
From men's sight, blotted with her blood? . . .

Again he vows, too late, after the mother-murder, that his Father's Ghost, if it had known all, would never have urged him to such a deed; it would rather

have knelt down
And hung his wreath of prayers about my beard,
To leave him unavenged

(*Or.* 288–93). In Hamlet this belief is made a fact; the Ghost specially charges him not to kill Gertrude:

Taint not thy mind, nor let thy soul contrive
Against thy Mother aught

(*Hamlet*, I. 5; cf. also the tone in III. 4).

Is it too much to say that, in all these strangely characteristic speeches of Orestes, every line might have been spoken by Hamlet, and hardly a line by any other tragic character except those directly influenced by Orestes or Hamlet?

Now what do we find in the sagas? Both in Saxo and in *Ambales* the madness is assumed, entirely or mainly, but in its quality also it is utterly different. Hamlet in both sagas is not a highly wrought and sensitive man with his mind shaken by a terrible experience, he is simply a Fool, a gross Jester, covered with dirt and ashes, grinning and mowing and eating like a hog, spared by the murderer simply because he is too witless to be dangerous. The name 'Amlođi' itself means a fool. This side is emphasized most in *Ambales*, but it is clear enough in Saxo also and explains why he has combined his hero with the Fool Brutus. Hamlet is a Fool, though his folly is partly assumed and hides superhuman cunning.

4. The Fool. It is very remarkable that Shakespeare, who did such wonders in his idealized and half-mystic treatment of the real Fool, should also have made his greatest tragic hero out of a Fool transfigured. Let us spend a few moments on noticing the remains of the old Fool characteristics that subsist in the transfigured hero of the tragedies. For one thing, as has often been remarked, Hamlet's actual language is at times exactly that of the regular Shakespearian Fool: e.g. with Polonius in II. 2 ; just before the play in III. 2, and after. But apart from that, there are other significant elements.

(a) The Fool's Disguise. Amlođi and Brutus and Shakespeare's Hamlet feign madness ; Orestes does not. Yet the element of disguise is very strong in Orestes. He is always disguising his feelings: he does so in the *Choephori*, Sophocles' *Electra*, Euripides' *Electra* and *Iphigenia in Tauris*. In two passages further, *Andromache* 980 and *I.T.* 956, he narrates how, in other circumstances, he had to disguise them :

I suffered in silence and made pretence not to see.

I suffered, Oh, I suffered ; but as things drove me I endured.

This is like Shakespeare's Hamlet. It is also very like the saga Hamlet, who laughs in pretended idiocy to see his brother hanged.

Again, it is a marked feature of Orestes to be present in disguise, especially when he is supposed to be dead, and then at some crisis to reveal himself with startling effect. He is apt to be greeted by such words as 'Undreamed of phantom!' or 'Who is this risen from the dead?' (*Or.* 879, 385, 478 f. ; *I.T.* 1361, cf. 1321 ; *Andr.* 884). He is present disguised and unknown in the *Choephori*, Sophocles' *Electra*, Euripides' *Electra* and *Iphigenia in Tauris* ; he is in nearly every case supposed to be dead.   In the *Choephori* and Sophocles' *Electra* he brings the funeral urn that is supposed to contain his own ashes; in the *Iphigenia* he interrupts his own funeral rites.

No other character in Greek Tragedy behaves in this extraordinary way.   But Saxo's Amloði does.   When Amloði goes to England he is supposed to be dead, and his funeral feast is in progress, when he walks in, 'striking all men utterly aghast' (Saxo, 95).

In *Hamlet* there is surely a remnant of this motive, considerably softened.   In Act V. 2, the Gravedigger scene, Hamlet has been present in disguise while the gravedigger and the public thought he was in England, and the King and his confidants must have believed him dead, as they do in Saxo.   Then comes the Funeral—not his own but Ophelia's; he stays hidden for a time, and then springs out revealing himself: 'This is I, Hamlet the Dane!'   The words seem like an echo of that cry that is so common in the Greek tragedies: '' Tis I, Orestes, Agamemnon's son!' (*Andr.* 884; *I. T.* 1361; cf. *Cho.* 212 ff.; *El.* 220; also the recognition scenes).   And one is reminded, too, of the quotation from the pre-Shakespearian *Hamlet* in Dekker's *Satiromastix* of 1602: 'My name's Hamlet! Revenge!'   I suspect that these melodramatic appearances were perhaps more prominent in the tradition before Shakespeare.

(*b*) The Disorder of the Fool.   This disguise motive has led us away from the Fool, though it is closely connected with him. Another curious element of the Fool that lingers on is his dirtiness and disorder in dress.   Saxo says that Amloði 'remained always in his mother's house, utterly listless and unclean, flinging himself on the ground and bespattering his person with foul dirt' (Saxo, 88). Ambales was worse; enough to say that he slept in his mother's room and 'ashes and filth reeked off him' (*Ambales*, pp. 73–5, 77). We remember Ophelia's description of Hamlet's coming to her chamber

> his doublet all unbraced;
> No hat upon his head; his stockings fouled,
> Ungartered and down-gyvèd to the ankle,
> Pale as his shirt . . .

Similarly Orestes, at the beginning of the play that bears his name, is found with his sister, ghastly pale, with foam on his mouth, gouts of rheum in his eyes, his long hair matted with dirt and 'made wild with long unwashenness'.   'Poor curls, poor filthy face', his sister says to him (*Or.* 219–26).   In the *Electra*, too, he is taken for a brigand (*El.* 219), which suggests some lack of neatness in dress; in the *I. T.* we hear of his foaming at the mouth and rolling on the ground (307 f.).   In both plays, it is true, Orestes carries with him an air of princely birth, but so, no doubt, did Hamlet, whatever state his stockings were in.

(c) The Fool's Rudeness of Speech.   Besides being dirty and talking in riddles the Fool was abusive and gross in his language.   This is the case to some degree in Saxo, though no doubt the monk has softened Amloði's words.   It is much emphasized in Ambales. That hero's language is habitually outrageous, especially to women. This outrageousness of speech has clearly descended to Hamlet, in whom it seems to be definitely intended as a morbid trait.   He is obsessed by revolting images.   He does

> like a whore unpack his heart in words
> And fall a-cursing like a very drab,

and he rages at himself because of it.

(d) The Fool on Women.   Now the general style of Greek tragedy will not admit any gross language.   So Orestes has lost this trait.   But a trace of it perhaps remains.   Both Orestes and Hamlet are given to expressing violently cynical opinions about women (Or. 246–51, 566–72, 935–42).   The Orestes bristles with parallels to the ravings of Hamlet's 'Get-thee-to-a-Nunnery' scene (III. 1).   The hero is haunted by his ' most pernicious woman '.   All women want to murder their husbands; it is only a question of time.   Then they will fly in tears to their children, show their breasts and cry for sympathy. We may, perhaps, couple with these passages the famous speech (Or. 552 ff. based on Apollo's ruling in the Eumenides), where he denies any blood relationship with his mother; and the horrible mad line where he says he could never weary of killing evil women (Or. 1590).

Both heroes also tend—if I may use such an expression—to bully any woman they are left alone with.   Amloði in Saxo mishandles his foster-sister—though the passage is obscure—and utters violent reproaches to the Queen.   (The scene is taken over by Shakespeare.) Ambales is habitually misbehaving in this way.   Hamlet bullies Ophelia cruelly and 'speaks daggers' to the Queen.   He never meets any other woman.   Orestes is very surly to Iphigenia (I. T. 482 ff.); draws his sword on Electra in one play, and takes her for a devil in another (El. 220 ff.; Or. 264); holds his dagger at the throat of Hermione till she faints (Or. 1575 ff.); denounces, threatens, and kills Clytemnestra, and tries to kill Helen.   There are not many tragic heroes with such an extreme anti-feminist record.

The above, I think, are all of them elements that go deep down into the character of the hero as a stage figure.   I will now add some slighter and more external coincidences.

1. In both traditions the hero has been away from home when the main drama begins, Orestes in Phocis, Hamlet in Wittenberg.   This point, as we shall see later, has some significance.

2. The hero in both traditions—and in both rather strangely—goes on a ship, is captured by enemies who want to kill him, but escapes. And as Hamlet has a sort of double escape, first from the King's treacherous letter, and next from the pirates, so Orestes in the *Iphigenia* escapes once from the Taurians who catch him on the shore, and again from the pursuers in the ship.   Ambales has similar adventures at sea ; and the original Amloði seems to have had nautical connexions, since the sea was his meal-bin, and the ship's rudder his knife.[1]

3. Much more curious, and indeed extraordinary, is the following point, which occurs in Saxo, *Ambales*, and the Greek, but not in Shakespeare.   We have seen that the hero is always a good deal connected with the dead and graves and ghosts and funerals.   Now in the sagas he on one occasion wins a great battle after a preliminary defeat by a somewhat ghastly stratagem.   He picks up his dead—or his dead and wounded—and ties them upright to stakes and rocks, so that when his pursuers renew their attack they find themselves affronted by an army of dead men standing upright, and fly in dismay.   Now in *Electra*, 680, Orestes prays to his Father :

> Girt with thine own dead armies wake, Oh wake,

or, quite literally, ' Come bringing every dead man as a fellow-fighter '. One would almost think here that there was some direct influence—of course with a misunderstanding.   But the parallel may be a mere chance.

4. I would not lay much stress on the coincidence about the serpent. Clytemnestra dreams that she gives birth to a Serpent, which bites her breast.   Orestes, hearing of it, accepts the omen : he will be the serpent.   And at the last moment Clytemnestra so recognizes him :

> Oh, God ;
> This is the serpent that I bore and suckled.

We are reminded of the Ghost's words :

> The serpent that did sting thy Father's life
> Now wears his crown.

However, Shakespeare abounds in serpents, and I have found no trace of this serpent motive in the sagas (*Cho.* 527–50, 928 ; *Or.* 479 ; *Hamlet*, I. 5).

---

[1] See also a pamphlet *Grotta Söngr and the Orkney and Shetland Quern*, by A. W. Johnston, 1912.

5. Nor yet would I make anything of the point that both Hamlet and Orestes on one occasion have the enemy in their power and put off killing him in order to provide a worse death afterwards. This is important in *Hamlet*, III. 3 : ' Now might I do it pat, now he is praying ', but only occurs as a slight incident in Sophocles' *Electra*, 1491 ff., and may be due merely to the Greek rule of having no violent deaths on the stage. Nor is there much significance in the fact that in both traditions the hero has a scene in which he hears the details of his father's death and bursts into uncontrollable grief (*Cho*. 430 ff. ; *El*. 290 ; *Hamlet*, I. 5, ' Oh, all you host of heaven ', &c.). Such a scene is in both cases almost unavoidable.

Let us now follow this Father for a little while. He was, perhaps naturally, a great warrior. He ' slew Troy's thousands ' ; he ' smote the sledded Polacks on the ice '. It is a particular reproach that the son of such a man should be so slow-tempered, ' peaking like John-a-dreams ', and so chary of shedding blood (*El*. 245, 336 ff., 275 ff., 186 ff.). The old king was also generally idealized and made magnificent. He had some manly faults, yet ' He was a man, taking him all in all '. . . . He was ' a king of kings ' (*El*. 1066 ff.). A special contrast is drawn between him and his successor (*El*. 320 ff., 917, 1080) :

> It was so easy to be true. A King
> Was thine, not feebler, not in any thing
> Below Aegisthus ; one whom Hellas chose
> Above all kings.

One might continue : ' Look on this picture and on this.'

We may also notice that the successor, besides the vices which are necessary, or at least desirable, in his position, is in both cases accused of drunkenness (*Hamlet*, I. 4 ; *El*. 326), which seems irrelevant and unusual.

Lastly, and more important, one of the greatest horrors about the Father's death in both traditions is that he died without the due religious observances. In the Greek tragedies, this lack of religious burial is almost the central horror of the whole story. Wherever it is mentioned it comes as something intolerable, maddening ; it breaks Orestes down. A good instance is the scene in the *Choephori*, where Orestes and Electra are kneeling at their father's grave, awakening the dead and working their own passion to the murder point.

ELECTRA

Ah, pitiless one, my mother, mine enemy ! With an enemy's

burial didst thou bury him : thy King without his people, without
dying rites ; thine husband without a tear !

ORESTES'

All, all, in dishonour thou tellest it, woe is me ! And for that
dishonouring she shall pay her punishment: by the will of the Gods,
by the will of my hands : Oh, let me but slay, and then perish !

He is now ripe for the hearing of the last horror :

LEADER OF THE CHORUS
His body was mangled to lay his ghost !   There, learn it all . . .

and the scene becomes hysterical (*Cho.* 435 ff. ; cf. Soph., *El.* 443 ff. ;
Eur., *El.* 289, 323 ff.).

The atmosphere is quite different in the English. But the lack of
dying rites remains and retains a strange dreadfulness :

> Cut off even in the blossom of my sin,
> Unhouselled, disappointed, unannealed.

To turn to the other characters ; in both the dramatic traditions
the hero has a faithful friend and confidant, who also arrives from
Phocis-Wittenberg, and advises him about his revenge. This friend,
when the hero is threatened with death, wishes to die too (*Or.* 1069 ff. ;
I. T. 675 ff.), but is prevented by the hero and told to ' absent him
from felicity awhile '. This motive is worked out more at length in
the Greek than in the English.

Also the friendship between Orestes and Pylades is more intense
than between Hamlet and Horatio ; naturally, since devoted friendship plays always a greater part in antiquity. But Hamlet's words
are strong :

> Give me the man
> That is not passion's slave, and I will wear him
> In my heart's core, yea, in my heart of hearts ;
> As I do thee.

I find no Pylades-Horatio in the sagas ; though there is a brother
to Hamlet, sometimes older and sometimes a twin, and in some of
the variants, such as the stories of Helgi and Hroar, there are pairs
of avengers, one of whom is mad or behaves like a madman.

Next comes a curious point. At first sight it seems as if all the
Electra motive were lacking in the modern play, all the Ophelia-
Polonius motive in the ancient. Yet I am not sure.

In all the ancient plays Orestes is closely connected with a strange
couple, a young woman and a very old man. They are his sister

Electra and her only true friend, an old and trusted servant of the dead King, who saved Orestes' life in childhood. This old man habitually addresses Electra as 'my daughter'—not merely as 'Child', παῖς, but really 'daughter', θυγάτηρ (*El.* 493, 563). She in return carefully avoids calling him 'Father'; that is to her a sacred name, and she will never use it lightly, at least in Euripides. But in Sophocles she says emphatically: 'Hail, Father. For it is as if in thee I saw my Father!' (*S. El.* 1361).

In the Elizabethan play this couple—if we may so beg the question—has been transformed. The sister is now the mistress, Ophelia; the old servant of the King—for so we must surely describe Polonius or Corambis—remains, but has become Ophelia's real father. And their relations to the hero are quite different.

The change is made more intelligible when we look at the sagas. There the young woman is not a sister but a foster-sister; like Electra she helps Amloði, like Ophelia she is his mistress. The old servant of the King is not her father—so far like the Greek; but there the likeness stops. He spies on Amloði in his mother's chamber and is killed for his pains, as in the English.

We may notice, further, that in all the Electra plays alike a peculiar effect is got from Orestes' first sight of his sister, either walking in a band of mourners or alone in mourning garb (*Cho.* 16; *S. El.* 80; *El.* 107 ff.). He takes her for a slave, and cries, 'Can that be the unhappy Electra?'· A similar but stronger effect is reached in *Hamlet*, V. 1, when Hamlet, seeing an unknown funeral procession approach, gradually discovers whose it is and cries in horror: 'What, the fair Ophelia?'

Lastly, there is something peculiar, at any rate in the Northern Tradition—I will take the Greek later—about the hero's mother. Essentially it is this: she has married the murderer of her first husband and is in part implicated in the murder, and yet the tradition instinctively keeps her sympathetic. In our *Hamlet* she is startled to hear that her first husband was murdered, yet one does not feel clear that she is perfectly honest with herself. She did not know Claudius had poisoned him, but probably that was because she obstinately refused to put together things which she did know and which pointed towards that conclusion. At any rate, though she does not betray Hamlet, she sticks to Claudius and shares his doom. In the First Quarto she is more definitely innocent of the murder; when she learns of it she changes sides, protects Hamlet and acts in confidence with Horatio. In Saxo her attitude is as ambiguous as in the later *Hamlet*; she is friendly to Hamlet and does not betray him, yet does not turn against Feng either.

A wife who loves her husband and bears him children, and then is wedded to his slayer and equally loves him, and does it all in a natural and unemotional manner: somewhat unusual.

And one's surprise is a little increased to find that in Saxo Amloði's wife, Hermutrude, does the same as his mother has done. On Amloði's death she marries his slayer, Wiglek. Again, there is an Irish king, historical to a great degree, who has got deeply entangled with the Hamlet story. His name is Anlaf Curan. Now his wife, Gormflaith, carried this practice so far that the chronicler comments on it. After Anlaf's defeat at Tara she marries his conqueror Malachy, and on Malachy's defeat marries Malachy's conqueror Brian. We will consider later the Greek parallels to this enigmatic lady. For the present we must admit that she is very unlike the Clytemnestra of Greek tragedy, whose motives are studied in every detail, who boldly hates her husband and murders him. There are traces in Homer of a far less passionate Clytemnestra.

III

Now I hope I have not tried artificially to make a case or to press my facts too hard. But I think it will be conceded that the points of similarity, some fundamental and some perhaps superficial, between these two tragic heroes are rather extraordinary; and are made the more striking by the fact that Hamlet and Orestes are respectively the very greatest or most famous heroes of the world's two great ages of tragedy.

The points of similarity, we must notice, fall into two parts. There are first the broad similarities of situation between what we may call the original sagas on both sides; that is, the general story of Orestes and of Hamlet respectively. But secondly, there is something much more remarkable; when these sagas were worked up into tragedies, quite independently and on very different lines, by the great dramatists of Greece and England, not only do most of the old similarities remain, but a number of new similarities are developed. That is, Aeschylus, Euripides, and Shakespeare are strikingly similar in certain points which do not occur at all in Saxo or Ambales or the Greek epic. For instance, the hero's madness is the same in Shakespeare and Euripides, but is totally different from the madness in Saxo or Ambales.

What is the connexion? Did Shakespeare study these Greek tragedians directly? No, all critics seem to be agreed that he did not. And, if any one should suggest that he did, I have further objections to urge, which would, I think, make that hypothesis unserviceable. Of course it is likely enough that some of Shakespeare's university friends, who knew Greek, may have told him in conversation of various stories or scenes or effects in Greek plays. Miss Spens suggests the name of Marston. She shows that he consciously imitated the Greek—for instance, in getting a special effect out of the absence of funeral rites—and probably had considerable influence on Shakespeare. This is a highly important line of inquiry. But such an explanation would not carry us very far with Shakespeare, and would be no help with Saxo.

Can it be indirect imitation through Seneca? No. Orestes only appears once in the whole of Seneca, and then he is a baby unable to speak (*Agamemnon*, 910–43). And in any case Saxo does not seem to have studied Seneca.

Will Scandinavian mercenaries at the Court of Byzantium help us? Or, simpler perhaps, will the Roman conquest of Britain? Both these channels were doubtless important in opening up a connexion between the North and the Mediterranean, and revealing to the Northmen the rich world of classical story. But neither explanation is at all adequate. It might possibly provide a bridge between the traditional Orestes and Saxo's Amloði; but they are not in any pressing need of a bridge. It does not provide any bridge where it is chiefly wanted, between the Orestes of tragedy and Shakespeare's Hamlet.

There seems to have been, as far as our recorded history goes, no good chance of imitation, either direct or indirect. Are we thrown back, then, on a much broader and simpler though rather terrifying hypothesis, that the field of tragedy is by nature so limited that these similarities are inevitable? Certain situations and stories and characters—certain subjects, we may say, for shortness—are naturally tragic; these subjects are quite few in number, and, consequently, two poets or sets of poets trying to find or invent tragic subjects are pretty sure to fall into the same paths. I think there is some truth in this suggestion; and I shall make use of something like it later. But I do not think that in itself it is enough or nearly enough to explain such close and detailed and fundamental similarities as those we are considering. I feel as I look at these two traditions that there must be a connexion somewhere.

There is none within the limits of our historical record; but can there be any outside? There is none between the dramas, nor even

VI   E e

directly between the sagas; but can there be some original connexion between the myths, or 'the primitive religious rituals, on which the dramas are ultimately based? And can it be that the ultimate similarities between Euripides and Shakespeare are simply due to the natural working out, by playwrights of special genius, of the dramatic possibilities latent in that original seed? If this is so, it will lead us to some interesting conclusions.

To begin with, then, can we discover the original myth out of which the Greek Orestes-saga has grown? (I do not deny the possible presence of an historical element also; but if history is there, there is certainly myth mixed up with it.) It contains two parts:

(1) Agamemnon, 'king of men', is dethroned and slain by a younger kinsman, who is helped by the Queen. (2) His successor, in turn, dreads and tries to destroy the next heir to the throne, who however comes home secretly and slays both him and the Queen.

The story falls into its place in a clearly marked group of Greek or pre-Greek legends. Let us recall the primaeval kings of the world in Hesiod.

First there was Ouranos and his wife Gaia; Ouranos lived in dread of his children and 'hid them away' till his son Kronos rose and cast him out, helped by the Queen-mother Gaia.

Then came King Kronos with his wife Rhea. He, too, feared his children and 'swallowed them', till his son Zeus rose and cast him out, helped by the Queen-mother Rhea.

Then thirdly . . . but the story cannot continue. For Zeus is still ruling and cannot have been cast out. But he was saved by a narrow margin. He was about to marry the Sea-maiden Thetis, when Prometheus warned him that, if he did so, the son of Thetis would be greater than he and cast him out from heaven. And, great as is my love for Thetis, I have little doubt that she would have been found helping her son in his criminal behaviour.

In the above cases the new usurper is represented as the son of the old King and Queen. Consequently the Queen-mother, though she helps him, does not marry him, as she does when he is merely a younger kinsman. But there is one great saga in which the marriage of mother and son has remained, quite unsoftened and unexpurgated. In Thebes King Laïus and his wife Jocasta knew that their son would slay and dethrone his father. Laïus orders the son's death, but he is saved by the Queen-mother, and, after slaying and dethroning his father, marries her. She is afterwards slain or dethroned with him, as Clytemnestra is with Aegisthus, and Gertrude with Claudius.

What is the common element in all these stories? You will doubtless have recognized it. It is the world-wide ritual story of what we may call the Golden-Bough Kings. That ritual story is, as I have tried to show elsewhere, the fundamental conception that lies at the root of Greek tragedy; as it lies at the root of the traditional Mummers' Play which, though deeply degraded and vulgarized, is not quite dead yet in the countries of Northern Europe; as it lies at the root of so large a part of all the religions of mankind.

I must not encumber my argument by any long explanation of the Vegetation Kings or Year-daemons. But there are perhaps two points that we should remember, to save us from confusion later on. First, there are two early modes of reckoning: you can reckon by seasons or half-years, by summers and winters; or you can reckon with the whole year as your unit. On the first system a Summer-king or Vegetation-spirit is slain by Winter and rises from the dead in the Spring. On the second each Year-king comes first as a wintry slayer, weds the queen, grows proud and royal, and then is slain by the Avenger of his predecessor. These two conceptions cause some confusion in the myths, as they do in most forms of the Mummers' Play.

The second point to remember is that this death and vengeance was really enacted among our remote ancestors in terms of human bloodshed. The sacred king really had 'slain the slayer' and was doomed himself to be slain. The queen might either be taken on by her husband's slayer, or else slain with her husband. It is no pale myth or allegory that has so deeply dyed the first pages of human history. It is man's passionate desire for the food that will save him from starvation, his passionate memory of the streams of blood, willing and unwilling, that have been shed to keep him alive. But for all this subject I must refer you to the eloquent pages of Sir James Frazer.

Thus Orestes, the madman and king-slayer, takes his place beside Brutus the Fool, who expelled the Tarquins, and Amlođi the Fool, who burnt King Feng at his winter feast. The great Greek scholar Hermann Usener some years since, on quite another set of grounds, identified Orestes as a Winter God, a slayer of the summer.[1] He is the man of the cold mountains who slays annually the Red Neoptolemus at Delphi; he is the ally of death and the dead; he comes suddenly in the dark; he is mad and raging, like the winter god Maimaktes and the storms. In Athenian ritual, it seems, a cloak was actually woven for him in late Autumn, lest he should be too cold (Aristophanes, *Birds*, 712). Thus he is quite unlike the various bright

---

[1] *Heilige Handlung*, in the *Archiv für Religionswissenschaft*, 1904.

E e 2

heroes who slay dragons of darkness.; he finds his comrade in the Bitter Fool—may we say the bitter Amloði ?—of many Mummers' Plays, who is the Slayer of the Joyous King.

But can we talk thus of Hamlet-Amloði ? I mean, can we bring him into the region of myth, and myth of the same kind that we find in Greece ? Here I am quite off my accustomed beat, and must speak with diffidence and under correction from my betters. But it seems beyond doubt, even to my most imperfect scrutiny of the material, that the same forms of myth and the same range of primitive religious conceptions are to be found in Scandinavia as in other Arian countries.

There are several wives in the Ynglinga saga who seem to belong to the Gaia-Rhea-Clytemnestra-Jocasta type. For instance, King Vanlandi was married to Drifa of Finland, and was killed by her in conjunction with their son Visburr, who succeeded to the kingdom. (The slaying was done by witchcraft; but no jury could, I think, exculpate Visburr.)

Visburr in turn married the daughter of Aude the Wealthy. Like Agamemnon he was unfaithful to his wife, so she left him and sent her two sons to talk to him and duly, in the proper ritual manner, to burn him in his house. Just as the Hamlet of Saga burned King Feng, just as the actual northern villagers at their festival burned the Old Year.

Again, there are clear traces of kings who are sacrificed and are succeeded by their slayers. Most of the Yngling kings die in sacrificial ways. One is confessedly sacrificed to avert famine, one killed by a sacrificial bull, one falls off his horse in a temple and dies, one burns himself on a pyre at a festival. Another—like Ouranos and Kronos and the other child-swallowers—sacrifices one of his sons periodically in order to prolong his own life. I cite these cases merely to show that such ideas were apparently current in primitive Norse society as well as elsewhere. But the matter is really clinched by Saxo himself. He not only gives us the tale of Ole, King of the Beggars, who came in disguise, with one servant dressed as a woman, to King Thore's house, got himself hailed as king in mockery and then slew Thore and took the crown [254]. He definitely tells us, in a story about the Sclavs, that 'By public law of the ancients the succession to the throne belonged to him who should slay the king' [277].

So that when we find that the Hamlet of Saga resembles Orestes so closely ; when we find that he is the bitter fool and king-slayer ; when especially we find that Hamlet's mother, whatever her name, Gerutha,

Gertrude, or Amba, and Amloði's mother and Ambales' mother, and the mother of divers variants of Hamlet, like Helgi and Hroar, and Hamlet's wife, and the wife of Anlaf Curan, who is partly identified with Hamlet, all alike play this strange part of wedding—if not helping—their husband's slayer and successor, we can hardly hesitate to draw the same sort of conclusion as would naturally follow in a Greek story. Hamlet is more deeply involved in this Clytemnestra-like atmosphere than any person I know of outside Hesiod. And one cannot fail to be reminded of Oedipus and Jocasta by the fact, which is itself of no value in the story but is preserved both in Saxo and the Ambales Saga, that Amloði slept in his mother's chamber [1] (Saxo, 88; *Ambales*, p. 119 *et ante*, ed. Gollancz).

There is something strangely characteristic in the saga-treatment of this ancient King's Wife, a woman under the shadow of adultery, the shadow of incest, the shadow of murder, who is yet left in most of the stories a motherly and sympathetic character. Clytemnestra is an exception, and perhaps Gormflaith. But Gaia, Rhea, and even Jocasta, are all motherly and sympathetic. So is Gerutha, the wife of Ørvandil and the mother of Amleth, and Amba the mother of Ambales. And if Gerutha is the same as Groa, the usual wife of Ørvandil, 'Groa', says Professor Rydberg, 'was a tender person devoted to the members of her family'. The trait remains even in Shakespeare. 'Gertrude', says Professor Bradley, 'had a soft animal nature. . . . She loved to be happy like a sheep in the sun, and to do her justice she loved to see others happy, like more sheep in the sun.' Just the right character for our Mother Earth! For, of course, that is who she is. The Greek stories speak her name openly; Gaia and Rhea are confessed Earth-Mothers, Jocasta only a stage less so. One cannot apply moral disapproval to the annual re-marriages of Mother Earth. Nor yet possibly to the impersonal and compulsory marriages of the human queen in certain very primitive stages of society. But later on, when life has become more fully human, if once a poet or dramatist gets to thinking of the story, and tries to realize the position and feelings of this eternally traitorous wife, this eternally fostering and protecting mother, he cannot but feel in her that element of inward conflict which is the seed of great drama. She is torn between husband, lover, and son; and the avenging son, the mother-murderer, how is *he* torn?

English Tragedy has followed the son. Yet Gerutha, Amba, Gertrude, Hermutrude, Gormflaith, Gaia, Rhea, Jocasta—there is

[1] In the extant form of the Ambales Saga Amba's personal chastity is preserved by a miracle : such an exception approves the rule.

tragedy in all of them, and it is in the main the same tragedy. Why does the most tragic of all of them, Clytemnestra, stand out of the picture?

One can only surmise. For one thing, Clytemnestra, like Gertrude in some stories, has both the normal experiences of the primitive King's Wife. Married to the first king, she is taken on by the second and slain by the third; and both parts of her story are equally emphasized, which is not the case with the other heroines. Their deaths are generally softened or ignored. But, apart from this, I am inclined to lay most stress on the deliberate tragic art of Aeschylus. He received from the tradition a Clytemnestra not much more articulate than Gerutha; but it needed only a turn of the wrist to change her from a silent and passive figure to a woman seething with tragic passions. If Saxo had had a mind like Aeschylus, or if Shakespeare had made Gertrude his central figure instead of Hamlet, Clytemnestra would perhaps not have stood so much alone.

And what of Hamlet himself as a mythical character? I find, almost to my surprise, exactly the evidence I should have liked to find. Hamlet in Saxo is the son of Horvendillus or Ørvandil, an ancient Teutonic god connected with Dawn and the Spring. His great toe, for instance, is now the Morning Star. (It was frozen off; that is why it shines like ice.) His wife was Groa, who is said to be the Green Earth; he slew his enemy Collerus—Kollr the Hooded or perhaps the Cold—in what Saxo calls 'a sweet and spring-green spot' in a budding wood. He was slain by his brother and avenged by his son. The sort of conclusion towards which I, on my different lines, was groping had already been drawn by several of the recognized Scandinavian authorities; notably by Professor Gollancz (who especially calls attention to the part played by the hero's mother), by Adolf Zinzow, and by Victor Rydberg. Professor Elton is more guarded, but points, on the whole, in the same direction.[1]

Thus, if these arguments are trustworthy, we finally run the Hamlet-saga to earth in the same ground as the Orestes-saga; in that prehistoric and world-wide ritual battle of Summer and Winter, of

---

[1] Gollancz, *Hamlet in Iceland*, Introduction; Zinzow, *Die Hamletsaga an und mit verwandten Sagen erläutert*, 1877; Rydberg, *Teutonic Mythology*, Engl. tr. by Anderson, 1889; Elton, Appendix ii to his translation of Saxo, edited by York Powell. Rydberg goes so far as to identify Hamlet with Ørvandil's famous son Swipdag. 'Two Dissertations on the Hamlet of Saxo and of Shakespeare' by R. G. Latham contain linguistic and mythological suggestions. I have not come across the works of Gubernatis mentioned in Ward, *English Dramatic Literature* [2], ii, p. 165.

Life and Death, which has played so vast a part in the mental development of the human race and especially, as Mr. E. K. Chambers has shown us, in the history of mediaeval drama. Hamlet also, like Orestes, has the notes of the Winter about him. Though he is on the side of right against wrong he is no joyous and triumphant slayer. He is clad in black, he rages alone, he is the bitter Fool who must slay the King.[1]

IV

It seems a strange thing, this gradual shaping and re-shaping of a primitive folk-tale, in itself rather empty and devoid of character, until it issues in a great tragedy which shakes the world. Yet in Greek literature, I am sure, the process is a common, almost a normal, one. Myth is defined by a Greek writer as τὰ λεγόμενα ἐπὶ τοῖς δρωμένοις, ' the things said over a ritual act '. For a certain agricultural rite, let us suppose, you tore a corn-sheaf in pieces and scattered the grain ; and to explain why you did so you told a myth. There was once a young and beautiful Prince who was torn in pieces. . . . Was he torn by hounds or wild beasts in requital for some strange sin ? Or was he utterly innocent, torn by mad Thracian women or devilish Titans, or the working of an unjust curse ? As the group in the village talks together, and begins to muse and wonder and make unconscious poetry, the story gets better and stronger and ends by being the tragedy of Pentheus or Hippolytus or Actaeon or Dionysus himself. No doubt history comes in as well. Things happened in antiquity as much as now ; and people were moved by them at the time and talked about them afterwards. But to observe exactly, and to remember and report exactly, is one of the very latest and rarest of human accomplishments. By the help of much written record and much mental training we can now manage it pretty well. But early man was at the time too excited to observe, and afterwards too indifferent to record, and always too much beset by fixed forms of thought ever to take in concrete facts exactly. (As a matter of fact he did not even wish to do so ; he was aiming at something quite different.) In any case, the facts, as they happened, were thrown swiftly into the same crucible as the myths. Men did not research. They did not keep names and dates distinct. They talked together and wondered and followed their musings till an historical king of Ireland grew very like the old mythical Amloði, an historical king of Mycenae took on part of the story of a primitive Ouranos or

[1] I believe this figure of the Fool to be capable of further analysis, but will not pursue the question here.

Sky-King wedded to an Earth-Mother. And in later times it was the myth that lived and grew great rather than the history. The things that thrill and amaze us in *Hamlet* or the *Agamemnon* are not any historical particulars about mediaeval Elsinore or prehistoric Mycenae, but things belonging to the old stories and the old magic rites, which stirred and thrilled our forefathers five and six thousand years ago ; set them dancing all night on the hills, tearing beasts and men in pieces, and joyously giving up their own bodies to the most ghastly death, to keep the green world from dying and to be the saviours of their own people.

I am not trying to utter a paradox, nor even to formulate a theory. I am not for a moment questioning or belittling the existence or the overwhelming artistic value, of individual genius. I trust no one will suspect me of so doing. I am simply trying to understand a phenomenon which seems, before the days of the printed book and the widespread reading public, to have occurred quite normally and constantly in works of imaginative literature, and doubtless in some degree is occurring still.

What does our hypothesis imply ? It seems to imply, first, a great unconscious solidarity and continuity, lasting from age to age, among all the Children of the Poets, both the Makers and the Callers-forth, both the artists and the audiences. In artistic creation, as in all the rest of life, the traditional element is far larger, the purely inventive element far smaller, than the unsophisticated man supposes.

Further, it implies that in the process of Tradition—that is, of being handed on from generation to generation, constantly modified and expurgated, re-felt and re-thought—a subject sometimes shows a curious power of almost eternal durability. It can be vastly altered; it may seem utterly transformed. Yet some inherent quality still remains, and significant details are repeated quite unconsciously by generation after generation of poets. Nay, more. It seems to show that there often is latent in some primitive myth a wealth of detailed drama, waiting only for the dramatist of genius to discover it and draw it forth. Of course we must not exaggerate this point. We must not say that *Hamlet* or the *Electra* is latent in the original ritual as a flower is latent in the seed. The seed, if it just gets its food, is bound to develop along a certain fixed line ; the myth or ritual is not. It depends for its development on too many live people and too many changing and complex conditions. We can only say that some natural line of growth is there, and in the case before us it seems to have asserted itself, both in large features and in fine details, in a rather extraordinary way. The two societies in which the Hamlet and Orestes tragedies arose were very dissimilar, the poets were quite different in character and quite independent, even the particular plays themselves differed greatly in plot and setting and technique and most other qualities; the only point of contact lies at their common origin many thousand years ago, and yet the fundamental identity still shows itself, almost unmistakable.

This conception may seem strange; but after all in the history of religion it is already a proven and accepted fact, this 'almost eternal durability' of primitive conceptions and even primitive rites. Our hypothesis will imply that what is already known to happen in religion may also occur in imaginative drama.

If this is so, it seems only natural that those subjects, or some of those subjects, which particularly stirred the interest of primitive men, should still have an appeal to certain very deep-rooted human instincts. I do not say that they will always move us now; but, when they do, they will tend to do so in ways which we recognize as particularly profound and poetical. This comes in part from their original quality; in part, I suspect, it depends on mere repetition. We all know the emotional charm possessed by famous and familiar words and names, even to hearers who do not understand the words and know little of the bearers of the names. I suspect that a charm of that sort lies in these stories and situations, which are—I cannot quite keep clear of metaphor—deeply implanted in the memory of the race, stamped, as it were, upon our physical organism. We have forgotten their faces and their voices; we say that they are strange to us. Yet there is something in us which leaps at the sight of them, a cry of the blood which tells us we have known them always.

Of course it is an essential part of the whole process of Tradition that the mythical material is constantly castigated and rekindled by comparison with real life. That is where realism comes in, and literary skill and imagination. An element drawn from real life was there, no doubt, even at the beginning. The earliest mythmaker never invented in a vacuum. He really tried—in Aristotle's famous phrase—to tell 'The Sort of Thing that Might Happen'; only his conception of 'What Might Happen' was, by our standards, a little wild. Then, as man's experience of life grew larger and calmer and more intimate, his conception of 'The Sort of Thing that Might Happen' grew more competent. It grew ever nearer to the truth of Nature, to its variety, to its reasonableness, to its infinite subtlety. And in the greatest ages of literature there seems to be, among other things, a power of preserving due proportion between these opposite elements—the expression of boundless primitive emotion and the subtle and delicate representation of life.   In plays like *Hamlet* or the *Agamemnon* or the *Electra* we have certainly fine and flexible character-study, a varied and well-wrought story, a full command of the technical instruments of the poet and the dramatist; but we have also, I suspect, a strange unanalysed vibration below the surface, an undercurrent of desires and fears and passions, long slumbering yet eternally familiar, which have for thousands of years lain near the root of our most intimate emotions and been wrought into the fabric of our most magical dreams.   How far into past ages this stream may reach back, I dare not even surmise; but it sometimes seems as if the power of stirring it or moving with it were one of the last secrets of genius.

MYTH AND RITUAL: A WASTELAND OR
A FOREST OF SYMBOLS?

HANS H. PENNER

My concern in this essay is to present a brief description of two methods for understanding myth and ritual. Both of the methods I want to describe exclude theology. I am not excluding theology because I think it subjective, unscientific, or non-cognitive. I am excluding it for the simple reason that I know of no theological description of myth (or ritual) that is not itself based upon one of the two methods I want to describe. My best examples, of course, are those modern theologians who are concerned with faith without god, or to put it in other terms, faith without myth.

Now the two methods I propose to discuss are associated with disciplines concerned in different ways with religion. The first is anthropology, the second is the history of religions. It is interesting that both disciplines originated at about the same time with the same interests. Both disciplines have an identity crisis, to borrow a phrase from Erikson, since they have trouble defining themselves. Their uncertainty, however, may be very healthy, since once the definition is found they may become bored to death with what they are.

My description of what anthropologists have said about myth and ritual will include such scholars as Harrison and Hooke. They were not anthropologists by profession; nevertheless, the assumptions of the discipline explicitly influenced their work. Although the description refers for the most part to the Anglo-American development of this science we might begin with a quotation of C. Levi-Strauss: "Of all the chapters on religious anthropology probably none has tarried to the same extent as studies in the field of mythology. From a theoretical point of view the situation remains very much the same as it was fifty years ago, namely, a picture of chaos. Myths are still widely interpreted in conflicting ways: collective dreams, the outcome of a kind of aesthetic play, the foundation of ritual. . . . Mythological figures are considered as personified abstractions, divinized heroes, or decayed gods. Whatever the hypothesis, the choice amounts to reducing mythology to an idle play or to a coarse kind of speculation."[1] Levi-Strauss is convinced that,

---

1. C. Levi-Strauss, *Structural Anthropology* (New York, 1963), 207.

as a result of this chaos, "all kinds of amateurs who claim to belong to other disciplines have seized this opportunity to move in, thereby turning into their private playground what we have left as a wasteland."[2] By "amateurs" he presumably means literary critics, folklorists, classicists, biblical scholars, historians of religions, and psychologists.

One of the ironies in this situation is that many of the amateurs have taken their premises from Levi-Strauss's own discipline. If these premises happen to belong to the development of anthropology in the late nineteenth century, it is not entirely the fault of those who moved in and made a playground of the wasteland. It is only since the appearance of Levi-Strauss's article, in fact, that anthropology has returned to religion by means of a study of myth and ritual. I am not saying that he alone is responsible for the return. Since 1960, however, we have had a number of books, anthologies, and articles on anthropological approaches to "religion" — which means myth and ritual.[3] Whether this new interest has resulted in a new understanding of myth and ritual remains a debatable point.

The description and comparison of the two methods will be based upon four premises. First, the new interest in anthropology concerning myth and ritual, though revised after the gap between, let us say, Tylor and the studies of Leach, Turner, Wallace, Evans-Pritchard, Douglas, and Spiro (that is, from the late 1950's onward) has not involved an essential change in methodological assumptions. Second, these assumptions provide a striking contrast with at least some of the more important interpretations of myth and ritual provided by historians of religions. The contrast or difference can be seen in the statement of Wallace that, in order to explain the phenomena, anthropology, like all scientific explanation, must be "unashamedly reductionistic."[4] By contrast, Wach, Eliade, and van der Leeuw, as historians of religions, attempt to show that religion as manifested in myth and ritual must be understood without reduction. From their point of view the method must fit the phenomena. This is a way of affirming a difference between those disciplines which assume that "explanation" is central to any successful science and those which assert that "understanding" is the primary concern. The split between the natural and human sciences characteristic of the Kantian tradition underlies the historian of religions' concern

2. *Ibid.*, 206.

3. Among recent studies not included below, cf. *Myth and Cosmos,* ed. John Middleton (New York, 1967); *Gods and Rituals,* ed. John Middleton (New York, 1967); *The Structural Study of Myth and Totemism,* ed. E. R. Leach (London, 1967); *Symposium on New Approaches to the Study of Religion* (American Ethnological Society, Proceedings of the 1964 Annual Spring Meeting, Univ. of Washington Press); *A Discussion on Ritualization of Behavior in Animals and Man* (Philosophical Transactions of the Royal Society of London, Series B, Vol. 251, No. 772); V. Turner, *The Forest of Symbols* (New York, 1967).

4. A. F. C. Wallace, *Culture and Personality* (New York, 1967), 199.

with "understanding." The empirical naturalism of the English tradition, on the other hand, attempts to overcome this dualism by viewing history and society as factors within the natural process. The task of science is to explain the variables of this process. To reduce or not to reduce the phenomena can be explained or understood as approaches which developed from these two philosophical traditions. Third, the contrast between the two approaches to myth and ritual can be described as a difference between a psychological-sociological point of view and one that might be called an ontological basis for interpreting myth and ritual. This contrast is both recognized and exemplified by Wallace, who states in relation to his own discipline that "ontological definitions are the bane of science. They postulate Platonic essences, states of being in a realm of absolutes, about which argument may rage endlessly without any resolution but that of authority. Discussion of such definitions is sterile, as Hume pointed out long ago. . . ."[5] And fourth, even though the two methods assume different beginnings they agree, for different reasons, that myth is non-cognitive.[6] This shift in emphasis involves new insights into myth and ritual as symbols. Although there is little agreement between the two disciplines on the meaning of such symbols, both are faced with the problem of symbolic reference in relation to myth and ritual.

Let us then turn very briefly to the two approaches. I think it is fair to make the general assumption that the history of anthropology has its origin in Spencer and Tylor, if not as persons, at least in their methods. Structure, function, and evolution are the central ideas of Part II of Spencer's *Principles of Sociology*. Evans-Pritchard has pointed out that Spencer's early work with the relations of social structure to social function was of prime importance in developing the use of these concepts in anthropology. If Spencer provides us with the beginning of an analysis based upon structure and function, Tylor marks the beginning of a psychological analysis in anthropology. Both, of course, assumed an evolutionary hypothesis as necessary for their explanations, even though their basic principles did not logically entail the hypothesis itself. J. W. Burrow, in his very interesting book called *Evolution and Society,* has pointed out one of the reasons why the evolutionary hypothesis was needed: the awareness that analysis without the concepts of evolution or natural law would lead to a relativism vis-à-vis all phenomena, including nineteenth-century British culture itself.[7] In any case, Tylor's analysis led to an understanding of myth as produced by individual thoughts and fears and based upon the dream world. Both types of analysis

5. *Ibid.,* 8.
6. "Non-cognitive" in the strict sense that myth is not regarded as making knowledge claims about the world.
7. J. W. Burrow, *Evolution and Society* (Cambridge, England, 1966), 218.

continue to refine themselves in the development of the study of myth and ritual in anthropology. Contemporary studies, for example, tend to combine the two, but in general we can say that the emphasis on structure and function can be traced to Spencer, while the vitality of the myth-ritual school, with its emphasis on the psychological-survival factor in myth and ritual, can be traced to Tylor. This, of course, would need some qualification in cases where the two approaches are combined into a complex method with or without the evolutionary hypothesis.

The myth-ritual school is the continuing heritage not only of Tylor, but of one other grand figure in the history of anthropology. That is, of course, James Frazer, and anthropologists still debate whether what he wrote was a golden bough or a gilded twig.[8] His popularity and influence remain with us in spite of the many criticisms of his work. Although his popularity may never be fully understood, the many uses of *The Golden Bough* certainly rest on the fact that Frazer was not consistent or systematic in his description of myths. His work may be viewed as a summary of the various positions concerning myth during his lifetime. In some instances myths were understood by Frazer as personifications of nature or as euhemeristic expressions of history. We may also find myth described as a libretto for ritual, as well as an explanation for ritual whose original meaning has been either forgotten or misunderstood. Whatever definition we choose, the basic assumption throughout all of these descriptions of myth remains rationalistic; Frazer, like Tylor, understood myth as primarily an attempt to explain something.

Though Frazer was not the first to correlate myth with ritual, the work of Jane Harrison was explicitly indebted to this emphasis in his work. The basic assumption in her study of Greek religion is that myth is the spoken correlative of the thing done or acted out.[9] Myth, according to Harrison, is the thing said over the thing done. This notion that ritual is the basis for myth is a recurrent theme in many contemporary studies.

Harrison's formulation of the correlation of myth and ritual certainly followed the work of Frazer. However, there is one important difference. Harrison moved away from the rationalism of Frazer and Tylor by denying that the myth as a libretto functions as an explanation for ritual. The two phenomena, according to Harrison, are simply two poles of one expression. What must be emphasized for understanding her position is the fact that the "thing done," the ritual, receives her full attention. She describes this action as: 1) the result of emotion, 2) the representation of an emotion

8. E. R. Leach, "The Golden Bough or Gilded Twig" in *Daedalus* (Spring, 1961).
9. J. E. Harrison, *Themis* (New York, 1962), 327 ff., and 485 ff.

which is basically collective, and 3) the imitation of some unsatisfied desire. In psychoanalytic terms we may describe Harrison's notion of ritual as the result of repression. The repression, however, is to be understood in terms of Durkheim's description of the collective conscience. Ritual is a certain kind of action which represents, or presents once again, a collective emotion or desire which has been blocked even though the emotion is intense. Ritual as such has no pragmatic function other than to express those collective desires which have no practical outlet. The recurrence of the rites eventually led to a conceptualized narrative concerning the gods, since, according to Harrison, what the Greeks called the *dromenon* is prior to the god. Given this description of ritual we may notice that Harrison agreed with Frazer's assumption that ritual preceded myth. The pattern which she thought could be found at the very heart of Greek religion was based upon the above hypothesis, and the theme of recurrence was expressed in the famous pattern of a spring festival, a death or defeat, and an epiphany.

The same understanding of myth can also be found in the study of the ancient Near East. Among many scholars the name of S. H. Hooke is usually associated with this pattern as applied to the myths and rituals of kingship and New Year's festivals. Elements of Frazer's description of the dying-rising god-king can also be seen as influencing this approach to the religions of the Near East. The ritual drama of the annual dethronement and re-enthronement of the king was enacted to secure the well-being of the community. At one time, according to this theory, the king was ritually killed as an imitation of the dying-rising god portrayed in the myth. The myth is the narrative of what was ritually enacted, and the words or narrative of the myth bring about or recreate a secure situation. Myths provide or secure the efficacy of the ritual. This pattern involves the same themes as Harrison's. There is an annual drama in which a contest, death, and epiphany take place. The protagonist of course is the god-king, and this pattern, according to the scholars of this school, is found in much of the Old Testament literature.

The criticisms of this school do not seem to have had much effect on it. After J. Frankfort wrote an explicit attack against it in 1951, Hooke wrote in 1958: "I still find no cause to abandon the main outlines of the position laid down in *Myth and Ritual*."[10] How bare the outlines have become can be seen in T. Gaster's *Thespis*. Once again, Frazer is the primary influence, but Gaster must admit that the myth-ritual structure, which can be divided into rites of mortification, purgation, invigoration, and jubilation, cannot be found in any complete sense in any of the ancient Near Eastern cultures. Yet his definition of myth is a continuation of the myth-ritual school. The function of myth, he says, "is . . . to bring out in articulate fashion the

10. S. H. Hooke, *Myth, Ritual and Kingship* (Oxford, 1958), 19.

inherent durative significance of the ritual program. . . . Its effect is to turn presentation into REpresentation."[11] His revision of the myth-ritual pattern involves an understanding of a parallelism of myth and ritual which is inherent in myth-ritual from the very beginning. Myth translates the punctual, real acts presented in ritual into durative, ideal representations. In this revised sense, however, myth is not just an outgrowth of ritual, nor is it merely the narrative of things done. Gaster's understanding of myth as the durative and ideal correlative of the punctual and real, therefore, moves in the direction of understanding myth as ideology.

The criticisms directed against the myth-ritual school have been twofold. First, it is impossible to show that all myths originate in ritual. Gaster, for example, is aware of this criticism when he denies that myths arise from ritual. Kluckhohn's essay on "Myth and Ritual: A General Theory" shows very clearly that the theory cannot be generalized.[12] Frankfort and J. Fontenrose have also proved rather conclusively that the evidence for the myth-ritual theory in the Near East is simply not there.[13] Not only is there no evidence for a ritual killing of a king, but, as Fontenrose has shown, there is no evidence that the famous Ekitu Festival was a libretto for the Babylonian New Year's Festival, even though it may have been narrated during the festival.

Though very few scholars now affirm the position that all myths arise from rituals, most would agree with Kluckhohn that it would be absurd to deny that some myths are related to ritual activity. But in the revised view, myth is regarded not as an explanation for a ritual but rather as a charter or justification for this kind of action. Myth in this sense is the rationalization of ritual activity for the sake of the security or solidarity of the social structure.

Now the myth-ritual school has not received much attention from contemporary anthropology, but we can easily demonstrate that they share one basic assumption. This is the assumption that myths and rituals are to be explained by reference to their function for the solidarity or unity of society and the psyche.

We do not have to stay with Harrison, Hooke, or Gaster to make this statement. Malinowski, Kluckhohn, Wallace, Spiro, and Leach assume the same position in their understanding of myth and ritual. The case of Malinowski needs no comment. For Leach, as another example, myths in the last analysis are "nothing more than ways of describing the formal relation-

11. T. Gaster, *Thespis* (Garden City, N.Y., 1961), 77; cf. also 23-25.
12. C. Kluckhohn, "Myths and Rituals: A General Theory" in *Harvard Theological Review* 34 (1942), 45-79.
13. Cf. Joseph Fontenrose, *The Ritual Theory of Myth* (Univ. of California Folklore Studies, No. 18, Berkeley, 1966).

ships that exist between real persons and real groups in ordinary society."[14] Kluckhohn's position is also clearly based upon an analysis of sociological and psychological needs and the relations created by these needs. This is fully documented in his essay "Myth and Ritual: A General Theory." Though Spiro is much more critical of this position, he also uses both functional analysis and psychological analysis in explaining myth and ritual, and defines religion in the same terms as Tylor. For Spiro, religion is "the belief in supernaturals or superhumans"; Tylor defined religion as the "belief in spiritual beings."[15]

Historians of religions have claimed that unashamed reduction of phenomena leaves the phenomena unexplained. To say with Leach that religious symbols, or myths, are nothing more than ways of describing formal relationships existing between individuals and groups leaves the particular symbols and the specific myths unexplained. I am not bothered by someone who tells me that he is not ashamed of being a reductionist. What does bother me is his failure to perceive that he has not *explained* myths or rituals by being unashamed of reduction.

Let me try to explain what I want to call the functional fallacy, which is usually involved in reduction. The reference of myth and ritual for most anthropologists is social solidarity or social relations. Now if, as Spiro has shown, the function of myth is social solidarity, or the symbolic expression of social relations, and if this social function is an unintended consequence of both myth and ritual, then it is illogical to explain myth and ritual by reference to social solidarity. The cause of social solidarity cannot be explained by reference to an unintended consequence.[16] Even if we accept the truism that religion has a social function, it is an *ignoratio elenchi* to infer that this unintended consequence of religion is the explanation of religion. Spiro in much that he has written is aware of this error. For, as he has pointed out, "the functional explanation of religion does not explain religion, rather it explains a dimension of society . . . by reference to religion." And, he adds, the anthropologist "must then recognize what he is doing; he is not explaining religion, he is explaining society."[17] Whether Spiro escapes his own criticisms is a question I cannot answer at the present time. What is clear, I hope, is that anthropology as one of the social sciences has persistently used functionalism as an explanation of religion. This implies that statements such as "I believe in Christ" or "Vishnu," or "I have attained Nirvana," mean "I believe or adhere to the social system of which this statement is a symbolic expres-

14. E. R. Leach, *Political Systems of Highland Burma* (London, 1954), 182.

15. M. E. Spiro, "Religion: Problems of Definition and Explanation" in *Anthropological Approaches to the Study of Religion*, ed. M. Banton (New York, 1966), 94; and E. B. Tylor, *Religion in Primitive Culture* (New York, 1958), 8.

16. M. E. Spiro, "Religion: Problems of Definition and Explanation," 108.

17. M. E. Spiro, *Burmese Supernaturalism* (Englewood Cliffs, N.J., 1967), 66.

sion." I know of no field worker, regardless of his methods, who has been able to extract this from his informants. This is a good example of what I mean by an unintended consequence becoming the cause of, or the explanation for, a social structure. Crude as it may seem, it fits the positions of such scholars as Durkheim and Leach, if not Freud and Tylor.

It must be emphasized that if we supply the correct empirical information for the myths and rituals, regarded as the symbolic expressions of real relations and fears, religion should be replaceable by the correct information itself. In this sense, anthropology remains what Tylor thought it was, "a reformer's science."

Historians of religions have for the most part avoided the old controversy about the origin of religion. Most will agree with contemporary anthropology that this is a dead issue. One of the problems within the history of religions, however, is that it continues to borrow some of its descriptions from anthropology both old and new, thereby throwing into total confusion its own quest for self-definition. Van der Leeuw, for example, cites with approval Harrison's view that a living myth is itself a celebration certifying a ritual. Myth celebrates reality; it takes the temporal instant in the form of an action and transforms it into its own realm. Thus, according to van der Leeuw, myth lifts the temporal act into an eternal now and always.[18] This description is reminiscent of Gaster's notion of myth and ritual as the polar expressions of the real and ideal. For van der Leeuw, however, myth is not a reflective contemplation but an actuality in itself.

Joachim Wach, who will perhaps be remembered more for his work on Dilthey, Troeltsch, and the problem of historical understanding than for what he wrote on the actual history of religions, tends to remain in the rationalist tradition. The main problem with his writing is the constant quotation of various scholars with whom he agrees but who contradict one another in their complete viewpoint. Myths for Wach are not explanations, and they are not even discursive. Yet they express in symbolic form the meaning of man's confrontation of Ultimate Reality. He agrees, on the one hand, with W. M. Urban that "symbols are taken from the narrower and more intuitable relations which because of their pervasiveness and ideality, cannot be directly expressed." On the other hand, he affirms Malinowski's statement that myths are "a statement of primeval and more relevant reality." However, he seems to take an opposite position to this viewpoint when he says that myths answer such questions as "Why are we here?, Where do we come from?, For what purpose?, Why do we act this way?, Why do we die?"[19] Doctrines, according

18. G. van der Leeuw, *Religion in Essence and Manifestation*, II (New York, 1963), 413-414 (Ch. 60 in one-volume edition).

19. J. Wach, *The Comparative Study of Religions* (New York, 1958), 65-66.

to Wach, systematically explicate what symbols imply and myths illustrate. Ritual is the practical expression of religious experience as a total response to Ultimate Reality in action. Since myth and doctrine are so closely related, it would seem that Wach would affirm the priority of ritual to myth in his agreement with Scheler: "Religious cognition is an understanding which does not exist fully prior to its cultic expression."[20]

What is explicit in Wach's description of both myth and ritual is that they function as expressions of encounters with Ultimate Reality. This, obviously, is not the function of either myth or ritual in the positions we have already described. We shall return to this difference of function later.

The basic concern of the historian of religions has been with the meaning of myth, not with ritual. One of the reasons for this may be the assumption that myth is the interpretation of the rite, or at least that it helps us decipher what is involved in ritual meaning. One of the well-known historians of religions, Mircea Eliade, has put the problem the following way: "Symbol and myth will give a clear view of the modalities [of the sacred] that a rite can never do more than suggest. A symbol and a rite are on such different levels that the rite can never reveal what the symbol reveals."[21] The emphasis in his studies of religions clearly reflects this persuasion. One of the differences between the approach of the historian of religions and those of the social sciences can be seen in this emphasis. The predominant concern among most historians of religion has been with the meaning of myth as a manifestation of the sacred. In terms of our description, this is an emphasis upon the eternal, the ideal, the durative aspect of myth. For Eliade and others it is symbol and myth which are invariable. For many anthropologists — Boas included — it is the ritual which is uniform while myths are variable.

Myths, for Eliade, are units of symbols combined in narrative form. His own clarification of the meaning of symbol and myth is given in six general remarks on the function and characteristics of religious symbols.[22] First, religious symbols have the capacity of opening modalities of the real or structures of the world that are not manifest in immediate experience. This capacity is not a rational process since it is anterior to conscious reflection. This is one of his most important premises. The notion that symbolic meaning is anterior to reflection implies that the rational process itself presupposes some symbolic meaning. Conscious reflection, in other words, is founded upon some symbolic framework through which reality is understood and an orientation in the world is posited. These symbolic orientations are expanded or lead to later reflection "on the ultimate foundation of the world, i.e., to all cos-

20. *Ibid.*, 98.
21. M. Eliade, *Patterns in Comparative Religion* (New York, 1958), 9.
22. "Methodological Remarks on the Study of Religion" in *The History of Religions*, ed. M. Eliade and J. Kitagawa (Chicago, 1959), 86-107.

mologies and ontologies, from the time of the Vedas to the pre-Socratics." It is important to emphasize that for Eliade religious symbols reveal a reality or structure not given in immediate or everyday experience. This is an obvious reference to his well-known definition of religion as "the sacred is opposite the profane." We shall return to this contrast later.

The second characterization is a clarification of symbol and religious symbolism, especially in primitive religions. For Eliade the two are synonymous in archaic traditions, "for the primitive *symbols are always religious* because they point to something *real,* or to a structure of the world." The real is equivalent to the sacred. The notion that a symbol points to something real is a fundamental but implicit assumption concerning the reference of a symbol. That is to say, a symbol is referential in that in and of itself it does not constitute the real. This symbolic reference, according to Eliade, implies an ontology even though it is pre-systematic in archaic traditions.

The third characteristic of a religious system is its multivalence. This is the capacity of a symbol to express any number of meanings not evident in immediate experience, reflection, or the particular historical context of the symbol itself. The task of the historian of religions is to understand and integrate the multivalent meanings as he finds them manifested in history. Eliade's well-known book, *Patterns in Comparative Religion,* shows best how to try to carry out this enterprise.

The fourth characteristic or function of religious symbolism is its capacity to manifest a coherent unity of the world in which the self is an integrating factor. This capacity follows from the description of a symbol as multivalent in its meaning. The stress here is on the unity of the multivalent meanings correlated with the self. This description of the meaning of religious symbols is an exact parallel of Eliade's description of the historian of religions' task. It is the best example I know of where the meaning of religious symbolism as an integrated, coherent unity and the interpretative work as an integration of the various religious phenomena form a single and consistent correlation. It is the exemplification of the maxim that the "method should fit the phenomena." This correlation prevents a reduction of the meaning of religion as it appears in and for itself, and it thus represents the aim of all phenomenologies of religion.

The fifth function Eliade singles out as "perhaps the most important." It is the capacity of a symbol to express "paradoxical situations or certain structures of ultimate reality otherwise quite inexpressible." His examples of this function are found in the symbolisms of the Symplegades and the notion of *coincidentia oppositorum.* The significance of this characteristic is once again its capacity to reveal a mode of being which is not accessible through immediate experience.

The sixth and last function of a religious symbol, according to Eliade, is that it "always aims at a reality or structure in which human existence is engaged." There is a double edge to religious symbols. On the one hand, they open, unveil, or point to a structure of reality or the real. On the other hand, and insofar as they have the first capacity, they also bring meaning into existence.

Any reading of the books and articles Eliade has written will show that his main concern is with symbolic systems or archetypes. In this sense, we find descriptions such as the symbolism of "The Cosmic Tree," "Ascension," "Water," "Lunar," and "Solar" symbolic systems. What is important to remember is that these systems do not manifest themselves as such and that any particular symbol such as the Asvatta tree in India or the cross in Christianity shares the multivalent meaning of the archetypal system. Understanding these archetypal systems as some deductive typology is an error. In speaking of the coherence of the symbolic system, Eliade states:

we have good cause to look upon these various symbolisms [i.e., of earth, sun, space, time, etc.] as autonomous 'systems' in that they manifest more clearly, more fully, and with greater coherence what the hierophanies manifest in an individual, local, and successive fashion. . . . It is not a question of arbitrarily 'deducing' any sort of symbolism from an elementary hierophany; [nor] of rationalizing a symbolism to make it clear and consistent. . . . Only one thing matters in the history of religions . . . the fact that all these myths and all these rituals fit together, or in other words, make a symbolic system which in a sense pre-existed them all.[23]

Many similar statements could be adduced to show Eliade's interpretation of symbolism in this archetypal sense.

Myths and rituals represent or repeat symbolically the model or prototype for meaningful existence. It must be remembered, however, that myths are complex symbol structures. That is to say, specific myths and particular symbols manifest or repeat a system or an archetype which is universal. As Eliade says:

Of course the water symbolism is nowhere concretely expressed, it has no central core, for it is made up of a pattern of independent symbols which fit together into a system but it is none the less real for that. . . . This system is obviously implied in every water hierophany on however small a scale, but it is more explicitly revealed through a symbol ('the flood' or 'baptism') and is only fully revealed in water symbolism as displayed in *all* the hierophanies.[24]

The levels or structures of symbolic meaning which we have described above refer to the sacred. The sacred as such never appears in immediate experience; in fact, it is paradoxical that it should manifest itself at all. Eliade translates this paradox as the manifestation of being — the absolute, the unconditioned, and the eternal — in the profane. It stands over against becoming — the relative, contingent, and temporal world. The dialectic which

23. M. Eliade, *Patterns in Comparative Religion*, 449-450.
24. *Ibid.*, 449.

truth in closest words shall fail, / And truth embodied in a tale / Shall enter in at lowly doors." He says that the term *myth* may be applied in this sense to the sacred story of Christian tradition, and so employed should give offense to none.[2]

According to Hooke, then, a myth with its associated ritual is something which meets a recurrent human need, and we can safely say that this need is for life and prosperity in one form or another. This applies to every genuine myth. Even in so simple a myth as that of Guy Fawkes, the implication of "I see no reason why gun-powder treason should ever be forgot" is that if it were forgotten things might be easier for traitors. Hocart has shown that, in the case of the Hindu myths, "the myth itself confers, or helps to confer, the object of men's desire—life."[3] We can then extend our definition and say that myth is not merely a narrative associated with a rite, but a narrative which, with or without its associated rite, is believed to confer life.

But some readers may say that this is not at all what they mean by myths. What they mean are highly imaginative stories about the miraculous rescue of a princess from a monster, or the vengeance of the gods on a king who has incurred their wrath; how could such stories be supposed to confer life? Anyone who makes this objection has obviously limited his study of mythology to those myths which the classical writers abstracted from their religious context and used as a basis for poetry and romance. Myths in their proper context are seen differently, as will appear presently.

Those who regard myths as the products of the imagination have clearly not considered how the imagination works. Nobody can possibly imagine anything which has not been suggested to him by something which he has seen, heard, or read. Poets and novelists, by selecting from and combining ideas which have reached them in various ways, produce what are called works of the imagination, but those who formulated or recorded the myths could not have acted in this way. For the myths were so sacred that they could have been altered or added to only by those who believed themselves inspired, and even then to a very limited extent.

The kind of imagination which the myth-maker is, according to some, supposed to have possessed is in fact something which nobody has ever possessed. When Grote, for example, says that the ancient Greek, instead of seeing the sun as we see it, "saw the great god Helios, mounting his chariot in the morning in the east, reaching at midday the height of the solid heaven, and arriving in the evening at the western horizon with horses fatigued and desirous of repose,"[4] he is postulating a type of mind which has never existed. The chariot of the sun was a ritual chariot, and the god Helios was seen in the ritual in the form of a priest who drove the chariot. The Christian believes that the consecrated wafer is the body of Christ, but what he sees is a wafer. In the same way, we may be sure, the ancient Greek believed that the sun was the god Helios, but what he saw was just the sun.

It has often been suggested that there is a myth-making stage through which all communities pass; but in that case all but the most primitive communities would have a mythology or traces of it, and if H. J. Rose is right that is not so. For he assures us that the earlier Romans had no mythology, and that the myths told of their gods by the later Roman writers were borrowings from the Greeks.[5] The Romans had many

[2] E. O. James, *Christian Myth and Ritual* (London, 1933), p. viii.
[3] A. M. Hocart, *The Life-giving Myth* (London, 1952), p. 16.
[4] Quoted by A. M. Hocart, *Social Origins* (London, 1954), p. 5.
[5] H. J. Rose, *Primitive Culture in Italy* (London, 1926), p. 43.

rites, but these were not associated with myths because the gods were not fully personified, and without full personification there can hardly be mythology. But if the Romans had no mythology, how comes it that the Greeks, their neighbors and kinsmen, had such an elaborate mythology? The reason, unpopular with classical scholars but noted by many writers from Herodotus to Sir Arthur Evans and Hooke, is that many of the Greek myths were not native, but imported from Egypt, Syria, and Mesopotamia. Herodotus, as is well known, assigned an Egyptian origin to many elements in Greek religion and mythology; Hooke identifies Perseus with the. Canaanite god Resheph; and Evans traces the Minotaur to the Euphrates. And in this connection Hooke notes that "both the Minotaur and Perseus myths involve an underlying ritual pattern of human sacrifice, and take us back to a stage in which the myth and ritual were united."[6]

Even those scholars who are in general hostile to the view put forward in this paper have been driven to realize that in some cases at least myth is linked with ritual. Thus H. J. Rose, dealing with the mythical quarrel of Zeus and Hera, and the Plataean rite which "commemorated" it, says that "the legend has pretty certainly grown out of the rite, as usually happens."[7] And Sir William Halliday says "that the story of Lycaon, connected as it undoubtedly was with some form of human sacrifice which seems to have persisted up to the time of Pausanias, is an hieratic legend connected with the savage ritual of Lycaean Zeus, appears to me almost certain. The story of the serving up of Pelops by Tantalus may also have had a ritual origin and have been in the first place connected with some rite of human sacrifice and sacrament."[8]

A. B. Cook refers the legend of Ixion, who was bound to a wheel, to a ritual in which a man was bound to a wheel and sacrificed in the character of the sun-god, and the legend of Triptolemus, who was borne over the earth in a winged chariot from which he introduced the blessings of corn, to a rite at Eleusis. "The *protégé* of the goddess, mounting his winged seat, was swung aloft by means of a *geranos* or scenic crane."[9]

We end our quotations from the classical scholars with one from J. A. K. Thomson, who says: "Not only is the Myth the explanation of the rite, it is at the same time, in part at least, the explanation of the god. To primitive minds it is of such transcendent importance to get the ritual exactly right (for the slightest deviation will ruin everything) that the worshippers will not proceed one step without authority. And who is their authority? In normal circumstances the oldest man in the tribe, the worshipper who has been most frequently through this particular ceremony before. And his authority? Well, the oldest tribesman within his memory. And so the tradition goes back and back. . . . But it must end somewhere, and it ends, as a thousand instances show, in an imaginary divine founder of the rite, who becomes the centre of the Myth."[10]

We may doubt whether the actual process was as Thomson suggests, but he correctly emphasizes the importance of the myth for the purpose of validating the rite. Hocart makes the same point when he writes: "If we turn to the living myth, that is

---

[6] *Myth and Ritual*, ed. S. H. Hooke (London, 1933), pp. 2, 6.
[7] H. J. Rose, *A Handbook of Greek Mythology* (London, 1933), p. 104.
[8] W. R. Halliday, *Indo-European Folktales and Greek Legend* (Cambridge, 1933), p. 103.
[9] A. B. Cook, *Zeus*, I (Cambridge, 1925), 211, 218.
[10] J. A. K. Thomson, *Studies in the Odyssey* (Oxford, 1914), p. 54.

the myth that is believed in, we find that it has no existence apart from the ritual. . . . Knowledge of the myth is essential to the ritual because it has to be recited at the ritual."[11]

Elsewhere, discussing Hindu mythology, he says that "we gradually come to realise that the sacrificer's object is to get control of the whole world—not temporal but ritual control; that is, he seeks to bend the forces of nature to his will so that they may produce plenty for him. . . . As the gods did, so must the sacrificer, for the sacrificer and his acolytes represent the gods. It is necessary that he should know the myth which describes how the gods succeeded. . . . The myth is a precedent, but it is more than that. Knowledge is essential for the success of the ritual."[12]

Let us now turn to mythology as it is dealt with by students of the present-day savage, and begin with Malinowski. He says: "Myth, studied alive, is not symbolic but a direct expression of its subject-matter. . . . Myth fulfills in primitive culture an indispensable function; it expresses, enhances and codifies belief; it safeguards and enforces morality; it vouches for the efficiency and contains practical rules for the guidance of man."[13]

Malinowski's views have been amplified by Haimendorf in his account of the Raj Gonds, an Indian jungle tribe. He says: "The social norms regulating the tribal life of the Gonds are firmly rooted in mythology. They derive their validity from the rulings of culture-heroes and from the actions of deified ancestors recounted in epics and countless songs. The myths that tell of the origin of the Gond race and the establishment of the four phratries are more than history or folklore; they are the pragmatic sanction for institutions that determine the behaviour of every Gond towards his fellow-tribesmen, they are the vital forces inspiring the performance of the great clan feasts, and they define and authorise man's relations with the divine powers on whom his welfare depends. A relationship of mutual enlivenment links myth and ritual: as the myths lend power to the ritual acts, so the symbolic enactment of mythical occurrences during the cardinal rites of the clan feasts endows the myths with reality. . . . It is in the sacramental rites based on the clan-myth that the unity of the clan attains realisation."[14]

Of the Santals, a tribe of Northeastern India, Culshaw tells us that "many of the social activities of the Santals are based on myths, and the strength of their clan organisation is due in no small measure to its foundations in mythology. . . . When for any reason a piece of ritual associated with a myth falls into disuse, knowledge of the myth begins to die out; conversely, when the myth is looked upon as outmoded, the activity with which it is linked begins to lose its hold on the people's imagination. . . . The decay of the ritual is leading to the disappearance of the ancient myth. It is nevertheless true that these stories do reveal the Santal view of the world. When they are told they call forth assent, and frequently in ordinary conversation the myths are cited in order to point a moral or clinch an argument."[15]

Among the Tallensi of the Gold Coast, so Fortes tells us, "the complementary functions of chiefship and *tendana*-ship are rooted directly in the social structure, but

[11] A. M. Hocart, *The Progress of Man* (London, 1933), p. 223.
[12] Hocart, *The Life-giving Myth*, p. 13.
[13] B. Malinowski, *Myth in Primitive Psychology* (London, 1926), p. 13.
[14] C. von F. Haimendorf, *The Raj Gonds* (London, 1948), p. 99.
[15] W. J. Culshaw, *Tribal Heritage* (London, 1949), p. 64.

are also validated by myths of origin and backed by the most powerful religious sanctions of the ancestor cult and the cult of the earth."[16]

Other examples could be given, but these should suffice to show that myth and ritual are as closely linked among modern savages as they were in the ancient civilizations. Are we justified, however, in concluding that every rite has or once had its associated myth and every myth its associated rite? I do not suggest that this can be proved, but I do suggest that it can be shown to be probable.

Let us first consider rites which have no myths, as, according to Rose, those of the early Romans. Had they lost their myths, or had they never had any? The Roman rites were largely of the character which is commonly called magical. Frazer and his followers took the view that magic was, to put it shortly, primitive religion, and since many magical rites have no myth, this if true would prove ritual to be older than myths. But I have elsewhere given reason to think that Frazer was mistaken, and that magic, far from being primitive religion, is really degenerate religion, a form of religion, that is to say, in which people go on performing rites, but have forgotten why.[17] In Europe and, I believe, in America, many people perform such rites as "touching wood" after boasting, throwing three pinches of spilled salt over the left shoulder, saluting a magpie, turning money in their pockets when they see the new moon. They do not know why they perform them, except that failure to do so would be followed by "bad luck." It is difficult to believe that rites could have come into existence in such a vague and meaningless way, and it is probable that they were once associated with some deity or hero.

Evans-Pritchard spent some years in studying two tribes of the Southern Sudan, the Zande and the Nuer. Of the former he tells us that they have very few myths, and those he mentions have no close connection with the ritual.[18] The Nuer, on the other hand, have many myths. Some of these explain the mythological relationships of the lineages, and "also explain the ritual symbols and observances of the lineages mentioned in them."[19] It seems more likely that the Zande myths should have become lost or detached from the ritual than that the Nuer myths and rites should have originated independently and then been fitted together.

We come now to what is perhaps the more important and interesting question, whether every myth once had its associated rite. That many myths, ancient and modern, have been associated with rites we have seen, but are or were there myths which were never associated with rites? That there are now such myths is obvious, but my suggestion is that these myths were once associated with rites, and that the rites ceased to be performed but the myths survived in the form of stories. Having become divorced from their rites and recited for other purposes, they gradually changed their character. How this comes about is discussed by W. J. Gruffydd. Of one story in the *Mabinogion* he says that "the four stages through which the tale has grown to its present form can be set down as follows: 1st. stage—Mythology. Of Lugh-Leu as a god we have considerable evidence. 2nd. stage—Mythology becomes history. 3rd. stage—Mythological history becomes folklore. 4th. stage—Folklore is

[16] M. Fortes, *The Web of Kinship Among the Tallensi* (Oxford, 1949), p. 3.
[17] Lord Raglan, *The Origins of Religion* (London, 1949).
[18] E. E. Evans-Pritchard, *Witchcraft among the Azande* (Oxford, 1937), p. 442.
[19] E. E. Evans-Pritchard, *The Nuer* (Oxford, 1940), p. 442.

utilised to form literary tales."[20] A deity or ritual figure may, that is to say, become in succession a pseudo-historical character, a fairy prince, and the hero of a saga or novel, and unscientific mythologists will assign to each of these four personages a totally different origin. It seems legitimate, however, to regard as myths such narratives, whether quasi-historical or quasi-fictitious, as suggest a ritual origin, and we shall now consider some such myths.

Human sacrifice, real or symbolical, has been a prominent feature of most religions. Nobody has succeeded in explaining it, and I shall make no attempt to do so, but its evolution seems to have been in four main stages. In the first it was the divine king who was regularly sacrificed; in the second somebody else was regularly sacrificed as a substitute for the divine king; with the progress of civilization came a third stage, in which a human victim was sacrificed in times of emergency, but at other times a pretense was made of killing him, but some other victim was substituted. In the fourth stage the victim was never human, but was usually treated in such a way as to indicate that it once had been.

Many myths describe or refer to the sacrifice of a human victim. Some of them, those of Lycaon, Pelops, and Ixion, have already been mentioned. I wish now to draw attention to some myths which suggest the pretended killing of a human victim. The best known of these is of course that of Abraham and Isaac. What happened at one time, no doubt, was that a human victim was brought to the sacrificing priest, who made a pretense of killing him but instead killed a ram, which was substituted at the last moment. The myth, in the usual way, explains and justifies this procedure by reference to an ancient hero.

A story which has a wide distribution in Europe and Asia is that of the Faithful Hound, which in its simplest form is as follows: "The master's child is attacked by a wolf, but a hound which is guarding the child kills the wolf. The master on returning fails to see the child, but sees the hound covered with blood and believes that it has destroyed the child. He rashly kills the hound, but finds out his mistake when he discovers the child safe and the wolf killed. . . . It is generally agreed that this marchen is of Oriental origin."[21] I suggest that this was originally a myth describing and authorizing the substitution of an animal for a human victim.

The story of William Tell seems to have been told in many parts of Northern Europe long before it reached Switzerland,[22] and is probably a myth, that is to say the account of a pretended or substitute human sacrifice.

I have already mentioned the Minotaur. His death is depicted on many Greek vases, where we see a man with a bull's head being slain unresisting. He is said to have been the son of Queen Pasiphae, whom, incidentally, we know to have been a goddess worshipped in Laconia, by her intercourse with a bull. This does not suggest ritual until we compare it with the Vedic horse-sacrifice. Here, as so often, the wildest dreams of myth become the facts of ritual. A stallion was killed, the queen was made to lie beside it, and her next child was supposed to be its offspring. The king took part in this ritual, which most probably represents the substitution of a stallion for

[20] W. J. Gruffydd, *Math vab Mathonwy* (Cardiff, 1928), p. 81.

[21] W. J. Gruffydd, *Rhiannon* (Cardiff, 1953), p. 59; cf. S. Baring-Gould, *Curious Myths of the Middle Ages* (London, 1892), p. 134.

[22] Baring-Gould, *Curious Myths*, p. 119.

the king as victim. To be a ritually effective substitute the stallion had to be married to the queen. And at Athens the Queen Archon was married annually, in a building called the Ox-stall, to the bull-god Dionysus. (J. G. Frazer, *The Golden Bough*, VII [London, 1915] 30.) That these rites provide the clue to the myth of the Minotaur can scarcely be doubted.

Before considering myths which it is less easy to explain as narratives associated with ritual, we must discuss briefly two types of narrative which are not usually regarded as myths, the fairy tale and the saga. If we can show that these are, or were originally, associated with ritual, and can therefore on our definition be regarded as myths, we can avoid a good deal of hair-splitting. We can put all traditional narratives as regards their origin into one category, though it may be convenient to subdivide them according to the form which they have assumed.

Saintyves, in his study of Perrault's Tales, has given us good reason to think that such familiar stories as Bluebeard, Cinderella, Sleeping Beauty, and Little Red Riding-hood are associated with rites, either seasonal rites or rites of initiation. He starts with the story called "The Fairies." This story, variants of which are found in many countries, is of two sisters. One of them is kind to a fairy disguised as an old woman, and gives her food and drink; as a reward a jewel falls from her mouth whenever she speaks, and she marries a prince. The other sister is rude to the old woman and refuses to give her anything; as a punishment a frog falls from her mouth whenever she speaks, and she dies in misery. Saintyves shows that this story illustrates a ritual still performed in remote parts of France. On New Year's Eve the women of the household prepare a room, with a table on which are a clean tablecloth, food, drink, and a lighted candle. The door and window are left open for the fairies to come in. Those who are punctilious in this will be prosperous throughout the year and if unmarried will make a successful marriage; those who are neglectful will meet with dire misfortunes.[23]

This must suffice for the fairies, and we now turn to the sagas. It was formerly supposed that these were historical narratives, but it is now coming to be generally realized that they are novels based largely on myth. Danielli has found a pattern in many of the sagas, which briefly is as follows: The hero in youth is exiled and goes to the court of a king or chief, where he is insulted and treated with contempt. After some time a band of twelve berserks (which may mean "bear-men") arrives under the leadership of one called Bjorn (Bear). These put the hero through various ordeals, and challenge him to fight one of them; he does so and is victorious. After this he successfully undertakes to kill a great bear or other monster which has been ravaging the neighborhood. He is then taken into favor by the chief, and is given a valuable sword and in some instances the chief's daughter in marriage. The details vary, but there is enough regularity to leave little room for doubt that these are features of an installation ritual which have been adapted by the sagamen to their purpose of telling a good story.[24] In my book, *The Hero,* I have noted a number of other ritual features in the sagas.[25]

The rites to which I refer are known to have existed, so that we may safely infer

[23] P. Saintyves, *Les contes de Perrault et les récits parallèles* (Paris, 1923), p. 13.

[24] Mary Danielli, "Initiation Ceremonial From Norse Literature," *Folk-Lore,* LVI (1945), 229-245.

[25] Lord Raglan, *The Hero* (London, 1936), pp. 256, 264, 272, 278.

that the stories told in the sagas, in whatever form they reached the sagamen, were once genuine myths. There are, however, many stories in myth form which are not known to have had associated rites; are we justified in assuming that such rites once existed? It is useless to discuss such questions in the abstract; let us take an example. Malinowski tells the Trobriand story of the origin of death. In the olden days people did not die when they grew old, but were able to rejuvenate themselves by taking off their skins. They lost this power because once a girl failed to recognize her rejuvenated grandmother, and the latter in pique put her old skin on again.[26] This story is not an explanation; the Trobrianders, as Malinowski tells us, take no interest in explanations, and it obviously does not explain the fact of death. I suggest that it is a reminiscence of a new year ritual in the course of which an officiant, by taking off an old garment and putting on a new one, symbolically rejuvenated the world. I know of no such rite, but it may safely be postulated as the prototype of the many rites in which a change of dress symbolizes beginning of a new life.

In the foregoing I have drawn my evidence from books readily accessible to me, which unfortunately include few American ones. A cursory survey of American literature suggests, however, that in America as elsewhere many ethnologists have no idea that myths may have a function, and tell them as so many "Just So Stories." I have found some exceptions. Thus Parsons, discussing the Hopi "emergence" myth, says "this myth is too explanatory of the ceremonial life to be told to rank outsiders."[27] Wheelwright says of the Navaho: "in the most complete versions of the myths the different forms of ceremonies are mentioned and often described."[28] And Park, dealing with certain tribes of Colombia, says that the songs and dances conferred on the priests are among the themes which stand out in the myths.[29]

In conclusion, I would ask what are the objections to the view which I have put forward. There are few students of mythology, I suppose, who would deny that there is in some cases a connection between myth and ritual, but there is what seems to me a surprising reluctance to accept the simple scientific principle that similar causes produce similar effects, and a belief that a wide range of causes, from the wildest speculation to the soberest regard for historical truth, may produce stories sufficiently similar to be classed together as myths. To explain this phenomenon some theorists invoke a mysterious force called convergence, which is apparently supposed to get hold of all kinds of different things and force them into the same mold. But it is divergence, rather than convergence, which obtains in matters of culture; hence the variety of sects and dialects, and of objects in our museums. Myths are similar because they arise in connection with similar rites. Ritual has been, at most times and for most people, the most important thing in the world. From it have come music, dancing, painting, and sculpture. All these, we have every reason to believe, were sacred long before they were secular, and the same applies to storytelling.

Cefntilla Court, Usk
Monmouthshire, England

[26] Malinowski, *Myth in Primitive Psychology*, pp. 41, 81.
[27] E. C. Parsons, *Pueblo Indian Religion*, I (Chicago, 1939), 216.
[28] M. C. Wheelwright, *Navaho Creation Myth* (Santa Fe, 1942), p. 19.
[29] W. Z. Park, *Handbook of South American Indians*, II (Washington, 1946), 886.

LECTURE I.

INTRODUCTION : THE SUBJECT AND THE METHOD OF
ENQUIRY.

THE subject before us is the religion of the Semitic peoples,
that is, of the group of kindred nations, including the Arabs,
the Hebrews and Phœnicians, the Aramæans, the Babylonians and Assyrians, which in ancient times occupied the
great Arabian Peninsula, with the more fertile lands of
Syria Mesopotamia and Irac, from the Mediterranean
coast to the base of the mountains of Iran and Armenia.
Among these peoples three of the great faiths of the
world had their origin, so that the Semites must always
have a peculiar interest for the student of the history of
religion. Our subject, however, is not the history of the
several religions that have a Semitic origin, but Semitic
religion as a whole in its common features and general
type. Judaism, Christianity and Islam are *positive* religions,
that is, they did not grow up like the systems of ancient
heathenism, under the action of unconscious forces operating
silently from age to age, but trace their origin to the
teaching of great religious innovators, who spoke as the
organs of a divine revelation, and deliberately departed
from the traditions of the past. Behind these positive
religions lies the old unconscious religious tradition, the

A

body of religious usage and belief which cannot be traced
to the influence of individual minds, and was not propagated
on individual authority, but formed part of that inheritance
from the past into which successive generations of the
Semitic race grew up as it were instinctively, taking it as
a matter of course that they should believe and act as their
fathers had done before them. The positive Semitic
religions had to establish themselves on ground already
occupied by these older beliefs and usages; they had to
displace what they could not assimilate, and whether they
rejected or absorbed the elements of the older religion,
they had at every point to reckon with them and take up
a definite attitude towards them. No positive religion that
has moved men has been able to start with a *tabula rasa*,
and express itself as if religion were beginning for the first
time; in form, if not in substance, the new system must
be in contact all along the line with the older ideas and
practices which it finds in possession. A new scheme of
faith can find a hearing only by appealing to religious
instincts and susceptibilities that already exist in its
audience, and it cannot reach these without taking account
of the traditional forms in which all religious feeling is
embodied, and without speaking a language which men
accustomed to these old forms can understand. Thus to
comprehend a system of positive religion thoroughly, to
understand it in its historical origin and form as well as in
its abstract principles, we must know the traditional
religion that preceded it. It is from this point of view
that I invite you to take an interest in the ancient religion
of the Semitic peoples; the matter is not one of mere
antiquarian curiosity, but has a direct and important
bearing on the great problem of the origins of the spiritual
religion of the Bible. Let me illustrate this by an example.
You know how large a part of the teaching of the New

Testament and of all Christian theology turns on the ideas of sacrifice and priesthood. In what they have to say on these heads the New Testament writers presuppose, as the basis of their argument, the notion of sacrifice and priesthood current among the Jews and embodied in the ordinances of the Temple. But, again, the ritual of the Temple was not in its origin an entirely novel thing; the precepts of the Pentateuch did not create a priesthood and a sacrificial service on an altogether independent basis, but only reshaped and remodelled, in accordance with a more spiritual doctrine, institutions of an older type, which in many particulars were common to the Hebrews with their heathen neighbours. Every one who reads the Old Testament with attention is struck with the fact that the origin and *rationale* of sacrifice are nowhere fully explained; that sacrifice is an essential part of religion is taken for granted, as something which is not a doctrine peculiar to Israel but is universally admitted and acted on without as well as within the limits of the chosen people. Thus when we wish thoroughly to study the New Testament doctrine of sacrifice, we are carried back step by step till we reach a point where we have to ask what sacrifice meant, not to the old Hebrews alone, but to the whole circle of nations of which they formed a part. By considerations of this sort we are led to the conclusion that no one of the religions of Semitic origin which still exercise so great an influence on the lives of millions of mankind can be studied completely and exhaustively without a subsidiary enquiry into the older traditional religion of the Semitic race.

You observe that in this argument I take it for granted that, when we go back to the most ancient religious conceptions and usages of the Hebrews, we shall find them to be the common property of a group of kindred peoples, and not the exclusive possession of the

tribes of Israel. The proof that this is so will appear
more clearly in the sequel; but, indeed, the thing will
hardly be denied by any one who has read the Bible with
care. In the history of old Israel before the captivity,
nothing comes out more clearly than that the mass of the
people found the greatest difficulty in keeping their
national religion distinct from that of the surrounding
nations. Those who had no grasp of spiritual principles,
and knew the religion of Jehovah only as an affair of
inherited usage, were not conscious of any great difference
between themselves and their heathen neighbours, and fell
into Canaanite and other foreign practices with the greatest
facility. The significance of this fact is manifest if we
consider how deeply the most untutored religious sensi-
bilities are shocked by any kind of innovation. Nothing
appeals so strongly as religion to the conservative instincts;
and conservatism is the habitual attitude of Orientals.
The whole history of Israel is unintelligible if we suppose
that the heathenism against which the prophets contended
was a thing altogether alien to the religious traditions of
the Hebrews. In principle there was all the difference in
the world between the faith of Isaiah and that of an
idolater. But the difference in principle, which seems so
clear to us, was not clear to the average Judæan, and the
reason of this was that it was obscured by the great
similarity in many important points of religious tradition
and ritual practice. The conservatism which refuses to
look at principles, and has an eye only for tradition and
usage, was against the prophets, and had no sympathy
with their efforts to draw a sharp line between the religion
of Jehovah and that of the foreign gods. This is a proof
that what I may call the natural basis of Israel's worship
was very closely akin to that of the neighbouring cults.

The conclusion on this point which is suggested by the

facts of Old Testament history, may be accepted the more
readily because it is confirmed by presumptive arguments
of another kind. Traditional religion is handed down from
father to child, and therefore is in great measure an affair
of race. Nations sprung from a common stock will have
a common inheritance of traditional belief and usage in
things sacred as well as profane, and thus the evidence
that the Hebrews and their neighbours had a large common
stock of religious tradition falls in with the evidence
which we have from other sources, that in point of race
the people of Israel were nearly akin to the heathen
nations of Syria and Arabia. The populations of this
whole region constitute a well-marked ethnic unity, a fact
which is usually expressed by giving to them the common
name of Semites. The choice of this term was orginally
suggested by the tenth chapter of Genesis, in which most
of the nations of the group with which we are concerned
are represented as descended from Shem the son of Noah.
But though modern historians and ethnographers have
borrowed a name from the book of Genesis, it must be
understood that they do not define the Semitic group as
coextensive with the list of nations that are there reckoned
to the children of Shem. Most recent interpreters are
disposed to regard the classification of the families of
mankind given in Genesis x. as founded on principles
geographical or political rather than ethnographical; the
Phœnicians and other Canaanites, for example, are made to
be children of Ham and near cousins of the Egyptians.
This arrangement corresponds to historical facts, for, at a
period anterior to the Hebrew conquest, Canaan was for
centuries an Egyptian dependency, and Phœnician religion
and civilisation are permeated by Egyptian influence.
But ethnographically the Canaanites were akin to the Arabs
and Syrians, and they spoke a language which is hardly

different from Hebrew. On the other hand, Elam and Lud, that is, Susiana and Lydia, are called children of Shem, and doubtless these lands were powerfully influenced by Semitic civilisation, but there is no reason to think that in either country the mass of the population belonged to the same stock as the Syrians and Arabs. Accordingly it must be remembered that when modern scholars use the term Semitic, they do not speak as interpreters of Scripture, but as independent observers of ethnographical facts, and include all peoples whose distinctive ethnical characters assign them to the same group with the Hebrews, Syrians, and Arabs.

The scientific definition of an ethnographical group depends on a variety of considerations; for direct historical evidence of an unimpeachable kind as to the original seats and kindred of ancient peoples is not generally to be had. The defects of historical tradition must therefore be supplied by observation, partly of inherited physical characteristics, and partly of mental characteristics habits and attainments such as are usually transmitted from parent to child. Among the indirect criteria of kinship between nations, the most obvious, and the one which has hitherto been most carefully studied, is the criterion of language; for it is observed that the languages of mankind form a series of natural groups, and that within each group it is possible to arrange the several languages which it contains in what may be called a genealogical order, according to degrees of kinship. Now it may not always be true that people of the same or kindred speech are as closely related by actual descent as they seem to be from the language they speak; a Gaelic tribe, for example, may forget their ancient speech, and learn to speak a Teutonic dialect, without ceasing to be true Gaels by blood. But, in general, large groups of men do not readily change their language, but go on from generation to generation speaking the ancestral dialect with such gradual modification as the lapse of time brings about.   As a rule, therefore, the classification of mankind by language, at least when applied to large masses, will approach pretty closely to a natural classification; and in a large proportion of cases, the language of a mixed race will prove on examination to be that of the stock whose blood is predominant.   Where this is not the case, where a minority has imposed its speech on a majority, we may safely conclude that it has done so in virtue of a natural pre-eminence, a power of shaping lower races in its own mould, which is not confined to the sphere of language, but extends to all parts of life.   Where we find unity of language, we can at least say with certainty that we are dealing with a group of men who are subject to common influences of the most subtle and far-reaching kind; and where unity of speech has prevailed for many generations, we may be sure that the continued action of these influences has produced great uniformity of physical and mental type.   When we come to deal with groups which have long had separate histories, and whose languages are therefore not identical but only cognate, the case is not so strong.   A Scot, for example, whose blood is a mixture of the Teutonic and Celtic, and a North German, who is partly Teutonic and partly Wendish, speak languages belonging to the same Teutonic stock, but in each case the non-Teutonic element in the blood, though it has not ruled the language, has had a perceptible effect on the national character, so that the difference of type between the two men is greater than the difference of their dialects indicates. It is plain, therefore, that kinship in language is not an exact measure of the degree of affinity as determined by the sum of race characters; but on the whole it remains true, that the stock which is strong enough, whether by numbers or by genius, to impress its language on a nation, must exercise a predominant influence on the national type in other respects also; and to this extent the classification of races by language must be called natural and not artificial. Especially is this true for ancient times, when the absence of literature, and especially of religious books, made it much more difficult than it has been in recent ages for a new language to establish itself in a race to which it was originally foreign. All Egypt now speaks Arabic—a Semitic tongue—and yet the population is very far from having assimilated itself to the Arabic type. But this could not have happened without the Coran and the religion of the Coran, which have given what I may call an artificial advantage to the Arabic language. In very ancient times the language of a conquering people had no such artificial help in preserving and propagating itself. A tongue which is spoken and not written makes way only in proportion as those who speak it are able to hold their own without assistance from the literary achievements of their ancestors.

As regards the Semitic nations, which, as I have already said, are classed together on the ground of similarity of language, we have every reason to recognise their linguistic kinship as only one manifestation of a very marked general unity of type. The unity is not perfect; it would not, for example, be safe to make generalisations about the Semitic character from the Arabian nomads, and to apply them to the ancient Babylonians. And for this there are probably two reasons. On the one hand, the Semite of the Arabian desert and the Semite of the Babylonian alluvium lived under altogether different physical and moral conditions; the difference of environment is as complete as possible. And on the other hand, it is pretty certain that the Arabs of the desert have been from time immemorial a race practically unmixed, while the Babylonians, and other members of the same family settled on the fringes of the Semitic land, were in all probability largely mingled with the blood of other races, and underwent a corresponding modification of type.

But when every allowance is made for demonstrable or possible variations of type within the Semitic field, it still remains true that the Semites form a singularly well marked and relatively speaking a very homogeneous group. So far as language goes the evidence to this effect is particularly strong. The Semitic tongues are so closely related to one another, that their affinity is recognised even by the untrained observer; and modern science has little difficulty in tracing them back to a common speech, and determining in a general way what the features of that speech were. On the other hand, the differences between these languages and those spoken by other adjacent races are so fundamental and so wide, that no sober philologist has ventured to lay down anything positive as to the relation of the Semitic tongues to other linguistic stocks. Their nearest kinship seems to be with the languages of North Africa, but even here the common features are balanced by profound differences. The evidence of language therefore tends to show that the period during which the original and common Semitic speech existed apart, and developed its peculiar characters at a distance from languages of other stocks, must have been very long in comparison with the subsequent period during which the separate branches of the Semitic stock, such as Hebrew Aramaic and Arabic, were isolated from one another and developed into separate dialects. Or, to draw the historical inference from this, it would appear that before the Hebrews, the Aramæans, and the Arabs spread themselves over widely distant seats, and began their course of separate national development, there must have been a long period in which the ancestors of all these nations lived together and spoke with one tongue. And as Hebrew Aramaic and Arabic are all much liker to one another than the old common Semitic can possibly have been to any of the languages of surrounding races, it would seem that the separate existence of the several Semitic nations up to the time when their linguistic distinctions were fully developed, can have been but short in comparison with the period during which the undivided Semitic stock, living in separation from other races, formed its peculiar and distinctive type of speech.

The full force of this argument can hardly be made plain without reference to philological details of a kind unsuited to our present purpose ; but those of you who have some acquaintance with the Semitic languages will readily admit that the development of the common Semitic system of triliteral roots, not to speak of other linguistic peculiarities, must have been the affair of a number of generations vastly greater than was necessary to develop the differences between Hebrew and Arabic. If, now, the fathers of all the Semitic nations lived together for a very long time, at the very ancient date which preceded the separate history of Hebrews Aramæans and Arabs,—that is, in the infancy of the races of mankind, the period of human history in which individuality went for nothing, and all common influences had a force which we moderns can with difficulty conceive,—it is clear that the various swarms which ultimately hived off from the common stock and formed the Semitic nations known to history, must have carried with them a strongly marked race character, and many common possessions of custom and idea, besides their common language. And further let us observe that the dispersion of the Semitic nations was never carried so far as the dispersion of the Aryans. If we leave out of account settlements made over the seas, — the South Arabian colonies in East Africa, and the Phœnician colonies on the coasts and isles of the Mediterranean,—we find that the region of Semitic occupation is continuous and compact. Its great immovable centre is the vast Arabian peninsula, a region naturally isolated, and in virtue of its physical characters almost exempt from immigration or change of inhabitants. And from this central stronghold, which the predominant opinion of modern scholars designates as the probable starting-point of the whole Semitic dispersion, the region of Semitic speech spreads out round the margin of the Syrian desert till it strikes against great natural boundaries, the Mediterranean, Mount Taurus, and the mountains of Armenia and Iran. From the earliest dawn of history all that lies within these limits was fully occupied by Semitic tribes speaking Semitic dialects, and the compactness of this settlement must necessarily have tended to maintain uniformity of type. The several Semitic nations, when they were not in direct contact with one another, were divided not by alien populations but only by the natural barriers of mountain and desert. These natural barriers, indeed, were numerous, and served to break up the race into a number of small tribes or nations; but, like the mountains of Greece, they were not so formidable as to prevent the separate states from maintaining a great deal of intercourse, which, whether peaceful or warlike, tended to perpetuate the original community of type. Nor was the operation of these causes disturbed in ancient times by any great foreign immigration. The early Egyptian invasions of Syria were not accompanied by any attempt at colonisation; and though the so-called Hittite monuments, which have given rise to so much speculation, may afford evidence that a non-Semitic people from Asia Minor at one time pushed its way into Northern Syria, it is pretty clear that the Hittites of the Bible, *i.e.* the non-Aramaic communities of Cœle-Syria, were a branch of the Canaanite stock, and that the utmost concession that can be made to modern theories on this subject is that they may for a time have been dominated by a non-Semitic aristocracy. At one time it was not uncommon to represent the Philistines as a non-Semitic people, but it is now generally recognised that the arguments for this view are inadequate, and that, though they came into Palestine from across the sea, from Caphtor, *i.e.* probably from Crete, they were either mainly of Semitic blood or at least were already thoroughly Semitised at the time of their immigration, alike in speech and in religion.

Coming down to later times, we find that the Assyrian Babylonian and Persian conquests made no considerable change in the general type of the population of the Semitic lands. National and tribal landmarks were removed, and there were considerable shiftings of population within the Semitic area, but no great incursion of new populations of alien stock. In the Greek and Roman periods, on the contrary, a large foreign element was introduced into the towns of Syria; but as the immigration was practically confined to the cities, hardly touching the rural districts, its effects in modifying racial type were, it would seem, of a very transitory character. For in Eastern cities the death-rate habitually exceeds the birth-rate, and the urban population is maintained only by constant recruital from the country, so that it is the blood of the peasantry which ultimately determines the type of the population. Thus it is to be explained that after the Arab conquest of Syria, the Greek element in the population rapidly disappeared. Indeed, one of the most palpable proofs that the populations of all the old Semitic lands possessed a remarkable homogeneity of character, is the fact that in them, and in them alone, the Arabs and Arab influence took permanent root. The Moslem conquests extended far beyond these limits, but except in the old Semitic countries, Islam speedily took new shapes, and the Arab domination soon gave way before the reaction of the mass of its foreign subjects.

Thus the whole course of history, from the earliest date to which authentic knowledge extends down to the time of the decay of the Caliphate, records no great permanent disturbance of population to affect the constancy of the Semitic type within its original seats, apart from the temporary Hellenisation of the great cities already spoken of. Such disturbances as did take place consisted partly of mere local displacements among the settled Semites, partly, and in a much greater degree, of the arrival and establishment in the cultivated lands of successive hordes of Semitic nomads from the Arabian wilderness, which on their settlement found themselves surrounded by populations so nearly of their own type that the complete fusion of the old and new inhabitants was effected without difficulty, and without modification of the general character of the race. If at any point in its settlements, except along the frontiers, the Semitic blood was largely modified by foreign admixture, this must have taken place in prehistoric times, or by fusion with other races which may have occupied the country before the arrival of the Semites. How far anything of this sort actually happened can only be matter of conjecture, for the special hypotheses which have sometimes been put forth—as, for example, that there was a considerable strain of pre-Semitic blood in the Phœnicians and Canaanites—rest on presumptions of no conclusive sort. What is certain is that the Semitic settlements in Asia were practically complete at the first dawn of history, and that the Semitic blood was constantly reinforced, from very early times, by fresh immigrations from the desert. There is hardly another part of the world where we have such good historical reasons for presuming that linguistic affinity will prove a safe indication of affinity in race, and in general physical and mental type. And this presumption is not belied by the results of nearer enquiry. Those who have busied themselves with the history and literature of the Semitic peoples, bear uniform testimony to the close family likeness that runs through them all.

It is only natural that this homogeneity of type appears to be modified on the frontiers of the Semitic field. To the West, if we leave the transmarine colonies out of view, natural conditions drew a sharp line of local demarcation between the Semites and their alien neighbours. The Red Sea and the desert north of it formed a geographical barrier, which was often crossed by the expansive force of the Semitic race, but which appears to have effectually checked the advance into Asia of African populations. But on the East, the fertile basin of the Euphrates and Tigris seems in ancient as in modern times to have been a meeting-place of races. The preponderating opinion of Assyriologists is to the effect that the civilisation of Assyria and Babylonia was not purely Semitic, and that the ancient population of these parts contained a large pre-Semitic element, whose influence is especially to be recognised in religion and in the sacred literature of the cuneiform records.

If this be so, it is plain that the cuneiform material must be used with caution in our enquiry into the type of traditional religion characteristic of the ancient Semites. That Babylonia is the best starting-point for a comparative study of the sacred beliefs and practices of the Semitic peoples, is an idea which has lately had some vogue, and which at first sight appears plausible on account of the great antiquity of the monumental evidence. But, in matters of this sort ancient and primitive are not synonymous terms; and we must not look for the most primitive form of Semitic faith in a region where society was not primitive. In Babylonia, it would seem, society and religion alike were based on a fusion of two races, and so were not primitive but complex. Moreover, the official system of Babylonian and Assyrian religion, as it is known to us from priestly texts and public inscriptions, bears clear marks of being something more than a popular traditional faith; it has been artificially moulded by priestcraft and statecraft in much the same way as the official religion of Egypt; that is to say, it is in great measure an artificial combination, for imperial purposes, of elements drawn from a number of local worships. In all probability the actual religion of the masses was always much simpler than the official system; and in later times it would seem that, both in religion and in race, Assyria was little different from the adjacent Aramaic countries. These remarks are not meant to throw doubt on the great importance of cuneiform studies for the history of Semitic religion; the monumental data are valuable for comparison with what we know of the faith and worship of other Semitic peoples, and peculiarly valuable because, in religion as in other matters, the civilisation of the Euphrates-Tigris valley exercised a great historical influence on a large part of the Semitic field. But the right point of departure for a general study of Semitic religion must be sought in regions where, though our knowledge begins at a later date, it refers to a simpler state of society, and where accordingly the religious phenomena revealed to us are of an origin less doubtful and a character less complicated. In many respects the religion of heathen Arabia, though we have few details concerning it that are not of post-Christian date, exhibits an extremely primitive character, corresponding to the primitive and un-

changing character of nomadic life. And with what may
be gathered from this source we must compare, above all,
the invaluable notices, preserved in the Old Testament, of
the religion of the small Palestinian states before their
conquest by the great empires of the East. For this
period, apart from the Assyrian records, we have only a
few precious fragments of evidence from inscriptions, and
no other literary evidence of a contemporary kind. At a
later date the evidence from monuments is multiplied and
Greek literature begins to give important aid; but by
this time also we have reached the period of religious
syncretism—the period, that is, when different faiths and
worships began to react on one another, and produce
new and complex forms of religion. Here, therefore, we
have to use the same precautions that are called for in
dealing with the older syncretistic religion of Babylonia
and Assyria; it is only by careful sifting and comparison
that we can separate between ancient use and modern
innovation, between the old religious inheritance of the
Semites and things that came in from without.

Let it be understood from the outset that we have
not the materials for anything like a complete comparative history of Semitic religions, and that nothing of
the sort will be attempted in these Lectures. But a careful
study and comparison of the various sources is sufficient
to furnish a tolerably accurate view of a series of general
features, which recur with striking uniformity in all parts
of the Semitic field, and govern the evolution of faith and
worship down to a late date. These widespread and
permanent features form the real interest of Semitic
religion to the philosophical student; it was in them,
and not in the things that vary from place to place and
from time to time, that the strength of Semitic religion
lay, and it is to them therefore that we must look for help

in the most important practical application of our studies, for light on the great question of the relation of the positive Semitic religions to the earlier faith of the race.

Before entering upon the particulars of our enquiry, I must still detain you with a few words about the method and order of investigation that seem to be prescribed by the nature of the subject. To get a true and well-defined picture of the type of Semitic religion, we must not only study the parts separately, but must have clear views of the place and proportion of each part in its relation to the whole. To this end it is very desirable that we should follow a natural order of enquiry and exposition, beginning with those features of religion which stood, so to speak, in the foreground, and therefore bulked most largely in religious life. And here we shall go very far wrong if we take it for granted that what is the most important and prominent side of religion to us was equally important in the ancient society with which we are to deal. In connection with every religion, whether ancient or modern, we find on the one hand certain beliefs, and on the other certain institutions ritual practices and rules of conduct. Our modern habit is to look at religion from the side of belief rather than of practice; a habit largely due to the fact that, till comparatively recent times, almost the only forms of religion which have attracted much serious study in Europe have been those of the various Christian Churches, and that the controversies between these Churches have constantly turned on diversities of dogma, even where the immediate point of difference has been one of ritual. For in all parts of the Christian Church it is agreed that ritual is important only in connection with its interpretation. Thus within Christendom the study of religion has meant mainly the study of Christian beliefs, and instruction in religion has habitually begun with the creed,

B

religious duties being presented to the learner as flowing from the dogmatic truths he is taught to accept. All this seems to us so much a matter of course that, when we approach some strange or antique religion, we naturally assume that here also our first business is to search for a creed, and find in it the key to ritual and practice. But the antique religions had for the most part no creed; they consisted entirely of institutions and practices. No doubt men will not habitually follow certain practices without attaching a meaning to them; but as a rule we find that while the practice was rigorously fixed, the meaning attached to it was extremely vague, and the same rite was explained by different people in different ways, without any question of orthodoxy or heterodoxy arising in consequence. In ancient Greece, for example, certain things were done at a temple, and people were agreed that it would be impious not to do them. But if you had asked why they were done, you would probably have had several mutually contradictory explanations from different persons, and no one would have thought it a matter of the least religious importance which of these you chose to adopt. Indeed the explanations offered would not have been of a kind to stir any strong feeling; for in most cases they would have been merely different stories as to the circumstances under which the rite first came to be established, by the command or by the direct example of the god. The rite, in short, was connected not with a dogma but with a myth.

In all the antique religions, mythology takes the place of dogma, that is, the sacred lore of priests and people, so far as it does not consist of mere rules for the performance of religious acts, assumes the form of stories about the gods; and these stories afford the only explanation that is offered of the precepts of religion and the prescribed

372

rules of ritual.   But, strictly speaking, this mythology was
no essential part of ancient religion, for it had no sacred
sanction and no binding force on the worshippers.   The
myths connected with individual sanctuaries and ceremonies were merely part of the apparatus of the worship ;
they served to excite the fancy and sustain the interest of
the worshipper ; but he was often offered a choice of
several accounts of the same thing, and provided that he
fulfilled the ritual with accuracy, no one cared what he
believed about its origin.   Belief in a certain series of
myths was neither obligatory as a part of true religion, nor
was it supposed that, by believing, a man acquired religious
merit and conciliated the favour of the gods.   What was
obligatory or meritorious was the exact performance of
certain sacred acts prescribed by religious tradition.   This
being so, it follows that mythology ought not to take the
prominent place that is too often assigned to it in the
scientific study of ancient faiths.   So far as myths consist
of explanations of ritual their value is altogether secondary,
and it may be affirmed with confidence that in almost
every case the myth was derived from the ritual, and not
the ritual from the myth ; for the ritual was fixed and the
myth was variable, the ritual was obligatory and faith in
the myth was at the discretion of the worshipper.   Now
by far the largest part of the myths of antique religions
are connected with the ritual of particular shrines, or with
the religious observances of particular tribes and districts.
In all such cases it is probable, in most cases it is certain,
that the myth is merely the explanation of a religious
usage ; and ordinarily it is such an explanation as could
not have arisen till the original sense of the usage had
more or less fallen into oblivion.   As a rule the myth is
no explanation of the origin of the ritual to any one who
does not believe it to be a narrative of real occurrences,

and the boldest mythologist will not believe that. But, if
it be not true, the myth itself requires to be explained,
and every principle of philosophy and common sense
demands that the explanation be sought, not in arbitrary
allegorical theories, but in the actual facts of ritual or
religious custom to which the myth attaches. The conclusion is, that in the study of ancient religions we must
begin, not with myth, but with ritual and traditional usage.

Nor can it be fairly set against this conclusion, that
there are certain myths which are not mere explanations
of traditional practices, but exhibit the beginnings of larger
religious speculation, or of an attempt to systematise and
reduce to order the motley variety of local worships and
beliefs. For in this case the secondary character of the
myths is still more clearly marked. They are either products of early philosophy, reflecting on the nature of the
universe; or they are political in scope, being designed to
supply a thread of union between the various worships of
groups, originally distinct, which have been united into
one social or political organism; or, finally, they are due
to the free play of epic imagination. But philosophy
politics and poetry are something more, or something less,
than religion pure and simple.

There can be no doubt that, in the later stages of ancient
religions, mythology acquired an increased importance. In
the struggle of heathenism with scepticism on the one
hand and Christianity on the other, the supporters of the
old traditional religion were driven to search for ideas of
a modern cast, which they could represent as the true
inner meaning of the traditional rites. To this end
they laid hold of the old myths, and applied to them an
allegorical system of interpretation. Myth interpreted
by the aid of allegory became the favourite means of
infusing a new significance into ancient forms. But the

theories thus developed are the falsest of false guides as to the original meaning of the old religions.

On the other hand, the ancient myths taken in their natural sense, without allegorical gloss, are plainly of great importance as testimonies to the views of the nature of the gods that were prevalent when they were formed. For though the mythical details had no dogmatic value and no binding authority over faith, it is' to be supposed that nothing was put into a myth which people at that time were not prepared to believe without offence. But so far as the way of thinking expressed in the myth was not already expressed in the ritual itself, it had no properly religious sanction; the myth apart from the ritual affords only a doubtful and slippery kind of evidence. Before we can handle myths with any confidence, we must have some definite hold of the ideas expressed in the ritual tradition, which incorporated the only fixed and statutory elements of the religion.

All this, I hope, will become clearer to us as we proceed with our enquiry, and learn by practical example the use to be made of the different lines of evidence open to us. But it is of the first importance to realise clearly from the outset that ritual and practical usage were, strictly speaking, the sum total of ancient religions. Religion in primitive times was not a system of belief with practical applications; it was a body of fixed traditional practices, to which every member of society conformed as a matter of course. Men would not be men if they agreed to do certain things without having a reason for their action; but in ancient religion the reason was not first formulated as a doctrine and then expressed in practice, but conversely, practice preceded doctrinal theory. Men form general rules of conduct before they begin to express general principles in words; political institutions

are older than political theories, and in like manner
religious institutions are older than religious theories.
This analogy is not arbitrarily chosen, for in fact the
parallelism in ancient society between religious and
political institutions is complete. In each sphere great
importance was attached to form and precedent, but the
explanation why the precedent was followed consisted
merely of a legend as to its first establishment. That
the precedent, once established, was authoritative did not
appear to require any proof. The rules of society were
based on precedent, and the continued existence of the
society was sufficient reason why a precedent once set
should continue to be followed.

Strictly speaking, indeed, I understate the case when I
say that the oldest religious and political institutions
present a close analogy. It would be more correct to
say that they were parts of one whole of social custom.
Religion was a part of the organised social life into which
a man was born, and to which he conformed through life
in the same unconscious way in which men fall into any
habitual practice of the society in which they live. Men
took the gods and their worship for granted, just as they
took the other usages of the state for granted, and if they
reasoned or speculated about them, they did so on the
presupposition that the traditional usages were fixed
things, behind which their reasonings must not go, and
which no reasoning could be allowed to overturn. To
us moderns religion is above all a matter of individual
conviction and reasoned belief, but to the ancients it was
a part of the citizen's public life, reduced to fixed forms,
which he was not bound to understand and was not at
liberty to criticise. Society demanded of each of its
members the observance of the forms, not for his sake
but for its own, for if its religion was tampered with

the bases of society were undermined, and the favour of the gods was forfeited.   But so long as the prescribed religious forms were duly observed, a man was recognised as a pious man, and no one asked how his religion was rooted in his heart or affected his reason.   Religious like political duty, of which indeed it was a part, was entirely comprehended in the observance of certain fixed rules of outward conduct.

The conclusion from all this as to the method of our investigation is obvious.   When we study the political structure of an early. society, we do not begin by asking what is recorded of the first legislators, or what theory men advanced as to the reason of their institutions; we try to understand what the institutions were, and how they shaped men's lives.   In like manner, in the study of Semitic religion, we must not begin by asking what was told about the gods, but what the working religious institutions were, and how they shaped the lives of the worshippers.   Our enquiry therefore, will be directed to the religious institutions which governed the lives of men of Semitic race.

In following out this plan, however, we shall do well not to throw ourselves at once upon the multitudinous details of rite and ceremony, but to devote our attention to certain broad features of the sacred institutions which are sufficiently well marked to be realised at once.   If we were called upon to examine the political institutions of antiquity, we should find it convenient to carry with us some general notion of the several types of government under which the multifarious institutions of ancient states arrange themselves.   And in like manner it will be useful for us, when we examine the religious institutions of the Semites, to have first some general knowledge of the types of divine governance, the various ruling conceptions of the relations of the gods to man, which underlie the rites and ordinances of religion in different places and at different times. Such knowledge we can obtain in a provisional form, before entering on a mass of ritual details, mainly by considering the titles of honour by which men addressed their gods, and the language in which they expressed their dependence on them. From these we can see at once, in a broad, general way, what place the gods held in the social system of antiquity, and under what general categories their relations to their worshippers fell. The broad results thus reached must then be developed, and at the same time controlled and rendered more precise, by an examination in detail of the working institutions of religion.

The question of the metaphysical nature of the gods, as distinct from their social office and function, must be left in the background till this whole investigation is completed. It is vain to ask what the gods are in themselves till we have studied them in what I may call their public life, that is, in the stated intercourse between them and their worshippers which was kept up by means of the prescribed forms of cultus. From the antique point of view, indeed, the question what the gods are in themselves is not a religious but a speculative one ; what is requisite to religion is a practical acquaintance with the rules on which the deity acts and on which he expects his worshippers to frame their conduct—what in 2 Kings xvii. 26 is called the " manner" or rather the " customary law " (*mishpat*) of the god of the land. This is true even of the religion of Israel. When the prophets speak of the knowledge of God, they always mean a practical knowledge of the laws and principles of His government in Israel,[1] and a summary expression for

[1] See especially Hosea, chap. iv.

religion as a whole is " the knowledge and fear of Jehovah," [1]
i.e. the knowledge of what Jehovah prescribes, combined
with a reverent obedience. An extreme scepticism towards
all religious speculation is recommended in the Book of
Ecclesiastes as the proper attitude of piety, for no amount
of discussion can carry a man beyond the plain rule to
" fear God and keep His commandments." [2] This counsel
the author puts into the mouth of Solomon, and so
represents it, not unjustly, as summing up the old view of
religion, which in more modern days had unfortunately
begun to be undermined.

The propriety of keeping back all metaphysical questions
as to the nature of the gods till we have studied the
practices of religion in detail, becomes very apparent if we
consider for a moment what befel the later philosophers
and theosophists of heathenism in their attempts to construct a theory of the traditional religion. We find that
they were not able to give any account of the nature of
the gods from which all the received practices of worship
could be rationally deduced, and accordingly those of them
who had any pretension to be orthodox were compelled to
have recourse to the most violent allegorical interpretations in order to bring the established ritual into
accordance with their theories.[3] The reason for this is
obvious. The traditional usages of religion had grown up
gradually in the course of many centuries, and reflected
habits of thought characteristic of very diverse stages of
man's intellectual and moral development. No one conception of the nature of the gods could possibly afford the
clue to all parts of that motley complex of rites and
ceremonies which the later paganism had received by
inheritance, from a series of ancestors in every stage of

[1] Isaiah xi. 2. [2] Eccles. xii. 13.
[3] See, for example, Plutarch's *Greek* and *Roman Questions.*

culture from pure savagery upwards. The record of the religious thought of mankind, as it is embodied in religious institutions, resembles the geological record of the history of the earth's crust; the new and the old are preserved side by side, or rather layer upon layer. The classification of ritual formations in their proper sequence is the first step towards their explanation, and that explanation itself must take the form, not of a speculative theory, but of a rational life-history.

I have already explained that, in attempting such a life-history of religious institutions, we must begin by forming some preliminary ideas of the practical relation in which the gods of antiquity stood to their worshippers. I have now to add, that we shall also find it necessary to have before us from the outset some elementary notions of the relations which early races of mankind conceived to subsist between gods and men on the one hand, and the material universe on the other. All acts of ancient worship have a material embodiment, the form of which is determined by the consideration that gods and men alike stand in certain fixed relations to particular parts or aspects of physical nature. Certain places, certain things, even certain animal kinds are conceived as holy, i.e. as standing in a near relation to the gods, and claiming special reverence from men, and this conception plays a very large part in the development of all religious institutions. Here again we have a problem that cannot be solved by à priori methods; it is only as we move onward from step to step in the analysis of the details of ritual observances that we can hope to gain full insight into the relations of the gods to physical nature. But there are certain broad features in the ancient conception of the universe, and of the relations of its parts to one another, which can be grasped at once, upon a merely preliminary survey, and we shall find it profitable to give attention to these at an early stage of our discussion.

I propose, therefore, to devote my second lecture to the nature of the antique religious community and the relations of the gods to their worshippers. After this we will proceed to consider the relations of the gods to physical nature, not in a complete or exhaustive way, but in a manner entirely preliminary and provisional, and only so far as is necessary to enable us to understand the material basis of ancient ritual. After these preliminary enquiries have furnished us with certain necessary points of view, we shall be in a position to take up the institutions of worship in an orderly manner, and make an attempt to work out their life-history. We shall find that the history of religious institutions is the history of ancient religion itself, as a practical force in the development of the human race, and that the articulate efforts of the antique intellect to comprehend the meaning of religion, the nature of the gods, and the principles on which they deal with men, take their point of departure from the unspoken ideas embodied in the traditional forms of ritual praxis. Whether the conscious efforts of ancient religious thinkers took the shape of mythological invention or of speculative construction, the raw material of thought upon which they operated was derived from the common traditional stock of religious conceptions that was handed on from generation to generation, not in express words, but in the form of religious custom.

In accordance with the rules of the Burnett Trust, three courses of lectures, to be delivered in successive winters, are allowed me for the development of this great subject. When the work was first entrusted to me, I formed the plan of dividing my task into three distinct parts. In the first course of lectures I hoped to cover the whole field of practical religious institutions. In the second I proposed to myself to discuss the nature and origin of the gods of Semitic heathenism, their relations to one another, the myths that surround them, and the whole subject of religious belief, so far as it is not directly involved in the observances of daily religious life. The third winter would thus have been left free for an examination of the part which Semitic religion has played in universal history, and its influence on the general progress of humanity, whether in virtue of the early contact of Semitic faiths with other systems of antique religion, or—what is more important— in virtue of the influence, both positive and negative, that the common type of Semitic religion has exercised on the formulas and structure of the great monotheistic faiths that have gone forth from the Semitic lands. But the first division of the subject has grown under my hands, and I find that it will not be possible in a single winter to cover the whole field of religious institutions in a way at all adequate to the fundamental importance of this part of the enquiry.

It will therefore be necessary to allow the first branch of the subject to run over into the second course, for which I reserve, among other matters of interest, the whole history of religious feasts and also that of the Semitic priesthoods. I hope, however, to give the present course a certain completeness in itself by carrying the investigation to the end of the great subject of sacrifice. The origin and meaning of sacrifice constitute the central problem of ancient religion, and when this problem has been disposed of we may naturally feel that we have reached a point of rest at which both speaker and hearers will be glad to make a pause.

THE MYTH AND RITUAL APPROACH
TO SHAKESPEAREAN TRAGEDY

Herbert Weisinger

THE "MYTH AND RITUAL" approach to literature is now one of the high gods in the pantheon of contemporary criticism, and it numbers among its devotees not a few eminently respectable names. This was not always so, however, and even as Zeus himself had laboriously to struggle up the ladder of divine acceptance, so the myth and ritual approach to literature now grows fat on quarterly hecatombs. So much so, indeed, that the very word *myth* has acquired a mana of its own and has been elevated into a substitute, less precise, less bold, and I dare say, less honest, for religion, though in this guise it has given many the courage of their conversion. As with other methods for the study of literature, the myth and ritual approach has its values, and they are distinctive and useful, but it also has its limitations, for it is certainly not a panacea concocted to cure all critical complaints.

What I want to do in this paper is to describe the myth and ritual approach to literature as I understand it and to show what new light it can throw on Shakespeare's tragedies, and presumably to illuminate them afresh. For the purposes of this analysis, I take the myth and ritual pattern as fundamental and anterior to tragedy, and I pass Shakespeare's tragedies over this pattern, as tracings over the original drawing, in order to reveal his changes, modifications, and alterations of it; that is to say, I try to distinguish the uniquely Shakespearean from the generally tragic. But I do not wish to be understood as suggesting that the myth and ritual pattern is either the *ur*-tragedy from which all others descend or the ideal tragedy toward which all others tend. Nor would I want to give the impression that the myth and ritual approach to Shakespearean tragedy excludes other established methods of interpreting the plays. The character analysis in ethical terms of Bradley, the visualization of the plays in action on the stage of Granville-Barker, the linking of Elizabethan tragedy with medieval traditions of Farnham, the study of Shakespearean characterization in the light of Elizabethan psychology of Campbell, the examination of the images and image-clusters of the plays as clues to their meaning of Spurgeon, the close reading of the text for structure and texture of Empson, the probing of character in Freudian psychoanalytic categories of Jones, the working-out of the Elizabethan world picture and its role in the Shakespearean ethos of Tillyard, the re-estimation of the extent and use of Shakespeare's learning of Baldwin, the utilization of the new texts established by the scientific bibliographers, the application of Christian ritual to the understanding of the plays of Knight, the placing of Shakespeare within the practices and economy of Elizabethan acting companies of Chambers, the syncretism of the *Scrutiny*-Penguin group—the achievements of these schools of Shakespearean criticism the myth and ritual approach endeavors to assimilate within its own methodology.

Certainly I am not the first to suggest such a correlation; on the contrary, many critics have seen the connection and have in fact gone beyond the tragedies to the later plays in an effort to prove that the pattern of rebirth and reconciliation is fundamental to virtually the whole of Shakespeare's plays. But, while the myth and ritual pattern so used makes, if I may say so, a Christian Olympian out of Shakespeare, it does so only at the expense of the myth and ritual pattern and of the substance of the plays themselves. It is my contention that while the last plays of Shakespeare do indeed carry forward the tragic pattern established in *Hamlet, Othello,*

King Lear, and *Macbeth,* they neither heighten nor deepen it but on the contrary reject and even destroy it. In fact, I would go so far as to argue that the tragic pattern in the tragedies themselves is scarely maintained equally strongly over each of the plays. For, on the basis of a comparison between the myth and ritual pattern as I have described it in *Tragedy and the Paradox of the Fortunate Fall* and the tragedies, I think that Shakespeare's tragic vision, which he was able to sustain but tentatively in *Hamlet,* most fully in *Othello,* barely in *King Lear,* and hardly at all in *Macbeth,* failed him altogether in the last plays, and that this failure is manifested by the use of the elements of the myth and ritual pattern as mere machinery, virtually in burlesque fashion, and not as their informing and sustaining spirit. The instinct of the critics in applying the myth and ritual pattern to the plays has been sound, but their superimposition of the pattern on the plays has been inexact and, I suspect, prompted more by religious rather than by critical motives, with the result that both the method and the plays have been falsified.

I

If I begin with some diffidence, it is because I am always acutely aware that the myth and ritual pattern, upon which the myth and ritual approach to literature must be founded, is as uncertain in its origins as it is unrealized in actuality. I have tried to account for the persistence and power of the myth and ritual pattern by retracing it generally to that initial impact of experience which produced the archetypes of belief, and specifically, to the archetype of rebirth as crystallized out of the archetype of belief) Unfortunately no real proof of this process is possible, for the events which generated the primary shock of belief are now too deep and too dim in the racial memory of man to be exhumed by archaelogical means, though the psychoanalytic probings of

Freud have cleared a path through this labyrinth, with reluctant confirmation coming from the anthropologists and
classicists. Similarly, we must not forget that there is really
no such thing as the myth and ritual pattern *per se;* at best,
it is a probable construction of many varieties and variations
of a number of beliefs and actions so closely related to each
other that it is reasonable to construct—reconstruct would
be a misleading word here—an ideal form of the myth and
ritual pattern more comprehensive and more realized than
any variations of it which we actually possess.

The myth and ritual pattern of the ancient Near East,
which is at least six thousand years old, centers in a divine
king who was killed annually and who was reborn in the
person of his successor. In its later development, the king
was not killed, but went through an annual symbolic death
and a symbolic rebirth or resurrection. Starting out as a
magical rite designed to ensure the success of the crops in
climates where the outcome of the struggle between water
and drought meant literally the difference between life and
death, the pattern was gradually transformed into a religious
ritual, designed this time to promote man's salvation, and
finally became an ethical conviction, freed now of both its
magical and religious ritual practices but still retaining in
spiritualized and symbolic form its ancient appeal and emotional certitude. Because it begins with the need to survive,
the pattern never loses it force, for it is concerned always with
survival, whether physical or spiritual. So far as can be as-
certained at present, the pattern had a double growth, one
along the lines of the ancient civilizations of the Near East,
the Sumerian, the Egyptian, the Babylonian, both South and
North, the Palestinian—first with the Canaanites, and then
with the Hebrews—and from thence into Christianity; the
other along the lines of the island civilizations of the Aegean,
from Crete to the mainland of Greece, from thence to Rome,
and once more into Christianity, the two streams of develop-

ment flowing into each other and reinforcing themselves at this crucial juncture.

Despite the differences between the religions of the ancient Near East (as, for example, between those of Egypt and Mesopotamia, and between that of the Hebrews and of the others), nevertheless they all possessed certain significant features of myth and ritual in common. These features, in their turn, stemmed from the common bond of ritual, characteristic (in one form or another) of all together, though, as I have said, none possessed completely all the elements, which varied in some degree from religion to religion. In this single, idealized ritual scheme, the well-being of the community was secured by the regular performance of certain ritual actions in which the king or his equivalent took the leading role. Moreover the king's importance for the community was incalculably increased by the almost universal conviction that the fortunes of the community or state and those of the king were inextricably intermingled; indeed one may go so far as to say that on the well-being of the king depended the well-being of the community as a whole. On the basis of the evidence covering different peoples at different times, we know then that in the ancient Near East there existed a pattern of thought and action which gripped the minds and emotions of those who believed in it so strongly that it was made the basis on which they could apprehend and accept the universe in which they lived. It made possible man's conviction that he could control that universe for his own purposes; and it placed in his hands the lever whereby he could exercise that control.

From an analysis of the extant seasonal rituals, particularly the new year festivals, and from the coronation, initiation, and personal rituals of the ancient Near East, it is possible to make a reconstructed model of the basic ritual form. Essentially the pattern contains these basic elements: 1. the indispensable role of the divine king; 2. the combat between the God and an opposing power; 3. the suffering of the God; 4. the death of the God; 5. the resurrection of the God; 6. the symbolic recreation of the myth of creation; 7. the sacred marriage; 8. the triumphal procession; and 9. the settling of destinies. We must remember, however, that the dying-rising-God theme constitutes but one illustration, so to speak, of the greater cycle of birth, death, and rebirth. The many and various rites connected with birth, with initiation, with mariage, and with death in the case of the individual, as well as the rites concerned with the planting, the harvesting, the new year celebrations, and with the installation ceremonies of the king in the case of the community, all these rites repeat each in its own way the deep-rooted and abiding cycle of death and rebirth. Not only do these rituals *symbolize* the passage from death to life, from one way of life to another, but they are the actual *means* of achieving the changeover; they mark the transition by which—through the processes of separation, regeneration, and the return on a higher level—both the individual and the community are assured their victory over the forces of chaos which are thereby kept under control.

The purpose of these rituals is by enaction to bring about a just order of existence in which God, nature, and man are placed in complete and final rapport with each other; they are both the defence against disorder and the guarantee of order. In the myth and ritual pattern, then, man has devised a mighty weapon by which he keeps at bay, and sometimes even seems to conquer, the hostile forces which endlessly threaten to overpower him. In the early stages of the development of the myth and ritual pattern, however, the best that man could hope for was an uneasy truce between himself and chaos, because the cycle merely returned to its beginnings; the God fought, was defeated, was resurrected, was momentarily triumphant, and thus ensured the well-being of the community for the coming year, but it was inevitable that in the course of the year he would again be defeated and would again have to go through his annual agony. Thus nothing new could be expected nor was anticipated, and year after year man could hope for no more than a temporary gain which he was sure would soon be turned into an inevitable loss. To achieve genuine faith, therefore, was an act of courage difficult and infrequent to attain, and it is no wonder that we detect in the myth and ritual pattern of the ancient Near East before the Hebraic-Christian tradition takes over, too strong a reliance on the mere machinery of ritual, ultimately leading not to faith but to superstition, as well as the melancholy notes of despair and pessimism. But the Hebraic-Christian tradition in the very process of adapting the pattern, transformed it, for by virtue of its unique and tenacious insistence on the mercy and judgment of its transcendent God, it introduced a new and vital element in the pattern, that of the dialectical leap from out of the endless circle on to a different and higher stage of understanding. The crucial moment in this transformation of the myth and ritual pattern comes when man, by himself, undertakes on his own to make the leap; to him remains the decision and his is the responsibility; by making the leap, he makes himself. The Hebraic-Christian tradition utilized the cycle of birth, life, death, and rebirth to conquer chaos and disorder, but it made its unique contribution to the pattern by giving man the possibility of defeating chaos and disorder by a single, supreme act of human will which could wipe them out at one stroke. In so doing it preserved the potency of the pattern and retained its ancient appeal and, at the same time, ensured its continued use by supplying the one element it had hitherto lacked to give it its permanent role as the means whereby man is enabled to live in an indifferent universe; it showed that man can, by himself, transcend that universe.

II

This, then, is the myth and ritual pattern as I understand it. What are its implications for tragedy? To start with, I would suggest that in the myth and ritual pattern we have the seedbed of tragedy, the stuff out of which it was ultimately formed. Both the form and content of tragedy, its architecture as well as its ideology, closely parallel the form and content of the myth and ritual pattern. But having said that, I must also say that the myth and ritual pattern and tragedy are not the same. Both share the same shape and the same intent, but they differ significantly in the manner of their creation and in the methods of achieving their purposes. The myth and ritual pattern is the group product of many and different minds groping on many and different levels over long and kaleidoscopic periods of time under the stimulus of motivations quite different from those which produce tragedy. I am not suggesting anything like the formerly accepted communal origin of the ballad, for we know that myth in its form as the complement to ritual must have been devised by the priest-astrologer-magicians of the ancient world. The intent of the myth and ritual pattern is control, its method that of mimetically reproducing the rhythm of birth, death, and birth again to gain that control. But imitation here means, not acting alike, as we think of the term—a parallel and similar yet at the same time a distinct and different attitude and behavior toward the thing imitated—but rather the interpenetration of and union with the imitator, the thing imitated, and the imitation, all three being one and the same thing.

Tragedy, on the other hand, is a creation compounded of conscious craft and conviction. If we describe the myth and ritual pattern as the passage from ignorance to understanding through suffering mimetically and at first hand, then we must describe tragedy as the passage from ignorance to understanding through suffering symbolically and at a distance. To speak of symbolic meaning is already to have made the leap from myth to art. In the myth and ritual pattern, the dying-reborn God-king, the worshippers for whom he suffers, and the action of his agony are identical; in tragedy, the tragic protagonist undergoes his suffering at an aesthetic distance and only vicariously in the minds of his audience. And for that reason does Aristotle tell us that tragedy is an imitation of an action. You participate in a ritual but you are a spectator of a play.

Moreover, tragedy reconstitutes the myth and ritual pattern in terms of its own needs. Of the nine elements which make up the myth and ritual pattern as I have described it, four have been virtually eliminated from tragedy, namely, the actual death of the God, the symbolic recreation of the myth of creation, the sacred marriage, and the triumphal procession; two elements, the indispensable role of the divine king and the settling of destinies, are retained only by implication and play rather ambiguous roles in tragedy; while the remaining three—combat, suffering (with death subsumed), and resurrection—now give tragedy its structure and substance. I have already noted that one of the characteristics of the myth and ritual pattern is its adaptability, its ability to change shape while retaining it potency, and we should therefore not be surprised to find the same process at work in its relation to tragedy. What is revealing, however, is the direction of change, for we find, first, that the theme of the settling of destinies which is the highest point in the myth and ritual pattern—the goal of the struggle, since without it the passion of the God would be in vain, and chaos and disorder would be triumphant—this theme, so elaborately explicated in the ritual practices of the ancient Near East, is no more than implied in tragedy, just as the correspondence between the well-being of the king and the well-being of the community, again so detailed in ritual, is only shadowed forth, as a condition to be aimed at but not to be achieved in reality.

Second, we discover that even greater emphasis is placed on the small moment of doubt in tragedy than in the myth and ritual pattern itself. In the rituals of the ancient Near East, at the point between the death of the God and his resurrection, all action is arrested as the participants fearfully and anxiously wait for the God to be revived. After the din of combat, this quiet moment of doubt and indecision is all the more awful, for there is no assurance that the God will be reborn: "For a small moment have I forsaken thee." "But," continues Isaiah, "with great mercies will I gather thee." It is no wonder that the small moment is followed in the pattern by creation, the sacred marriage, and the triumphal procession as the peoples' expression of joy that the death of the God has not been in vain and that for another year at least: "the earth remaineth, seedtime and harvest, and cold and heat, and summer and winter, and day and night shall not cease."

And, clearly spelling out the implications of the second change made by tragedy in the myth and ritual pattern is the third, the freedom of choice of the tragic protagonist and the responsibility for the consequences of making that choice. For in that small moment of doubt and indecision, when victory and defeat are poised in the balance, only the moral force of man wills him on in action to success. The tragic protagonist acts in the conviction that his action is right, and he accepts the responsibility for that action; for him to do less than that means the loss of his stature as a moral, responsible agent. The tragic occurs when by the fall of a man of strong character we are made aware of something greater than that man or even than mankind; we seem to see a new and truer vision of the universe.

But that vision cannot be bought cheaply. It cannot be bought by blind reliance on the mere machinery of the myth and ritual pattern, and it cannot be bought by fixing the fight, as Handel's librettist fatuously puts it:

> How vain is man who boasts in fight
> The valour of gigantic might,
> And dreams not that a hand unseen
> Directs and guides this weak machine.

Better the indifferent Gods of Lucretius than the busybody *deus ex machina* of Vine Street and Madison Avenue. Only the deliberate moral choice of the tragic protagonist confronted by two equal and opposite forces and fully aware of the consequences of his choice can bring off the victory, and then only at the expense of pain and suffering: "He is despised and rejected of men; a man of sorrows, and acquainted with grief." But suffering can be made bearable only when at the same time it is made part of a rational world order into which it fits and which has an understandable place for it:

> I cried by reason of mine affliction unto the Lord, and he heard me; out of the belly of hell cried I, and thou heardest my voice.
> For thou hadst cast me into the deep, in the midst of the seas; and the floods compassed me about: all thy billows and thy waves passed over me.
> Then I said, I am cast out of thy sight; yet I will look again toward thy holy temple.
> The waters compassed me about, even to the soul: the depth closed me round about, the weeds were wrapped about my head.
> I went down to the bottoms of the mountains; the earth with her bars was about me for ever: yet hast thou brought up my life from corruption, O Lord my God.
> When my soul fainted within me I remembered the Lord: and my prayer came in unto thee, into thine holy temple.
> They that observe lying vanities forsake their own mercy.
> But I will sacrifice unto thee with the voice of thanksgiving; I will pay that that I have vowed. Salvation is of the Lord. (*Jonah* 2. 2-9)

Salvation is indeed of the Lord, but Jonah must deliberately look to the holy temple and must remember the Lord of his own free will; *then* salvation is of the Lord.

Tragedy therefore occurs when the accepted order of things is fundamentally questioned only to be the more triumphantly reaffirmed. It cannot exist where there is no faith; conversely, it cannot exist where there is no doubt; it can exist only in an atmosphere of sceptical faith. The protagonist must be free to choose, and though he chooses wrongly, yet the result of the wrong choice is our own escape and our enlightenment. Yet nothing less than this sacrifice will do, and only the symbolic sacrifice of one who is like us can make possible our atonement for the evil which is within us and for the sins which we are capable of committing. Nevertheless, in western thought, if man is free to choose, in the end he must choose rightly. He is free to choose his salvation, but he is punished for his wrong choice. Man is free, but he is free within the limits set for him by his condition as a man. So great is the emphasis placed on freedom of choice in tragedy that the settling of destinies, which in the myth and ritual pattern is the tangible reward of victory, recedes more and more into the background, and the messianic vision implicit in the settling of destinies is personalized and humanized in tragedy in the form of heightened self-awareness as the end of the tragic agony. In short, what I have been saying is that the myth and ritual pattern pertains to religion which proceeds by assertion, tragedy to literature which proceeds by assessment.

To sum up, then, the structure of tragic form, as derived from the myth and ritual pattern may be diagrammed in this way: the tragic protagonist, in whom is subsumed the well-being of the people and the welfare of the state, engages in conflict with a representation of darkness and evil; a temporary defeat is inflicted on the tragic protagonist, but after shame and suffering he emerges triumphant as the

symbol of the victory of light and good over darkness and
evil, a victory sanctified by the covenant of the settling of
destinies which reaffirms the well-being of the people and
the welfare of the state. In the course of the conflict there
comes a point where the protagonist and the antagonist appear to merge into a single challenge against the order of
God; the evil which the protagonist would not do, he does,
and the good which he would, he does not; and in this
moment we are made aware that the real protagonist of
tragedy is the order of God against which the tragic hero
has rebelled. In this manner is the pride, the presumption
which is in all of us by virtue of our mixed state as man,
symbolized and revealed, and it is this *hybris* which is vicariously purged from us by the suffering of the tragic protagonist. He commits the foul deed which is potentially in us,
he challenges the order of God which we would but dare not,
he expiates our sin, and what we had hitherto felt we had
been forced to accept we now believe of our free will, namely,
that the order of God is just and good. Therefore is the tragic
protagonist vouchsafed the vision of victory but not its at-
tainment:

> But the Lord was wroth with me for your sakes, and would
> not hear me: and the Lord said unto me, Let it suffice thee;
> speak no more unto me of this matter.
> Get thee up into the top of Pisgah, and lift up thine eyes
> westward, and northward, and southward, and eastward, and
> behold it with thine eyes: for thou shalt not go over this
> Jordan. (*Deuteronomy* 3. 26-27)

III

Seen from this point of view, *Hamlet* is a particularly fascinating example of the relationship between the myth and ritual
pattern and tragedy, because it shows within the action of the
play itself the development of Shakespeare's awareness of
tragedy as a heightened and secularized version of the pattern. Hamlet begins by crying for revenge which is personal

and ends by seeking justice which is social. Shakespeare deals with the problem of the play—how shall a son avenge the injustice done his father?—by presenting it to us in four different yet related ways simultaneously, each consistent within its pattern of behavior, yet each overlapping and protruding beyond the other, like the successive superimpositions of the same face seen from different angles in a portrait by Picasso. First, there is Hamlet-Laertes who, incapable of seeking more than revenge, dies unchanged and unfulfilled, no better nor no worse than when he had begun. Then there is Hamlet the Prince, caught midway between revenge and justice, who passes from ignorance to understanding but too late. Third, there is Hamlet-Fortinbras who avenges his father's wrongs by joining the warring kingdoms into a single nation under his able rule. And finally, containing all these Hamlets, is Hamlet the King, idealized by his son into the perfect king whom he must replace. From this dynastic destiny stems Hamlet's ambivalence towards his father: he loves him for the man he wants to be himself and hates him for the King who stands in the way of the Prince and for the father who stands in the way of the son. Seeking his father's murderer, Hamlet finds himself. The same necessity holds Hal and Hamlet alike, but where Hal sees a straight line between his father and himself—"You won it, wore it, kept it, gave it me; / Then plain and right must my possession be." (*II Henry IV.* IV.v.222-23)—and is therefore sure of himself and of his actions, Hamlet finds himself in a labyrinth whose walls are lined with trick doors and distorting mirrors: "O cursed spite, / That ever I was born to set it right!"

Hamlet's ambivalence is reflected in the fragmentation of his character; there are as many Hamlets as there are scenes in which he appears, and each person in the play sees a different Hamlet before him. But of the contradictions in his character, two stand out as the major symptoms of his incompleteness. The first is Hamlet's yearning to be able to act, not for the sake of action alone, but rightly, in the clear cause of justice; for while no tragic protagonist acts more frequently and more vigorously than Hamlet, he is more and more perplexed to discover that the more he would do good—that is, cleanse Denmark by avenging his father's death—the more evil he in fact accomplishes; hence his envy of Fortinbras' ability to act resolutely and without equivocation (IV. iv.). Second, though he is nominally a Christian, yet in the moments of sharpest crisis Hamlet turns instead to the consolations of Stoicism: "If it be now, 'tis not to come; if it be not to come, it will be now; if it be not now, yet it will come; the readiness is all. Since no man has aught of what he leaves, what is't to leave betimes?" (V.ii.231-35). And it is not enough: his mission succeeds only by mischance, his cause is still not understood, and with his dying breath he calls on Horatio, the true Stoic, to tell his story to the unsatisfied. Hamlet's vision is still clouded at his death— "Things standing thus unknown"; Horatio's own version of the events is surprisingly but an advertisement for a tragedy by Seneca (V.ii.391-97); and there is something too cold and callous in the way Fortinbras embraces his fortune. In short, the myth and ritual elements have not been completely assimilated into the tragedy: the suffering of the tragic protagonist is neither altogether deserved nor altogether understood by him, the rebirth is not quite inevitable nor necessary, and the settling of destinies in the person of Fortinbras is somewhat forced and mechanical. The genuine sense of tragic loss is somewhat vulgarized into regret: Hamlet has been too-fascinating.

In *Othello*, Shakespeare mixed his most perfect amalgam of the myth and ritual elements with tragedy. Where in *Hamlet* he was almost too fecund and profusive in characterization—invention inundating integration—in *Othello* he ruthlessly simplified and organized; if *Hamlet* is linear, proceeding by the method of montage and multiple exposure, *Othello* is monolithic and nuclear: the opposites of good and evil in human nature are forcibly split and then fused together in the fire of suffering. By overvaluing human nature, Othello destroys the balance between good and bad which is the condition of man; by undervaluing human nature, Iago brings about the same destruction from the equal and opposite direction. Each in his own way is an incomplete man: where Othello responds emotionally, Iago reasons; where Othello feels that men are better than they are, Iago knows that they are worse; each, in short, believes only what he wants to, and they are alike only in that both lack tolerance and understanding. Othello must be made to realize that the perfect love which he demands—"My life upon her faith!" "And when I love thee not, Chaos is come again."— is nothing more than the perfect hate which Iago practices:

> *Othello.* Now art thou my lieutenant.
> *Iago.* I am your own for ever. (III.iii.478-89)

If Iago is motivated by pride, will, and individualism, so then is Othello in his own way. Iago is the external symbol of the evil in Othello, for everything that Othello would stand for is negated and reversed in Iago: the subverter of the order of God whose coming is after the working of Satan, the man who rejects principle, and who denies virtue, love, and reputation. To him, ideals are but a mask which conceals the sensuality, the brutality, and the greed for money, power, and sex, which he believes constitute man's true nature.

As the opposites of character in Othello and Iago meet and merge in Act III, scene iii, Othello becomes for the moment Iago: he reverts to paganism and calls on the stars for help, he orders his friend murdered, he spies on and humiliates and at the last repudiates his wife: "She's like a liar, gone to burning hell." But this is for him the bottom

of the pit, and by a supreme effort of will he purges the
Iago from within him; and in that awful moment of self-
awareness, he recreates himself as he might have been, he
realizes his potential as a human being. Having by his rash-
ness put the well-being of the people and the welfare of the
state in jeopardy, as Brabantio had foretold, perhaps better
than he knew,—

> Mine's not an idle cause. The Duke himself,
> Or any of my brothers of the state,
> Cannot but feel this wrong as 'twere their own;
> For if such actions may have passage free,
> Bond-slaves and pagans shall our statesmen be. (I.ii.95-99)

—Othello is inevitably punished. And Iago is defeated by the
one force which he is incapable of understanding, the power
of principle. What he fails to see is that Othello's love for
Desdemona is the symbol of Othello's faith in the goodness
and justice of the world. What Othello seeks, therefore,
when that faith is called into question, is not revenge, which
is Iago's goal, but the cleansing of evil and the reaffirmation
of goodness and justice: "It is the cause, my soul." From the
depth of his self-awareness, bought at so dear a price, there
emerges the theme of the settling of destinies, not embodied
in the person of a successor, but filling as it were with its
vision the entire stage, the sign of evil purged and the good
restored, the image of man in his full stature as responsible
man: "Speak of me as I am." "And when man faces destiny,"
Malraux writes, "destiny ends and man comes into his own."

IV

Both *Hamlet* and *Othello* possess three features in common
which by contrast are not present in *Lear* and *Macbeth*.
First, both *Hamlet* and *Othello* are for the Elizabethan audience contemporary plays laid in contemporary or nearly contemporary settings. No great historical distance separates
them from their audience as it does in *Lear* and *Macbeth*,

which are laid in pre-Christian England and Scotland. Second, both *Hamlet* and *Othello* operate within the Christian framework, recognized and apprehended as such by the audience for which they were written. But in *Lear* and *Macbeth* the pagan background is insistent. From the depth of their suffering Lear and Gloucester can appeal no higher than to the heathen gods: "As flies to wanton boys, are we to th' gods,/ They kill us for their sport" (IV.i.38-39); and Edgar's wisdom is but cold comfort in the Stoic manner: "Bear free and patient thoughts" (IV.vi.80). In *Macbeth,* the witches play the same role as do the gods in *Lear:*

> But 'tis strange;
> And oftentimes, to win us to our harm,
> The instruments of darkness tell us truths,
> Win us with honest trifles, to betray 's
> In deepest consequence. (I.iii.122-26)

Finally, the theme of the settling of destinies—present directly in *Hamlet* and indirectly in *Othello*—fades away in *Lear* and disappears altogether in *Macbeth.* These changes reveal a significant shift in Shakespeare's use of the myth and ritual pattern and seem to be symptomatic of his increasing inability to bear the burden of the tragic vision. Having confronted the face of evil in *Othello* with an intensity unmatched even by the man staring at Death in Michelangelo's "Last Judgment," and having in the face of that evil been able to reassert the good, Shakespeare seems to have fallen back exhausted, so to speak, the effort of holding off evil weakening with each successive play.

Lear begins with the abdication of responsibility already accomplished; that a king could even contemplate, let alone achieve, the division of his kingdom must have struck an Elizabethan audience with fear and horror. By his own act, Lear deliberately divests himself of power and retains only the trappings of power, which in turn are one by one inexorably stripped from him until he stands naked on the heath in the rain. The waters of heaven give him wisdom, but his insight into the hypocrisy of this great stage of fools comes to him only in his madness, and he realizes at last that clothes —the symbols of his *hybris*—make neither the king nor the man. Having been purged of the pride of place, he sees himself as he is:

> I am a very foolish fond old man,
> Fourscore and upward, not an hour more nor less;
> And, to deal plainly,
> I fear I am not in my perfect mind. (IV.vii.60-63)

But this moment of illumination, of heightened self-awareness, so like Othello's, occurs not at the end of Act V, where it would be normally expected, but at the end of Act IV. Having said "Pray you now, forget and forgive; I am old and foolish" (IV.vii.85), what is left for Lear to say? Yet Shakespeare forces the action on to the shambles of the Grand Guignol of Act V, completely cancelling the calming and cleansing effect of the tragic vision already attained with Lear's self-awareness. The play ends not with the hope that this suffering has not been in vain, but with the defeatism of Kent's "All's cheerless, dark, and deadly" and Edgar's "The oldest hath borne most; we that are young/ Shall never see so much, nor live so long." The order of nature has been turned topsy-turvy; the old who cannot bear suffering have endured too much of it; the young who should be able to bear it are too weak.

But at least *Lear* gives us the consolation of the settling of destinies, mishandled and misplaced as it is. There is none in *Macbeth*. The action of the play begins with the figure of the bloody man and ends with the figure of the dead butcher, and nothing between mitigates the endless horrors of the progression from one to the other. Macbeth accepts the evil promise of the witches' prediction because they so neatly match the evil ambition already in him. Nor does his desire for the crown even pretend that it is for the well-being of the people and the welfare of the state, that excuse which gives some color to Bolingbroke's ambition: "I have no spurs/ To prick the sides of my intent," Macbeth confesses to himself, "but only/ Vaulting ambition." The country suffers under Macbeth's iron rule; "Things bad begun make strong themselves by ill" (III.ii.55), says Macbeth, and Malcolm confirms him:

> I think our country sinks beneath the yoke;
> It weeps, it bleeds; and each new day a gash
> Is added to her wounds. (IV.iii.39-41)

More—while Malcolm stands behind Macbeth as Fortinbras stands behind Hamlet, can we seriously accept him as the doctor who can "cast/ The water of my land, find her disease,/ And purge it to a sound and pristine health" (V.iii. 50-52)? What are we to make of a potential successor to the throne whose own ambivalence towards himself confounds even his strongest supporter? Is Macduff—are we—really persuaded that Malcolm is in fact capable of exhibiting "The king-becoming graces,/ As justice, verity, temp'rance, stableness,/ Bounty, perseverance, mercy, lowliness,/ Devotion, patience, courage, fortitude" (IV.iii.91-94)? Surely his black scruples, coupled with his innocence and inexperience, bode ill for Scotland, whatever the outcome, so that when at last Malcolm is hailed King of Scotland, and, like Hal and Fortinbras, emerges as the symbol of the settling of destinies, our eyes do not see the vision of peace rising from suffering, and our ears hear only the echo—

> for, from this instant,
> There's nothing serious in mortality.
> All is but toys; renown and grace is dead;
> The wine of life is drawn, and the mere lees
> Is left this vault to brag of. (II.iii.96-101)

—repeated in the dying close of Macbeth's reply to Seyton. The witches have indeed triumphed:

> He shall spurn fate, scorn death, and bear
> His hopes 'bove wisdom, grace, and fear;
> And, you all know, security
> Is mortals' chiefest enemy. (III.v.30-33)

Man's security, for which he has fought so feverishly, the guarantee of rebirth, has at the very last moment been snatched away from him. Tragedy may be much more and much different from what I have been suggesting here, but one thing it cannot be and that is a tale signifying nothing.

V

A few words must be said about the Roman tragedies. Though *Timon of Athens* and *Coriolanus* provide almost too easy confirmation of the point I am making, *Julius Caesar* and *Antony and Cleopatra* would seem substantial stumbling-blocks in the path of my argument. But the obstructions are not in the plays themselves so much as in our uncritical acceptance of the liberal view of Brutus as the champion of liberty laying down his life to free Rome from the shackles of tyranny, and of the romantic adulation of Antony and Cleopatra as lovers whose passion is so much beyond the ordinary that it justifies their indifference to mere mundane obligation. Having learned to read the histories as an aesthetic and ideological unity, so we must read *Julius Caesar* and *Antony and Cleopatra* as the continuous exposition of a single theme, that of the responsibility of rule. The clue to the Elizabethan judgment of Brutus is to be found in Canto 34 of the Inferno, where, in Judecca, "quite covered by the frozen sheet," and ceaselessly devoured by Satan, hang the ultimate traitors to sworn allegiance—Judas and Brutus and Cassius. For, whatever his defects—and Shakespeare does not minimize them—Caesar is the embodiment of legitimate authority, the source and guarantor of the order and stability of the state. He is, in

Elizabethan terms, the anointed king, God's vicar on earth, from whom flow the blessings of peace, justice, and security to his grateful people; and if we want to see the problem of power through Elizabethan eyes, we must not permit our vision to be blurred by our own political preconceptions. By his pride and arrogance, then, by his insistence that he can set his judgment above that of his ruler and try him and condemn him, by his vanity, by his susceptibility to flattery, by his obstinacy—all traits which Shakespeare is at pains to make clear again and again—Brutus murders Caesar and thereby destroys the continuity and stability of the state. Into the vacuum left by the death of Caesar pour hatred, jealousy, and betrayal, and from the Senate House of Rome death spreads in ever-widening circles to the utmost confines of the Empire.

The imminent dissolution of the then known world is the backdrop against which Antony and Cleopatra play out their passion, and it is in terms of the responsibilities of rule which this setting imposes on them that they are judged and found wanting. Four claimants to the authority that was Caesar's now confront each other: Lepidus, Pompey, Antony, and Octavius. Each is brought to the test of power and the first two fail quickly, Lepidus because he cannot raise his eyes above his ledgers, Pompey because he is a credulous fool. Antony and Octavius remain, and the very first lines of the play foretell Antony's inevitable failure:

> Nay, but this dotage of our general's
> O'erflows the measure. Those his goodly eyes,
> That o'er the files and musters of the war
> Have glow'd like plated Mars, now bend, now turn
> The office and devotion of their view
> Upon a tawny front; his captain's heart,
> Which in the scuffles of great fights hath burst
> The buckles on his breast, reneges all temper,
> And is become the bellows and the fan
> To cool a gipsy's lust. (I.i.1-10)

There is no one who does not share this opinion of Cleopatra. Even "the noble ruin of her magic" reviles her: "I found you as a morsel cold upon/ Dead Caesar's trencher." But Antony is besotted by the passion of his last love: "Come,/ Let's have one more gaudy night." The luxury of Egypt has corrupted the Roman virtues, and Octavius, that calculating and priggish youth looking down his nose at human weakness ("the wild disguise hath almost/ Antick'd us all"), so like Hal and Fortinbras, alone remains at the end to wield the power of Caesar. The peace of Augustus is about to heal an empire diseased by pride and passion.

But, as with *Lear,* the construction of *Julius Caesar* and *Antony and Cleopatra* is at variance with their content. *Julius Caesar* presents the strange spectacle of a conflict between a ghost representing an idea and a man of flesh and blood, for though Caesar is the protagonist of the play, his early death removes his physical presence from the stage and forces Brutus into the center of our interest. The result of this unsuccessful dramaturgic experiment is that for half the play the antagonist is able to claim and gain our sympathy; the belated appearance of Caesar's ghost cannot turn the flow of our increasing affection for Brutus; and the motifs of *Antony and Cleopatra* already dominate *Julius Caesar.* And if the last act of *Lear* disturbs us as intellectually unnecessary, what are we to say of the end of *Antony and Cleopatra* from Act IV, scene 14 on? Defeated by Cleopatra's betrayal, Antony seeks an honorable death, yet he can find no one to kill him. He attempts his own life and even here he fails, and, as he lies mortally wounded, he begs the guards to end his misery; they refuse. The sight of the great Antony, dying of a self-inflicted wound, crying in vain for release, is surely one of the most moving and most bitter scenes in all Shakespeare. Nor is this the end of his trial: he is deceived by Cleopatra once more, he is ignominiously hauled up to her tower, and even his last words are all but silenced by Cleopatra's false lamentations. No wonder Caesar, on being informed of Antony's death, exclaims: "The breaking of so great a thing should make/ A greater crack." Yet, with Antony dead, the play continues for another act, an act which makes the death of Antony appear noble in comparison, which degrades both Cleopatra and Octavius, and makes a mockery of the promise of his forthcoming reign.

VI

The limitations of the subject of this paper prevent me from showing that the disintegration of the tragic pattern which we have seen take place in the major tragedies is paralleled in the three middle comedies, *Troilus and Cressida, All's Well That Ends Well,* and *Measure for Measure,* and comes to its culmination in the four last plays, *Pericles, Cymbeline, The Winter's Tale,* and *The Tempest.* Nevertheless, I think that the configuration of Shakespeare's thought was for the most part sympathetically conformable to the shape of the myth and ritual pattern. Yet having raised the pattern to the heights of its most moving and significant expression, Shakespeare was unable to hold it there for long. This does not mean that we must regard him as less than, say, Sophocles or Milton, neither of whom seems to have given way to doubt, nor does it mean that the myth and ritual pattern is inadequate either to its purposes or as a means of elucidating tragedy. On the contrary, the application of the pattern to Shakespeare's plays discriminates between them with nicety, it intensifies our awareness of the unique qualities of the individual plays, and it enables us to respond to Shakespeare on a most profound level of understanding. Recent critics of Shakespeare have enjoyed many a laugh at the expense of their predecessors who labored to box Shakespeare's plays under the neat labels "in the workshop," "in the world," "out of the depths," and "on the heights"—to use Dowden's terms—but I cannot see that they themselves have done anything more than to say the same thing in perhaps more fashionable language. But the myth and ritual approach converts a Progress into a Calvary.

Shakespeare paid for the cost of the tragic vision by its loss. He looked long and directly into the face of evil. In the end, he shut his eyes. Writing of another artist who found himself in the same dilemma, Sir Kenneth Clark says: "The perfect union of Piero's forms, transcending calculation, rested on confidence in the harmony of creation; and at some point this confidence left him." As it seems to me, at some point Shakespeare too lost his confidence in the harmony of creation. I do not know when Shakespeare reached that point, but I think that it perhaps came at the moment of his greatest expression of faith in the harmony of creation, in *Othello* when he realized that he had left Iago standing alive on the stage. When in the bottommost circle of Hell, Virgil steps aside from Dante and reveals to him that creature fairest once of the sons of light: "Behold now Dis!", the poet is moved to cry out: "This was not life, and yet it was not death." So in the end Iago: "Demand me nothing; what you know, you know./ From this time forth I never will speak word." The rest is silence.

ACKNOWLEDGMENTS

Bascom, William. "The Myth-Ritual Theory." *Journal of American Folklore* 70 (April-June 1957): 103–14. Reproduced with the permission of the American Folklore Society. Not for further reproduction.

Brandon, S.G.F. "The Myth and Ritual Position Critically Considered." In S.H. Hooke, ed., *Myth, Ritual, and Kingship* (Oxford: Clarendon Press, 1958): 261–91. Reprinted with the permission of Clarendon Press.

Cornford, F.M. "A Ritual Basis for Hesiod's *Theogony.*" In W.K.C. Guthrie, ed., *The Unwritten Philosophy and Other Essays* (Cambridge: Cambridge University Press, 1950): 95–116. Reprinted with the permission of Cambridge University Press.

Fergusson, Francis. "*Oedipus Rex*: The Tragic Rhythm of Action." In Francis Fergusson, *The Idea of a Theater* (Princeton: Princeton University Press, 1949): 13–41. Reprinted with the permission of Princeton University Press.

Frazer, James George. "The Myth of Adonis." In James George Frazer, *The Golden Bough, Adonis Attis Osiris: Studies in the History of Oriental Religion*, Vol. 5, 3rd ed. (London: Macmillan, 1914): 3–12.

Frazer, James George. "The Ritual of Adonis." In James George Frazer, *The Golden Bough, Adonis Attis Osiris: Studies in the History of Oriental Religion*, Vol. 5, 3rd ed. (London: Macmillan, 1914): 223–59.

Frazer, James George. "Introduction." In Apollodorus, *The Library,* Vol. 1 (New York: Putnam, 1921): ix–xxxiii.

Hardin, Richard F. "'Ritual' in Recent Criticism: The Elusive Sense of Community." *Proceedings of the Modern Language Association* 98 (1983): 846–62. Reprinted with the permission of the Modern Language Association of America. Copyright 1983 The Modern Language Association of America.

Harrison, Jane Ellen. "Introduction." In Jane Ellen Harrison, *Themis* (Cambridge: Cambridge University Press, 1912): xi–xxv.

Hooke, S.H. "The Myth and Ritual Pattern of the Ancient East." In S.H. Hooke, ed., *Myth and Ritual* (London: Oxford University Press, 1933): 1–14. Reprinted with the permission of Oxford University Press.

Hyman, Stanley Edgar. "The Ritual View of Myth and the Mythic." *Journal of American Folklore* 68 (October-December 1955): 462–72. Reproduced with the permission of the American Folklore Society. Not for further reproduction.

Kaberry, Phyllis M. "Myth and Ritual: Some Recent Theories." *Bulletin of the Institute of Classical Studies* 4 (1957): 42–54. Reprinted with the permission of the Institute of Classical Studies.

Kluckhohn, Clyde. "Myths and Rituals: A General Theory." *Harvard Theological Review* 35 (January 1942): 45–79. Copyright (1942) by the President and Fellows of Harvard College. Reprinted by permission.

Marlow, A.N. "Myth and Ritual in Early Greece." *Bulletin of the John Rylands Library* 43 (March 1961): 373–402. Reprinted with the permission of the John Rylands University Library of Manchester.

Murray, Gilbert. "Hamlet and Orestes: A Study in Traditional Types." *Proceedings of the British Academy* (1913–14): 389–412. Reprinted with the permission of The British Academy.

Penner, Hans H. "Myth and Ritual: A Wasteland or a Forest of Symbols?" *History and Theory,* Beiheft 8 (1968): 46–57. Reprinted with the permission of *History and Theory*.

Raglan, Lord. "Myth and Ritual." *Journal of American Folklore* 68 (October-December 1955): 454–61. Reproduced with the permission of the American Folklore Society. Not for further reproduction.

Robertson Smith, William. "Introduction: The Subject and the Method of Enquiry." In William Robertson Smith, *Lectures on the Religion of the Semites, First Series: The Fundamental Institutions* (Edinburgh: Black, 1889): 1–28.

Weisinger, Herbert. "The Myth and Ritual Approach to Shakespearean Tragedy." *Centennial Review* 1 (Spring 1957): 142–66. Reprinted with the permission of the *Centennial Review*.

WITHDRAWN